CALIFORNIA SERIES IN PUBLIC AN

The California Series in Public Anthropology en   ..pulogist's role as an
engaged intellectual. It continues anthropology's ...mitment to being an ethnographic
witness, to describing, in human terms, how life is lived beyond the borders of many readers' experiences. But it also adds a commitment, through ethnography, to reframing the
terms of public debate—transforming received, accepted understandings of social issues
with new insights, new framings.

Series Editor: Robert Borofsky (Hawaii Pacific University)

*Contributing Editors: Philippe Bourgois (University of Pennsylvania), Paul Farmer
(Partners In Health), Alex Hinton (Rutgers University), Carolyn Nordstrom (University
of Notre Dame), and Nancy Scheper-Hughes (UC Berkeley)*

University of California Press Editor: Naomi Schneider

1. *Twice Dead: Organ Transplants and the Reinvention of Death*, by Margaret Lock

2. *Birthing the Nation: Strategies of Palestinian Women in Israel*, by Rhoda Ann
   Kanaaneh (with a foreword by Hanan Ashrawi)

3. *Annihilating Difference: The Anthropology of Genocide*, edited by Alexander
   Laban Hinton (with a foreword by Kenneth Roth)

4. *Pathologies of Power: Health, Human Rights, and the New War on the Poor*, by
   Paul Farmer (with a foreword by Amartya Sen)

5. *Buddha Is Hiding: Refugees, Citizenship, the New America*, by Aihwa Ong

6. *Chechnya: Life in a War-Torn Society*, by Valery Tishkov (with a foreword by
   Mikhail S. Gorbachev)

7. *Total Confinement: Madness and Reason in the Maximum Security Prison*, by
   Lorna A. Rhodes

8. *Paradise in Ashes: A Guatemalan Journey of Courage, Terror, and Hope*, by Beatriz
   Manz (with a foreword by Aryeh Neier)

9. *Laughter Out of Place: Race, Class, Violence, and Sexuality in a Rio Shantytown*,
   by Donna M. Goldstein

10. *Shadows of War: Violence, Power, and International Profiteering in the Twenty-First
    Century*, by Carolyn Nordstrom

11. *Why Did They Kill? Cambodia in the Shadow of Genocide*, by Alexander Laban
    Hinton (with a foreword by Robert Jay Lifton)

12. *Yanomami: The Fierce Controversy and What We Can Learn from It*, by Robert
    Borofsky

13. *Why America's Top Pundits Are Wrong: Anthropologists Talk Back*, edited by Cath-
    erine Besteman and Hugh Gusterson

14. *Prisoners of Freedom: Human Rights and the African Poor*, by Harri Englund

15. *When Bodies Remember: Experiences and Politics of AIDS in South Africa*, by
    Didier Fassin

16. *Global Outlaws: Crime, Money, and Power in the Contemporary World*, by
    Carolyn Nordstrom

17. *Archaeology as Political Action*, by Randall H. McGuire

18. *Counting the Dead: The Culture and Politics of Human Rights Activism in
    Colombia*, by Winifred Tate

Illegality, Inc.

Illegality, Inc.

Clandestine Migration and the Business of Bordering Europe

Ruben Andersson

UNIVERSITY OF CALIFORNIA PRESS

University of California Press, one of the most distinguished
university presses in the United States, enriches lives around the
world by advancing scholarship in the humanities, social sciences,
and natural sciences. Its activities are supported by the UC Press
Foundation and by philanthropic contributions from individuals and
institutions. For more information, visit www.ucpress.edu.

University of California Press
Oakland, California

Library of Congress Cataloging-in-Publication Data

Andersson, Ruben, 1977–
    Illegality, inc.: clandestine migration and the business of
bordering Europe / Ruben Andersson.
        pages cm. — (California series in public anthropology; 28)
        Summary: "In this groundbreaking ethnography, Ruben
Andersson, a gifted journalist and anthropologist, travels with a
group of African migrants from Senegal and Mali to the Spanish
North African enclaves of Ceuta and Melilla. Through the voices of
his informants themselves, Anderson explores, viscerally and
emphatically, how migration meets and interacts with its target—
the clandestine migrant. This vivid, rich work examines the
subterranean migration flow from Africa to Europe, and shifts the
focus from the concept of 'illegal immigrants' to an exploration of
suffering and resilience. This fascinating and accesible book is a
must-read for anyone interested in the politics of international
migration and the changing texture of global culture"—Provided by
publisher.
        Includes bibliographical references and index.
    ISBN 978-0-520-28251-3 (hardback)
    ISBN 978-0-520-28252-0 (paper)
    ISBN 978-0-520-95828-9 (e-book)
        1. Illegal aliens—Spain—Cueta—Case studies.   2. Illegal
aliens—Spain—Melilla—Case studies.   3. Ceuta (Spain)—
Emigration and immigration—Case studies.   4. Melilla (Spain)—
Emigration and immigration—Case studies.   5. Mali—Emigration
and immigration—Case studies.   6. Senegal—Emigration and
immigration—Case studies.   I. Title.
    IV8259.Z6C482 2014
    364.1′370964—dc23

                                                         2014010244

Manufactured in the United States of America

23   22   21   20   19   18   17   16   15   14
10   9   8   7   6   5   4   3   2   1

In keeping with a commitment to support environmentally
responsible and sustainable printing practices. UC Press has printed
this book on Natures Natural, a fiber that contains 30% post-
consumer waste and meets the minimum requirements of ANSI/NISO
Z39.48-1992 (R 1997) (Permanence of Paper).

To those who have died trying

Contents

PART THREE. CONFRONTATIONS

ONLINE CONTENT

The appendix "A Global Front: Thoughts on Enforcement at the Rich World's Borders" is available online from the University of California Press website, www.ucpress.edu/go/illegality.

Illustrations

MAP

Acknowledgments

A great many people and institutions have helped make this book possible, too numerous to mention here.

First of all, I am very grateful to the young repatriates of the Dakar neighborhood I call Yongor for welcoming me despite their difficult circumstances and for setting my whole project on a new track. I am greatly indebted to all the migrants who have shared their stories with me, in Senegal, Mali, Morocco, and Spain: protecting their identities prevents me from mentioning them by name here.

In Ceuta, I am indebted to Pepi Galván, without whose hospitality, kindness, and help my experience in the city would have been completely different. I am also grateful to the director of the enclave's migrant reception center and its workers for receiving me, as well as to the Spanish Red Cross staff and volunteers in Ceuta.

A great many journalists, aid workers, academics, and activists have helped shape this project. While many of them will not be mentioned here by name in order to safeguard anonymity, I do wish to thank Melanie Gärtner and Max Hirzel for their great collegiality; Pepe Naranjo and Nicolás Castellano for their contacts and inspiration; and Papa Demba Fall for receiving me at l'Institut Fondamental d'Afrique Noire in Dakar. Among the numerous organizations that have helped make this research possible, I wish to extend special thanks to the team at Aracem for their warm welcome in Bamako. I am also thankful to the

Spanish Guardia Civil and the Senegalese border police for having received me on numerous visits.

The PhD project on which this book is based was funded by a U.K. Economic and Social Research Council Studentship, and I am very grateful for this generous assistance.

At the London School of Economics and Political Science, I am deeply indebted to my supervisors, Mathijs Pelkmans and Deborah James, for their unfailing support and guidance over many years. Both have been incredibly patient and helpful and have provided me with constructive criticism and stylistic advice that has fundamentally helped shape this book. I also wish to thank Chris Fuller for his supervision during the initial stages of this project, as well as Katy Gardner and Nicholas De Genova for their very helpful comments and encouragement.

I wish to thank colleagues at Stockholm University's anthropology department, which provided a welcoming environment for continuing my work on the manuscript during 2013, as well as the Civil Society and Human Security Research Unit in LSE's Department of International Development, my current host institution.

Warm thanks to the team at the University of California Press: Naomi Schneider and Chris Lura for taking me through the whole process of publishing, and Rachel Berchten for getting the manuscript ready for print. Thanks to Robin Whitaker for her detailed copyediting. Thanks, too, to Rob Borofsky for his dedication to the publicly engaged anthropology that underpins this book series as a whole.

The feedback of friends and colleagues at LSE and elsewhere has been most useful. I especially wish to thank Moctar Ba, Agnes Hann, Polly Pallister-Wilkins, Laura Shin, Luca Pes, Markus Roos Breines, and Ana Paola Gutierrez Garza, among many more. The book's peer reviewers have provided enormously valuable input, as have article reviewers of earlier versions of some of the material included in it.

My parents, Sara and Vincent, have been a constant source of support and encouragement. My brother, Hjalmar, would have loved to have seen me finish this book and would have enjoyed challenging my ideas; my son, Aaron, might as well, in due course.

Above all, I am grateful to Cristina for her inspiration throughout, as well as for her almost superhuman levels of patience with me during the research, writing, and editing phases of this project. Besides offering me her constant support, she has been a sounding board for my ideas and has even taken some of the pictures—the better ones, to be sure—in this book. Without her, this project would never have been finished, let alone begun.

Author's Note

This book is based on several hundred interviews, extensive participant observation conducted in a range of settings throughout 2010 and early 2011, and numerous visits to border agencies and other key groups working on migration along the Euro-African border. While the stories in the coming chapters often read like reportage, they have been selected for the purpose of illustrating these broader findings. I have carried out interviews or in-depth field conversations with more than a hundred migrants, around eighty nongovernmental organization and international officials, over fifty border guards, and forty Red Cross workers, to name a few categories of research participants; I have also talked informally to many more, while developing close relationships with key informants. I have carried out participant-observation among deported migrants in Dakar, as a volunteer in a Spanish migrant reception center, and among deportees and activists in Bamako. My large number of visits to the Spanish Guardia Civil has given me a gradual grasp of the border agency's work and thinking on migration, even though these visits have by their nature taken place under rather "controlled" conditions. Questions of access, as well as my approaches to research and theory, are discussed further in the appendix.

In keeping with a "public" anthropological style, all references have been relegated to footnotes, along with links to relevant websites and articles: readers who wish to look at the larger debates behind the book are encouraged to explore these notes. Research participants are all referred to by first name or nickname in the chapters and have all been anonymized. While quotes are usually verbatim, they are sometimes based on fieldnotes written as soon as possible after an encounter. This applies to many discussions with migrants, as well as to quotes from Ceuta's reception camp in chapters 5 and 6.

Selected Abbreviations

AECID   Agencia Española de Cooperación Internacional para el Desarrollo, the Spanish official development agency

AME   Association Malienne d'Expulsés (Malian association of expelled migrants)

AQIM   Al Qaeda in the Islamic Maghreb

Aracem   Association des Refoulés d'Afrique Centrale au Mali (association of central African deportees in Mali)

CCRC   Centro de Coordinación Regional de Canarias, the Frontex regional coordination center in the Canaries

CEAR   Comisión Española de Ayuda al Refugiado, a Spanish refugee assistance organisation

CETI   Centro de Estancia Temporal de Inmigrantes (temporary reception center for immigrants); exists in Ceuta and Melilla

CIE   *centro de internamiento de extranjeros*, foreigners' detention center

CIGEM   Centre d'Information et des Gestions des Migrations (center for information and management of migration), in Bamako

CIRAM   common integrated risk analysis model, used by Frontex in building its risk assessments for the external borders xvi | Selected Abbreviations

CIREFI   Centre for Information, Discussion and Exchange on the Crossing of Frontiers and Immigration

CPIP   common prefrontier intelligence picture, Frontex-produced intelligence syntheses under Eurosur

DMSF   Direction de la Migration et de la Surveillance des Frontières (directorate of migration and border surveillance), in Morocco

DPAF   Direction de la Police de l'Air et des Frontières, Senegal's directorate of border police

ECOWAS   the Economic Community of West African States

ENP   European Neighbourhood Policy, a framework for bilateral cooperation between the European Union and neighboring states

ERIE   Equipo de Respuesta Inmediata en Emergencias, Red Cross emergency response team

Eurosur   the European external border surveillance system

Frontex   the E.U. border agency, whose full name is European Agency for the Management of Operational Cooperation at the External Borders of the Member States of the European Union

FSC   Frontex Situation Centre

GMES   Global Monitoring for Environment and Security, the E.U. program for the establishment of a European capacity for Earth Observation

ICC   International Coordination Centre for Frontex operations in Spain

ICMPD   International Centre for Migration Policy Development, headquartered in Vienna

ICRC   the International Committee of the Red Cross

IFAN   l'Institut Fondamental d'Afrique Noire Cheikh Anta Diop, located in Dakar

IOM   International Organization for Migration

JO   joint operation of Frontex for migration controls

NCC   national coordination center for Frontex operations. The Madrid ICC is also referred to as the NCC in terms of Eurosur

PP   Partido Popular, the Spanish conservative party

RAU   the Risk Analysis Unit of Frontex

SAR   search and rescue

SIVE   *sistema integrado de vigilancia exterior,* the Spanish integrated system for external surveillance of the coastlines and seas

SOLAS   the International Convention for the Safety of Life at Sea

TFA   tactical focused assessment prepared before the commencement of Frontex joint operations

TRA   tailored risk analysis prepared by Frontex on regions or topics of concern

UAV   unmanned aerial vehicle or drone, planned for use in sea surveillance

UNHCR   United Nations High Commissioner for Refugees

UNODC   United Nations Office on Drugs and Crime

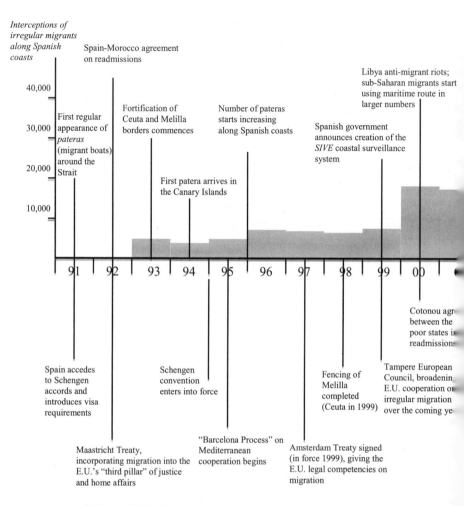

Interceptions of irregular migrants along Spanish coasts

40,000

30,000

20,000

10,000

Spain-Morocco agreement on readmissions

First regular appearance of *pateras* (migrant boats) around the Strait

Fortification of Ceuta and Melilla borders commences

Number of pateras starts increasing along Spanish coasts

First patera arrives in the Canary Islands

Libya anti-migrant riots; sub-Saharan migrants start using maritime route in larger numbers

Spanish government announces creation of the *SIVE* coastal surveillance system

91 | 92 | 93 | 94 | 95 | 96 | 97 | 98 | 99 | 00

Cotonou agr between the poor states i readmission:

Spain accedes to Schengen accords and introduces visa requirements

Schengen convention enters into force

Fencing of Melilla completed (Ceuta in 1999)

Tampere European Council, broadenin E.U. cooperation or irregular migration over the coming ye

Maastricht Treaty, incorporating migration into the E.U.'s "third pillar" of justice and home affairs

"Barcelona Process" on Mediterranean cooperation begins

Amsterdam Treaty signed (in force 1999), giving the E.U. legal competencies on migration

TIMELINE: Policy and Migration Events

Sources: Frontex 2010; Serón et al. 2011; Gabrielli 2011; E.U. websites; and chronology by Migreurop (www.migreurop.org/article1961.html?lang=fr). Migrant interception data adapted from Gabrielli 2011:425, itself based on an earlier study (http://echogeo. revues.org/index1488.html), for 1993–2000; data from MIR 2013 for 2001–12.

Notes: This is just a selection of policy milestones and significant migration events at the external border since Spain's Schengen accession in 1991. Migrant interception data should be used with caution, since methods for calculating these differ among agencies and over different periods.Arrivals in Ceuta and Melilla excluded. Comparable data not available for 1991 and 1992.

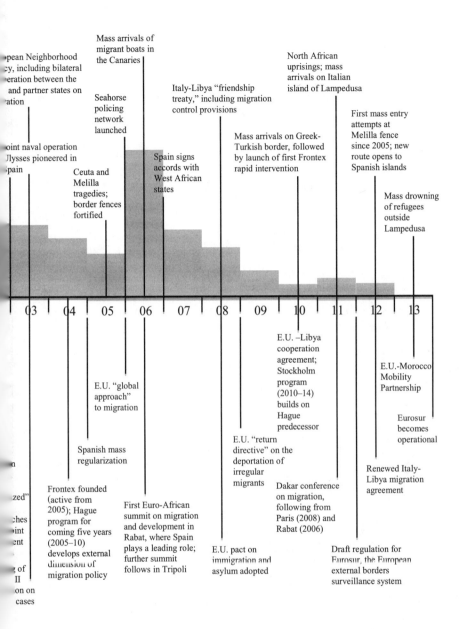

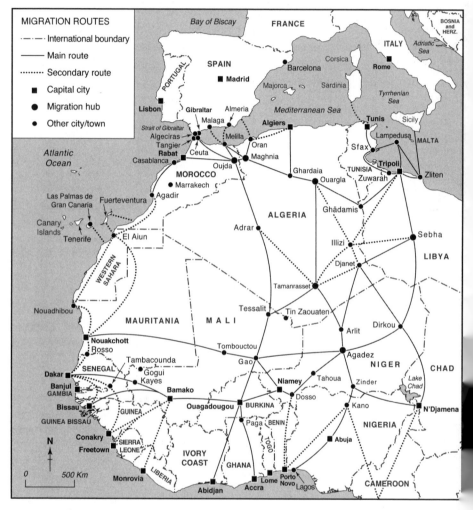

Irregular migratory routes between Africa and southern Europe. Based on 2012 version of MTM i-Map, imap-migration.org.

Introduction

The Illegality Industry at Europe's African Frontier

The border is as tall as a fence and as deep as the sea, yet across it migrants and refugees keep coming. This is the latest phase in the tragic spectacle of "illegal" migration from Africa to Europe, a broadcast set on repeat at the fault line between continents:

MELILLA, NORTH AFRICA. OCTOBER 2005. *It was after darkness had fallen that the migrants came running towards the Spanish enclaves of Ceuta and Melilla. Hundreds of road-weary Africans descended from their Moroccan forest encampments, threw makeshift ladders onto the border fences circling the territories, and scrambled to climb across. Silhouetted figures crowded in between the fences, cameras capturing their blurry movements between reams of barbed wire. Journalists called it* el asalto masivo, *the massive assault: newscasts and front pages showed the black migrants, many "violent" or "desperate," advancing swiftly and silently. Then Moroccan or Spanish security forces—it was never clear who was responsible—fired into the crowds. At least fourteen people died.*[1] *The ramshackle migrant encampments outside the enclaves were razed and burned by Moroccan soldiers; their inhabitants were rounded up, detained, and put on buses bound for the faraway Sahara. Many were never heard from again. Then controls tightened, the border was cleaned up, the media moved on. But soon a new front would open up in Europe's "fight against illegal migration": the sea route to the distant, improbable destination of the Spanish Canary Islands, where in*

2006 more than thirty thousand boat migrants landed among sunbath-ers, Red Cross volunteers, and throngs of journalists and police. After years of increasing migrant arrivals on southern European shores, the chaos at Europe's external borders had begun in earnest.
LAMPEDUSA, ITALY. MARCH 2011. The tragedy happened at the time of the Libyan uprising. An increasingly desperate Colonel Gaddafi had promised to unleash an "unprecedented wave of illegal immigration" on southern Europe as a riposte against impending NATO attacks. Soon African refugees set out, boatload after boatload, their blank faces filmed by the BBC, Al Jazeera, and CNN as their rusting, creaking, or leaking vessels approached the Italian island of Lampedusa with its waiting crowds of aid workers, journalists, and police. The spectacle of boat migration was routine by now, European audiences hardened and blasé—and so, it turned out, were the coastguards and soldiers. The tragedy—one among many—began when a dinghy set sail from Tripoli with seventy-two passengers onboard. Its distress calls went unheeded. A military helicopter air-dropped water and food and then disappeared, never to return; the boat drifted for two weeks through NATO's mari-time military zone before washing up on Libyan shores. By then all but nine of those onboard had died of thirst or starvation. The tragedy was a "dark day for Europe," concluded an official investigation. Yet migrants keep waking up to new dark days at Europe's southernmost fringes—whether outside Lampedusa, where hundreds drowned as their boats capsized in autumn 2013; in the treacherous riverbed of the Greek-Turkish border; outside Ceuta and Melilla; or in the straits of Gibraltar and Sicily. Barely a decade after the debacle at the Spanish fences, the border now promises constant chaos.[2]

Gruesome tales of migrant deaths abound at the gates of the West, whether at the southern frontiers of Europe, at the U.S.-Mexican bor-der, or along Australia's Pacific shores. The scenes of this story are famil-iar: "illegal immigrants" crammed into unseaworthy boats, squeezed into rusty trucks trundling across the Sahara, walking through the dis-tant deserts of Arizona, or clinging onto Mexican cargo trains.[3] Thou-sands have perished on these grueling treks, with one incomplete tally listing almost twenty thousand deaths at the gates of "Fortress Europe" since 1988.[4] Yet the misery does not end there for today's migrant out-casts. The media, populist politicians, and zealous bureaucrats have seized upon the illegal immigrant as a bogeyman, a perennial outsider who in waves and floods invades Western countries. In their accounts, a global pariah is emerging: alternately an object of deep fascination and utter indifference, of horror and pity, he stalks the borders of the rich world, sowing panic, wrecking election campaigns, and generating headlines as he goes.

Much has been written about this "threat" lurking outside the gates: news stories, documentaries, policy papers, academic tracts, and funding reports in which the irregular migrant is followed, scrutinized, probed. This book takes a different approach. It casts an eye on the observers and investigates the workings of what I will call an illegal migration industry—or "illegality industry" for short—in the emerging Euro-African borderlands.[5] It moves across the domains in which this industry works on its captive human material: from the control rooms of Europe's new border regime and the shelters where humanitarians care for migrants under the watchful eye of the state to the police patrols scouring African terrains for a sighting of their elusive prey.

This cannot be done, however, without considering the target of these interventions—the irregular migrants and, in particular, the sub-Saharan travelers among them who increasingly find themselves marooned in the no-man's-lands springing up like weeds in the interstices between Europe and Africa. Running the gauntlet of border controls that now stretch across deserts and high seas, North African cities and dusty Sahelian dumps, these travelers are subject to what the director of a Spanish migrant reception center called a Darwinian selection. It is a selection of the most brutal kind, in which shriveled bodies disappear in Saharan dunes and bloated corpses float ashore at the Strait of Gibraltar. Luckier travelers get stuck in newly cosmopolitan border towns and fringe neighborhoods of Tangier and Oujda, Tripoli and Tamanrasset. Others get deported, time and again. Yet whether they succeed or fall short of their goals, these travelers increasingly end up collaborating in their own making as illegal immigrants on the infernal production line of the illegality industry.

This book is an ethnography of the industry's operations along the western edge of Europe's external border: between West Africa, the Maghreb, and Spain. In these emerging borderlands, the coming chapters will show, the European response to "illegal" African migration has sparked conflicts and contradictions that speak volumes about rich countries' relations with their southern neighbors. Only rarely does the story touch down on European soil; for the business of bordering Europe now thrives well beyond the confines of the continent's geographical borders.

CONJURING A MENACE

The moving, questing people were migrants now. Those families
which had lived on a little piece of land, who had lived and died on
forty acres, had eaten or starved on the produce of forty acres, had
now the whole backyard of the West to rove in. And they scampered
about, looking for work; and the high seas were boatfuls of people,
and the border ditches were lines of people. Behind them more were
coming. The desert and borderlands streamed with moving
people. . . . The movement changed them: the highways, the camps
along the road, the fear of hunger, and the hunger itself, changed
them. The children without dinner changed them, the endless moving
changed them. They were migrants. And the hostility changed them,
welded them, united them—hostility that made the rich nations
group and arm as though to repel an invader, border guard squads
with patrol boats, African police with rifles, guarding the world
against their own people.
—John Steinbeck's *The Grapes of Wrath*, freely adapted

The world, we are often told, is on the move. Millions of dollars are
transferred, invested, and squandered at the click of a trader's button.
Commodities and contraband cross borders in endless, unchecked trails
of trucks, pickups, and freight containers.[6] Businesses outsource their
labor force to low-wage countries and settle their tax affairs in offshore
havens, while the rich threaten to move their fortunes abroad unless
governments keep their stay sweet and smooth. People of relatively
modest means, too, move as never before, physically or virtually—zip-
ping across continents for business, work, and leisure or tweeting their
way across cyberspace.

Globalization, theorists argue, involves such "time-space compression" on an unprecedented scale. Yet while some travelers—whether
executives, "expats," or tourists—are celebrated for their powers to
shrink distances and connect territories, others are fretted about for the
same reasons.[7] The label "migrants" is usually, and paradoxically,
reserved for them. These migrants haunt the rich world, but it is rarely
clear who they are or why they provoke such fear. What they have in
common is their relative poverty and the suspicion attached to their
movements—a suspicion that, for some, comes to subsume their whole
identity in the eyes of their reluctant hosts. These are the "illegal immigrants," the absolute Others to the dream of a mobile world: those who
cannot—or should not—move.

From Spanish beaches to American deserts, the "illegals" are massing
at the borders of the West. We know it—we see it on our newscasts and
front pages. We hear it in our politicians' stump speeches or in embit-

tered voices from the southern frontiers. The wetbacks, *ilegales,* or *clandestins* squat in rundown border dens, lurk in forest "jungles" or on dark hillsides, wade across rivers, or clamber over fences erected to keep them out.[8] They mock the state's sovereign powers and ridicule its border patrols. They carry diseases, strange customs, and a backpack full of poverty. They leech goodwill and resources out of the nation. Their invasion must be halted at all costs.

While unwarranted fears about irregular migration thrive on both sides of the Atlantic, a fundamental absurdity underlies Europe's response to it in particular. The "invasion" has not materialized. The highways to the gates of the West are not crowded with the desperate and the poor. In the States, up to a million migrants make it across the border each year—a high figure, yet not rising and not disproportionate to the exchanges that have always characterized this large border region. In Europe, fears of "Africa pushing upwards," expressed by border workers and fueled by reports of the continent's swift demographic growth, remain spectacularly unfulfilled.

Indeed, the starting point of this book is the peculiar mismatch between the vast industry around irregular entry by land and sea—what I will gloss as "clandestine migration"—and the phenomenon's small statistical importance.[9] Amid the wild official estimates and the absence of firm data, it has long been clear to migration scholars that such movements towards Europe are tiny relative to other means of unauthorized entry and residence. In Spain, the country's latest immigrant census shows that, for all the media hysteria, fewer than 1 percent of those entering the country since 1990 have done so by means of irregular boat migration. Instead the majority of Europe's irregular migrants are visa overstayers—something even recognized by Frontex, the E.U. border agency of which more will be said in subsequent chapters. The political impact of the "boat people" approaching Europe's southern borders, in short, greatly surpasses their actual numbers.[10]

This mismatch applies particularly to the case of the sub-Saharan migrants and refugees, whose journeys in groaning boats or across fences have captured prime-time television slots, stoked political fears, and fueled border guards' imaginations despite their tiny numbers. In Spain, other Europeans make up almost half of the country's foreign-born population, with sub-Saharan Africans but a fraction of the remainder next to large Latin and Moroccan groups.[11] In West Africa itself, movement *within* the region has long outstripped intercontinental migration, while so-called transit states in North Africa are increasingly important destinations in their own right. With this in mind, a disturbing question lurks beneath the stories of this book: why have such massive efforts been expended to target black Africans in the borderlands, and what racial and colonial legacies underpin these efforts?

This book, then, is about the making of illegal immigrants as refracted through one particular case—the West African travelers, the extensive borderlands through which they move, and the system that pursues them all the way to Europe. The extreme ordeals these travelers endure—and European powers' extreme response to their statistically minuscule movements—highlight larger patterns in the making of migrants, whether these hail from Senegal or El Salvador, Afghanistan or Nicaragua. Their exclusion, like their illicit mobility, is now a global condition.

From the U.S.-Mexican border to Australia's offshore detention centers, hostilities unfold in a pattern reminiscent of the Depression-era migrations evoked in John Steinbeck's *The Grapes of Wrath*, updated to the early twenty-first century in the epigraph above. In the 1930s, poor "Okies" of the American dust bowl faced spite and violence on their westward escape towards California; today's illegal immigrants endure similar ordeals. In Arizona, a maverick sheriff lines up his shackled "illegals" in the sweltering sun, dragged up in pink like Guantánamo detainees for the benefit of the news cameras. Vigilantes patrol America's southern borders, while in Greece, extremists torch and ransack migrant dwellings. The deepening economic crisis has, in some quarters, found its scapegoat—not the mobile banker or trader with his squandered billions, but the impoverished, immobilized "migrant" stuck in the borderlands.

Yet something has changed since Steinbeck's time. Now the vigilantes are but a sideshow: instead, powerful border regimes seek to keep the undesirables out. Inland, unprecedented investments allow for increased surveillance and incarceration of those deemed dangerous or unwelcome. In the United States, about two million irregular migrants have been deported so far in the Obama years. In northern E.U. countries such as the United Kingdom and Sweden, police stand accused of stopping those who "look" undocumented; in Spain, Italy, and Greece, security forces raid migrants' homes and lock up the "illegals" they find in detention centers, which are now spreading, virus-like, across the European body politic.[12] And this body's outer frontiers, its skin, is hardening into a seemingly impenetrable carapace. Military planes, helicopters, satellites, and patrol boats circle the external E.U. border. Radars, advanced information systems, and intricate policing networks map the routes of potential intruders. Asylum seekers are pushed back to North Africa or corralled in enclaves, on islands, and in distant retention centers. "Fortress Europe" has, activists allege, unleashed a "war" on refugees and migrants fleeing poverty, conflict, and disaster. In North America, Israel, and Australia, the battle lines are similarly drawn. Understanding this "conflict" and its ramifications is more pressing than ever at a time of global economic crisis, with the resentment such downturns and depressions have stirred since Steinbeck's times.

Beyond the crisis and its scapegoats, more is at stake, too, in assessing rich states' efforts to shut out the unwanted. These efforts bring into stark relief the uneven distribution of mobility under globalization; moreover, they shine a light on the role of movement in our understanding of what it means to be a fulfilled, rights-bearing human being. In our high-speed world of resurgent international borders, mobility is paradoxically becoming both a privilege and a stigma.

Thoughtful voices in academia, journalism, and politics deploy a set of well-worn arguments against today's attempts to control unauthorized human movement, worth listing in passing here. The West—and especially an aging Europe—needs more, not less, low-skilled labor. The divide between global rich and poor, inherited from colonial times and worsened by unjust economic policies, pushes people to seek fortunes abroad. Goods and money move in a near-frictionless fashion, while people do not. As a result, some companies set up shop beyond the border, drawing on a cheap workforce deprived of its right to move; others "insource" tasks that cannot be shipped abroad, such as cleaning offices, picking fruit, or caring for the elderly. While migration crackdowns rarely succeed, they do serve to keep the undocumented workforce pliable. They also bring easy votes at no risk, since those targeted are disenfranchised.[13] These crackdowns and controls clash with the human rights credentials of Western polities such as the European Union, the Nobel Peace Prize winner of 2012. They also reveal a surly inhospitality at a time when the vast majority of the world's refugees are housed by those least able to cope with them—poor neighboring states to countries racked by conflicts that are, moreover, often unleashed by Western states themselves.

A vast scholarly literature on migration—some of which is given in endnotes here and throughout this book—has elaborated on these injustices and irrationalities surrounding migratory flows.[14] Rather than rehearsing and rehashing these arguments, however, this book will instead cast a sideways anthropological glance at today's attempts to control human movement, highlighting not the repressive but the *productive* nature of such controls. In short, it focuses on the products and excesses of an "illegality industry" rather than on the apparent injustice and violence of a "border regime." This industry, it is argued, produces what it is meant to eliminate, curtail, or transform—more migrant illegality. In this loop, more funding is assured in a vicious circle reminiscent of the "war on terror"; the more specter-like the threat at the border, the higher the potential gains from this phantom menace.[15]

Yet this "menace" is also a living person, a traveler of flesh and blood. And, like Steinbeck's Okie, the African illegal immigrant of the early twenty-first century undergoes profound and distressing changes as he hits the road. Setting out with a small backpack and big hopes, he—for it is usually a he, even though women are increasingly common on clandestine routes—soon finds himself dragged along a darkening and narrowing tunnel of detentions, border posts, and legal exclusions. As he moves, he also has to deal with the slot or mold reserved for him: that of illegal immigrant. The illegality industry, it seems, reduces and flattens its migrant "product" in the borderlands by funneling a wide array of personal stories and cultures into this one generic mold of migrant illegality.

The category of illegality may seem clear-cut—as the U.S. bumper sticker would have it, "What part of illegal don't you understand?"—yet it is riddled with unspoken assumptions. In the imaginations of European border workers and citizens, as in the United States, the illegal immigrant is indeed a specific figure. As already seen, this migrant is increasingly racialized in Spain and beyond, feeding into revived fantasies about Africa as the West's Other, a hopeless continent beset by poverty and war, disease and disaster. Much like a mirror image of the feminized African "refugee," this migrant is also male, but he is a specific type of male evoking a peculiar constellation of attributes. He is anonymous and out of place, homeless and bereft of clear national belonging; he alternates between untrustworthiness and innocence, the roles of villain and victim.[16] On the road, the traveler comes to inhabit the category of migrant illegality, *incorporating* such contradictory traits into his very bodily self. The ways in which this incorporation of illegality comes about—often unexpectedly, frequently absurdly—will be the topic of the chapters that follow.

IN SEARCH OF THE BORDER

In a Spanish control room equipped with all the latest technology, a border guard spies an approaching migrant boat on his digital radar screen; in a sandy Senegalese courtyard thousands of kilometers away, a young deportee recalls, each day, his failure to reach Europe in such a boat. In the Canary Islands, his one-time destination, a melancholy detention center chief stares across his empty domains now that routes have moved elsewhere, into the desert. There, in the Algerian Sahara, one migrant hides in the back of a lorry, tucked in under a stash of contraband cigarettes; in northern Morocco, another lies in wait outside the razor-wire fence blocking his path into Ceuta. The border guards patrol the fences of Ceuta and Melilla; they scour the open seas; they enlist their African colleagues in a regionwide manhunt. Inside the enclaves and on Spanish shores await, for those astute enough to make it, journalists and aid workers. One of these workers takes a bedroll out of a cupboard, hands it to a migrant fresh off his raft, and escorts him into the strange world of Ceuta's migrant reception center. In the enclave's port a Portuguese border guard, wearing a blue Frontex armband, sets his sniffer dog on lined-up trucks in search of hidden travelers. Far from there, in the Malian Sahel, African and European activists march through the borderlands, protesting against the Portuguese guard and his Frontex colleagues. The players are lined up, each in his slot, along the Euro-African border: let the border game begin.[17]

This game unfolds across such apparently disparate places and time frames, united by invisible threads in the patchwork of connections that is the emerging Euro-African border. The coming chapters will reach across this large field, from Bamako in Mali to Frontex headquarters in Warsaw; they will travel in time, too, from the run-up to the 2005 tragedies at the fences of Ceuta and Melilla to the latest "attacks" on these barriers in the crisis-racked Spain of 2014. At times it is a fast-paced ride, flicking back and forth between control centers and African border posts; at other times it enters into the slow-moving world of deportees or stranded migrants. Datelines, along with the map and timeline at the start of the book, should help ease the ride. So should the chapter progression, which roughly follows the migratory journey northwards, from the West African Sahel towards North Africa and southern Spain.

Each chapter explores one interface where the illegality industry rubs against its targets, highlighting the excesses, contradictions, and absurdities that define Europe's response to clandestine migration. We will meet a bereaved Senegalese mother with her lucrative anti-migration association (chapter 1); a Spanish *comandante* running a state-of-the-art border operation while fantasizing about complete border surveillance (chapter 2); the African subcontractors who reluctantly do

Europe's dirty borderwork in exchange for cash, junkets, and gifts of night-vision goggles (chapter 3); the Spanish gatekeepers who drag migrants aboard their patrol boats while ambivalently showing off the high-tech fences of Ceuta and Melilla (chapter 4); "Mamá," a reception camp worker caring for her captive "sons" (chapter 5) who are treated as mere numbers by the police (chapter 6); and activists descending on the Sahel for a show of solidarity with migrant victims and a fruitless search for Europe's borders (chapter 7). Among these characters circulate shadowy presences—journalists and jailers, smugglers and spooks, defense industry contractors and policy makers—as well as the anthropologist, himself part of the industry that has grown up around the illegal immigrant.

THE CRACKED MIRROR: RESEARCHING THE ILLEGALITY INDUSTRY

Like many of the academics and journalists descending on the Euro-African border in recent years, I came to the topic of clandestine migration with a double sense of anger and intrigue. Anger, because of the tragedy unleashed upon poor travelers embarking upon life-changing journeys only to face border patrols and deadly desert and sea crossings—or what, in the U.S. context, has been called the willful and cruel "optimization of natural obstacles" for the purposes of migration control.[18] In European capitals, as in Washington, migration crackdowns are an easy vote-winner for the hard right—but few voters pay much attention to the untold deaths and miseries in the borderlands resulting from these crackdowns. Part of my task as ethnographer, as I saw it, was to expose the state-sanctioned violence occurring in the no-man's-lands that migrants traverse.

Yet for me as for other writers, beyond this task of exposure was an abiding *fascination* with the figure of the clandestine migrant. The trans-Saharan *aventure* (adventure), as some Francophone Africans call their long journeys towards Europe, reminded me of my own years of traveling the world. Setting out as a young man in the late 1990s on the one-time overland hippie trail to Asia from my suburban Swedish home, hitchhiking with a tiny backpack, a bit of money, and a piece of cardboard saying "India" held up to passing cars, I knew firsthand what it was like to head towards the unknown on a quest of discovery. The thrilling arrival in dark border towns in Iran or Pakistan without guidebook or language skills was quite like the trials of African adventurers or their Latin American counterparts seeking *el sueño americano*, albeit in a much more privileged position. Clandestine migration, I sensed, was not all gloom: it was also a journey of self-realization that revealed the resilience, restlessness, and striving of a very contemporary human condition. In my fieldwork, I would seek to explore this condition by following migrants on their overland adventures, sharing in their exhilaration, fear, and eventual transformation. "You think you are making a trip," the Swiss travel writer Nicolas Bouvier once said, "but soon it is making you—or unmaking you." Keeping his words in mind, my research question was, quite simply: what it is like to *become* "illegal"?[19]

This romantic and dramatic side to the overland "adventure" was not lost on other writers from the frontier. The Italian journalist Fabrizio Gatti, who joined migrants on their Saharan journeys, told his African travel companions they were, to him, the "protagonists of a modern heroism."[20] I expressed a similar admiration in my writing from another overland route—the Central American passage to the United States—where I had ended up in 2003, a few years after my Asian adventure, while doing research for a migrants' rights NGO. The migrants seeking shelter in the southern Mexican town of Tapachula, I wrote as I left them for Mexico City, were "the real travellers of the twenty-first century, the intrepid ones, full of horrors and stories, defying every border: if the northerner wishes for adventure, here is his disavowed mirror, cracks and all."[21]

As I arrived in Senegal in 2010 for fieldwork on the parallel routes on the other side of the Atlantic, however, I was soon up for an unwelcome realization. The mirror was not just cracked, but the face in it was staring back at me with an inquiring, angry, even accusatory gaze. Sitting in sand-swept Dakar courtyards and parrying questions about my objectives from the Senegalese "repatriates" booted out of Spain after their failed boat migration, I soon saw that my research hinged upon a helplessly romantic fascination with the unfortunate African traveler. What's more, I realized that this fascination writ large underpinned the whole spectacle of clandestine migration—the stacks of newsreels, documentaries, articles, academic tracts, and policy reports produced in the wake of the migrant boats. And the Senegalese repatriates—like their adventurer brethren I would later encounter on the overland route—were thoroughly sick of being the protagonists, heroic or otherwise, of this tawdry and tragic spectacle.

I should have been prepared for this early revelation in fieldwork, detailed in the first chapter of this book. After all, several writers have sounded a note of caution on the research topic of irregular migration.

The anthropologist Nicholas De Genova says that the act of constituting undocumented migrants and "the migrant experience" as objects of study is a form of "epistemic violence," reducing a wide array of people to an ethnographic gaze beholden to a state-centric vision. The French ethnographer Michel Agier similarly argues, in the case of encamped refugees, that studying these in their role as refugees "would mean confusing the object of research with that of the intervener who creates this space and this category"—that is, the "humanitarian government" that runs the camps and manages the lives of their inhabitants.[22]

In a similar vein, it soon dawned on me in Dakar's backyards that I should not let my fascination with the clandestine migrant direct my research, but that I should rather explore this fascination—or, more accurately, *obsession*—itself and the new realities it had helped create. I started reorganizing my fieldnotes, drawing diagrams of the actors who until then had been secondary to my concerns: aid workers and journalists, police and politicians, activists and academics such as myself. My aim, mapped out from my initial Dakar base, became to explore ethnographically how clandestine migration has been constituted as a field of intervention and knowledge gathering in the past decades. In this field careers are now made, networks created, knowledge and imagery circulated, and money channeled in increasing amounts. Why this obsession with clandestine migration into Europe by sea and land, and what are its effects? Why and how has a range of sectors—aid and media organizations, academic and defense industries, African and European security forces—become implicated in assessing, quantifying, and controlling irregular migratory flows in recent years? To answer these questions I realized that it was not enough to simply approach "the migrant" as an object of study, as anthropologists often do. Rather, I had to focus on the *system* in which illegal migration is both controlled and produced—its configuration, its workings, and its often distressing consequences.

This book gives a particular perspective on this system that should be briefly spelled out in relation to the vast literature on borders and migration. First of all, it does not ask who "should" be able to enter, a favorite topic among pundits and politicians. As will be seen, this question is far from straightforward, based as it is on the fantasy that border crossings *can* be optimally "managed" while economies remain deregulated and social networks across borders grow ever more intricate.[23] Nor does it look in detail at the systems of control on their global or even Europe-wide levels, like other recent works, such as journalist Jeremy Harding's far-reaching foray into the frontiers around the West, *Border Vigils*.[24]

Rather, it drills down into one particular section of the Euro-African frontier, the Spanish one, in order to grasp the day-to-day workings of the border. Here it approaches the system from an oblique angle, where the migrants themselves often provide the analytical and narrative push. The aim is to bring into a single frame the illegality industry's three principal fields on the frontline—policing and patrolling, caring and rescuing, and observing and knowing—alongside the migrants they target. These functions largely correspond to three key sectors treated in the book: the border guards, especially the Spanish Guardia Civil; the aid workers, in particular the Red Cross; and the media and academia.

Given this frame, there are again several things that this book does *not* attempt. It is not an ethnographic study of the migratory journey from the travelers' perspective, and little space will be spent on explicating the complex reasons behind the decision to migrate. Instead, the focus is on the system that makes these travelers observable, controllable—and, as migrants themselves insist, profitable. For this reason, those who are "invisible" to the industry—particularly female migrants and unaccompanied children—will remain somewhat invisible in the book as well.[25]

Certain strong beneficiaries and coproducers of migrant illegality similarly end up on the ethnographic margins. First among these are European employers, whose structural need for cheap and unorganized labor is usually seen as the reason why irregular migration flows are allowed to persist. Next are the smuggling (and trafficking) networks, as well as the security companies that increasingly handle detention and deportation or develop new "solutions" in the fight against migratory flows. While both smugglers and private businesses will be considered, their presence is more comprehensively dealt with by other recent work, including the academic volume *The Migration Industry and the Commercialization of International Migration* and activist author Claire Rodier's coruscating *Xénophobie Business*.[26] Finally, the world of politics and policy making—amply studied elsewhere—will be touched upon only tangentially in the coming chapters.[27] For this perspective, anthropologist Gregory Feldman's *The Migration Apparatus* provides important ethnographic insights into Europe's policy-making machinery. In his book, he charts how apparently disparate policy agendas converge in a nebulous apparatus that produces a profound indifference towards the migrants it targets.[28]

These omissions have allowed me to focus on the migratory "frontline," where clandestine migrants appear not as objects of indifference but rather as a source of fascination and preoccupation out of all proportion to the numbers. Put in a simplified manner, for the police, clandestine migrants are of concern as a source of risk; for the media, they represent newsworthiness and drama; for aid workers, they are of interest because of their assumed vulnerability; and their marginality renders them worthy of study in academia. This multipronged obsession with clandestine migration—forged in a feedback loop between the patrols and pictures of the frontline and the politics of European capitals—is in fact essential to the migration policy machinery and its production of indifference, since it ensures the political, financial, and media clout needed for the sector to flourish.

In part, the term *illegality industry* simply highlights how the "management" of irregular migration is a particularly expensive—and lucrative—field within the larger migration industry. Funding figures remain opaque, thanks to the multiple pots involved, from Interior Ministry funds to rerouted development aid; however, a few sums are worth mentioning. The European Union has allocated 60 percent of its total Home Affairs budget for 2007–13, or four billion euros, to the "solidarity and management of migratory flows"—with funding set to rise steeply, despite European austerity, in coming years. Besides central E.U. sums, member states spend large amounts on reception, detention, surveillance, and patrols. Spain, which lists the fight against irregular migration as one of its main security objectives, has in recent years built new detention, reception, and control centers; upped spending on sea rescues sixfold to one billion euros over 2006–9; and increased its border and migration forces from 10,239 officers in 2003 to 16,375 seven years later. Beyond such investments are the tied "aid" deals sealed with African states, whether in the five-billion-dollar Italy-Libya "Friendship Pact" of 2008 or the disbursements in West and North Africa that will be discussed in this book.[29]

This bonanza benefits not only African governments but also the security forces, research institutes, and aid organizations that increasingly compete for funds in the new Europe of outsourced public services. Incidentally, it also boosts the coffers of the people smugglers. Widely labeled "mafias" by politicians, these are nowhere near as organized as such a term implies—yet their trade, which grows alongside tougher controls, generates revenues estimated in the billions.[30] These profits are matched by the defense groups that are increasingly tied into the fight against illegal migration as active participants rather than passive beneficiaries. As will be seen, the companies involved in controls—many of which remain partly state-owned, such as the pan-European, French-backed Airbus Group and Finmeccanicca of Italy—lobby for new security "solutions" and priorities, and their stands line international conferences where Europe's security forces likewise mingle and compete for attention, money, and power.[31]

Yet while such gains are important—not least in migrants' understandings of their condition, as will be seen in the coming chapters—the term *illegality industry* also highlights other, deeper features of the structures developing around clandestine migration. Above all, it foregrounds productivity, or how the multifarious agencies purportedly working on "managing" illegality in fact produce more of it, like bickering workers on an assembly line. Yet the assembly line metaphor does not quite do justice to the geographical dispersal of this work—an aspect that is also highlighted by the term *industry*. In an industry, employees and machinery work in concert to manufacture and process products across factories, offices, and points of sale that add value through a division of labor. The term *illegality industry* here pinpoints several interrelated features of Europe's migration response: it foregrounds interactions among humans, technology, and the environment; it highlights how illegality is both fought and forged in concrete, material encounters; and it allows for the consideration of a dispersed "value chain," or the distinct domains in which migrant illegality is processed, "packaged," presented, and ultimately rendered profitable.[32]

This "productive" perspective—discussed further in the appendix—may raise some eyebrows. First, it could be objected that the *industry* term rolls too many disparate actors together, from defense contractors to aid workers and even the activists and academics protesting against them. Critical voices are certainly marginal to the industry—*in* it rather than *of* it—yet still awkwardly bound to its core through shared sources of funding, commonalities of concern, or similarities in working methods. Moreover, those at the receiving end—migrants and their families—often perceive these groups as part of a shared endeavor, as will be seen in chapter 1. As for critical research such as my own, the words of an anthropologist writing on the global anti-corruption industry spring to mind: "The final sign that an industry has come of age is that it spawns an academic critique." This book, then, is inevitably caught up in the system that it sets out to analyze.[33]

Second, the "productive" perspective may suggest a passive role for the travelers targeted by controls, yet they actively participate in their making as migrants. As self-designated "adventurers," some migrants take pride in their clandestine skills; others launch loud protests against their incarceration or immobilization; others again seek funds from the industry by claiming they are bona fide *clandestins*. To explore these dynamics, I will draw upon the philosopher Ian Hacking's notion of "making up people." To Hacking, scientific and policy categories such as that of "illegal immigrant" are not simply discursive constructs but help create "new way[s] to be a person." Hacking's point, succinctly put, is that "ways of classifying human beings interact with the human beings who are classified." The "interactive classifications" of social science and public policy feed back into the experiences of people so classified through what Hacking terms the "matrix" of the social and material setting—including, in this case, the paperwork, passports, patrols, and other material features of the clandestine encounter.[34] The "illegal immigrant," it will be seen, is not just a convenient political label fretted about in European capitals; it also becomes a lived-in category in the borderland "matrix" of the illegality industry.

The study of the industry involves methodological considerations too. While these are dealt with in the appendix, suffice to say here that I have departed from more traditional anthropological methods by drawing up an "extended field site" that reaches across the whole Spanish section of the Euro-African border. This has involved fieldwork on the move, switching between sites of departure and deportation (Dakar and Bamako, the Senegal-Mauritania border), ports of entry and reception (the Canaries and Andalusian coasts), points of blockage en route (Ceuta and Melilla, Oujda and Tangier in Morocco), and command and control centers (Frontex in Warsaw, Guardia Civil headquarters in Spain). The coming chapters aim to "link the phenomenal and the political," as the anthropologist Robert Desjarlais has framed the contemporary ethnographic challenge, by moving along these scales: from policy and journalistic discourses to the blips on screens in radar control rooms and a policeman's firm grip around the shoulders of a rescued migrant.[35]

TALES OF HUNGER: ILLEGALITY IN CONTEXT

Illegal migration is a recent phenomenon with a long and complicated past. Yet for me as for other anthropologists studying highly political events of the present, the question of how far one should dig into history, how many layers and fragments one should unearth, is battled out on each page of our ethnography. In recent years, many anthropologists have used history to unsettle their object of investigation, drawing upon the "genealogical" approach of the French philosopher Michel Foucault. Such digging into the past shows how categories, systems, or ideas that are now taken for granted—whether sexual and racial labels or forms of punishment and diagnosis—are contingent and contested. Things could have been otherwise.

This book does not follow such a genealogical approach; instead it is firmly ensconced in the present and recent past, leaving history—and especially colonial history—as the silent backdrop to the stories unfolding at the Euro-African border. Yet the contingency of illegal migration needs to be grasped, even if in the broadest sense, before embarking on the overland journey of the coming chapters.

First, it should be made clear that term *illegal immigrant*—used in this book as a popular (or "folk") term—is pejorative, stigmatizing, and even incorrect, implying as it does that migrants are criminals when they have usually only committed an administrative infraction. While the creeping criminalization of migration is changing this, *illegal* remains insidious when used to label *people* rather than actions, as the Associated Press noted in dropping *illegal immigrant* from its vocabulary in 2013. Moreover, the term masks the legal complexities pertaining to entry, residence, and employment in which travelers such as those of the coming chapters are caught; as will be seen, some of them have clandestinely crossed fences and seas and yet managed to register with local authorities once in Spain or have been rounded up in expulsion raids in Morocco despite carrying bona fide asylum application documents.[36]

Not only is it a blunt term: look back only a few decades, and the *illegal immigrant* vanishes from view altogether. It was only from the 1970s, with the draconian migration controls inaugurated by the oil crisis, that this category started taking on broad importance in the United States and Europe.[37] Outside the rich world, "illegal migration" is moreover a foreign imposition ill-suited to local contexts of human movement. In the West African case at the heart of this book, it is but a recent phenomenon superimposed upon older and larger patterns—including circular migration within the region, ancient trade routes across the Sahara, and transnational circuits borne of the colonial encounter. Illegality, however, threatens these older patterns. It twists aid priorities, inhibits licit movements, and sours regional relations—all the while drawing upon colonial history and stirring memories from the darkest chapter in West Africa's past, the slave trade ferreting human chattel across the Sahara and the Atlantic.[38]

. . .

Ever since the boats started bringing black migrants into southern Spain, sympathetic journalists and border guards have glossed the reason behind their seemingly senseless journeys as "hunger." Hunger in barren home countries, hunger among peoples racked by droughts and brutal civil wars: the migrants here appear as survivors, threatening and pitiable by turns, escaping a sinking continent. Yet the reasons behind their long journeys are to be found in altogether more subtle, and more insidious, hunger pangs than those imagined by the media.

Many years ago, during my undergraduate studies, I spent a summer in Mali, the cultural heart of West Africa and one of the world's poorest countries. As a good anthropologist I sought full immersion in this new world and had found myself a relatively well-to-do host, a Soninké trader, who generously welcomed me to his two-room family home on the outskirts of Bamako. I recall starting the days with baguettes and Nescafé, politely refusing the big tins of Nestlé condensed milk that my host and his wife poured, liberally and with a flourish, into their cups. Then the days began, languorous and eventless, with time marked by the tock-tock of women pounding grain in the backyard and the sipping of glass after tiny glass of bittersweet Chinese "gunpowder" tea. In the patches of shade dotting the neighborhood's mud lanes sat clusters of unemployed men who all itched to invite the stranger to talk and take down addresses, to discuss the state of the nation and George W. Bush's still recent presidency. In the evenings, as the mosquitoes began to circle and the tinny call to prayer subsided, I roamed streets illuminated only by the warm flicker of television screens showing Latin American *telenovelas,* dubbed in French, the old colonial language. At home my host's nephew, Modibo, would join me on the couch, laying out his ambitious plans to leave Mali by any means: by plane, by road, by using fake documents. What could I suggest? Occasionally the rattle of my host's old car—bought with proceeds from his itinerant vending on the streets of Paris—interrupted Modibo's musings or the evening debates among neighbors on the porch, bringing the promise of an excursion to the swish *supermarché* or an empty nightclub. Soon enough, my anthropological self had reached a point of no return: I was nowhere near as far away from "home" as I had perhaps wanted to imagine.

The Mali I visited was simultaneously profoundly connected to and disconnected from the world economy. Its clusters of tea drinkers constituted a spare labor pool happily ignored by global markets, yet these men and their families were also full-fledged consumers of imagery, goods, and desires from these very markets. It was a country where young men such as Modibo found themselves torn between their hunger for the world they saw on-screen and their home world of rusty cars and muddy lanes. As a result, some of them felt the peculiar claustro-phobia of the immobilized that left no space for thoughts other than joining the two worlds by the only means possible: to leave.

Ethnographers have documented this hunger for leaving across West Africa, relating it to a sense of social death among those who can nei-ther find work nor move. Among Soninké villagers of Mali and Sene-gal—whose life cycles have long been structured around the rhythms of labor migration—young immobile men are taunted by women for being "stuck like glue"; in neighboring Gambia, their brethren experience a state of "nerves" as they hear the tall tales of success brought back by visiting emigrants. As in other postcolonial regions, access to foreign lands has become a source of increased polarization, with Europe ren-dered as a mythical repository of wealth and transformative power.[39]

This predicament again harks back to the 1970s. The oil crisis did not just lead European states to close off migratory channels for workers from former colonies; it also brought soaring debt to West African nations. In the IMF-imposed structural adjustment programs that ensued in the coming two decades, state assets were sold off, formal employ-ment fell, and price controls on basic goods were abolished. Meanwhile dwindling regional fisheries, the droughts of the Sahel, and sagging prices for regional commodities such as cotton pushed formerly self-sufficient farmers and fishermen closer to penury. Then the sharp 1994 devalua-tion of the regional franc CFA currency—still controlled by Paris, the former colonizer—reduced spending power and so pushed more West Africans to look for better fortunes abroad: that is, in the European countries that had largely been responsible for their economic predica-ment and whose borders now came with a "no entry" sign attached.

As I embarked on fieldwork in 2010 in Dakar, I would again see the hunger firsthand in young men like Malick, a broad-shouldered guy with natty dreads whose quiet demeanor failed to hide an utter determina-tion. In Malick's shared room, his friends' voices rose as they took turns at playing cards or a combat game on the old Dell computer in the cor-ner. Malick was itching to leave his Dakar existence behind—his cramped room with its endless games and whiff of lingering adolescence, his fruit-less trade selling secondhand mobile phones. In fact, he had tried to leave repeatedly already. With no possibility of acquiring a European visa, he had attempted the clandestine sea journey three times: first detained by Spain and deported, next intercepted by the Senegalese Navy and locked up for forty-five days, and finally caught and expelled by Mauritanian police. Still, he kept scheming to leave. His friends giggled at the pictures he had posted of himself on the Internet, sultry eyes and bare torso, to appeal to foreign girls. No one had so far been in touch. "It doesn't matter what work I do once I get there," he said, his plans vague at best. As with his small mobile "business," he would fend for himself in Europe as best he could—a notion neatly encapsulated in the Wolof verb *góor-góorlu,* or "doing one's best," from the word for "man" *(góor).* Like other young Senegalese, Malick had an acute sense of how what was once a normal part of becoming a man—earning his keep, moving out, founding a family—had become next to impossible. Migration, as he saw it, was his only remaining option. "One day, I'll have three hundred thousand CFA (six hundred dollars) again, and I will leave. You have to try, even for the tenth time, you have to keep on trying." By 2014, he was in Morocco, scheming to finally make the dash across to Europe.[40]

"Hunger," then, is at the heart of clandestine migration, yet not in the sense of absolute want. Indeed, the poorest of the poor remain within the region; it is those with at least some access to contacts and cash— often family funds—who can set off on long, uncertain journeys towards the north. It is in this context that the clandestine routes from West Africa need to be seen: as but one extreme response to the closed borders, economic turmoil, and globalized imaginations of a new era. As anthropologist Hans Lucht puts it in his evocative ethnography of impoverished Ghanaian fishermen migrating across the Sahara, "high-risk immigration from West Africa to Europe is an attempt to revitalize life by *reestablishing connections"* between unfulfilled desires and an unresponsive external world.[41]

The hunger behind these migrations is twofold, however—not just as a means of sating the desires of young men such as Malick, Modibo, and their families, but also as a response to the voraciousness of Western labor markets. In setting off in flimsy boats or overloaded desert trucks, clandestine migrants have provided a small but supremely expendable labor force for the construction and farming sectors of new immigration countries such as Italy and Spain.[42] And as southern Europe's economic bubble burst, they would also come to play a new and complementary role: as guinea pigs for the illegality industry.

. . .

The story of Spain since the death of dictator Francisco Franco in 1975 is one of swift "Europeanization"—not least of the country's borders. In preparation for E.U. entry in 1986, Madrid introduced the country's first Aliens Law and soon began fortifying its southern frontiers. Controls and clandestinity have since then accompanied each other. It is no coincidence that the first reported arrivals of *pateras,* or migrant boats, around the Strait of Gibraltar occurred in 1991, the year when Spain joined the Schengen Agreement for free movement within the European Union and introduced visa requirements for Moroccans.[43]

Yet it was not the North African *harragas,* or "burners of borders," who provided the spark for the illegality industry on the Spanish frontier; it was the media spectacle of sub-Saharan migrants arriving in rickety rafts a few years later. By 2000, Spain's conservative government had started extracting substantial political capital from irregular migration and was swiftly taking Spain from being Europe's weak and pressurized entry point towards the migration control vanguard—a task continued, with new rhetorics and techniques, by the Socialists during their eight-year spell in power. In a parallel to U.S.-Mexico and Italy-Libya collaboration at the time, Spain and the European Union enlisted North African countries in controls and stepped up patrolling—eventually pushing migrants onto the longer, more dangerous route towards the Canary Islands. The result was growing numbers of arrivals, culminating in the 2006 "boat crisis," in which exhausted migrants staggered ashore on the archipelago's beaches among startled sunbathers, Red Cross volunteers, and journalists.

Spain's recent migration experience has been both exemplary and unique among Western states. Unique, because the country has gone from being an *emigration* country in the 1980s to seeing one of the rich world's highest rates of immigration two decades later—yet has proven more welcoming to these new arrivals than most other European countries. Exemplary, because the Socialist government's embrace of multiculturalism, humanitarianism, and international cooperation accompanied an extraordinary success in halting the migrant boats. In 2005, the Socialists inaugurated their years in power with a mass regularization of irregular migrants to criticism of a "call effect" from the opposition and other E.U. member states; soon after, the tragic "mass assaults" at Ceuta and Melilla seemed to prove the critics right. Yet the government, whose liberal politics at home was accompanied by a swift reinforcement on the southern front, soon got the upper hand. Only a few years after the chaos in the enclaves and the Canaries, Spain's interior minister declared that 2010 had been the best year in a decade for migration control, and the country's methods were envied and emulated by its southern European neighbors.[44]

The Spanish "front," then, is about much more than a single state's efforts to control human movement; it is a key site for investigating the

European, or indeed Western, "fight against illegal migration" in all its contradictions. For contradictions suffuse the E.U. border regime. This is a regime in which repressive policing awkwardly coexists with invocations of human rights and the political leadership of a Swedish card-carrying member of Amnesty International (Cecilia Malmström, the E.U. commissioner for Home Affairs) who insists that "no human being is illegal."[45] It is a regime, too, in which development money is used to "fight migration," ignoring any ethical quandaries as well as evidence that points to *increased* migration as countries develop.[46] And it is a regime that has willfully fomented the pressure at the European Union's land and sea borders—most importantly via draconian visa and flight controls as well as via the "Dublin regulation," which requires asylum cases to be processed by the first E.U. member state the claimant enters. A ground-level perspective on such contradictions is at the heart of this book.

The apparent "success" on the Spanish front must also be measured against "failure" elsewhere along the *shared* external border of the European Union. Irregular entry by air continues apace from West Africa and elsewhere, through the use of fake or loaned passports, black-market visas, or other creative means. The Greece-Turkey and Libya-Italy routes remain constantly on the verge of "crisis," and Spain's southern shores see regular bouts of police violence, protests, or new waves of arrivals, as the coming chapters will show.[47] The diplomatic deal making underlying Spain's "closure" of the border is also fragile—not least after the Socialist government that negotiated these deals lost power in 2011. Yet regardless of the changing political winds, the problem runs deeper. Much as in colonial times, when French dominance in Africa failed to embrace the rural hinterland, the European border regime cannot control the borderlands despite the dazzling surveillance machinery and innovative policing networks at its disposal. The state's "monopolization of the legitimate means of movement," as the sociologist John Torpey shows in *The Invention of the Passport,* is not just a recent historical phenomenon; it is also a maddeningly ambitious undertaking that cannot but fail in its task of controlling thousands of kilometers of coastlines and terrestrial borders.[48]

ILLEGALITY, INC.

Like the migratory journey, this book moves gradually north, with the stops and starts, setbacks, and shifts of perspective that characterize the clandestine circuit. Starting in the migration world of Dakar, the chapters roam across the Euro-African borderlands, where they chart how contradictory modalities of illegality are forged in the industry's interfaces of deportation, surveillance, patrolling, rescues, reception, and activism. Upon reaching the gates of Europe in chapter 6, the story heads south again, eventually returning to Dakar and the confrontation with the illegality industry staged by activists there. Brief forays into scenes from elsewhere along the border accompany the chapters, contrasting high and low, the near and the far, workers and the migrants they target.

The first part, "Borderlands," maps the industry's scattered geography and its absurd local consequences. The story begins at journey's end, among the Senegalese youth who embarked for the Canaries during the boat migration boom only to be swiftly sent back home. The resentment among these repatriates in chapter 1 provides a window onto the inequities and bizarre workings of the illegality industry that rolled into Dakar in 2006. In this absurd industry, it will be seen, repatriates come to collaborate—as self-identified *clandestins*—in their own making up as illegal migrants.[49]

Chapter 2 moves away from the trickle-down economics of the Dakar aid world for a bird's-eye view on the big money in the illegality industry. The security forces and subsidized defense companies fast at work building the Euro-African border, it is argued, render clandestine migration as a source of "risk" both to human life and the European external border—in the process creating a depoliticized security threat from which maximum value may be extracted.

Chapter 3 dives back into the Sahel, shifting the focus to the African policing partners' crucial role in the "fight against illegal migration." It follows migrants and those who police them on the overland journey northwards, through a very different borderland from that of the high-tech European regime: a world of wild desert stretches and derelict border posts where the "illegal migrant" is alternately conjured as a hunted prey and a ghost like, prohibited presence.

Part 2, "Crossings," meets the migrants at the final hurdle: the European external border. Chapter 4 explores the two-faced spectacle awaiting them there—humanitarian rescues at sea versus the hidden show of force at the land borders of Ceuta and Melilla. The border spectacle, the section shows, is constantly threatened by its own inconsistences as well as by protests and subversion from within and without, with control over it increasingly slipping away from its presumed directors.

Buffeted by border controls, migrants and their associates also fight back. Part 3, "Confrontations," starts in Ceuta, among migrants who have finally crossed into "European" space. Or so they think—in fact, they soon find themselves stranded indefinitely in this tiny territory hemmed in between the sea and the fence. Chapter 5 follows the stranded migrants as they launch a protest against their captivity, in which they end up giving a distressing twist to their racialized role as captive "illegals." Chapter 6 steps back from the melee and analyzes how migrants are subject to a politics of time in Ceuta and Melilla, wherein their months or years stuck in limbo constitute, to the Spanish authorities, a form of deterrence against more entries. Stuck in an arbitrary landscape of time, migrants have little choice but to reach for absurd or desperate solutions.

Chapter 7 heads back south and into another confrontation sparked by the illegality industry. Activists are increasingly converging on the Euro-African border, and the chapter follows one such group on a "caravan for the freedom of movement" leaving Mali for the World Social Forum of Dakar in early 2011. The activists soon face a problem, however: the absence of a clear target and a concrete border at which to protest. Like the migrant demonstration in Ceuta, their efforts highlight the difficulties marring attempts to confront the nebulous border regime at Europe's southern edges.

Taken together, these interfaces show how the work-in-progress of the illegality industry is a fraught and contradictory enterprise. The industry, feeding on the illegality it is meant to control, only produces more and increasingly distressing forms of it. From the world of precarious guest workers has emerged, over barely two decades, a confusing array of phenomena—wooden fishing boats packed to the brim; migrants marooned on tiny islands; bodies clinging to barbed wire or sinking on their inflatable rafts. As old routes close down, strange sights also abound in the industry itself. Fences and sea patrols guard against migrant boats that no longer appear on the horizon while detention centers stand empty, migration documentaries remain unsold, good Samaritans lose their beneficiaries, and "migration management" centers squander their last funds. Such ruins and remnants—explored in the scenes set between chapters—may seem to broadcast "success" in the fight against illegal migration, yet they also stand as testament to a deeper futility. The problem they address has simply moved elsewhere: to Greece or Italy, to European airports, to the buffer zones of the borderlands. This merry-go-round in turn hints at an absurdity at the heart of the industry's endeavors, despite the steely logics at play. Not "absurdity" as colloquial dismissal or utter senselessness, but absurdity in a more specific analytical sense: as a perpetual mismatch between measures and targets that inflates the fears it seeks to address, raises the stakes, and spawns unforeseen conflicts while opening up an existential abyss for the travelers it targets. The conclusion will reflect further on this absurdity and what can be learned from it.

While this book explores one "front" in a shared Western endeavor to shut out the unwanted, the parallels with developments elsewhere are striking—whether in Greece and Italy, in the U.S.-Mexico borderlands, at Israel's frontiers, or on Australian shores. Set at a time when southern Europe was descending into chronic crisis, it charts a crucial phase in the consolidation of the illegality industry as the boom-year demand for cheap labor was being paired with other, darker logics developed in the industry itself. With this in mind, what lessons can be drawn from the Spanish experience, and is there any hope for a different approach in the future? What does it say about the West's contradictory relations with its neighbors and about the consolidation of the European Union through a fortified external border? Finding humane answers to these questions is key to the future of inclusive democracy in the West and elsewhere, and it is hoped that this book will contribute to these debates—if not with answers, at least with critical ground-level insights.

Beyond these political questions, however, lurks an all-too-human account riven with deep contradictions. As will be seen in the coming pages, the growth of the illegality industry is in part a story about hardworking men and women—most of them earnest and good-hearted—who together have produced an anti-mobility machine in which today's ultimate pariahs are stuck, in an infernal warp.

The Lonely Jailer

A FOREIGNERS' DETENTION CENTER, THE CANARY
ISLANDS, SPAIN, EARLY 2010

The centro de internamiento de extranjeros *(CIE) lay far off the beaten track and did not even appear on that all-seeing cartography of our times, Google Maps. My taxi driver, a garrulous Argentinian, kept talking about his impending London migration as he finally found a dug-up road along the highway and labored uphill until the track forked in two. To the right, a military zone. To the left, the empty CIE parking lot. I walked up to the perimeter wall, and a guard slid the massive entrance gate open.*

Spain's migrant detention centers are the southernmost outposts in what has been called a "new carceral archipelago" of internment camps for foreigners—about 400 and counting—in Europe.[1] *Few independent observers have made it into these Spanish centers: my brief glimpse of life inside, in my first month of fieldwork, would give me a disconcerting view of the new realities created by Europe's illegality industry. Here was a poignant display of the massive structures for shutting out and corralling the unwanted; here, too, was the strange mix of visibility and invisibility, of neglect and attention, and of humanitarianism and violence that define Europe's anti-migration efforts; and here I would see, above all, how the illegal immigrant was taking shape as a racial figure endowed with an essential set of characteristics, carrying distressing echoes from the presumably long-forgotten colonial past.*

We walked through the empty courtyard. Downhill the Atlantic Ocean beckoned, from where migrants once came in their wooden fishing boats. "The sunrise is pretty here," the guard said wistfully. I nodded and looked about, wondering if any early blush of sun would make it past the looming walls.

In the waiting hall, plastic chairs were grafted onto the empty walls, and a notice gave the timetable for visits to internos (detainees). Eventually the chief arrived and excused himself: he had gone for a coffee at the shopping center a few kilometers down the road, the closest place for refreshment in these parts. He was affable, but there was something disconcerting in the broad smile across his lips as he led me to his first-floor office.

"Do you mind if I smoke?" The chief sat down, lighting a cigarette. On his desk rested a memento mori made up of a plastic skull and a book: all too fitting in a center that raked up the migrants fortunate enough to have survived the dangerous sea journey across the Atlantic. He walked up to a big map of Africa on the wall, tracing movements along the continent's coasts with his finger. "Why don't they come any longer?" he asked, genuinely perplexed. The officer in charge of housing boat migrants was at a loss to explain their sudden disappearance from the coasts of the Canary Islands.

When the migrant boats first arrived in the Canaries, there had been no structures in place for holding their passengers. Military tents were erected, old aircraft hangars filled with litters. Then the new CIEs were built. Here migrants could be kept for up to sixty days for identification followed by deportation, or liberation if their nationality had not been ascertained.[2] In the beginning, West African arrivals had swiftly been sent on to mainland Spain and set free with an expulsion order; then deportations began in 2006, carrying planeload after planeload of boat migrants back to Mauritania and Senegal. The conflicts triggered by these "repatriations" remained unresolved five years on, as will be seen in chapter 1.

The chief sat down, puffed on his cigarette, and explained the routines: "At 8:00 A.M. we get up, with half an hour for a shower and so on," he said. Breakfast followed, then workshops run by the Red Cross, before lunch and an afternoon rest. Dinner at 8:00 P.M., lights out at 10:00. Throughout he talked in first person plural: the image he projected was of a holiday camp, perhaps, or a home-away-from-home where he was the resident leader.

The chief was hardly popular among the aid workers outside the walls. "He thinks it's a playground, but he's really a jailer," sighed one. Popular *or not, the jailer was certainly stuck in what seemed a punishment posting by the standards of Spain's national police, in a center that, according to a mounting chorus of critical reports and campaigns, offered fewer guarantees than a normal prison.[3] Everything inside depended on the judgment of the director, the aid worker said. "It's his castle."*

The time for visiting the castle finally came. Downstairs the corridors lay bare and gloomy: hardly a clandestine migrant in sight. The crowds, the people sleeping under open skies back in 2006—all gone. In the canteen sat a morose club of a dozen or so migrants, lunching under the watchful eyes of a few policemen. Crayon drawings adorned the walls: a Red Cross worker had been running creative classes for detainees. The corridors were plastered with notices on detainees' rights in Spanish, French, and English; torn A4 printouts rendered the text in Wolof, Senegal's main language.

"We can find out when they lie to us," said the jailer while showing me the doctor's room. "You see from the sores they have on their behind and their back." If the detainees had sores on their buttocks, they had endured a shorter trip; if they had back injuries, it could be a boat journey of up to fifteen days, during which the salt of the sea rubbed against the skin. The clandestine body, like a lie detector, revealed the secrets of the journey thanks to the duty of care and in spite of the migrant's intentions.

The jailer took me to the patio, all drab concrete and strategically positioned surveillance cameras. The CIE was set in a depression, so no horizon offered itself up beyond the looming fences. Here they once organized football tournaments, with teams divided by age, nationality, or boat, or "depending on how we feel that day." The jailer glanced across his domains with a hint of pride. "The only privation here is that they cannot go free," he said. "All this," he used to tell detainees, sweeping his hand across the empty courtyard, "is not mine, it's yours!"

In 2006, the whole place was packed: people slept outside, some in tents and others outside the fences. "They could have jumped across the wall easily," the jailer said. "But no one fled. Why?" he asked rhetorically. "El negro es una persona buena por naturaleza": the black man is by nature good.

Not sensing my unease, the jailer warmed to the topic of race. "We corrupt them (les pervertimos nosotros)," he continued. "We educate them in greed, we educate them in consumerism." To prove his point, he pointed to their simple dress upon arrival. "They all come in a jogging suit, their clothes are like a uniform, they all come the same. Here, inside, one of them might say, 'I want those trainers,' 'I want a pair of jeans'—they start changing." Why? "They have the television, they see us, they see me arriving on a motorcycle or in a big car."

There was sympathy in the jailer's voice and ambivalence about the provisions in his castle. People bad-mouthed the sub-Saharan migrants, he said, calling them dangerous and lazy. *"It's just because they are black,* nada más, *just plain ignorance."* Lack of resources meant there was not much to do here, he said, so the detainees *"lie on the floor all day long. If this was a center where we had a gym . . . but we don't. What can you do? What would you do for five hours here? They are lazy because of that? No."* His defense speech of the African migrant was directed at the hostile voices outside the walls but simply twisted their accusations of the lazy, dangerous black man into its opposite image: that of the noble savage.

The jailer led me into the female living "modules." "Cells" seemed a more apt description for the dark, empty rooms strung out along a narrow corridor. Inside each were three double-bed bunks under a low, oppressive metal mesh ceiling. The shared bathroom's new granite walls had been labeled "luxurious" in the media, the jailer said with disdain: yet the old, cheap walls had crumbled and fallen apart, eroding with overuse. Scattered around the sinks lay the lone woman detainee's toiletries. Why had he taken me here, to the women's bathroom? Why had I come here at all? I felt sickened, like a voyeur.

On the way out, we walked past the glazed-in TV rooms, and there she was, in the room reserved for women. She put her face up against the glass pane, her eyes following us as we walked, piercing or pleading. The jailer told the guard she wanted to be let out for a toilet visit: How did he know? And why was she locked in the TV room, alone?

We headed for the exit, where the jailer stopped for a moment before opening the heavy gates. *"I have changed a lot here,"* he suddenly said. *"Before I had this hatred* (aborrecimiento), *this fear"* of black people. *"But we are the ignorant ones, the* blanquitos," he said, using an affectionate diminutive for white people in a mirroring of the negritos under his care. *"We can learn a lot from them, something as simple as saying* buenos días." He smiled, recalling his earlier ignorance. *"It's we who have corrupted them"* (les hemos viciado nosotros), he repeated as he ventured into the guard cabin and commandeered the gate, which creaked and slid open with a rattle. We shook hands; I was free. I went out into the dreary parking lot, stranded in the middle of nowhere, and called the taxi. As my driver arrived, the jailer still stood there, at the other side, smoking a cigarette and looking out across the metal gate, alone in his empty castle.

PART ONE

Borderlands

CHAPTER 1

Mohammadou and the Migrant-Eaters

Mother Mercy arrived one hour late. Her car stopped on the sandy Senegalese backstreet right outside the doorway; she stepped out of the passenger seat and strode into the bare, ramshackle locales of her collective for women who had lost their sons to boat migration. A crisp black dress laced with silvery strands flowed around her as she sashayed past, talking loudly into her mobile; on her wrist glittered a large watch. *"Ah, excusez-moi,"* she said, switching from Wolof on the phone to French, momentarily addressing me as I waited behind a wooden table in the corner. "The traffic jams . . ." She sat down and snapped her fingers to command the attention of her assistant, a rotund woman behind a rickety counter at the back of the room. The assistant promptly brought her calendar, whose pages already spoke of visits to France, Italy, and Spain: Mother Mercy was a busy, busy woman. She flipped through the pages with one hand as she clutched her mobile with the other, giving orders and managing appointments in an executive stream of Wolof and French while jotting down the details of another trip abroad.

It was at this point that I realized something strange was happening in the world of clandestine migration.

Middle-aged women in flowing reds, greens, and yellows trickled into the office, went up to the counter, and gave 525 francs CFA (one dollar) to the assistant, daily debt payments in the microcredit scheme Mother

Mercy had set up for the members of her Dakar-based collective. Many of them had, like her, lost a son to the waves. A poster on the wall next to the counter trumpeted, *"Non aux pirogues de la mort!"* (Say no to the boats of death!)

Eventually Mother Mercy hung up and slid a brochure across the table. "Our collective started its work with our sons losing their lives." She had switched to a soft, maternal voice that sounded as though it had been through hundreds of rehearsals. As it turned out, this was indeed the case. Her outfit had been fêted by journalists and politicians from London to Las Palmas since the fateful days of 2006, when fishing boats packed with migrants had departed from Senegal for the faraway Canary Islands. "Mother Mercy," which the media soon insisted on calling her because of her brave "battle against migration," had graced the screens and pages of the BBC and France2, *Glamour* and *Elle* magazines, the *Washington Post*, France's *Libération* and *Le Monde*, Spain's *El País* . . . the list was endless.[1] She flicked through the brochure detailing the collective's good works, temporarily ignoring the incessant ring of her mobile. "Our campaigns have put a stop to illegal migration," she said, despite the "meager means" at their disposal. "We have to work hard to *fixer les jeunes* (keep the youth in place)."

The media and politicians had praised her efforts to keep the youth in place through so-called *sensibilisation* (sensitization), awareness-raising campaigns about the "risks of illegal migration." Her work was "more effective than all the warships and planes sent to the Atlantic Ocean by the European Union," the BBC had said in 2006. If so, Mother Mercy was a victim of her own success. By 2010, the boats had stopped departing, and funding was slowly leeching away. "We have to continue our work," she said. "If we do sensitization here, people just depart from elsewhere," which meant they had to spread the message across the whole country, even over the whole region! *"La sensibilisation n'a pas de deadline,"* she said distractedly while typing a number into her mobile, then calling. My brief audience was over.

I went outside and called Mohammadou. "Tell him you got the number from me," Mother Mercy had said, scribbling it on a piece of paper. Soon enough Mohammadou came ambling towards the office. He was the president of the local association of young repatriates from Spain but cut a poor figure for such a lofty title in his loose jeans, plastic sandals, and old jacket, a cap resting on his head. He said a brief, unsmiling hello and then led me into the sand-swept lanes of his neighborhood. Yongor, as I will call it, was a fishing village swallowed by the urban sprawl of Dakar that had been particularly hard hit by boat migration. It was from here that Mohammadou and his friends had once set off, and it was here that they now lingered, jobless and immobile, nursing the wound of their one-time deportation.[2]

"What can you offer us?" Mohammadou blurted out as we walked towards the beach, the stale air carrying smells of putrid fish and gasoline. "And what do you want?" The order of his questions seemed topsy-turvy, but it was so for a reason: he had seen too many visitors already. On a corner, two women in bright robes squatted next to a cart piled high with mangoes, children scuttling round them in the pale, hot sand. Walking past, I tried to think of suitable replies but had none to offer him.

At the family home of Ali, a brawny repatriate in his twenties, the crash of the waves whispered through narrow lanes whose walls were scrawled with the phone numbers of neighbors' relatives in Spain and France. Ali wedged a wooden bench into the sand, and Mohammadou sat down and got his notebook out. He flicked through page after page of names, numbers, and e-mails of all those who had come to see his repatriates' association. The contact details of journalists, researchers, students, NGO workers, even an E.U. delegate adorned the pages. He had never heard back from any of them. "A lot of people have passed by here, but every time they go back to Europe, there's nothing." Ali nodded and shared out his only cigarette, Mohammadou drawing the last bit of smoke from its dying embers. "*Ils mangent sur nous*" (they eat from us), Mohammadou said, his mouth twisting into what would soon become a familiar frown. Even the aid organizations ate their money, while the repatriates got nothing. "I am the president, and I have to ask him for a cigarette. Do you think this is normal?" Mohammadou said angrily, nodding towards his friend.

The repatriates had had enough. They did not want to speak to researchers or reporters any longer. They felt embittered and angry with the fact finders and delegations—not to mention with the interlocutor of these *toubabs,* or white people, in Yongor, Mother Mercy. "Why did she send you to us?" Mohammadou asked with a twisted smile. It was a rhetorical question that was to become a standing joke during the coming year. "Because you don't bring any money. If you had come in a four-wheel drive, she would have invited you to her house."

THE BIRTH OF A TRAGEDY

The wave of clandestine migration hit the shores of Senegal and the front pages of European newspapers in the summer of 2006. The sudden sight of brashly painted wooden boats groaning under the weight of disheveled Africans had come as a shock and surprise to the news-reading public and Spanish police alike, but the signs and premonitions had been there. The previous year, sub-Saharan migrants stuck in Morocco had launched the infamous mass attempt to climb the fences surrounding Ceuta and Melilla. The ensuing crackdown pushed clandestine routes southwards: first to Morocco-occupied Western Sahara, then to the desert state of Mauritania along the Atlantic coast, and finally farther south to Senegal and beyond. A direct route had suddenly opened up from West Africa to Europe, and youth from Senegal and farther afield saw their chance to hitch a ride. In 2006 almost thirty-two thousand people landed in the Canary Islands, fifteen hundred kilometers of rough Atlantic to the northwest of Dakar.[3]

Boats had landed in earlier years in the archipelago's smaller easterly islands, often carrying Sahrawis and Moroccans, but it was with the West African arrivals in Tenerife and Gran Canaria that an extraordinary spectacle unfolded. Tourists in swimsuits rushed to assist exhausted migrants on the beaches, and soon the media "set up a show" in port, as one local migration scholar recalled. A moral panic over the human "tsunami" or "avalanche" washing over the islands was reinforced with each day's fresh tally. Never mind that in 2006, amid the clamor over that year's thirty-two thousand boat arrivals, about ten million travelers passed through just Gran Canaria's airport, including large numbers of labor migrants from Europe and Latin America: the storyline about irregular migration was set and framed through racial images of an unstoppable invasion.[4]

The media hysteria also reached West Africa, where newscasts showed how a new route had suddenly opened to Spain—and was soon to close down with the deployment of European sea patrols. It was now or never.[5]

"This is the big chance, we mustn't lose it," young men reasoned in Senegal's seaside fishing hamlets, according to Ousmane, a theater producer and community leader. "It was generalized madness." Women scrambled their savings together to finance the trip; young men bartered their family belongings. The captains of the boats became sudden heroes, and women sang their praise. Everyone wanted to leave on *mbëkë mi*, the Wolof term for the journey that literally means "hitting one's head." "At that time, everyone talked of the forecast," Ousmane recalled: people checked obsessively for the best weather conditions in which to depart. Rumors were spreading. Spain wanted more migrants to come and work! The expressway to Europe was open! Fishermen-turned-smugglers loaded their large wooden canoes with cans of petrol, bottles of water, and supplies of dry food. They consulted the *marabouts* (Muslim religious leaders), collected the money for the "tickets," set their GPS for Tenerife, and off they went, boatload after boatload of willing workers. *Barça walla barzakh* was their motto: "Barcelona or the afterlife." Men who hesitated to join in the boat craze were ridiculed as effeminate and weak of will. People said *"Jéleen gaal yi, jigeen yi jél avion yi!"* Ousmane reminisced: take the boat, [only] women take the plane!

After the mania came the fall. Police detained and imprisoned those who had been forced to return while the death count added up at high sea. Relatives' phone calls were left unanswered. Boats disappeared with their human cargo, never to be heard of again. Thousands died in the waves; no one knows exactly how many.

Mohammadou's fishing village was a pioneering terrain for mbëkë mi, and its youth suffered worse knocks than those of other coastal communities. While some local *convoyeurs* (smugglers) and marabouts had made good money out of the boat craze, losses were adding up across the neighborhood. Wives, children, and parents were left bereaved and often bereft of income. Walking along the lanes of Yongor, Mohammadou invoked the dead at every turn. "Do you see her?" he said as we passed a woman in her thirties carrying a bucketful of goods on her head. "She lost her husband, she lost five family members, that's why she has to work now." He nodded towards friends, saying, "He was in my boat" or "In his house three people died." He had tried counting the dead, but his mother had told him to stop when he reached 475—the effort was ripping open barely healed wounds. "Everyone has lost someone here."[6]

If the boat arrivals in the Canaries had triggered the first media frenzy, the tragedy back in Senegal now set off another. Journalists descended on the country's seaside communities in search of stories on the dead, the missing and the deported—and Yongor was at the center of their attentions. A 2006 visit to the neighborhood by the French presidential hopeful Ségolène Royal spurred the reporters on and put Mother Mercy and her association in the spotlight. Yongor went "from dire anonymity to world fame," as one news report put it: it was becoming a privileged stage for what the Spanish media and politicians liked to call the "drama of immigration."

By 2010, the wave of clandestine migration had receded. But in its wake a confrontation had spread across Yongor and beyond, pitting mothers against sons and former migrants against one another. I had come there looking for stories about the fraught sea journeys and the brief, extraordinary arrival of Senegalese fishing boats at the heart of Western leisure migration, the *playas* of Tenerife and Gran Canaria. So had hundreds of other researchers and journalists. The repatriates' tragedies had been told and retold to countless visitors, but their resentment about this retelling opened a new line of inquiry. As I left Ali and Mohammadou on their bench, I was already intrigued by their simple, recurrent question: who benefits from illegal migration, and how?

Mohammadou and his repatriated friends would in the coming year help me analyze who the winners and losers were in the illegality industry at Europe's southern frontier. This industry, built around the fight against illegal migration and drawing in the media, defense contractors, civil society, politicians, academics, and police, has—among other achievements—put the unemployed repatriates to work. The repatriates deter any "potential candidates for illegal migration" from even trying the journey; they bring in money for local associations, NGOs, and politicians; and they provide compelling stories for journalists and academics alike.

But it is not enough to consider how, in Mohammadou's words, everyone "ate" from migration. His question about illicit gains led to other, deeper quandaries. Why this fascination with the unfortunate travelers of the high seas? And why, *despite* this fascination among aid workers, journalists, and politicians, were they sidestepped as the illegality industry rolled into Dakar and other West African departure points from 2006? Beyond its much-vaunted "success" in fighting migration, what social realities did this industry leave behind in Senegal's seaside neighborhoods? During my visits to Yongor in 2010 and 2011 that structure this chapter, I would try to find answers to these questions.

MIGRANTS AS HUMAN DETERRENTS

Mohammadou often picked me up at the highway roaring out of Dakar as I came back after my fieldwork excursions along migrant routes through Morocco, Mali, and Spain. A Ford billboard towered over the fume-choked junction: "Drive one," it exhorted, next to a picture of a slick four-wheel drive. If such a car ever slogged up the sand-whipped lanes of Yongor it was bound to belong to either a local dignitary, an expatriate in Dakar's booming aid industry, or a *modou-modou*, the

Wolof term for rags-to-riches emigrants who in recent decades have come to embody success in Senegal. On our walks of Yongor, we sometimes met modou-modou back on visits from Europe, big-boned and well-fed men sporting new jeans and confident smiles. Their houses, built with remittances from Spain, Italy, or France, reminded the repatriates of their failed journeys at every turn.[7]

If the modou-modou advertised the benefits of departure, the repatriates were their abject inverse: walking billboards testifying to the futility of boat migration. Failure was broadcasted by their sullen faces, their empty pockets, their shattered dreams. They had used up their savings to pay up to five hundred thousand CFA (one thousand dollars) for a journey in a packed boat only to be intercepted, detained, and sent back from detention centers such as the one I had visited in the Canaries. Their friends had died in the rough seas. Some had turned back before reaching the archipelago; others, like Mohammadou, had been diverted to Western Sahara, where internment and expulsion to the Mauritanian border awaited. Mohammadou told me how he had spent days walking back and forth in the desert no-man's-land between Moroccan and Mauritanian border posts, soldiers forcing the migrants to retreat at gunpoint, until Senegal's president intervened. Eventually Mohammadou made it back home, penniless. The migrants' dreams had swiftly turned into the stuff of nightmares.

The shame of return was shattering. Sometimes tricked onto their deportation flights by police who told them they were being sent to mainland Spain, sometimes promised a money envelope that ended up containing as little as ten thousand CFA, the repatriates eventually made it home. Some slept on beaches or hid with acquaintances, too ashamed to face their families. Their shame was not just a family disaster, however. It was also a dissuasive weapon, as I would learn in the Spanish embassy, a world away from Yongor and its miseries.

• • •

The embassy, a whitewashed edifice in central Dakar's Plateau District, was an operation in constant expansion. As the migrant boats kept coming in 2005 and 2006, Spain suddenly "discovered" sub-Saharan Africa.[8] The country's Socialist government embarked on a political offensive in West Africa and opened new embassies across the region. Under its first Africa Plan, launched amid the growing boat crisis in the Canaries, Madrid also doubled overseas development aid to sub-Saharan Africa between 2006 and 2010. The Dakar expansion was part of this. In the years following the visits of ministers and the Spanish premier in 2006, a new consulate had been built, an export promotion office had opened, and Interior and Labor Ministry attachés had set up shop.

Raúl was one of these attachés, a friendly police officer who had years of experience in migration controls in Senegal. He had lived through the heady times of 2006. "The waiter in the café where I go for breakfast told me one morning, 'Tomorrow I'm leaving, I'm heading to Spain!'" Raúl laughed. The media fed the phenomenon, he said, spreading rumors from the Canaries, where those who had arrived "told of how you call the police as you arrive to the coast, then the police take you to a room where you get food three times a day, you can even repeat, and after some time they bring you to Spain." Then the repatriations began, tentatively in early summer and with full force a few months later. "Now you knew that you might be selected for repatriation, so will you risk losing your job here only to be sent back?"

The migration patrols launched in 2006 by Frontex and the Spanish Guardia Civil had of course contributed to the fall in arrivals, Raúl said, but the repatriations were even more important. According to him, these were "the principal weapon of dissuasion" in the fight against illegal migration. "It's tough but it's the best option." The repatriate "is worth much more than whatever publicity campaign you can think of doing," he said. Repatriation is "very difficult, very painful, very tough," but it "transmits the idea that you shouldn't leave."

His colleagues hammered home the same message. Raúl's fellow attaché, the head of the Guardia Civil's patrolling operations in Senegal, called repatriation an "efecto llamada al revés" (reverse "pull" effect). The Spanish ambassador likewise saw it as the principal form of dissuasion. "There are villages that have received people back who have risked their lives, who have risked their money, and who have failed." Now, thanks in part to the repatriates, he made clear, people thought twice about even trying.

The Canaries repatriations were but one instance of the rise of what migration scholars have called a global "deportation regime." In a pattern repeated across the rich world, states increasingly defend and enact their sovereignty against those who violate the boundaries of the nation—poor migrants and refugees whose subjection to discrimination, abuse, and disciplinary power is being catalogued from Israel to El Salvador.[9] The intentional use of mass repatriation as weapon of dissuasion in the Canaries gave a performative angle to the workings of this international deportation regime. Rather than simply being disciplined, the Senegalese repatriates were put to work as human deterrents within the illegality industry.

To implement repatriation-as-deterrence, Spain had entered into a grand bargain with Senegal. In exchange for joint patrols and repatriations, Spain promised money and favors. This created a virtuous circle for officialdom. Development cooperation smoothed the way for police initiatives while humanizing the cold, dissuasive logic of repatriation. In its "new generation" of migration accords, signed across the West African region from 2006, Spain followed the European Union's so-called global approach to migration, launched after the 2005 tragedies at Ceuta and Melilla. Through this three-pronged approach—encompassing migration controls in sending countries, the promotion of legal migration, and development assistance—Madrid padded the steeliness of policing and deportation with financial rewards and warm diplomatic words. And it soon seemed to be working perfectly. Between 2006 and 2010, arrivals in the Canaries dropped from thirty-two thousand to two hundred a year. The Spanish model of "externalization," increasingly emulated by other European countries, seemed to have cracked the code of how to control migration in a humane, cooperative fashion.[10]

The path to cooperation had not been smooth, however. The Senegalese president, Abdoulaye Wade, was faced with a conundrum in the summer of 2006. Elections were approaching, and the opposition was ready to exploit the humiliation of repatriations. As more Senegalese migrants were sent back from the Canaries, the anger boiled over among them. "We called on all of the youth, everyone came out," recalled Moctar, the president of the national association of repatriates. "We decided to make some noise . . . we will burn the country!" Riots raged on the roads of Dakar, and repatriates fought with police. They were finally summoned to see the president, who had briefly wavered on allowing repatriations but was now swiftly forging a coherent response to the crisis. To placate the repatriates, he had an offer: Spanish-sponsored development projects and work visas would come their way. More important, these deals would also help calm the opposition.

First out in this softer part of the Spanish-Senegalese migration strategy was Plan REVA (Retour vers l'Agriculture, or "back to agriculture"). This plan, a brainchild of Wade's, was meant to integrate returned migrants into a modernized farming sector. In September 2006, Senegal's interior minister announced a firm Spanish offer of twenty million euros of development aid—initially broached at the time of the first repatriations in

June—in part destined for this plan. REVA would be beset by accusations of squandered money, government nepotism, and propaganda. The repatriates, briefly wooed by the president, also refused to endorse it. They were fishermen, not farmers, and dreamed of real jobs, not tilling the soil. The Spanish money, it was widely rumored, had, instead of helping the youth, funded Wade's reelection campaign in 2007.[11]

Another aspect of the strategy was the handing out of "visas." Spain had launched a recruitment program *(contratación en origen)* "in order to prevent what was happening, people going to Spain by boat illegally," as Ismael, the Spanish Labor Ministry attaché, bluntly put it. But the repatriates were again sidelined, despite initial promises; they had an entry ban on Europe, and Madrid had no wish to encourage more departures by rewarding those sent back. Instead, the visa scheme became a high-stakes political game. While some relatives of repatriates were quietly offered places on the flights to Spain, visas were also bartered and sold by repatriate "leaders" or offered to members of Wade's party. Soon accusations flew in all directions.[12]

A few visas reached Yongor, where Mohammadou would play a part in selecting recipients. Sitting in his one-room home next to the beach, his little children coming and going as we spoke, he recalled the visa debacle in 2007. "One day they called me," he said. "They told me, 'You have won a visa, so you should come here tomorrow at eight o'clock.'" He went to the national youth employment agency, in charge of visa allocations, the following morning. "I did the paperwork, I did everything!" Still, no news came. The next month they called him again, saying he should wait for another round of contracts, this time for fishermen. Again, he said, "I did my paperwork with the Spaniards. After that, I've seen nothing." As the repatriates were sidestepped for visas, they became ever more resentful at their exclusion, from which Mohammadou still smarted, four years later.

The battle over visas sometimes took bizarre turns, as in the 2008 round of *contratación* of more than seven hundred women to go and work the strawberry fields of Andalusia. The tricky bit was to "break with the cultural schema of Senegal," Ismael said. The Senegalese had insisted that half ought to be male, but "we explained that a certain gentleness is needed in the harvesting of this product." The real reason, of course, was different. The women had to have "family charges in Senegal" so that they would be sure to return, the attaché explained, as had also been the case in similar programs between Morocco and Spain. The result was a bevy of well-connected women, all "high heels and makeup" as one Spanish NGO worker recalled, descending on the rough terrains of Andalusia. The strategy had backfired, and some women even stayed on. Ismael blamed the "disaster" on the Senegalese administration, whose preselection of candidates had been jumbled. But as could have been expected, the rich and well-connected had won out in the scramble for visas.[13] Then the crisis hit the Spanish economy, and no more contracts were being offered. The contracts were "an emergency system," Ismael admitted, but "the fact that there are no contracts now doesn't mean that we have abandoned Senegal."

A third aspect of the strategy was the awareness-raising campaigns, promoted by overseas development agencies and the International Organization for Migration (IOM). Based in the expatriate haven of Mamelles along Dakar's shoreline, this intergovernmental body—often erroneously thought of as a UN agency—regularly received government financing for its "migration management" programs, often targeting irregular flows. In 2010 alone, it raised $265 million worldwide for its work on "voluntary returns," countertrafficking, and border management. Now, amid the Senegalese "boat crisis," it received a "rapid response" injection of one million euros in E.U. funds to build state capacity on irregular migration, provide assistance to returned migrants, and conduct sensitization campaigns.[14]

The IOM's campaigns applied the *sensibilisation* format common across French-speaking West Africa on anything from desertification campaigns to disease prevention.[15] In public meetings, wise words from "community leaders" were mixed with testimony from former migrants, who sometimes were referred to as having been "vaccinated" against the wish to depart. "Sensitization shouldn't be only about the risks, not only 'you might die on the way,'" said one European IOM officer. "It should also be about the fact that you might not get a job in Spain, you might not have a nice life there." This positive spin on the campaigns betrayed a common unease among expatriate workers at the anti-migration effort. In previous years gruesome images of bloated bodies and sunken boats had appeared on Senegalese television in an effort by the Spanish government to stem the flow. While the IOM had run similar television campaigns across the region, it also followed a softer strategy incorporating cartoons, theater, and speech-making competitions. It had first conducted campaigns in fishing hamlets before branching out to sending zones inland, where people still did not know much about the risks, according to the officer. "There's never enough sensitization," she concluded, echoing Mother Mercy's words.

Amid the proliferation of local actors in the deterrence game, Mother Mercy stood out from the competition with her grassroots appeal. After the death of her only son on his journey towards the Canaries, she had converted her previous local development association into a women's collective fighting illegal migration. Besides focusing on *sensibilisation*, the association's women also kept an eye on Yongor's youth in case they tried a clandestine journey. This meant the women, once blamed for financing and encouraging their sons' fatal departures, now attracted a different kind of ire. As Mother Mercy recognized, the association's work was "very difficult," not least "because in fishing communities the woman does not have responsibility and should not take initiatives." But she had strong backers. Her forceful anti-departure narrative attracted the funders—and the police. "The mothers have helped quite a lot," quipped the Guardia Civil chief. One academic writer on the association noted how the mothers, caught like their sons between the promises of European wealth and the vagaries of Senegal's battered economy, could either choose to live off migrants' money transfers or rely on funds given for their cooperation in halting migration. By converting her association into a vehicle for anti-departure rhetoric, Mother Mercy had chosen the latter strategy, but her reasons for doing so were complex and sometimes at odds with those of her backers. Her collective was created "because we have lost so many youth," she later told me, in between criticism of how Europe was closing its doors while spending all its migration money on Frontex instead of on job-generating projects. "My son left with eighty friends, and they all disappeared at sea; that's what pushed me as a woman to call on my sisters who had suffered the same [fate] to organize a structure to fight this scourge." For a time, the priorities of bereaved Senegalese mothers and European police coincided—yet it was a fragile alliance that tragically divided families, genders, and generations who in fact held a *shared* concern with the injustices behind the fatal departures.

The repatriates, seeing the rapid and unequal spread of benefits from clandestine migration, had been deported, deceived, and made destitute. Now the work contracts and aid money bypassed them. The Senegalese president "has promised a lot of things that we haven't seen," Moctar said. "They have done nothing, nothing at all, absolutely nothing." But the initial anger had dissipated amid the undignified scramble for visas and funds. Soon the lure of the illegality industry would prove irresistible. Mohammadou and his repatriated colleagues wanted a share of the spoils. They wanted someone to listen. Above all, they wanted funding partners from Europe, and they knew that to find any they had to obey the rules of the deterrence game. As a result, they started fashioning themselves in the very guise preferred by Western donors and politicians: as real *clandestins* working to deter potential candidates for illegal migration.

On the corrugated iron door to the office of Mohammadou's association, a shack doubling up as mobile phone repair shop on the main road leading into Yongor, their motto had been printed atop a painting of a wooden boat: *halte à l'émigration clandestine* (halt illegal emigration), an increasingly present and pernicious slogan in the Dakar aid world.[16] "It's thanks to us that no one is leaving anymore," Mohammadou kept repeating, as did Mother Mercy. Yet her offices, some hundred meters away from the repatriates' shack, were a constant reminder of who the European donors believed: the logos of Spanish development agencies crowned her portico, and four-wheel-drives and taxis kept pulling up at her porch.

Mohammadou's association had no funding partners, and so their projects—on equipping Yongor's ailing fishing fleet, on creating chicken coops, on professional training for would-be or one-time *clandestins*—failed to take off. But in asserting their role in fighting illegal emigration, the repatriates signaled an awareness of their crucial role as human deterrents.

The beach, down Yongor's maze of lanes, was strewn with litter and crammed like a car park with wooden fishing boats. It was bigger versions of such boats—known as *gaal gi* in Wolof, *pirogues* in French, and *cayucos* in Spanish—that had once taken Mohammadou and his friends to the Canary Islands. The boats were long and slender, painted in brash, beautiful colors: red against yellow, deep green and black. The names of Senegalese wrestlers and marabouts had been written on the hulls. Occasional German or Spanish flags hung limply in the windless air. Industrial fishing boats rested on the horizon. Children scuttled past, deftly skirting fish bones, nets, and household debris.

"Look at the boat out there!" Mohammadou suddenly exclaimed. "It's the *garde espagnole.*" The Guardia Civil's patrolling vessel came every day, he said. It was just sitting there, observing, like a well-trained beast ready to pounce on any trespassers. "It can't stop us," he said. "If no money comes soon from Europe we will set off again. . . . This time we'll be one hundred thousand, or thousands of twelve-year-olds." It sounded like a warning from someone aware of both the depiction of migrants as a threatening force and the legal constraints in

FIGURES I AND 2. Pirogues on a Dakar beach and moored nearby.
Photos by author.

deporting the increasing number of unaccompanied children arriving along Spanish coasts.[17] The repatriates' effort to convince impatient youth to bide their time was the reason no one was leaving, Moham-madou made clear. This unpaid work of putting a brake on the runaway tales of the boat craze era was done silently, away from the spotlight.[18] "We are waiting now for any development projects to come through from Europe," insisted Mohammadou. Their patience would not last forever.

Mohammadou and his friends were recoiling from the passivity of their repatriation. They placed deterrence in their actions and speech, not just their bodies. It was a message that kept falling on deaf ears, however. Despite the European largesse, no partners appeared. Instead, their attempts to share in the spoils of the illegality industry had led to their being co-opted into Europe's human deterrence program.

MIGRANTS AS MONEY SPINNERS

It was late spring 2010, and Mohammadou and I sought refuge from the heat blowing in from the Sahelian plains in a mud-floor courtyard shaded by a *guerté toubab* tree. His friends leaned against a wall, fishing nets spread out at their feet that they mended with deft movements, threading cord through the frayed edges. Fishing had long been the main métier of Yongor's Lebou inhabitants, who, scattered in seaside hamlets across Dakar's Cap Vert peninsula, were the Senegalese capital's original population. Now a fishing crisis racked their neighborhoods. Mohammadou had once worked as a *mareyeur*, selling fish and seafood, but no longer. Stocks had depleted in part because of an explosion in small-scale fishing, caused by Senegal's worsening economy and the motorization of pirogues. The biggest culprit in the emptying of the seas, however, was the sale of fishing rights to other states, not least Spain. The foreign trawlers resting on Yongor's horizon swallowed tons of fish destined for European and Asian markets. This, Mother Mercy and Mohammadou agreed, was why so many had tried to leave in 2006, embarking in the very boats they had previously used for fishing: here there were no jobs to be had.[19]

Unlike other groups in Senegal, the Lebous had relatively little experience of long-distance migration. The Soninké of the Senegal River valley, for instance, had long depended on circular migration as a means of income and a rite of passage, while Wolof traders had lately branched out to Europe and elsewhere through tight-knit Mourid Muslim networks. The Lebous, by contrast, had at most embarked upon seasonal fishing expeditions towards Mauritania or Guinea, their lives structured by the sea. Yet as for fishermen elsewhere in West Africa, the dwindling fisheries and the sudden opening of clandestine routes had now pushed them to try their luck on the boats, where their familiarity with the sea made them useful as captains or helpers. The resulting journeys in sea-battered pirogues were but the most extreme outcome of a deepening global economic divide, policed by European sentinels off Dakar's coastline.[20]

Mohammadou leaned back, sipped some bittersweet *attaya*, and repeated what was soon to become a familiar sum of money. "Do you know how much Wade and his government have earned from illegal migration?" he asked. "Thirteen billion CFA! And what has he done for us? Nothing." The amount—referring to the twenty million euros in Spanish aid offered at the time of the 2006 deportations—was lambasted not just by Mohammadou but also by repatriates up and down Senegal's coastline. Word circulated on how much money Wade had received per repatriate. *"La migration clandestine a beaucoup d'argent,"* Mohammadou insisted (there is lots of money in illegal migration).

In Kayar, a fishing hamlet and tourist magnet north of Dakar, repatriates told the same bitter story. "Lots of NGOs came here after 2006," said the president of Kayar's repatriate association, "but we didn't realize at the time that they were just trying to fill their own bellies." We were careful to meet with his fellow repatriates in a large room, with everyone present so that there would be no suspicions of anyone receiving money for talking. "You have to say in your book that all those who have passed by here have done nothing for us!" one of them insisted. NGOs, journalists, researchers had all come. "What have we got out of it?" they asked, voices rising. "It's been four years of talking!"

An acute awareness of what they saw as the great gains from illegality pervaded the repatriates' migration experience. Mohammadou and his friends sensed that moneymakers trailed them on their journey, during repatriation and at home—"swindlers" and "liars" ready to make a killing from boat migration. They saw it in sea rescues and patrols, in which boats were diverted from Spanish waters to Morocco, since the latter would then "earn money from the European Union." They saw it in the visits of E.U. delegates who come, "promise us things," and leave. They saw it in the scrum of journalists and researchers who "take our stories." And they saw it in the Western NGO workers who "come here with their four-wheel-drives" only to speed off once they have received funding for their spurious migration projects.

I was no different from all those others, the more than one thousand people Mohammadou said had visited their association since 2006. What could I offer? Money? Partners? Contacts?

All I offered was to set up a website. Nothing as slick and stylish as that of Mother Mercy's collective, however. Not even a real website, mind, but a blog. The association's IT expert typed their posts onto his laptop in his bedroom after Mohammadou's attempts at hitting the right keys had failed. One of their first and only posts, in French, read like this:

> Subject: Letter Asking for Assistance
> First of all, please accept our warmest greetings. We would like to let you know that our association was created between 2006 and 2007 in order to try to fix the youth to stay in the country because after our repatriation we have seen that a big number of youth had died at sea, after some time of waiting we have started to do sensitization in the surrounding localities . . . but during this time we have received nothing from these promises even the European Union came to visit us last year with promises but none of that has been done. There are even people who talk about immigration without having experienced this scourge others content themselves with traveling to Europe by means of the repatriates and masquerade as people who come to find funding for the youth, while this is not the case because the money they bring in, they fill their bags with it. Even the projects and the visas that the Europeans gave to the repatriates have not arrived to those concerned. . . . This is why we turn to you so that at least we will have training centers to educate the youth, schools for the children of those who disappeared, and funding to find some kind of work. . . . We count on your understanding while waiting for assistance.
> *Thank You*

"You" did not come forward. No replies were forthcoming. With each attempt, and each visiting toubab, responsibility weighed heavier on Mohammadou's shoulders. He was the president; he should bring partners. *"Ana liggéey bi?"* (Where is the work?), members of the association asked, stopping to chat with him on the streets. Lacking a good response, Mohammadou grew increasingly bitter and angry; for, unlike some repatriate "leaders," he was sincere in seeking projects for the hundreds of repatriates in Yongor and their families, not just quick cash for himself.

Meanwhile Mother Mercy was raking in the money, as the repatriates saw it. They had initially trusted her, seeing her as the benevolent "mother of the migrants." Some even took loans she had negotiated, with sour aftereffects for both parties. As the repatriates were sidelined, acrimony grew. By 2010 the split was deep and definite. Before the boat crisis she had lived in a single room, the repatriates said; now she had a big, big house. She was driven around by a chauffeur and flew off to conferences in Europe, but she could not go down to the seafront because she would be hounded away. She was a liar. "All that she says is false," the repatriates kept repeating, like a record stuck in the same groove. She went and met funding agencies in Europe, then took the money but shared nothing. "One hundred thousand CFA bills, 150,000 CFA bills, she takes them out as if they were cigarettes," Mohammadou said with his trademark frown.[21]

The repatriates' anger towards Mother Mercy was, of course, not the whole story. It was rather a symptom of the double trauma visited upon Yongor's inhabitants: first the deaths at sea, then the injustice of deportation and the unequal gains that followed. Mother Mercy was herself aware of the accusations. "People here think that when you are with a white person, he brings money," she told me, echoing the concerns of Mohammadou with his moneyless trail of researchers and reporters. "This creates problems and tensions in the community. [People say] 'I collect money here, I collect money there,' but this is not the case!" Unlike Mohammadou's association, however, she at least maintained "vertical and horizontal relations" with Spanish donor organizations. The biggest funder was the Agencia Española de Cooperación Internacional para el Desarrollo (AECID), the official Spanish development agency, which channeled money through Spanish NGOs. Their funding priorities, as I would soon see, held further clues to the role of the repatriates in Dakar's illegality industry.

. . .

In the AECID offices in central Dakar, Rocío leafed through her files, looking for budget expenditure on migration-related projects that I had asked her about, with little luck. She was a Spanish development worker in her forties, brimming with enthusiasm for development. Projects were carried over from year to year, she explained; it was hard to get precise figures. I asked her why the repatriates got nothing. She shrugged. "We're a development agency," she said. The funds "were for families who had lost someone, not for repatriates." Indeed, their projects were presented as being about female empowerment or for the "mother victims of the cayucos." Brochures filled up with pictures of smiling African women sewing, dancing, shoveling, and preparing fish, in what

seemed a perfect example of the co-optation of once-radical development ideas by a larger state agenda.[22] Rocío was keen to stress the gulf
separating development aid and migration controls, however. "We don't
want to know anything about that since it's not our field," she said and
waved her hands as if pushing the patrols to one side. "That's all with
the Interior Ministry."

Such purification of development aid was a major cleanup operation.
Development assistance was independent from clandestine migration,
the Spanish ambassador insisted, and rather depended on the Africa
Plan's aim of fostering better relations with sub-Saharan nations. Leaving aside the fact that migration was already a fundamental part of this
plan, the ambassador's view also contrasted with recent findings on
Spanish aid to Africa. One comprehensive, AECID-funded study found
that the country's NGOs had expanded strongly in sub-Saharan countries since 2006 thanks to exponentially growing official aid; that more
than half of these NGOs had a tenuous previous connection to the continent; and that the official funds directed especially at Senegal, Mali,
and Mauritania were closely related to irregular migration concerns.
Another study focusing on these three countries similarly affirmed the
"subordination of official development aid to Spain's migration policy"
there while stating that Spanish funds might even have hampered the
stated policies of this aid—poverty reduction, human rights, and democratic governance.[23]

In the uneasy mixing of policing and poverty reduction, Spain's West
African experiment was but an extreme case of the perils of "codevelopment." This approach, initiated in France, has meant seeing migrants as
a factor in developing their home countries while contradictorily incorporating attempts to constrict such development-inducing migration
flows.[24] "Codevelopment," Rocío quipped, "is meant to prevent . . . or,
well . . ." She tried again. It "could contribute to . . ." She stumbled. "It
may or may not halt the departures." Migration concerns entered
AECID's remit under "vulnerable groups such as minors," she explained,
"who could later become fodder for illegal migration" *(carne de
migración clandestina)*. Maybe, she suggested, the repatriates could try
to attract funding by presenting themselves as being vulnerable?

Before I left, Rocío looked over her shoulder towards the corridor,
making sure no one was listening. "I say this since no one is here," she
began, lowering her voice, "but obviously, what are the links between
Spain and Senegal? There are none. Links usually come through a shared
language, a shared history, but with Senegal and Mali there is none of

that." She continued in a conspiratorial whisper: "It's clear there's a relation between [fighting] illegal migration and [funding] development
here for Spain . . . though this topic is taboo."

As in other international aid encounters, Spain's migration-backed
development push seemed like a case of "the emperor's new clothes."[25]
Everyone started speaking the language of fighting illegal migration,
perpetuating the illusion that the emperor was fully clothed. The irony
was that Spanish and E.U. politicians, in seeking to depoliticize their
anti-migration operations through recourse to the language of drama
on television and development on the ground, created a *politicized*
development interface drawing in brokers, entrepreneurs, and swindlers. They were no longer in full control.

Through a trickle down of development aid, local associations willing to take part in the fight would be co-opted and contained. This was
part of a pattern of clientelism and "everyday corruption" in Senegal, to
be sure, but the illegality industry extended beyond this nexus to encompass European security, media, and policy sectors as well.[26] The industry
also depended on a signifier amenable to infinite manipulation: the
"fodder for illegal migration," in Rocío's words. It was through this
figure, in its IOM-promoted incarnation as potential candidate for illegal migration, that the business of migration had filtered down to the
Senegalese grassroots.

International agencies, the Senegalese state, Western NGOs, and
local associations were all at it. On the top of the food chain were the
"expatriates" parachuted in from other diplomatic or IOM missions.
Tasked with tempering the illicit movements of their Senegalese hosts,
they mixed in Dakar's swish seaside restaurants and mingled on the
city's expat party scene, where Guardia Civil officers on their three-
month patrolling stints also made occasional appearances.

One step down the food chain followed a range of Senegalese ministries that had staked a claim in migration. While they in theory converged around the government's official line, honed over the summer of
2006, of "protecting" Senegalese citizens from the risks of the boat journey, economic and political incentives made them pull in different directions.[27] Chaos, as European aid workers complained, was the predict-
able result. Next came the European NGOs that had followed the
money scattered by Western governments in the pirogues' wake. At the
grassroots, again, the strategy was replicated. In a poor neighborhood
outside Dakar, a local development association had scribbled *migration
clandestine* at the end of its typed-up list of projects. A Senegalese

human rights NGO, once of a radical bent, did *sensibilisation* with the IOM in Dakar and remote Tambacounda; it had produced T-shirts saying "There is another choice" on the front and "NO to illegal migration" on the back, and its office was plastered with stickers sporting the same message. Theater troupes across Senegal did *sensibilisation* with cookie-cutter characters explaining the dangers of boat migration. In a Dakar fishing village, a branch of Mother Mercy's collective invoked, in a letter asking for funds to build an ice factory, "our unfailing fight to make the youth of Senegal in general, and of [our neighborhood] in particular, say no to illegal migration." No matter that out of its local five hundred members, only twenty at most had done mbëkë mi. Most of these, after all, fitted the IOM's suitably loose profile of a potential candidate: young, male, and unemployed.

No partners came looking for Mohammadou and his friends. While aid workers such as Rocío insisted—correctly—that former migrants were not necessarily worse off than other youth struggling along in Dakar's poor neighborhoods, the repatriates' sense of entitlement and frustration grew along with the parade of donors, brokers, and visitors. However, their ire was mainly directed at Mother Mercy and other competitors, not at the funding agencies and European politicians. A quiet battle was raging among local associations about who was *really* fighting clandestine migration. Everyone bickered with everyone, not just in Yongor, but across Senegal's seaside communities. Moctar, the head of the presumably national association of repatriates, was working only for himself rather than for a broader cause, local youth and repatriates said. In Kayar, one angry repatriate leader caught up with me in the back streets of the fish market. A rival association had received €6,500, "and they ate it all," he said while pointing at scrawled funding figures in his notebook. "Some people benefit from this money in the name of the illegal migrants," he said, waving a bunch of papers belonging to his association's members. The papers—presumably certificates from the migrant detention centers in the Canaries—proved they were bona fide *clandestins*, he insisted. He later turned out never to have made the boat journey.

Transcending this bickering was Mother Mercy, who played the funding game to perfection. As noted by other scholars, her success related to the combination of Western concerns that her collective represented: women's empowerment, development, and illegal migration. But she was no victim of European priorities. She had entered a virtuous circle in which media exposure, political clout, and more funding fed into one another. The women's soap making and handicraft projects found favor with donors, combining as they did female empowerment with a "back to the soil" strategy against migration. "Sometimes misfortune is good; we had never dared to speak out in our communities before," she told me. "It's thanks to migration, to the disappearance of our children, that we have integrated ourselves into male society."

We should perhaps ask, along with the development anthropologist David Mosse, not whether aid projects such as the Spanish migration-and-development drive succeed but how "success" is produced—and what the side effects of such success might be.[28] The sensitization drive, the mothers with their soap bars, and the high-heeled farmhands put success in Senegalese quarters, while diverting activist and "grassroots" attention away from the controversial European patrols and repatriations that Wade's government had approved. The illegality industry also created a role for former and potential migrants, but not as actors, brokers, or beneficiaries. Instead, the repatriates oiled the cogs of the anti-migration machinery with their tragic experiences at sea. To them befell the thankless task of repeating their stories to the visitors-without-funds descending on Yongor—the researchers, fact finders, and journalists.

MIGRANTS AS CONTENT PROVIDERS

We were sitting in the "office," people eating the peanut stew *mafe* from a shared platter, when a mobile phone rang. The association's treasurer stopped fiddling with old Nokia SIM cards and took the phone, talking in French, and then handed the phone to Mohammadou, who went outside to continue the conversation. It was a journalist, he explained afterwards. Her reporting team would come on Sunday to discuss a documentary they wanted to film in Yongor.

I left the office with Mohammadou and Ali, walking along the rail tracks that split Yongor in half. Mohammadou was thoughtful, silent. Then he said, "I will ask her, what will we get from participating? All the time, people come here to speak to us about migration, always migration." Ali nodded. "It's tiring . . . we need compensation, or to talk of something else." To him, "the most important thing is what happened *after* our migration." The debt to relatives for the journey, the loss of jobs and savings, and the fruitless funding battles—not to mention the day-to-day struggles for "migrant" and nonmigrant alike in Senegal's rattled economy—were not foremost in journalists' minds, as Ali and Mohammadou were well aware.

A few hundred meters along the tracks lay the office of Yongor's mayor. He had lost a brother and a cousin to mbëkë mi after paying for their fatal journey and was sympathetic to the repatriates' struggles. "Tell the journalists the truth," he advised Mohammadou as we sat in plush sofas in his reception room. Mohammadou listened and nodded, saying little more. As we walked back, Mohammadou mulled his tactics. "We will say we haven't seen any help from Europe, but without mentioning Mother Mercy," he said. "It's better that way."

The repatriates had already met hundreds of journalists, but little had come of all this attention except broken promises. "In 2007, journalists came here almost every day," said one member of the association. "They come and do their reports; all the time they come, then they just leave and we never hear from them again." Mohammadou used to wonder where his photo had ended up, in how many news reports. "If I go to England and I see my photo on a poster, I ask myself why."

The poster image for boat migration, however, was not Mohammadou or his fellow repatriates; it was Mother Mercy, whose qualities made for perfect feature stories. She was the strong and steadfast mother and also the bereaved, impoverished victim. Such media portrayals pandered to Western stereotypes of the African woman, as one analysis of her collective notes: Mother Mercy here appeared as a "consensual figure arousing the compassion of everyone" in fusing "the charisma of the victim and the activist." And the women played along, singing and showing pictures of their dead sons and husbands during journalists' visits. Some entrepreneurial young repatriates had also found a source of income in chasing contacts for the journalists, offering up smugglers and marabouts, bereaved relatives, and jobless fishermen, according to the needs of the story. Mohammadou and his friends had played this game too, but they were tired. Unlike Mother Mercy, they saw little outcome of the visits.

After the media stampede came the more slow footed researchers. Many were preparing their postgraduate theses; some worked for NGOs; others might have been undercover police. "I'll be completely honest," a UN official in Dakar told me, relishing his moment. "Around sixty researchers have come here in the past few years to study irregular migration. You'd better think of another topic."

This sudden academic "discovery" followed a familiar trend. Irregular migration, sociologist Alejandro Portes observed already in the 1970s, "is one of those issues in which the interests of scholars and of government agencies converge."[29] Yet while the U.S.-Mexican border had long been a vast field of inquiry, the Euro-African frontline was, until the Ceuta and Melilla tragedies of 2005, virtually unexplored. In the words of one Moroccan academic, irregular migration was an "empty field" on which migration researchers descended in the hope of quick data for articles, theses, and reports. In Senegal after the boat crisis, the pattern was repeated: here was a wide-open research frontier, an academic Klondike where any early studies were bound to attract disproportionate attention from editors, selection committees, and funders, including E.U. research bodies and the ever-present IOM. Predictably, an onward rush of policy-relevant papers proposing piecemeal "solutions" soon followed—but so did a quieter current of in-depth studies exploring the complexities of migratory flows. Yet to the repatriates, sensing the stakes at play, these varied efforts looked remarkably similar: they were all attempts at mining their stories to feed the demands of European funders.[30]

The repatriates had belatedly learned that the clandestine migrant was a valuable piece of merchandise, and they now wanted their slice of the business. Moctar, the repatriate president, said they had decided not to speak about their experiences unless they got something out of it. "For a small sum, I'll give you three or four guys," he told me. "Maybe ten thousand CFA is enough, since you are a research student." This was a discount, he made clear—self-appointed middlemen had been given one hundred thousand CFA or more by journalists keen on stories. While researchers such as I often refused, the journalists kept giving, sometimes in the form of a gift to Mother Mercy's collective, other times as a backhand fee to the fixers.

Except for these one-off payments, the repatriates were unable to monetize their media presence. Their stereotype within the illegality industry was not that of Africans needing empowerment; it was that of wild youth in need of domestication. The only thing they could sell was their story at sea, which made for a perfect piece of journalism—a package of suffering and high drama that worked both as hard news and feature fodder. And this story, as other researchers have also attested, became shrouded in ambivalences and resistance in its telling and retelling.[31]

One day I went with Mohammadou to see Momar, one of the association's spokesmen. He was a dreadlocked member of Baye Fall, the Muslim Mourid devotees famed throughout Senegal for their colorful ragged clothes and itinerant begging on behalf of their marabout. We sat down on a foam mattress in Momar's bare room as he emptied a "gunpowder" tea bag into a metal pot and put it on the coals. I asked if he wanted to speak about his journey. Momar was a kind man who found it hard to say no. "I do it for Mohammadou," he said eventually. "We have a policy not to speak to anyone." Mohammadou reiterated the figure of a thousand journalists and researchers visiting them since their return. Still, they kept yielding to demands for stories.

"It's harder now than before leaving," said Momar, who was a self-employed plumber. "In 2006, I could find clients, but after I left, my clients found other workers. I had to start from scratch again." This lack of funds, the repatriates often said, was another reason no one contemplated departing anymore; in 2006 at least they had some funds to draw upon for the trip.

Then Momar talked of his journey. "Only the brave ones *(nit ñu am jóm)* left," he said. His pirogue departed on 28 July 2006—everyone remembers the date they set off—and he summed up his ordeal in a few words: "I went on mbëkë mi, I lost all my money, I lost many friends, I returned with nothing, nothing, nothing."

On the seventh day water and food ran out, Momar explained as we sipped our tea. The passengers, desperate, started drinking seawater. Then the fuel tanks dried up, so they cut down the tarp covering the pirogue to make an improvised sail. They ripped chunks of wood off the boat's sides to make a mast and oars and spent hours rowing, twenty men on each side. There were ninety-two onboard, lost on the high seas. Eleven people died. Several among them passed away on Momar's lap.

"The fourteenth day they started dying," added Mohammadou, who had begun filling in Momar on the details. Soon they were bouncing elements of the story off each other, talking of how Momar's pirogue—or was it Mohammadou's?—had been intercepted. It was the Moroccans, not the Spaniards, who finally "came to the coasts of the Canary Islands to take us away." The more they talked, the blurrier the story became. It was a standardized account of their misery, I started to realize, a tale they had repeated so many times they knew it by heart, their individual tragedies melting into one another for the benefit of the visiting interviewers. Whose story was I hearing, and how many had heard it before me?

Repatriates from coastal Senegal, and especially those organized into associations, were in one sense the beneficiaries of the visitors' excessive attentions. Former migrants in impoverished inland regions such as Tambacounda or the remote southern Casamance saw few reporters, researchers, and aid workers. Besides, many deportees in Dakar and other seaside cities steered clear of repatriates' associations and the illegality industry. The reason was simple: they had no wish to revisit their misfortune or relive the shame that so often accompanied it. One such deportee, when I asked him about his harrowing journey, suddenly rose to his feet and started pacing up and down the room. "I've forgotten most of it," he said, glancing towards the door leading down to the car mechanic shop where his uncle had found him work after his deportation. The rescue happened on their ninth day at sea, he finally recalled, a day after the food had run out. "One guy onboard went mad. 'Let me leave!' he screamed. We had to tie him to the boat . . . He was seeing his girlfriend in the waves." Then he stopped pacing and sat down, next to me, squeezed in close as on the boat, holding his head in his hands as the passengers would do at night. For this car mechanic as for others, mbëkë mi was lodged in bodily memory, not spoken about. Soon I thanked him and he headed downstairs, relieved of the duty of retelling.

For Yongor's organized repatriates, however, there was no such relief to be had. They had decided to stop speaking to visitors, Momar said, since so many had come, and because the journalists asked "if you are normal or crazy," questioning their sanity. What most shocked the journalists, Mohammadou said, was the descent from solidarity into chaos on the boat: how "yesterday we ate together, today we throw you into the water. But if you don't, everyone will die onboard." Yet despite their complaints and their policy of silence, the repatriates kept talking to the journalists and researchers. Their stories were, after all, the only product they could offer the illegality industry and their one remaining means of connection with the European world they had once sought to enter.

. . .

The French film team arrived in Yongor in early April. I caught up with Mohammadou and his friends at the shore, where they sat atop a beached pirogue, blankly watching the cameraman home in on a woman doing the laundry. "She lost her husband in mbëkë mi," Mohammadou said in his usual dry voice. Down at the beachfront, a pirogue was being prepared for a film trip at sea. The journalists had paid for the petrol, Mohammadou said. They had also paid for a meal of *cebujën* (rice and fish, Senegal's national dish) for everyone and had promised "something more" too. It was not clear what this was. Money? Contacts? Mohammadou said nothing more.

The conversation drifted on to the topic of funding partners. "You should help us find partners now that you're a member of the association," said Omar, their fast-talking, self-proclaimed spokesman who had suddenly shown up. The French documentary maker, hearing the exchange, came out from under a shaded canopy and joined us on the boat, notepad in hand. "Could you help us find contacts?" they asked her eagerly. "You should prepare a dossier with your projects," she suggested, looking skeptical. "We have done it already!" they insisted. Omar said an E.U. delegation had been there and promised things, but nothing came of it. He picked up his mobile and called the E.U. offices in Dakar, but the delegate was away. Conversation died off, and the repatriates sauntered down to the shoreline while the reporter lingered. "Why are they not leaving anymore?" she asked me, looking out over the waters, past the pirogues towards Gorée Island and the cargo ships. "Do people really know about the economic crisis in Europe?"

Besides their fascination with the tragedies onboard, visitors struggled to comprehend migrants' decision to depart. While academics analyzed the journey as a form of collective risk taking and an identity-forging experience, their journalistic colleagues usually resorted to a quicker, neater explanation: a mix of desperation and ignorance, with Europe pictured as a shimmering El Dorado on the horizon. This vision, shared by politicians and donors, justified the need for *sensibilisation* on both the risks of the journey and the perils of life in Europe—yet bore little resemblance to how the sea crossing was understood by migrants themselves. The migrants' motto of *Barça walla barzakh* did conjure an El Dorado, but like the term *mbëkë mi* it also rendered the journey as an expected headache. Rather than being ignorant of the risks, migrants *embraced* it in a quest to affirm their masculine prowess, as other ethnographers have noted.[32] In mbëkë mi, Lebou fishermen out of work had suddenly found themselves as the protagonists in a national drama: the heroic seeking of European shores in defiance of the Senegalese and Spanish governments.

Now, in the aftermath of their equally spectacular failure, ambivalence suffused the repatriates' relationship with the foreign visitors. They often evaded the questions thrown at them and at times came up with fake answers, but they still replied. Maybe this time, someone would listen. Maybe for once, the reporters could put them in touch with a partner. Mohammadou kept finding excuses for talking. "This is the last time," he said, or he got a business card out to show me that the reporter was worth the effort: "He is from France 3!" They always hoped, against experience, that this time would be different. With the French television team, they would yet again be sorely disappointed.

. . .

Autumn had come. I was back in Dakar, and Mohammadou met me as usual at the highway. On the corner someone had lined up stereos and radios, stacked a plastic plate with detergent bottles, and heaped old shoes onto a blanket. "It's the modou-modou who have brought it here," Mohammadou said as we made our way into the neighborhood. It was the time of *tabaski,* the Muslim festival Eid al-Adha, when many migrants came back to visit their families.

Outside the women's collective a shack had been erected, its top adorned with the now-familiar logos of AECID and Spanish NGOs. Inside sat a bored-looking woman in a blue dress, the shelves around her stacked with handmade soap, African dolls, and assorted souvenirs. "They do that every year," explained Mohammadou, "to sell to the visitors. But this year, no one is coming." The largesse was moving elsewhere.

Mohammadou nevertheless had some good news to share. The association had joined in the preparations for the World Social Forum, the large annual gathering of activists, NGOs, and politicians for an alternative globalization.[33] The turn had now come to West Africa to host this international event, and Dakar had been chosen as the venue. Mohammadou's association would, in part thanks to my contact with the forum, take part. "We had no idea there was a forum happening in Dakar," he told visitors later on. "A social forum here in Senegal without the immigrants, it's nothing at all."

Retreating from our usual shaded courtyard to watch a Chelsea football game, Mohammadou revealed he had recently hosted another team of reporters, who had come via the forum. "Next time I don't want to do it," he said. "I'll tell the forum that." The association and elders from Yongor had been invited to the prelaunch of the forum, traveling there in buses and taxis as a real delegation. "We won't ask for money at the forum, we'll go there to find contacts," Mohammadou said. "It's like with you. Do you remember the day I came looking for you at Mother Mercy's place? And see, now you bring cigarettes!" The delivery was deadpan as usual, but there was a new humor and bounce in his voice. Maybe things were soon to change.

As we walked back to the main road across the rail tracks, Mohammadou said they had still not heard back from the French reporters. One of his friends chipped in, saying his sister had seen them on TV in

Tunisia. "If we don't see a result everyone will think that we have got something out of it!" another repatriate added. We said good-bye at the main road, where trucks roared out of Dakar and Senegal's police went past on their nightly anti-migration patrols.

As anthropologists and other chroniclers of tragedies have noted, the telling of traumatic stories is often marred by silences and resistances. Survivors of conflict and disaster reel as visitors gain "fame from writing, filming, or reporting about us," in the words of one writer on the Bosnia war.[34] Unlike in the aftermath of conflict, however, the boat tragedy did not even raise the hope of bringing a perpetrator to account. There was no one to blame but the Atlantic waves, the "unscrupulous smugglers," and the repatriates themselves. With no result to show for their labors—not even a copy of the images, books, or films extracted from their accounts—the repatriates' retellings of their tragedies only mired them further in illegality, fueling resentment and distrust of those who ate from migration.

REPATRIATION AND THE ECONOMICS OF AFFLICTION

In February 2011 the World Social Forum descended on Dakar. The venue, Université Cheikh Anta Diop, had been invaded by cosmopolitan *altermondialistes,* Native American delegations, Moroccan nationalists, curious Dakarois students, and an ever-growing crowd of vendors flogging straw hats, beads, and postcards along the leafy roads of the campus. Amid the trinket stands and the swelling crowds, a theater piece was taking place. A quick glance at the props spread out on the pavement—a fishing net, planks depicting a boat—gave it away as *sensibilisation* on illegal migration; so did the wail of the female protagonist. As her sobs subsided, her male coprotagonist spoke, arguing forcefully against departure: to leave for Europe "without mastering the language, without profession" did not make sense, he admonished his audience. The play was done in French instead of Wolof for the benefit of the foreign visitors, explained an Italian worker from the NGO funding the show. The actors already had multilingual experience: besides performing for candidates for illegal migration, they also did sensitization shows for tourists whose "solidarity trips" financed the campaigns. "That way, the tourists know where their money's going."

Elsewhere on campus, the venerable Institut Fondamental d'Afrique Noire (IFAN) was to host the migration and diaspora section of the weeklong gathering. But nothing was going according to plan. Wade's government, suddenly unhappy with forum radicalism, had deposed the university's director, and the new one withdrew his support from the event. The halls of IFAN were closed, meetings got canceled, chaos reigned on campus.

Among the presenters was Yongor's repatriate association. The repatriates had lost their hall in the chaos and did not know where to go. I tagged along, as did two other researchers. Eventually we found an empty lecture hall. There was no one in the gloomy science classroom, only Mohammadou, two of his fellow repatriates, and us. A third, rival collective of "families affected by illegal migration" from Yongor had also made it there in the form of their spokesman, Alioune, and three women dressed in their finery. They had broken with Mother Mercy because of anger over funding and were still hoping against hope for news of their disappeared relatives. Like Mother Mercy, whom we had spotted earlier mingling in the migration and diaspora grounds, they also sought potential partners.

The room was oppressively hot in the late afternoon. We waited: maybe more people would arrive. Mohammadou wavered, not sure whether to go ahead. They had talked about this moment for months. Then a French woman in her fifties entered and sat down. Mohammadou decided to begin.

"I know very well that the people didn't want to have a conference about illegal migration, because they know that if I speak, they will know the reality of illegal migration." Mohammadou, resting on a school bench at the top of the room, cap on head, spoke in a deep voice that receded into a mumble. "There are people who earn a lot of money from illegal migration, but since 2006, the young repatriates haven't received anything from illegal migration." He found the French woman's eyes and held them as he told his own story of fourteen days at sea, nearly a hundred people packed together. "There are mothers here who have lost their sons while others say they have lost relatives, and go earn money in Europe." He fixed his gaze on the woman as he talked in a calm, steady tone about the lost lives. The dirty fans did not whirr, dust stuck to the walls, and sweat to our bodies. "Who is responsible, the European Union? Who?" Someone swallowed. Outside the closed door I heard the shuffle of feet, a reminder that soon this meeting would end and we could go back out to mingle among the careless students. "Here they have hidden everything, they have hidden everything, because people don't want to understand the reality." Still Mohammadou held the French woman's eyes. "They don't give any resources for keeping the youth in place," he said. I averted my gaze, instead scanning the walls where grimy posters hung depicting uranium chain reactions. "I'm not the association," he continued, gesturing to his fellow repatriates. "The association needs assistance . . . You have to go speak in Spain, in Italy, because we don't have the means to go there." He mentioned the journalists who had come, the French reporter team from last spring, people calling him to say they had seen him on television, books he had helped Europeans write. "But the money from that, where do they put it?" Two of the mothers of Yongor were slouching over their desks, slipping into an afternoon stupor in the airless hall. "It's finished, talking about illegal migration. . . . You have to help the youth and the mothers." A soft, short applause ensued, followed by a sad silence.

Then Alioune and the mothers talked of their tragedy under the pale lights of the hall. "They are eighty-six families who really want to talk," said Alioune, also addressing the French woman. As he handed out his business cards, she finally saw her chance and escaped from the room.

. . .

Amid their fruitless hunt for partners, the repatriates had been put to work in three ways in the illegality industry: as human deterrents, as commodities to be bartered by NGOs and authorities, and as an alluring presence ripe for journalistic or academic portrayal. The illegality industry was not a smooth operation forged by policy makers and politicians in their European offices, however. Instead it mutated and grew increasingly absurd as Spanish (and Senegalese) needs for depoliticizing controversial border operations co-opted development aid from above—a process that was, in turn, co-opted from below.[35] While Mother Mercy was an expert at this snagging and snaring of the funders, the repatriates also tried their best. Here, the voyeurism inherent in clandestine migration—a veiled presence to be discovered by police, journalists, or potential partners spurred new and shifting modes of self-presentation. Sometimes repatriates decided to render themselves visible as illegal migrants, much as they would tear off their invisibility amulets, or *gris-gris,* on the open sea once all hope was gone and they waited for a miraculous rescue. They did so when calling upon the Senegalese state to do justice to the repatriates, when selling their story to journalists and researchers, or when presenting themselves as pacifiers of candidates for illegal migration to Western funders. In the process, states, NGOs, and repatriates all conspired in what, following philosopher Ian Hacking, can be called the "making up" of the illegal migrant.[36]

But what type of migrant was being made up? As critical migration scholars have suggested, the global deportation regime allocates individuals to their designated slots across the world, maintaining the fiction of place-bound, discrete belonging. It was such a "territorial solution" that Spain had tried to achieve in Senegal.[37] A brief crack had opened in the armor of the West, but by 2010 order had been reestablished. The gate to Europe had slammed shut. The wild men who once steered towards European shores were back where they belonged, immobilized and resentful in their homeland.

Deportation had at first made the repatriates into tragic heroes. The ethnographer Caroline Melly, commenting on tales of "missing men" during Senegal's boat craze, says, "It was through repetition and reiteration of tales of failed migration attempts that men became spectacularly present as national adventurers, risk-taking entrepreneurs, and devoted family men who were willing to sacrifice themselves for others."[38] Yet their return had entangled the repatriates in a battle over funds and dignity, from which they emerged as diminished figures. As they were left to scramble for the spoils of the illegality industry, the imaginary of their one-time migrations mutated. No longer simply the stuff of heroic tales, mbëkë mi increasingly turned into a stigma. Illegal migration, prevented in sensitization campaigns and paraded by repatriates' morose and idle bodies, came to resemble less a sign of bravado and sacrifice than a disease-like affliction.

This served the authorities well, but Mohammadou and his friends were nonetheless no pawns bartered between NGOs and "community leaders," politicians and police, journalists and anthropologists. In their tragic attempts to reach the Canaries, they had thrown a line and hook across the waters to Europe, establishing a direct connection where before there was none. Their journeys not only created relations between Spanish and African politicians, journalists and NGOs, but also entitled the migrants to ask the Europeans for funds, reparations, and recognition.[39] By 2010, most of Yongor's former migrants were firmly ensconced at home, with little thought of leaving again because of the patrols, the poverty, and the tragedy they had faced. In their never-ending attempts to find partners, they nevertheless tried to convert their boat ordeal into political and economic capital. When this failed, only a wounded, resentful pride remained.

Down at the beach, looking out over the milky waters towards the Guardia Civil boat, Mohammadou fixed his eyes on me. "No one can stop us," he said. "We are Africans." To prove his point he unbuttoned his shirt to show a snake-like leathery amulet wrapped around his stomach. The gris-gris would protect him if he were ever to leave again. It would make him invisible to the prying eyes of Senegalese police and the Spanish coast guards, the radars, and the infrared cameras crisscrossing the wild waves all the way to the Canary Islands. There were new, stronger motors on the market, sixty-horsepower Yamahas that would take them there even faster than in 2006. "We have no fear," Mohammadou said. "We have no fear of the planes, we have no fear of the boats, we have no fear of the crisis."

Mohammadou and his fellow former migrants were not just dragged into the measly trickle-down world of Dakar's aid industry. They would also become capital in a high-stakes game of bordering Europe, whose webs of control were every bit as invisible and magical as those of Mohammadou's gris-gris. These invisible threads connected Mohammadou's coastline, his one-time destination in the Canaries, and European policing headquarters in a dispersed border regime of unprecedented proportions. This regime, and its extraction of the very "risk" once embraced by the repatriates, is the subject of the next chapter.

CHAPTER 2

A Game of Risk

MADRID, JUNE 2010. Deep in the bowels of the Guardia Civil headquarters, ten men sit around a small wooden table in an open-plan room. Uniformed marines, suited police, and green-clad *guardias* clutch their phones or type awkwardly on identical laptops lined up around the table. A Baltic policeman dials his head office, and a stern-looking officer speaks broken English down the line. The men are eastern European, Icelandic, Italian, Dutch, and Spanish. Their table is the nerve center of the European border agency Frontex's migration control operations off Spain's southern coasts.

Follow the wires and satellite networks as they spin away from this room and you will reach Las Palmas de Gran Canaria and the regional coordination center for migration surveillance along the Atlantic seaboard. Inside, on an electronic map in a guardia-manned control room, patrol boats appear as blips in the waters between the Canaries and Africa. Next door sit Senegalese, Moroccan, and Mauritanian officers who communicate with their African colleagues down the telephone cables and satellite links that reach, like the translucent strands of a great spider's web, all the way to Dakar and the coast outside Mohammadou's neighborhood.

A Euro-African border is under construction at the southern edge of Europe. Clandestine boat migration is a small phenomenon, yet vast amounts of money have been spent on radars, satellites, advanced computer systems, and patrols by sea, land and, air to prevent migrants from leaving the African coastline in the first place. From state-of-the-art control rooms in Europe to rundown West African border posts, from Atlantic coasts to the Mediterranean Sea, a new border regime is at work, aimed at tracking one principal target—the illegal immigrant.

Europe's emerging border regime underlines the "seismic shift" that scholars have detected at contemporary frontiers. Ballooning enforcement budgets, new technology, and tougher migration laws are leading to a rebordering of rich states even as these borders are migrating away from their territorial boundaries. Borders now exist in the ledgers of African police, in trucks scanned for migrant bodies, in surveillance software or remote visa controls. Amid such a proliferation, as the political scientist William Walters has noted, the borders of Europe seem less like the walls of a fortress and more like a fluid Internet firewall. Yet for all its recent dispersal, the border regime has a distinguished historical and geographical pedigree. It actively draws upon the Mediterranean and Atlantic waters with their ancient powers to both divide and unite while mimicking the Roman *limes,* the fortified imperial buffer beyond which the barbarians awaited. Limes is, in twenty-first-century Europe, the name of a border control program; Greek and Roman gods lend their names to joint patrolling operations.[1]

The coming pages will embark on a fast-paced ride through Europe's border surveillance machinery, interspersed with glimpses of migrants' clandestine crossings. The journey starts in Madrid, at the heart of Spain's border control operations; it then skips across to the Canaries and the coordination center created there to halt the migrant boats. Next it travels north to the Polish capital, the unlikely seat of Europe's border agency, before descending again on Spain's coasts and control centers. These fragments from below and above—from the hull of a migrant boat and the monitors where this boat is rendered as an errant cluster of pixels might make it possible to glimpse, as through a kalei doscope, the workings of the border through its disparate yet intricately linked fragments.[2]

The novelty of the emerging Euro-African border, it will be argued, lies in a gradual process of abstraction of both the border itself and the clandestine migrant who approaches it. This process in turn hinges on the rendering of the migrant and his boat as a peculiar kind of risk. The language of risk, as the sociologist Ulrich Beck has noted, is spreading globally: it fuels financial market panics, terrorist fears, and apocalyptic visions of climate change. Beck's recent work sees risk as the *anticipation* of catastrophe: it is manufactured, staged, and acted upon, in the process becoming ever more real.[3] The "game of risk" played out by Europe's border agencies on high seas and in control rooms is such a staging, in which experts and security forces labor under the sign of looming catastrophe. In doing so, they remove the migrants and their rickety boats from the political field and treat them as something new, something abstract: a security threat approaching the external E.U. border.

This process is known as "securitization," of which more will be said below. Securitization has two distinct meanings in international relations and global finance, but both of these kinds, as will be seen in Frontex headquarters and Spanish control rooms, try to disperse and reduce risk. Yet risk cannot be contained by the border regime—and neither can the conflicts spawned by the ever-higher stakes in the business of bordering Europe.

THE BIRTH OF A BORDER

Europe's border regime remains largely unknown even to law enforcement officers, tucked away as it is into the far corners of distant cities and historic buildings. At the fortress-like Guardia Civil headquarters in Madrid in the summer of 2010, none of the guardias manning the gate knew about the International Coordination Centre (ICC) for migration controls. "Ah, is that Indalo?" one guardia asked, finally dialing the comandante in charge. Indalo was one of two migration patrol operations along Spanish coasts, covering the Mediterranean coasts of Andalusia and Murcia. It took its name from an ancient good-luck charm from Spain's southern Almería region, said to ward off evil (figure 3).

Across the courtyard and down a corridor from the ICC control room sat Comandante Francisco behind his polished wooden desk, a large Spanish flag hanging in the corner. Francisco led the Guardia Civil on Indalo and also oversaw the second Frontex maritime joint operation in Spain: the patrolling of the Atlantic Ocean between West Africa and the Canary Islands.

The mass arrival of migrant boats in the Canaries had first taken Spain by surprise. "We weren't geared up in the beginning," Francisco said. "These were islands, an archipelago," said a guardia colleague in Tenerife. "What problems could we have? There were just no serious problems in border control here." But the Guardia Civil, responsible for patrolling land and sea borders in Spain, soon found their feet. While

FIGURE 3. The Indalo symbol.
Source: the World Wide Web.

the building blocks of the new border regime were already being put in place before 2006, efforts now redoubled with the boat crisis. Spain's Socialist government scrambled for E.U. support and signed secretive patrolling and readmissions agreements with Mauritania, Cape Verde, and Senegal.[4] Soon it also had Frontex, Europe's young border agency, onboard. Francisco left on a mission to the windblown port city of Nouadhibou in Mauritania, from where migrant boats had set off that summer, earning it the nickname *la ville des clandestins* (city of illegal migrants). His objective was the launch of unprecedented anti-migration patrols along African coasts. The Atlantic waters lapping against the Canary Islands would soon become the laboratory for a "migration management" model to be exported across Europe's south-ern borders.

Hera was the name given to the Frontex joint operation in the Atlantic. Erstwhile wife of Zeus, Hera is the Hellenic goddess of love and marriage, and she has achieved a perfect union between Spain, its E.U. partners, and West African states. Hera I, launched in July 2006, brought experts to the Canaries to help identify the nationalities of detained migrants. With Hera II, launched a month later, Frontex-funded and Guardia Civil patrol vessels descended on African coasts. For the first time, European and West African states were patrolling the external E.U. borders together.

Hera has pride of place in the Frontex pantheon. In the Frontex booklet *Beyond the Frontiers,* a sepia-tinted stocktaking five years on from the agency's creation, Hera is described as "pivotal in achieving success. Before Operation Hera everything was theory. But after Hera the way forward was clear . . . [it was] the birth of sea operations."[5] Hera, Comandante Francisco said, was "the prototype that Frontex would like to export to the other joint operations." They work "in the jurisdictional waters from where they are leaving, it's the ideal operation," he said. "You have to prevent them leaving, you can't wait for them to arrive. . . . That way you save many lives." Early interception meant you saved money as well, he added: if migrants arrive "you give them food, you have to take care of them."

The numbers reveal why Hera was so popular. Arrivals in the Canaries fell from around thirty-two thousand in 2006 to twenty-two hundred in 2009. By 2010, the flow had virtually stopped, with only a trickle of arrivals from the coasts of Western Sahara. The direct passage from West Africa to Europe had effectively been closed.

Hera was a first successful attempt at a Europeanized border regime centered on Frontex and its new powers. It had also for the first time drawn a clear borderline across the seas, separating Europe's southernmost reaches from the African coasts. Yet the line, as soon as it was drawn, was already becoming diffuse; it was but the first step in the business of bordering Europe in the boats' wake.

. . .

The Hera deployment had been impressive. By the summer of 2006, Guardia Civil vessels patrolled first the Mauritanian and then the Senegalese coast in alliance with their African colleagues; Frontex-funded and Spanish military planes circled the open Atlantic; and the Spanish sea rescue service Salvamento Marítimo scoured the high seas in search of boat migrants. The proliferation of agencies involved in patrolling needed a coordination center, and this took the form of the CCRC, or the "Regional Coordination Center of the Canaries" (Centro de Coordinación Regional de Canarias). *El Frontex,* as it became informally known among border workers, was to be run by the Guardia Civil, which as Spain's military-status police force was an ideal choice according to one guardia: "The military won't get upset and the civilians won't get angry, since the Guardia Civil has a civilian scope." One security analyst called the CCRC "an experiment in security that is ahead of its time . . . its mission represents a new generation of security: one that goes beyond what can be defined as purely internal or external, national or international, civilian or military." The CCRC's "multidisciplinary" model, since updated in the ICC in Madrid, enabled an unprecedented visualization and control of the southern maritime border.[6]

In 2010, the CCRC occupied the back offices of the Military Palace in central Las Palmas while waiting for new-built locales out of town. Its corridors were adorned with pictures that would soon become a familiar sight in other Guardia Civil control centers: drowning Africans being pulled onto the deck, patrol vessels racing through the waves. In the control room upstairs, a digital map projected onto the wall showed the six Canary Islands and a scattering of Guardia Civil boats and vehicles, with the seas divided into surveillance zones for military planes monitoring the Atlantic.[7] The control center oversaw the whole operational area, about 425,000 square kilometers of open sea between the Canaries, Cape Verde, and Senegal.

The CCRC's very architecture highlighted how migration has emerged in recent years as what the border theorist Didier Bigo calls a "global security problem" situated at the threshold of internal and external security. As rich states have shifted from war fighting to crime fighting at the borders since the end of the Cold War, the roles of security forces have become increasingly mixed. In this new security landscape, Bigo stresses that, contrary to commonsense opinion, "migration control is not an *answer* to a security problem." Instead, security agencies nervous about their future relevance "compete among themselves to have their objectives included in politicians' platforms." The CCRC stood not as just a monument to the winners in this battle on the Spanish front, the Guardia Civil. Rather, its placing at the back of the Military Palace, its new technology, and multiagency staff proved a *catalyst* in blurring the border between civilian and military means in the fight against illegal migration.[8]

A worthy cause was needed to justify this militarization. The solution was, as indicated by Comandante Francisco and confirmed by the pictures in the CCRC corridors, the task of "saving lives." Legal scholars have argued that Frontex maritime interceptions may be legally justified only if framed as rescues, and this seems to be a lesson that high-ranking border guards have taken to heart.[9] In the words of Giuseppe, an Italian coast guard and former project manager of Hera, "The priority is to save human lives, and this entails intercepting all the boats that try to arrive in Spain before they reach the coasts." The basis for interceptions, Giuseppe confirmed, was "rescuing lives" in accordance with SOLAS, the International Convention for the Safety of Life at Sea.

The bordering of southern Europe was aided by the diffuse nature of maritime borders and the patchwork of rules that governs them under international law.[10] While humanitarianism provided a legal justification for interceptions on the open or "free" seas, it also lent a preemptive rationale to the controversial policing of African territorial waters, in which Spanish memoranda of understanding signed with coastal states allowed the Europeans to patrol as long as local officers were formally in charge of the decision to intercept.[11] "What matters is helping people," said one guardia, "whether it's at one [nautical] mile, or fifteen, or thirty, or two hundred ... when helping a boat there is no limit."

This humanitarian urge seems at odds with the boat tragedies in the Mediterranean, where at least fifteen hundred migrants died in 2011 alone. Here, scholars note, loopholes in the international search-and-rescue regime (SAR) and SOLAS mean that European states can heave off responsibilities for rescuing migrant boats to their neighbors. The search-and-rescue laws, Human Rights Watch says, are moreover unclear on the concept of distress at sea, "allowing ships to ignore dangerously overcrowded and ill-equipped migrant boats."[12]

In contrast to states such as Malta, however, Spanish patrols saw any migrant vessel as a virtual shipwreck (náufrago). In the words of one Spanish sea rescue chief, a cayuco was a "danger for navigation" by definition, akin to a coach racing down a highway "without brakes." Such reasoning enabled early interventions across Spain's vast SAR zone of more than 1.5 million square kilometers, with the Canaries zone constituting two-thirds of this and reaching the African coastline. In the Mediterranean joint operation Indalo, the patrolling area followed the Spanish SAR zone rather than limiting itself to territorial waters. In the Strait, this zone in fact reached into Moroccan waters, meaning Spanish vessels routinely "rescued" migrant boats right up along Morocco's coasts—overriding the otherwise tense and militarized border.[13]

The Spanish use of humanitarianism is not unique. Charting the emergence of the "humanitarian border" elsewhere, William Walters notes how on the Italian island of Lampedusa, migrant boats have been greeted since 2005 by a joined-up effort from the police, coast guards, the Red Cross, the IOM, and UNHCR (the United Nations High Commissioner for Refugees). This "uneasy alliance" mixes reception and rejection, care and coercion, much as in Spain's joint operations. The Spanish case simply shows in the clearest fashion how humanitarianism, in dissolving the patchwork of maritime boundaries, has allowed border controls to migrate away from European shores. Security experts have argued that "police units both intercept and rescue, which undermines their image as a dissuasive force," but this very humanitarian-policing nexus is what legitimizes and lends efficacy to migration control operations in African and international waters.[14]

The Euro-African border might have started life as a line, but the rescues and patrols soon subverted this linear logic. Sea and air operations diced up the open sea into surveillance areas dependent on the patchwork of SAR zones and the African patrolling agreements. Surveillance was not an exercise in "holding the line," as the name of a border control operation in the United States once had it, but in "monitoring a grid."[15] This monitoring exercise depended upon a framing of boat migration as dangerous by definition, a "risk to life" in the words of one Guardia Civil captain. Migrants had to be "prevented from leaving" for their own good. Yet migrants were rendered a risk not only to themselves on the open seas but also to the integrity of the external E.U. border—and it fell upon Frontex, Europe's elusive border agency, to conceptualize them as such a risk.

FRONTEX AND THE DOUBLE SECURITIZATION OF MIGRATION

"Ah! You're writing about the pateras." Ali's smile lit up the rain-swept Canarian patio. "I know of some French journalists who went to Western Sahara and made a documentary there, they even took the boat to the Canary Islands, filming everything. If you want, I can help organize something. I have contacts. You could make good money with a film." Ali used to make good money too—his line of business was "transport, any kind of transport." He drove trucks full of contraband and smuggled people. Ali knew the routes, how to evade paying bribes to the Moroccan security forces, how to quick-inflate a Zodiac boat, how to steer the course from a Saharan beach to Gran Canaria's shores in twenty-four hours. "I always sent people here, I sent my two brothers before I came myself. . . . Before it was very easy, the police didn't bother me. I gathered the people, I got the Zodiac, we went down to the beach. I didn't even pay the police." Sometimes he took on clients from sub-Saharan Africa and Asia too. "They pay more, two thousand euros each, or three thousand euros for the Asians. Moroccans only pay a thousand euros in a Zodiac, five hundred euros in a patera." Then he decided to go himself. "I brought a chauffeur. . . . we call him al rais [the chief] but

he's really nothing, I buy all the material and pay the transport." Ali paused momentarily, high on the bravado of his trip. "I looked on the Internet, waiting for the right weather . . ." Then they set off. "When Spain was four hours away, the weather changed, high waves and lots of wind. The international seas are more dangerous, the water is black deep down, very deep. We saw fishing boats. The rais is clever; when he sees a boat he stops the motor so that we don't appear on radar." In the early morning, they reached an abandoned beach. Ali's brother was waiting there: he had done the same journey before, arriving in the exact same spot. "He made a note of it on the GPS and then sent the GPS to me by post," Ali said with a smile. "I went straight to his house, to have a shower, make some food, and sleep." The VIP commute was over.

WARSAW, JULY 2011. Frontex headquarters are far from the African coastlines and deserts, far from the Mediterranean and Atlantic seas. Its home, the Rondo1 skyscraper, is all sheer glass surfaces set in the corporate post-Communist landscape of the Polish capital. Its façade sports the logo of the accountancy firm Ernst & Young; only a limp Frontex flag at the entrance indicates this is the seat of the European Union's border agency.

Frontex remains little known among European publics. Charged with managing "operational cooperation" at the European Union's external borders, the agency's main task is halting irregular migrant flows, and for this it has been provided with an (until recently) rapidly growing budget, going from €19.1 million in 2006, its first full year of operations, to €84.9 million in 2012. Criticism has mounted over the legality of Frontex patrols and the pushback of asylum seekers, while activists have increasingly decried the agency's "war" on migrants. But Frontex, it soon became clear on my visits, is both more and less than this militaristic view would allow for.[16]

The glassed-in elevator pinged open on the eleventh floor, where a Frontex doormat welcomed me to the agency's swipecard-entry offices. On the wall behind reception was the Frontex logo, tastefully engraved in a wooden panel. A glass cabinet displayed Frontex T-shirts, Frontex torches, and Frontex ties nicely folded in their boxes. THINGS NOT FOR SALE, said a notice. I sat down and browsed Polish policing magazines as a staffer beeped her entrance card on a reader at the end of the room. A glass door slid open into what looked like a decompression chamber, where a camera read her face before the inner door let her through. This "mantrap," as workers called it, plus the policing magazines and the not-for-sale sign: these were the only indications this was not the head-quarters of an accountancy or law firm but the brains of Europe's bor-der regime, a "cop shop" in the words of one staffer.

Alessandra, the Frontex spokeswoman, dressed in a discreet gray suit with a Hermès shawl wrapped around her neck, led me to the offices of the deputy director. Spain had proposed Gerardo, a soft-spoken man with a background in the Spanish national police, as director when Frontex was in its infancy. A Finnish border guard, Ilkka Laitinen, secured the position, but Gerardo's being second in charge was still a coup for Madrid. Gerardo had a Spanish secretary, a strong Spanish accent, and Spanish priorities, talking warmly of his country's success in combating clandestine migration. As the interview unfolded I glanced at a poster of the sunny Pyrenees on his wall: its postcard rendering of his faraway home seemed an apt metaphor for the continued dominance of state loyalties in a supposedly Europeanized border regime.

The Spanish experience underpinned all subsequent Frontex opera-tions. While Gerardo called Hera the "benchmark" for all future joint operations, he immediately downplayed Frontex's role in the success. "The joint operation might have helped," he said, "but [this] was also the time when Spain was negotiating agreements" with African states. These deals for border surveillance, policing cooperation, repatriation, and "arresting smugglers" had a drastic impact, he insisted. "We do not pretend to be the key players in this success." Afterwards Alessandra echoed Gerardo's comments. "We have to be very careful when we talk about the reasons for the reduction," she said. "We can't take the glory."

This was surely a communications strategy that aimed to strike a bal-ance between visibility and invisibility—promoting Frontex just enough while letting it work in the shadows, leaving both glory and blame to the host state. But Frontex had indeed been a hanger-on, not a leader, in Hera. As one Frontex officer put it, the police officers who arrived to interview migrants in the Canaries "took it as vacations" and needed guidance, much as their Icelandic patrolling colleagues would in Senegal a few years later. Moreover, as Gerardo insisted, it is the host state that retains command in joint operations—and future Frontex agreements with non-E.U. countries might not even change this. Governments were simply too reluctant to let go of control over their slice of Europe's southern maritime border.[17]

The borders, then, remain a largely bilateral business, as Frontex's full name indicates: "European Agency for the Management of Opera-tional Cooperation at the *External Borders of the Member States* of the

European Union." In the words of one commentator, "Frontex is still an agency that lacks independence, whose performance depends on the political agenda of states such as Spain, who in this way transfer their domestic interests to a European level."[18] Indeed, Spain leads Hera patrols on the basis of Spanish bilateral deals; the CCRC is run not by *el Frontex* but by the Guardia Civil, until recently from the back offices of a Spanish military palace. Frontex here seems reduced to being a funnel for European funds and a megaphone for member states.

Yet this conclusion would miss Frontex's main impact in *rethinking* the border. Its "thought-work," to borrow a term from the anthropology of migration bureaucracies, has helped redraw the patchwork of borders in southern Europe within a larger narrative of the external border. Spain-Morocco, Italy-Libya, Greece-Turkey, and, to a lesser extent, the eastern land borders: these are now frontlines in a common European endeavor, and Frontex provides the language to make sense of and operationalize these frontlines in terms of migration. The agency's thought-work, as will be seen, again frames migration as a risk—although no longer just to human life, but also to the security of Europe's external borders.[19]

. . .

For Frontex, the border means business. In the words of one commentator, "Frontex wears suit not uniform."[20] Its operations are organized along the lines of corporate ventures. "Project teams" handle joint operations (JOs), drawing in staff from most Frontex units, including the Risk Analysis Unit (RAU), "returns" (forced deportation), and "ops" (operations). RAU first prepares thematic and area reports—tailored risk analyses (TRAs) and tactical focused assessments (TFAs)—before a draft operational plan is circulated to member states and "to legal, PR, and so on," as one risk analyst explained. The host state gets a say, and a full operational plan follows, outlining the assets—staff or vessels, for example—that member states can contribute. The JO is ready to go.

JO and RAU, TRA and TFA, assets and ops: Frontex lingo is as impenetrable as any business jargon. The agency's reports speak of "business fields" active in the (military-style) "operational theater" of the external border. The "operational portfolio" includes delivery of "strategic and operational risk analysis products" to "customers," also known as the border guards of member states.[21] Despite Alessandra's protestations ("business implies a profit, right?"), Frontex's business language with its splash of military metaphors points to the agency's dual view of itself: as a purveyor of "solutions" and "best practice" on the one hand and as a quick-footed emergency deployment force on the other.

Frontex, as the fulcrum in the European Union's strategy of "integrated border management," reconceptualizes the border through a range of tasks: it trains border guards, creates arenas for officers to talk shop in joint operations, and exports its jargon to member states for statistics collection. But it is risk analysis that is at the heart of Frontex's thought-work, underpinning all operations. The RAU collects intelligence via the Frontex Risk Analysis Network, whose nation-state contributors in turn gather data from immigration liaison officers stationed in "transit countries." As the language of risk spreads across these networks and filters down to border patrols, Frontex reprioritizes border-work towards halting migration.[22] Anything else—detecting oil spills, assisting boats in danger, intercepting drugs—is subordinated to that goal. As Alessandra put it: "[Joint Operation] Indalo [is] interesting in terms of ... side products. Our mandate is border controls as such, controlling illegal migration," but in Indalo they "seized four [metric] tons of hashish while they were at it."[23] Border controls *as such* mean irregular migration, first of all, and Frontex as an intelligence-driven agency has made its task the definition and understanding of this object through the concept of risk.

Risk, to Frontex, is defined as "a function of threat, vulnerability and impact": "[A] 'threat' is a force or pressure acting upon the external borders that is characterized by both its magnitude and likelihood; 'vulnerability' is defined as the capacity of a system to mitigate the threat and 'impact' is determined as the potential consequences of the threat."[24]

Through this three-pronged risk concept, Frontex seems to be providing one key piece in the "securitization" of migration. As mentioned, securitization refers to taking an issue out of politics and framing it as a security threat, whether through enunciation or practice. While recent academic studies have analyzed how Frontex contributes to the securitization of migration in Europe, relatively little attention has so far been paid to the organizing concept of risk. Risk bridges humanitarianism and crime fighting, enunciation and practice, politics and patrols: it provides the language shorn of politics needed to make migrant boats an abstract threat to the external border. As will be seen, risk also allows for thinking of migration in terms of a second "securitization"—in the banking sense of pooling and profiting from financial risk.[25]

Risk is made real through a world of arrows in which the migrant boats, still visible and tangible in sea patrols and rescues, reach a new level of abstraction. In a Frontex meeting room, one risk analyst spread printouts of a map for tracking clandestine migrant routes across the table. On the "i-Map," developed by the migration think-tank ICMPD (the International Centre for Migration Policy Development) and rendered in simplified form at the start of this book, arrows pointed across the deserts of Libya, Niger, Algeria, and Mauritania before converging on migrant nodes such as Nouadhibou, Oujda, and Agadez. In Frontex lingo, the routes are closed, displaced, and reactivated, while "transfers" of "pockets" of migrants are talked about in the imported academic language of push and pull factors. Here migrant routes morph into sharp arrows—"forces or pressures," as the Frontex risk definition puts it— threatening the European Union's "vulnerable" external borders.

The risk analyst traced her finger along the arrows, from Mauritania on the coast to the Algerian desert. "There was a displacement effect" in 2009 "from the Atlantic to the western Mediterranean route," she said. "Up to 2009, this was the most dangerous route migrants could take." With increasing pressure on both the Atlantic and eastern fronts—the route from Niger to Libya and Italy—this was the only path left. The "pocket" had to be transferred; Spain's Indalo area of operations was being "reactivated."

Those who do the transferring and reactivation—the people smugglers—are known in Frontex parlance as facilitators, a catch-all term covering anyone from taxi drivers on the Greek-Macedonian frontier to organized trafficking rings. Through "debriefings" with migrants in detention, Frontex finds out about their routes and facilitators' modus operandi, data that are later synthesized in risk assessments.[26]

The gradual abstraction in risk analysis—evident in both the i-Map visuals and the Frontex glossary—flattens the complex realities of the border. Is an Afghan refugee as much of a risk as a Senegalese boat migrant?[27] Are Macedonian taxi drivers and Nigerian trafficking gangs equal threats? Frontex lingo, through its neutrality, facilitates the swift translation of border terminology. When smuggling networks professionalize in response to increased controls, this change is also masked by the i-Map arrows and the Frontex jargon of reactivation and facilitation. Frontex thought-work, through its very neutrality, furnishes a unitary vision of the border as the place where homogenous migrants and facilitators are fought back and apprehended.

This unitary vision contrasts with the reality of boat migration, as the Spanish police know. The migrant networks of Senegal in 2006 and 2007 were spontaneous, according to Raúl, the Spanish police attaché in Dakar. "These were Senegalese fishermen who often wanted to migrate themselves. They had the boat, they had the motor, and clients offered themselves up." In fishing neighborhoods such as Yongor, a whole chain of workers was involved. The *coxeur* found clients on behalf of the convoyeur or *borom gaal,* the trip organizer and owner of the boat. Once all "tickets" were sold, the convoyeur contracted a *capitaine* or a guide for the boat, who would handle the GPS onboard, as well as several chauffeurs, who piloted the boat in exchange for free passage. To Frontex, the convoyeur, borom gaal, coxeur, capitaine, and chauffeur are all facilitators that, in Spain, can be denounced in the media as "mafias" and sentenced as *pasadores* (smugglers). In Morocco, the same applies to both al rais and his paymaster Ali.

The framing of migrants and facilitators as sources of risk, then, securitizes them through visual and linguistic abstraction. But risk is not just the anticipation of danger; it is also the source of potential profits. To understand this flip side of risk, it is useful to think about the second, financial meaning of "securitization" together with the term's policing sense.[28] To bankers, securitization refers to the bundling, slicing, and trading of debt. In the financial derivatives at the heart of the 2008 credit crunch, risky subprime mortgages were packaged into a bundle, pushed into an off-balance-sheet vehicle, and traded on global markets in "tranches" with different levels of exposure to risk. The trick was an unprecedented *dispersal* of risk; yet this very dispersal proved the system's undoing.[29]

Disconcertingly, the border regime seems to disperse and distribute risk in a similar fashion. It first securitizes migratory flows as a threat through Frontex intelligence networks and tools such as the i-Map, which let experts envision new "solutions" in a graphic interface. Here risk is securitized in ways analogous to the second, financial sense— bundled into pockets, routes, flows, and vulnerabilities and assigned to police forces and external investors. And this distribution, like that of financial securitization, generates new risk and growing tensions among "junior" and "senior" investors, as will soon be seen.

Frontex, much like a fast-moving financier or the "facilitators" it targets, both shuns and embraces risk. To keep up to date with migratory routes, it needs a lean and flexible operation. A few floors of a Warsaw skyscraper will do just fine for this purpose. Frontex has—for now, at least—no clumsy infrastructure to handle.[30] Instead of the stiff and clumsy working arrangements of Europe's old border guards, it provides quick, sharp interventions across the whole external border.

"Frontex," then, is not *el Frontex*—a control room in Las Palmas, a militarized border force. Like the blue Frontex armband its seconded officers wear in joint operations, it is flexible, moveable, and removable. In this lightweight fashion, in the shadow of still-powerful states, it quietly goes about its business of bordering the continent.

HARDWIRING THE AFRICAN FRONTIER

From a migrant boat, Europe first appears as light—a glimmer on the horizon, a glittering coastline—and to reach it you have to traverse the darkness of wild seas and deserts, shielded from the prying eyes of border guards. When setting off from Western Sahara, the lighthouse of La Entallada on Fuerteventura guides the pateras packed to the brim with people and battered by the rough winds that give their destination its name. Boat migrants who depart from northern Morocco seek the glimmer of the tiny Alborán Island, in the Mediterranean north of Melilla, and, if they pass it undetected, three sparks along the Spanish coast: the lighthouses of the coasts of Granada and Almería. In the Mauritanian port city of Nouadhibou, migrants say they can see the lights from Europe across the sea. But the light reaches farther, penetrating the desert. "Ah, Zouerate," said one Spanish policeman with a sigh, talking of a godforsaken mining town in deepest Mauritania. "That's where the migrants were left by the mafias; they pointed to the lights of Zouerate and told them that was Spain; they had to walk towards the light."

LAS PALMAS, APRIL 2010. It was the time of the big yearly gathering. Suited police, marines in white uniforms, and green-clad guardias congregated in the halls of Hotel Meliá in the Gran Canarian capital. The Euro-African policing conference on migration, attended by eighty-nine security chiefs from twenty-five countries, was redolent with the power of the state: straight-backed men, flags on tables, glossy police posters galore. Behind the podium was a large banner of the sun setting at sea, a potent symbol of Europe's external border; outside the big windows, sunbathers lounged on the city beach a few steps away.

Presentation followed presentation. Comandante Francisco spoke excitedly of "the surveillance system of the future" through a complete integration of sea border controls and "compatibility between all systems." The discussant, a tall Dutchman from Europol, exhorted African police in the hall to target human smugglers and "send us the information you have on these networks." "There's a model law on people smuggling for downloading on the UNODC [UN crime agency] web page," he said, encouraging the Africans to promote it in their capitals. "As we're building up so-called Fortress Europe, it's getting harder to get to Europe . . . [so] you face the same problem with illegal migration and illegal stayers," he said in a nod of sympathy to his North African colleagues.

In the break, African marines mingled with guardias on the hotel terrace, sipping coffee and tea and digging into patisserie trays. I went about collecting business cards: the general director of the Malian gendarmerie, the Senegalese navy's chief of operations, the Gambian immigration commissioner. They were all there, the top brass of Africa's border forces. Two officers—North African and Greek—snapped pictures of each other as souvenirs. The real action was in backroom talk: Malians laughed hard with guardias in the halls, a Mauritanian gendarme took down phone numbers on his battered Nokia mobile.

Journalists were let into the conference hall for the concluding session. They congregated at the back as the director of Spain's security forces strode to the podium. He spoke fast and assuredly of "the excellent climate of confidence that has prevailed at the conference." Illegal migration had gone down by 70 percent, he said, and the fight against this "scourge" was proceeding apace thanks to "the collaboration between all the institutions represented here." They needed to "persecute this crime" of "commerce with other people," he said, referencing the smuggling networks. It would be wrong to indulge in a "false sense of triumphalism," he warned, but his speech was strident. The view from the top was bright and shiny, the battle was being won. But at what price?

. . .

In the beginning, getting the Africans onboard had been difficult. "Maybe they didn't understand very well what we were trying to do," said the Guardia Civil chief in Dakar in a rather diplomatic understatement. In the first years, "there would even be policemen or gendarmes who would send their children" if they knew a boat was leaving, he said. "They saw it as a bus trip." Stories circulated about African officers absconding from policing conferences and migrant identification missions, never to be heard from again.

"All member states are aware that there's no other way to fight migration than to cooperate with third countries," insisted Comandante Francisco, and this was a lesson the Spaniards took to heart before anyone else. At the root of the migration agreements between West Africa and Spain discussed in the last chapter was policing cooperation. Enrique, a tough-talking Spanish policeman based in Morocco, had worked on pushing through these deals with state after state. "First there is always an accord between the foreign ministries on cooperation," he said, "something to cover things up" *(para tapar)*. Next came the memoranda of understanding between interior ministries. "Let's see," he said, remembering the countries where he helped push these through: "Senegal, Mauritania, Mali, Morocco already had one, Cape Verde, Gambia, Guinea, Guinea-Bissau, what else . . . oh yes, Niger. They are basically all the same; you cut and paste from one to the other." Through these deals, a vast policing network was quickly being built up around Europe's southern border.

Key to this network was the Seahorse Project. Starting in 2005, it received more than €6 million of E.U. funding, as part of the larger €120 million Aeneas program, to establish "an effective policy to prevent illegal migration."[31] Seahorse, managed by the Guardia Civil, aimed to tie police forces into a tighter network through conferences, training, and the increased deployment of liaison officers and joint patrols. The Seahorse secretariat had organized the Las Palmas conference for the fifth year running, in what was fast becoming a "tradition" according to the concluding remarks of the Spanish police chief. Spanish officers also trained African police on illegal migration in West African capitals and invited high-ranking officers to Spain for tours of control rooms and police academies. The conferences, courses, and visits not only served "to see how other countries work on migration," as the Spanish police attaché in Mali put it; they were also junkets for African officers that fomented a shared vision of the border while creating informal connections. In Las Palmas, cake and coffee did as much to boost the border network as endless PowerPoint presentations.

But Seahorse was, above all, a high-tech venture. It would not only expand the transnational policing networks around the figure of the illegal immigrant; it would also hardwire these networks into a secure communications system via satellite. Technology triggered cooperation. The secure system, the Seahorse Network, had by 2010 pulled in Spain, Portugal, Mauritania, Cape Verde, Senegal, the Gambia, Guinea-Bissau, and Morocco.[32]

Hera built on this network, which spun out from the CCRC in Las Palmas in a widening web. Senegal, Frontex's most eager collaborator, had created a national coordination center in Dakar's navy base, where a joint chiefs of staff communicated with Las Palmas via a second control center in the Senegalese Interior Ministry, as well as via the Spanish embassy attachés. The information did not stop in Las Palmas, how-

ever: by 2010, a steady stream of information was funneled from the
CCRC, Dakar, and elsewhere along the African coast into the control
room in Madrid and onwards to Warsaw.[33] Through such day-to-day
contact the communications network grew ever more intricate, its transnationalism increasingly taken for granted.

One thing stood out in this Seahorse-wired regime, however: all
information traveled through Spain. No lines of communication united
Mauritania and Senegal or Senegal and the Gambia. The information
network was a one-way street.

The border theorist Ladis Kristof long ago drew a distinction between
boundaries, which are "inner-oriented," distinguishing insiders and outsiders, and frontiers, which are zones of contact and "the spearhead of
light and knowledge expanding into the realm of darkness and of the
unknown."[34] Ironically, to close off, Spain first had to reach out. It had
to create a zone of contact—that is, a frontier. In doing so, the Spanish
government had used copied-and-pasted memoranda of understanding
to impressive effect. It had knocked on all the right doors in order to
close its own. But Spain's frontier making only got it that far: the smooth
satellite channels generated friction. And these tensions, however slight
and brief, sometimes broke into the open.

Before the Guardia Civil chief stepped up to the conference podium
to declare that the battle against illegal migration was being won, before
the journalists were let into the hall, there had been a brief time for
questions. One African officer spoke. "The police response is not the
only approach to resolving the phenomenon of illegal migration," he
said. Another West African officer also raised his hand. He spoke softly
in eloquent French, which was promptly translated. "The exchange of
information should be reciprocal," he said, otherwise it was not "cooperation." The Europol officer at the podium replied. He fully understood
the frustrations about access to confidential information, he said, but
there were strict rules for sharing. Maybe an open version could be
made available, he thought out loud. Then he realized there was something the African officers could use. The previous year's report from
ICMPD was comprehensive, he said; what's more, it was available to
the public, "free and available to download" from the center's website.
If they wanted, he offered, he could send his African colleagues a link.

. . .

The Euro-African border was in Seahorse no longer—or not only—a
line across the seas, a search-and-rescue area, or a complex field of risk

management. It was morphing into what William Walters calls a "strategic node within a transnational network," where Spain—unburdened by a colonial past in the region—was perfectly placed to create alliances with West African states around a shared concern with migratory risk. Yet instead of a smooth "risk community" across the maritime divide of the cosmopolitan kind envisioned by Ulrich Beck, here reemerged the asymmetrical relation familiar from the days of empire. Returning to the financial analogy, if the border regime apportioned risk, the African partners in the fight against illegal migration were left with the riskiest, most "junior" tranches. In Beck's terms, risk was "exported" from rich to poor. This is what the Europol officer acknowledged with his sympathetic words on the side effects of Fortress Europe; it was also implicit in the questions voiced by the African delegates. The larger gains from securitization, meanwhile, went elsewhere—into Europe's security industry with its technological "solutions" to the risk posed by clandestine migration.[35]

THE MEN WHO STARE AT SCREENS

At Café Hafa in Tangier, favored haunt of the Beat poets who once flocked to this "free city" at the tip of Africa, the Spanish coast is a mere thirty kilometers away. Serge and I sipped our mint tea and gazed towards the Spanish town of Tarifa on the horizon, a dollop of whitewashed Andalusia amid the sea haze and the clear blue sky. Serge was from Congo-Brazzaville but had fled twelve years earlier after his brother was nearly killed in the country's civil war; he had been in Morocco for one year now and was seeking asylum. "I only want to leave this place, that's all I want," he said. "But I would never go by boat, it's too risky." Serge knew a Nigerian man who lived on the edge of town in a big house built with people-smuggling money. "I asked him about the trips," Serge said. Nothing came of it. He had tried other options, foremost of which was flirting with European girls with the hope of love and a passage to Europe. He finished his tea, still pondering the possibility of a clandestine boat journey to Spain. "If I go, I'd go by Zodiac," he said, referring to the small, fast vessels that had replaced the wooden pateras used by pioneering Moroccan migrants in the 1990s.[36] Then he turned to me with a question. "Is it true that if you take a small boat from the beach here, they see you on the radar?"

If risk analysis is the "brains" of Europe's border regime, as Frontex would have it, the screens and surveillance machinery are its eyes. In the control rooms in Warsaw, Madrid, and the Guardia Civil *comandancias* dotting the Spanish coastline, the border is made visible, legible, and operational. In this endeavor, Spain is again in the vanguard. Its "integrated system for external surveillance," or SIVE *(sistema integrado de vigilancia exterior)*, combines radar, high-tech cameras, and patrols in a powerful surveillance network that is credited with the sharp decline in migrant boat arrivals. SIVE, which received E.U. funding once it shifted focus from drug control to illegal migration, has helped rebrand the Guardia Civil as a cutting-edge border force; it has also boosted the fortunes of the developers, including the Spanish companies Amper, Isdefe, and Indra. Indra, named after the Hindu god of war (who is, as it happens, cognate to Hera's husband, Zeus), has exported SIVE to destinations as diverse as Romania, Latvia, and Hong Kong.[37]

Walk into a SIVE control room—as many international delegates, security experts, and journalists have in recent years—and you will see rows of computer terminals manned by guardias staring at their monitors. Facing them are wall-mounted screens that project a real-time electronic map and camera shots of the coastline and seas. The operator monitors his terminal, looking for signs of migrants approaching the coastline. Suddenly something might appear: a pixelated boat, with a vector attached indicating its speed and direction. The guardia brings the map up on the wall projection, takes a closer look. It could be nothing, the guardia knows. Maybe the radar has just detected the crest of a wave, a small fishing boat, or even a whale. Determining signs of a patera relies on experience. What is the weather like? If the hard, easterly Levante wind blows across the Mediterranean, migrants rarely set out from Algeria and Morocco. How does the object move? A sinuous, zigzag path, represented by a trail of pixels, means it could be a patera. Is it moving fast? In the Canaries, where the large wooden cayucos groan under the weight of perhaps a hundred passengers, a slow speed gives migrant vessels away. In the Strait, if the object is small and moves fast, it could be drug smugglers or migrants in a lightweight Zodiac. With a right-click on the mouse, the operator can identify the patera and track its movements. As it approaches the coast, he steers the camera with his joystick into line with the object, as in a computer game. If it is a patera sighting, he activates the protocol and a Guardia Civil patrol boat shoots out, followed by a Salvamento Marítimo rescue ship. The four steps of an intervention are about to be completed: detection, identification, follow-up, and "interception or rescue." Finally, a crosshair marks the spot of a *patera* interception.

The Euro-African border on the SIVE screens appears as a diffuse area of intervention, devoid of clear borderlines.[38] What counts is the range of your radar, the specs of your cameras, the reach of your patrols—all represented visually on-screen. In this borderless world, the "abnormal vessel behavior" gives the patera away, seen in stops and starts or a zigzag, errant course.

The "life-saving" SIVE seems a roaring success: not only does it broadcast the border, promote Spanish technology, and stop pateras in their tracks; it also renders migrant risk as an on-screen abnormality. But the SIVE screens blind visitors to how surveillance of the seas has changed the cat-and-mouse game of the sea border. As a Guardia Civil book on SIVE acknowledges, the "substantial increase in surveillance and control of the areas covered by deployments has driven the irregular activities to move to less guarded areas"—meaning longer and riskier sea crossings.[39] But other strategies have also emerged in recent years. Now, most sub-Saharan migrants know that they might be spotted by the SIVE, and unlike their Moroccan and Algerian counterparts who fear immediate deportation, they *want* this to happen. In the border game that ensues, all actors—facilitators, migrants, rescue services, guardias, and police—have their assigned role. Migrants or their associates often call for help before departure, sea rescue boats search for them, and once found bring them to port for a medical check followed by detention and the hope of eventual liberation. Other migrants, at much greater risk, try to skirt the radars and limit costs by using tiny, inflatable "toy" boats to traverse the deep, rapid waters of the Strait. They, too, are usually detected. Again, their detection often depends on a simpler solution than the expensive SIVE, since the Spanish authorities encourage the thousands of ships passing through the Strait each year to inform them of any patera sightings. The result of this combination of high and low technologies meant that, by 2010, most migrant vessels were intercepted. The impromptu arrivals among sunbathers on Spanish beaches were a memory of the past.

Manning the SIVE could be stressful: the lives of dozens of travelers in a sinking boat depended on reading the on-screen signs correctly. During the mass arrivals of earlier years, reports surfaced of depression among guardias. The nationwide Guardia Civil workers' association has denounced the lack of SIVE staff and the working conditions in the control rooms, while aid workers whispered that the lack of manpower made the SIVE much less effective than it used to be.[40]

The solution to these limitations was, however—as across Europe's border regime—more technology. "We have to extend it much further," said Comandante Francisco, outlining his vision of border surveillance in three layers: first, the SIVE and patrols covering the coasts; second, planes, ocean-going ships, and satellites monitoring the high seas; and third, joint patrols scouring African territorial waters, as in Hera and to a lesser extent in Morocco.[41]

This full surveillance vision is already becoming reality. The European Maritime Safety Agency is providing satellite coverage in the first Frontex multiagency operation, Indalo. GMES, the European program for Earth observation, has launched a collaboration with Frontex under its fifteen-million-euro G-MOSAIC program for "situational awareness" of regional crises, its website showing footage of car tracks in the Algerian desert and color-coded maps of "border permeability."[42] GMES and other publicly funded initiatives have pulled in defense companies such as Indra that develop the technology at a healthy profit. And Frontex, through its research and development unit, is in the thick of it, coordinating research and linking up academia, E.U. authorities, security companies, and border guards. Electro-optical sensors for sea, land, and air surveillance, smaller sensors "for detecting humans and objects inside closed compartments," advanced command and control systems (C4I), and vessel tracking tools are all in the cards in a fruitful back-and-forth between the security industry and Europe's border regime. In the words of one commentator, migration control is "an opportunity for our industries to take advantage of an unbeatable laboratory to develop new research and development products." The creativity the Euro-African frontier has unleashed seems endless.[43]

One important spark for this creativity is the European Union's Seventh Framework Programme (FP-7), which has provided €1.4 billion for security research over 2007–13, with the aim of "improving the competitiveness of the European security industry." Yet the defense companies are far from passive recipients of subsidies and favors: like the border guards, they are actively *creating* a demand for their "solutions" in Brussels, Warsaw, and beyond. Lobby groups such as the European Organisation for Security have played a key role in the formulation of priorities in security research, and industry representatives have participated as "experts" in public-private dialogues such as the European Security Research and Innovation Forum. Meanwhile the European Union and its member states, keen to bolster the fragmented European defense sector, promote the industry's products to neighboring countries such as Libya, often guaranteeing sales through export credits. One academic contributor to *The Migration Industry*, detailing these dynamics, notes how "the militarization of Europe's borders is grounded not only in a desire to prevent immigration, but also in European politics of supporting military and control exports with public funds, even if this leads to increased debts in especially developing countries." The double securitization of migration here takes concrete shape: new debt is created out of the migration bubble, yet with little risk for defense companies or their shareholders and creditors—which, besides member states, include investment banks familiar from the subprime crisis.[44]

While a full treatment of the security industry's work is beyond the scope of this book, it is worth lingering on the vision for border surveillance that emerges from the collaborations among border guards, Frontex workers, policy makers, and defense companies. The full surveillance vision presented by new border "solutions" usually shares two features: a dynamic visualization of risk and a powerful rendering of the surveillance system itself as a generator of spatial order.[45] In one virtual demo of a new border control system seeded by FP-7 funds, an intruding illegal migrant is spotted inside a circular sensor area, highlighted as a threat, and targeted by an unmanned vehicle shooting out in a line of interception, much like the SIVE's radars, cameras, and boats follow the errant pateras. "Freeze!" the unmanned machine calls out; the traveler stops in his tracks, gripping his suitcase, until the border patrol arrives and the words *mission accomplished* light up on-screen.

Satellite systems and aerial drones are at the pinnacle in this drive to visualize the border, attracting policing dreams and triggering activist ire. With camera technology from the United States or Israel, Comandante Francisco mused, "we could cover maybe a thousand square kilometers with a small unmanned plane." The vision, in his words, is a complete surveillance cover of the border region and beyond.

This will be achieved through a project known as Eurosur, or the "European external border surveillance system." This "system-of-systems" brings to fruition a plan hatched already in the 1990s, initially inspired by the Spanish SIVE, for a European early-warning system on illegal crossings. Pushed by the European Commission and member states such as Spain, Eurosur has moved ahead at breakneck speed, going from a 2008 roadmap to a draft regulation and "big pilot" in 2011 and operational rollout in 2013. In Eurosur, the policing dream and activist nightmare of an omnipresent surveillance system for Europe's frontiers could soon become reality. But this all-seeing beast of the border, I was soon to find out, had an unlikely nemesis waiting for him in Frontex headquarters.[46]

KILL THE CYCLOPS

Ibra and Ndiogou squatted on the floor outside their room in Yongor as friends and relatives came and went, reggae bouncing out of the stereo. They were friends of Mohammadou's, repatriates sent back to Dakar from the Canaries in 2006. Ndiogou's journey had been terrifying, and to illustrate it he drew four boxes in a row: one each for Senegal, Mauritania, Morocco, and Spain. Then he pointed with the tip of the pen at the space between the Senegal and Mauritania boxes: no problems there, the sea is calm. Next, the pen slid towards the Mauritania-Morocco gap: that's where the boats are wrecked by massive waves, "twelve meters high . . . you think it's the sky. All the shipwrecks happen here." Other migrants spoke of the sea journey as heading "uphill," or of the desert winds blowing across the sea, or of the cold gusts indicating their arrival "at the coasts of Europe." In these accounts, the border appeared as a physical barrier or abyss, not an administrative divide. To Ndiogou and his friends, the clandestine journey was an arduous "climb" northwards, not the threatening downhill "flow" imagined by European border guards and officials.

WARSAW, JULY 2011. Back in the Rondo1 skyscraper, the elevator sped past the offices of Credit Suisse and Ernst & Young and stopped on the twenty-second floor. This was, finally, the beating heart of Europe's border regime: the management and operational offices of Frontex across two conjoined floors. Internal stairs rose at the side of the vast flag-lined reception, giving easy access between the managers on the twenty-second floor and "ops" on the twenty-third while enclosing the heart of Frontex in a safe bubble. And at the center of it all was the Frontex Situation Centre, the all-seeing eyes of the border.

The FSC was the latest generation of border control integration, a control-room-of-control-rooms that monitored all operations off Greek, Italian, and Spanish coasts. One of the screens showed deployments around the Italian island of Lampedusa; another covered Greek operations. "Once a week we update the maps," said the commander in charge. A third screen was blacked out. "Is this for Spain?" I asked. "No, it's just down," the commander said with a chuckle. There was no real-time communication with Spain from the FSC. The terminals stood empty, his colleagues had gone for lunch. Work hours were eight to five Monday to Friday, with an officer on call the rest of the time. Europe's virtual, all-seeing border still seemed a far cry.

Barely two years later, these "Stone Age" interfaces—as one FSC worker put it—had been replaced by a near-real-time system updated by Frontex-seconded border guards on mission in Italy, Greece, and Spain. But the limitations to full border surveillance would remain, at least according to Antonio, a bearded Spaniard with a Frontex badge round his neck and an endearingly brusque manner. As one of the principal architects of Eurosur, he showed palpable excitement for the next generation of controls, but his take on advanced technology was less than enthusiastic.[47]

"Let me tell you an anecdote," he said while sipping coffee in the breakout area, looking out over the rain-swept expanse below. "I went to Spain, to the navy control center in Cartagena, [and] they showed tracks of AIS [sea vessel tracking] on-screen. 'How nice!' I said. 'But what is the use of this?' 'Oh, we show it to the visitors,' they said!" He shook his head. "Why should we be exchanging this [information]?"

Industry lobbying was to blame for this excess of technology, according to Antonio. "Satellites are useless," he said, then told me of how GMES had sent around an e-mail with satellite pictures of the Libyan-Tunisian border. "But I've just seen this border on Al Jazeera, I've learnt they've been there for three days and don't have water, that is a *push!*"[48] And you know what they did? he asked with a laugh. They inserted *and* into their name, changing it to Global Monitoring for Environment *and* Security. "They need customers!" Unmanned flights were just as useless, Antonio continued, since they could not yet fly in civilian zones because of safety regulations. The key to border monitoring, he said, was to "establish Frontex liaison officers and give them money to bribe [local] authorities to give them information." Human intelligence provided 95 percent of the results, Antonio said, while satellite might provide just 5 percent—at a cost inverse to its proportion. "But the industries are happy and the commission is happy because they are subsidizing them." He finished his coffee. "The emperor is naked!" he exclaimed.

Other officers similarly called for caution in the rush towards new technology. The FSC and similar systems, like SIVE, are resource heavy and labor intensive, while satellites still do not provide continuous real-time information. "In Hera, maybe the information can be of some use if it gets to you within six, seven hours," said Giuseppe, the Italian ICC manager, "but in Greece or Italy, the [migrant] boat can cross the sea in this time; it doesn't have added value."

The "myth of mastering the frontiers," according to Didier Bigo, is perpetuated in the hopeless striving for full electronic security. Yet this striving achieves something else too, as Antonio made clear. In the double securitization of migration, Europe's industrial giants can be seen as the largest investors, buying the most "senior" tranches carrying next to no risk. For them, the dream of a virtual border is creating a free-for-all in which the risk represented by an errant migrant patera has become big business. Eurosur is at the pinnacle of this process, as noted by an independent 2012 report, *Borderline*. While criticizing the "technocratic process" shorn of political control behind Eurosur, the report's authors denounce the "blank cheque" given for its development, which could end up costing several times one conservative official estimate of €339 million between 2011 and 2020.[49]

In this frontier economy, information equals both power and money. The result, as with African states under Seahorse, is factionalism among competing border agencies and states. "Nobody wants to give up anything," Antonio sighed. "If I give up the information," the border agencies reasoned, "I will give up responsibility and my funding will be diminished." In Spain, the divide between the surveillance community, centered on the Guardia Civil, and the intelligence community, mainly the Spanish police, was deep at times. "Often they don't talk to each other," he said.

Border officers were aware of the skewed incentives and the constant threat of politicking. In fact, Eurosur was tailored to overcome these problems. Its first trick was to focus even more strongly on that one precious target at the border: the clandestine migrant. If the border was a field for information sharing and information was an expensive commodity, it had to be shared in just the right doses. Eurosur did so by filtering out most information as noise. The system's triple initial aim of fighting migration, combating cross-border crime, and saving human lives at sea in practice amounted to much the same thing: intercepting and rescuing migrants while detaining their smugglers.[50] Yet even this was proving tricky, Antonio noted. "It's not a technical problem, it's a political problem, a will problem," he said. This is why he always emphasized to national security forces that Eurosur was a decentralized network. "There's no central node," he said, "because they don't want to have a Big Brother."

Rumors that "Frontex will see everything that is happening in the border" were crazy, according to Antonio. "That system will be . . . what do you call that monster with one eye here?" he said, touching his forehead. "A cyclops . . . we'll be a hated cyclops!" Wanting to see everything was akin to the fate of a one-eyed monster, who saw only what his single eye allowed him to see.[51] "So let's make it decentralized!"

Antonio's face lit up. "We will not exchange drugs," he said, just "illegal immigration plus other common-interest information" such as "a ship on fire." The decentralized system, he exclaimed, "kills the cyclops!"

. . .

To Antonio, if technology was part of the problem, it was also part of the solution. He took me to a small room where fans whirred frantically; in it stood three big cabinets with glass doors, reaching almost to the ceiling. Inside each was a stack of black computer consoles, red lights occasionally blinking. These were the "nodes," the electronic hearts of Eurosur, allowing for the sharing of sensitive border information in a vast network eventually covering all European states. One of them, the "mother node," was producing two copies of itself—one for Frontex, one for Poland. Next others would follow. If Hera had been the birth of sea operations, it seemed we were witnessing yet another birth here: that of a fully integrated border surveillance system for Europe.

In Eurosur, each country will have one national coordination center (NCC) for border surveillance, "a very difficult thing to achieve." Antonio's strategy was to confront them with a choice. "I ask them, so where do you want the Eurosur node? Then I force them to fight between them." Technology, as with Seahorse, triggers compliance.

Through a seamless link between NCCs and Frontex, complete surveillance of the Euro-African border is for the first time a possibility. Antonio sketched his version of the Eurosur border regime (figure 4). In it, the new control centers are rendered as interlinked circles; the two upward-facing triangles represent member states with a shared border; and the arrows are information flows. "Frontex doesn't have a border, but it has another requirement," Antonio said while drawing the downward triangle labeled CPIP, the "common prefrontier intelligence picture." The prefrontier, in keeping with the technological obliteration of the borderline already seen on SIVE screens, refers to the areas lying beyond the surveillance reach of the border regime—African territorial waters, trucks traversing deserts, smugglers running a safe house or ghetto.

Look at the bottom arrows: they refer to maritime sensors, radars, and other surveillance, Antonio explained, but they point outwards from the E.U. external border towards African states. Sharing of information with African forces is already happening, of course. Spanish cameras spot a migrant boat setting off from Morocco and notify the Moroccan gendarmerie. Its surveillance systems locate a boat on open seas: the ICC calls the Algerians, who "rescue" the migrants if the boat

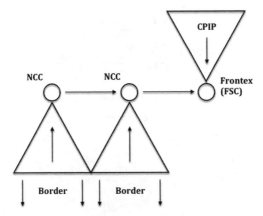

FIGURE 4. Sketch of information flows in Eurosur. Source: Adapted by author from interview material.

is still close enough to their coasts. To Frontex, however, the prefrontier has long been anathema. Although the agency's risk analysts gather data on migrant routes through Africa, its official mandate, staffers insist, ends at the external border. Eurosur will change this. Through its novel interfaces for information sharing beyond the border—and a planned future integration with Seahorse—the prefrontier will finally be made palatable.[52]

In Antonio's Eurosur vision, the border appears as something akin to a cell membrane, a permeable surface that communicates with nearby cells in a chain of signals. These signals are selective, however; there is politics aplenty in the software that sifts, filters, and chooses before presenting its data in a graphic interface.[53] On the interactive Eurosur map developed by the Spanish company GMV in Frontex headquarters, the system's principal target is rendered as an Illegal Entry sign, used to indicate where a significant attempt at crossing the Euro-African border is taking place (figure 5). Officers can add comments about the event in a chat box, as in Facebook or Messenger. It is a potent Keep Away sign, a modern equivalent of the ancient Spanish Indalo.

The interfaces and symbols—not least the illegal entry icon—hint at the magic of statecraft at work in Europe's border regime. As if by a conjuring trick, a wooden boat on the high seas has become a source of risk sold to African partners and industrial investors. This risk has been rendered on-screen as arrows and zigzag lines interrupting the straight logics of border controls, before finally being abstracted into

FIGURE 5. The Illegal Entry sign. Source: Eurosur presentation on the website of the European Day for Border Guards (www.ed4bg.eu).

the amorphous, three-dimensional fields of information flows of the Eurosur interface. Risk is here dispersed but not obliterated. Beyond the neat interfaces, migrants face a type of borders opposite to those built in Eurosur: untamed frontiers, rough seas, and scorching deserts, through which only the luckiest and toughest emerge unscathed. In their search for a virtual border, Europe's border workers are creating a new, postmodern wilderness.

THE MAKING OF A EURO-AFRICAN BORDER

MADRID, JUNE 2012. Amid the deepening eurozone crisis, the Spanish capital seemed to have come to a standstill. The scaffolds, skips, and Caterpillars—such a frequent sight during Spain's property-fueled boom—had long since been removed from the city's streets. But in one site, at least, the construction industry was defying the gloom. In the fortress-like headquarters of the Guardia Civil, cranes and excavators were at work digging up the vast courtyard to make space for the NCC under Eurosur. A new regional coordination center had been inaugurated in the southern port of Algeciras, where Comandante Francisco had jetted off to receive the Spanish king. Algeria had signed a new cooperation agreement, and so had the Spanish navy. Here was one sector that seemed to have escaped the age of austerity—the European illegality industry and its fight against illegal migration.

In the control room next to the courtyard, Guardia Civil officers were already feeding live data on illegal entries into the recently installed Eurosur interface, to which more member states were now connecting by the month—despite the European Parliament's approval for the system still being a year away and the official launch set for late 2013. Soon even African states might be able to join, any political qualms brushed aside by the technical language of the Eurosur interface, in which migration "events" were created as the "property" of one state that could then be "ceded" to another. In the words of one officer, "You'd just have to create another user." On the Eurosur monitor, illegal entry signs were scattered across the Mediterranean. "It's a bit slow," sighed the guardia at the terminal when her screen temporarily froze. "Another Brick in the Wall," by Pink Floyd, rang out from her colleague's computer: it was just another day in the business of bordering Europe.

· · ·

The emerging Euro-African border is an elusive creation of multiple logics. It is sharply drawn through the seas, but the closer you look the more it dissipates. It is fixed in place—in control rooms, patrol bases, and surveillance systems—while constantly bleeding outwards. At times, the border appears as an Indalo or as the illegal entry sign: here but no further. Other times, it appears in its guise of frontier, ever extendable and stretchable. It is everywhere and nowhere. In this way, as political scientist Nick Vaughan-Williams has noted, "the border-work of Frontex produces a border that is no longer at the border."[54]

As has been seen, this dispersal is accompanied by a distribution and management of migratory risk that breeds ever larger risks. "The hazardousness of risk analysis," Beck cautions, "consists in the fact that imagining dangers that were previously unthinkable can inadvertently help to bring them about."[55]

At first glance, Hera at least seems to disprove this conclusion. While the operation was devised as an emergency response, it had, by 2010, become permanent. A "recovery of the territory by law enforcement agencies" had fast been achieved, in the words of a Senegalese border police chief. No one left along these routes. The border was, as his words indicated, partly militarized. Hera, the divine matchmaker, had successfully tied the knot between police, military, and industry in Africa and Europe.

Hera might be the goddess of marriage in Greek lore, but her main traits are jealousy and vindictiveness. She had, as Frontex itself acknowledged, *displaced* routes into the even more dangerous Sahara Desert, punishing migrants for their transgression in crossing her seas. This way, Hera also brought trouble upon her fellow deities farther east—Hermes, Nautilus, and Poseidon, the Frontex operations in the eastern and central Mediterranean. Migration controls remain a zero-sum game, where the gains of one are the troubles of others. Mass arrivals hit the Greek land border with Turkey in 2010. In 2011, amid the Tunisian and Libyan uprisings, it was Italy's turn to see an unprecedented influx of boat people, followed by the widely reported tragedies outside Lampedusa two years later. "Migration is something that will never stop," said Comandante Francisco, echoing a sentiment often repeated by border officials. So why impose such a vast system to deal with the few brave men and women who try to arrive in Europe, cost what it may, by land and sea?

One reason was the preemptive task of preventing people from leaving. "We can't leave the deployment we have in Mauritania and Senegal," said Francisco. "If we leave, the avalanche will return in two days' time." Giuseppe agreed: "Both Spain and the African countries have said several times that it would be a big error to withdraw the deployment, because this could give a signal to the candidates for migration to try to leave again from there to the Canaries." Indeed, Hera operations in African waters were previously vaguely referred to as diversion and sometimes as interception: Frontex now labels them deterrence.

Such deterrence is not the whole story, however. As this chapter has shown, the Euro-African border is generating its own momentum, its own sense of necessity. Frontiers have always attracted entrepreneurs: gold diggers, bandits, and self-appointed sheriffs in the hunt for the bounties of a recently discovered wilderness. The Euro-African frontier is no different. Along with the smugglers and swindlers, the *passeurs* and coxeurs, the security and defense industries have marched into the frontier, sensing a great business opportunity. The border has become a site for ever-growing investments, a place where frontiersmen can look for quick gains and where European leaders can project their fears and visions. The African security forces and the Guardia Civil do not want to let Hera and the CCRC go, say bemused policemen: too much money and influence are at stake, too many agencies have tapped into the treasures buried in the borderlands.

Eurosur was not eliminating these frontier politics. Instead it created new battles along new fronts: among security forces, among member states, and even among Eurosur officers themselves. "It's very much about egos, about tradition, about power," was how one such officer glossed the power struggles at the 2013 European Day for Border Guards in Warsaw, before adding a strong note aimed at skeptics in his police audience: "The train has left the station." And at the helm of the train is Frontex. Despite the talk about "decentralization," Frontex will through Eurosur play an increasingly pivotal role at Europe's external borders, appropriating the data dutifully fed into the system by border guards along southern European coasts—and, even more bizarrely and expensively, from member states away from the Mediterranean region. The train may have left the station, but where it is heading and at what cost remain to be seen.

Besides these battles, there are deeper reasons behind the fortification as well. The nascent Euro-African border is the result of a symbolic and political urge to define the outer frontiers of the European Union—and, for Spain, a chance to reaffirm its European identity through a combination of humanitarianism, technological mastery, and political acumen. This double-edged Europeanization of the borders was always a fraught enterprise, as shown in the summer of 2011, when the Schengen Agreement was coming under unprecedented strain because of the migrant boats leaving Tunisia for Italy. In Warsaw, the Frontex deputy director did not want to be pushed on the consequences. "We are not an actor in this debate," he sighed. The idea of the space of free movement was that it "gives the feeling that you are an E.U. citizen," he added, pointing at his heart. But "as long as elections are approaching, everyone has to play this game."

It is often said that a "constitutive outside" is needed to bind a polity, but the European Union's way of doing this is nevertheless a most peculiar enterprise. Its target is, as in the illegal entry sign, people on the move, and it has created a complex industry for the purpose. While states such as Spain provide the parts and build the machinery, Frontex edits the manuals, oversees the work, evaluates the results. Pushing the securitization analogy, the agency works in some ways as the "special purpose vehicle" used in derivatives banking before the financial crisis—spreading risks off the balance sheet, diffusing accountability away from sovereign states and their elected governments. In this double securitization of migration, the junk risk is heaped onto the African borderlands. Here risk is reproduced and magnified, or as one European police attaché put it: "We're in the eye of the cyclone now. . . . When you bolt all doors, you'll have a pressure cooker." It is to this pressure cooker, and the fraught task of putting the lid on African mobility, that we will now turn.

CHAPTER 3

Hunter and Prey

Europe's high-tech border regime takes on a more profane guise on African soil, as I discovered back in Dakar in between visits to Yongor's repatriates and Spanish officials. Walk into the Cité Police complex along the capital's seafront corniche and look out for a torn A4 printout taped to a door two floors up announcing the "Division for the fight against irregular migrations." This is the home of Frontex's local police partner in patrolling Senegal's coastline. Inside the dark halls of the division, I knocked on a door with a broken handle indicating the offices of the research group on migrant smuggling networks. Jean-Pierre, the commissioner in charge of the division, opened and greeted me with a friendly handshake. His office was full of cartons packed with night-vision goggles and other border policing tools, gifts from the division's Spanish partners. A large copy of the i-Map familiar from Frontex's Warsaw offices lurked in a corner. Jean-Pierre started talking, unprompted, of the causes of clandestine migration. "The cause is poverty, the lack of work," he said. But now all routes were closed. "The maritime route has been bolted up, the air route has become more and more difficult. What's left? The land route, and this is more difficult too. They are closing over there as well, and there are lots of deaths." Jean-Pierre, who was of foreign West African stock himself, sounded sympathetic to the migrants' plight. "Everything's harder," he said. "Everything has changed now."

It was largely thanks to officers such as Jean-Pierre that boat migration had ground to a halt, Spanish officials never tired of repeating. This was not only meant as praise but was also a simple statement of fact. The success in halting irregular migration did not reside in slick Frontex machinery but rather was to be found in the Sahel and the Sahara, where African forces had been subcontracted to carry out migration controls. And it was the Spanish government, rather than Frontex or Brussels, that took most of the credit for oiling the wheels of the subcontracting machine. On a visit to Dakar in 2011, the Spanish state secretary of security waxed lyrical on policing cooperation on migration. "The policy promoted by Spain is a total, absolute and resounding success that everyone recognizes, and especially so the European Union," he said. "In 2006, I think we came here with an attitude that they were very thankful for," agreed the Spanish ambassador.[1] Spain's attitude of "dialogue and cooperation" contrasted sharply with that of the old colonial power, France, which kept strong-arming its way into its former African dominions. While Senegalese and Malian officers sourly accepted the French presence, they talked warmly of their Spanish colleagues. Praise and dialogue were not enough to bring the Africans onboard, however. The Spaniards rarely said as much, but key to the success of Frontex operations such as Hera was not just disbursing aid money but also providing incentives to local forces. Essentially, you had to outbid the smugglers.

As a result of such incentives, a hunt was on for the illegal migrant across the deserts, forests, and towns stretching beyond the Euro-African border. But this migrant is an elusive prey. Who is he? Where is he to be found? How can he be distinguished from his fellow travelers— the labor migrants, merchants, and sojourners who have moved around the region freely for decades? This chapter will seek to answer these questions by following the police "hunters" and their elusive clandestine prey on the journey north through the borderlands: first on the shores of Dakar, next at the Mauritania-Senegal border, and finally in the transit sites and dumping grounds of the Sahara and Morocco. On the African side of the border, it will be seen, Europe's subcontractors do not simply detect and prevent irregular crossings; they also help bring their target, the illegal migrant, into being.

This making of migrants is not simply about the assignation and appropriation of a social category, as was seen among Dakar's repatriates; it is also about travelers' progressive *embodying* of that category. Building on pathbreaking ethnographies of border controls in settings ranging from the U.S.-Mexico frontier to Israel, this chapter will thus consider how illegality comes to be lived—at times up to the point of death. "The border," anthropologist Michel Agier says, is now "everywhere that an undesirable is identified," including the indeterminate zone in which the traveler's body becomes the border, the site of enforcement.[2] Walking across stretches of desert, hiding in the undergrowth next to an abandoned beach, crawling into a truck meant for merchandise, and staring at the moving sky in a vast wooden boat are all ways of traveling that render the journey a bodily minefield. Contorted postures, stomachaches, dehydration, shivering, and sore feet become sensorial signposts indicating the gradual crossing of borders, and attempts to avoid these ailments start signaling illegality to police. In the back-and-forth between the bodily strategies of Africa's wayward travelers and police patrols and detections, the illegal migrant is conjured in increasing degrees of otherness, stigmatized by his very bodily presence.

RUCKSACKS AND BISCUITS: CLANDESTINE SPOTTING IN DAKAR

Nighttime on Dakar's shores. The headlights of the police van illuminate the lanes leading down to the beachfront. The patrol chief, dressed in a checkered shirt and relaxed trousers, steers the van with fast, careless movements that send it jolting and bouncing to the rhythm of Arabic music streaming out of the speakers. "Only the night guards are out now!" the chief shouts, honking his way towards the beach. His is one of the patrol units dedicated to tracking down illegal migrants on Europe's behalf. We step onto the abandoned beach, the officers leading me to a rocky section of the shore next to a French-owned hotel. "The illegal migrants were hiding here," they say while pointing to the undergrowth, as if on an archaeological tour. The hotel owner used to inform on the migrants-to-be, as did paid-off local informers. "In general, we take them before they depart," says one of the officers. "All the clandestine passengers, regardless of their nationality, we bring them in." In 2006 journalists published pictures of Senegalese police cells crammed with detainees almost piled atop one another. Migrants were detained for months to deter others from leaving; smugglers were sent to languish in jails.[3] By 2010, the *temps des clandestins,* the "time of the illegal migrants," was over, as one of the officers put it, not without a note of regret. Only this memory of departures and detentions remained in Dakar: a hiding place amid rocks and shrubs on a darkened beach. The border police's task had been accomplished.

The Direction de la Police de l'Air et des Frontières (DPAF), the Sen-egalese border police directorate encompassing Jean-Pierre's division for fighting irregular migration, was a European brainchild to begin with. It had been created in 2004 at the insistence of the French, "as if all this had been anticipated," said one inspector in reference to the 2006 boat crisis and the Frontex response that ensued. Since then, Spain had taken over as DPAF's main partner. Four Senegalese forces were involved in Frontex patrols in 2010: the air force, the navy, the gendar-merie, and DPAF. While the navy and air force monitored the seas and the gendarmerie the coastlines, DPAF patrolled Dakar's shores and Rosso and Oussouye near the Mauritanian and Guinea-Bissau border, respectively. DPAF was, in a sense, the poor cousin of the navy, the Guardia Civil's main partner. Its officers were, crudely put, the spivs, sweepers, and back-office staff in migration control—crucial to keep onboard but at one remove from the real action on high seas.

At sea unfolded the glamorous side to Hera patrols—roaring planes and boats aided by the technological wizardry of radars, satellites, and infrared cameras. Here was also the possibility of catching migrants in the act of setting out for Spain. The Guardia Civil or Frontex vessels would approach pirogues and look for signs of an imminent "illegal" trip, notwithstanding their being in Senegalese waters. A load of around thirty passengers was normal for a fishing trip, or *mare,* in which Sene-galese fishermen set out for days; lack of fishing gear in the hull raised suspicions, as did the presence of petrol canisters. The European border guards made a note of the captain and later checked that the boat had returned to the coast. All this was done under the "legal cover," as one comandante put it, of having a Senegalese officer onboard. The appear-ance of sovereignty was still intact, national boundaries respected. "We help them to fight illegal migration," said Comandante Francisco, no tongue in cheek.

Such "help" would look distinctly unhelpful on land, leaving patrol-ling Senegalese policemen—if not their bosses—at one remove from the joys of collaboration. DPAF's task was also more difficult than that of their seaborne colleagues, since it involved stopping migrants in their tracks, *before* they had even embarked towards Spain. The Guardia Civil chief in Dakar acknowledged this was a tough brief. "We can never demonstrate that fifty people in a bus are migrants," he said. Instead any suspect travelers were referred to as candidates for illegal migration, as in Senegal's sensitization campaigns. DPAF's patrols had the crucial task of defining and conjuring migrants out of the broad group of candidates before they revealed themselves on the open seas; it was also here that the unequal gains from the illegality industry were most keenly felt.

. . .

The Spanish-funded four-wheel-drive bounced along the road towards Hann-Maristes. I had joined a daytime patrol, made up of four police-men crammed into the car and one officer riding a quad bike, also donated by Spain for patrolling the beaches dotting Dakar's Cap Vert peninsula. The officers were part of the coastal surveillance brigade, whose principal task was to patrol the beaches in three shifts around the clock in search of illegal migrants. "There's no police or gendarmerie brigade that's more skilled than us on the theme of illegality [clandesti-nité]," said Abdoulaye, the gangly head of the unit, turning around to address me at the back as the car sped down a mud lane towards the beach. "We know everything that happens along the seashore."

On the beach, pirogues were pulled up in the white sands and locals occasionally sauntered by. No illegal migrant in sight. Alassane, a young officer with several years in the brigade, explained how to determine who was a migrant and who an innocent fisherman. "It's very easy to catch an illegal migrant," he said. "They don't come one by one, they come ten to fifteen of them together, all with a backpack." The backpack and the clustering were but two signs of migrant illegality on Dakar's beaches. The clandestins, Alassane explained, also stocked up on bis-cuits to avoid excessive bowel movements during the crossing; they wore trainers or plastic sandals, good if the boat got wet; sometimes they dressed in several layers of clothing against the winds and kept elaborate gris-gris for protection or invisibility. They were also identi-fied by their lack of movement. If a group descended on the beach and stayed there, waiting, Alassane knew they were migrants and would proceed to search them. Browsing through their backpacks, he would find euros, not franc CFA, and no mobile phones. All these signs were giveaways for police on the trail of today's footloose travelers.

The brigades' patrols were not concerned with the surveillance of abstract risk patterns familiar from the control rooms in Las Palmas, Madrid, and Warsaw. Instead, their task—as Alassane made clear—was to read embryonic signs of potential threats on behalf of Spain and Frontex. For this subcontracting to succeed, Spain had developed an intricate gift economy. First, the Spaniards provided a generous "expenses" pay (per diem, or indemnité) for working on illegal migra-

FIGURE 6. A Spanish-funded quad bike for patrolling clandestine migration. Photo by author.

tion. They also lavished African forces with policing gear—the night-vision goggles in Jean-Pierre's corner and also the brigade's vehicles and computers. The third incentive was the trips discussed in the last chapter. To get the anti-mobility machine rolling, Europe had to invest in the mobility of the higher echelons of African forces, who flitted between policing conferences and study visits, the better to police the cross-border movements of their countrymen.

I will talk about these incentives as gifts—rather than, say, as payments or even bribes—in a nod to long-running anthropological debates on gift exchange. The outsourcing of migration controls has involved a continuum of incentives, ranging from exchanges of border policing tools to large financial aid packages for the collaborating states. With this in mind, the term *gift economy* simply highlights three key features of police cooperation. First of all, Spain's *personalized* incentives created social bonds among colleagues, as well as an "obligation to reciprocate" for the Senegalese receivers—not in kind, but in deeds. But the gifts, as soon as they were given, nullified the supposed collegiality between the Europeans and Africans, instead creating a hierarchy of interests. This ambiguous status of the gifts helped spawn ever-increasing demands, along with tensions over who gained what—bringing into stark relief the unequal power relations between local police and their bosses, among competing border agencies, and between European giver and African receiver in a claims-making process carrying echoes from the colonial encounter.[4]

The Senegalese officers said Frontex paid for their resources, but the agency denied any involvement. Any incentives, according to Giuseppe, the former Hera manager, stemmed from the "bilateral agreement between Spain and Senegal; Frontex has no knowledge" of them. He also sounded a note of caution. "When we're with the Africans and you're about to give them money, it's not as easy as paying European police; you don't know how it's been spent," he said, hinting that some of it inevitably "gets lost." And the way money and resources trickled down, were unequally distributed, and finally disappeared was a source of resentment for the officers in the illegal migration brigade.

As I spoke to Alassane, his colleagues congregated around us. I asked them about the Spaniards. "We see them . . . the Spanish boat over there," said one of them, looking out over the gray still seas where the Guardia Civil patrolled, "but we have never met these people." He continued: "There are identification missions in Spain, but police agents never go! We should!" Then Abdoulaye weighed in. "If there are benefits like that, it's the office people who leave. But identification is the job of police agents!" The others all murmured in agreement.

Besides concerns about trips, the officers also demanded more resources. The brigade had received vehicles, including a speedboat, as well as gadgets that were more easily "retrieved" for private use, as one of the officers admitted with a smile: torches, an iPhone, two pairs of binoculars, mobile phone credit. But now funds were running dry. No more credit, no new gadgets. Vehicle upkeep stalled. The cars rusted or broke down after being exposed to sun and sand twenty-four hours a day, according to the officers. "Each brigade should have its own vehicle," said one of them. "They should give us the logistical means to be able to work at ease."

The biggest source of resentment, however, was pay. When the Spaniards and Frontex descended on Senegal in 2006, the per diem had been tantalizing. The officers said they had initially received forty euros per person per day—a fortune in Senegal. This only lasted for the first two months. "Afterwards everyone got implicated," said Abdoulaye. All the police directorates wanted their share of the illegal migration spoils, and the brigade's extra pay was slower and slower in coming. They had started receiving it once a week, then once a month, then once every forty-five days or every two months. Money from "Frontex" reached agencies and police chiefs who had nothing to do with the fight against illegal migration, Abdoulaye said, while "the agents suffer a lot" on their long shifts. The others chimed in, complaining about the cost of eating out during their breaks, the mosquitoes on the beaches, the night-time patrols. The list of grievances seemed endless. "In illegal migration, it's the police agents who do the bulk of the work, but they haven't gained anything at all," said one officer, sounding strangely like Mohammadou and his repatriate friends a few kilometers down the road.

For all my sympathies, I couldn't help asking myself: what work? We stood around the beach chatting, watched by a few fishermen. By 2010 the brigade's travails were no longer about spying for signs of illegal migrants, since no one left from these beaches any longer. The patrols were instead an exercise in what police chiefs called visibility—to show candidates and their families that the police were ready to cut short any attempted boat journey. This was boring, to be sure, but not quite the ordeal the brigade made it out to be.

The patrols were also about visibility in another sense. Much as the Guardia Civil's patrol boat rarely failed to rumble past the European tourist haunts of Gorée Island, the DPAF patrols were at least partly a show for the funders and the visiting researcher. Yongor's repatriates said they never saw the DPAF patrols, despite police reassurances of their existence. Moreover, they insisted that Frontex, which to them meant a hapless bunch of bribe-taking Senegalese state agents, could not stop them from departing. "For me, Frontex is things people do to make money," Mohammadou said with his trademark frown. "Because those people are not serious people, they are there, but if you give them money they let you pass. That's why, for me, Frontex doesn't exist. . . . Those people don't do their work!" he exclaimed. Even though repatriates ironically denounced the Senegalese forces for not doing their work, by 2010 no would-be migrants were attempting to leave Dakar's shores. Money instead circulated downwards, through payments to informers. A delicate financial balancing act was maintained among the European paymasters, African forces, local youth, and potential "smugglers," but how long it would last was another matter.

Beyond the unequal gains, Frontex was a source of friction on other fronts too. Jean-Pierre voiced concerns about national sovereignty when discussing Frontex patrols. So did Moussa, one of the jet-setting chiefs the coastal brigade looked upon with envy. Moussa was nearing retirement, and his regular trips to the Las Palmas coordination center, where I had first met him, were a boon at this stage in his career. The Senegalese forces involved in the Frontex mission rotated the liaison officer role among them, spreading the joy of a few months in the Gran Canarian capital equitably. To Moussa, it was "better for everyone" that boat migration had stopped because of the risks to life at sea, but he added a critical observation: frustrated youth stuck at home could spell trouble for those in power.

Moussa had other concerns as well, however subtly voiced. "It's very hard in Africa now," he said. "People have studies, diplomas, and so on, but afterwards there's no work." He was advising his sons, who studied in France, to stay put there. Life had become harder since the devaluation of the CFA franc in the 1990s. "We're not independent; the currency is still controlled by France," he complained, mentioning the strong French military presence in the capital. "Dakar is a strategic point, including for the Americans, the Arabs and so on . . . They come here, and afterwards they expand into the region. It's the same thing with Frontex," he concluded.

Moussa, Abdoulaye, and Jean-Pierre all expressed unease at their predicament as subcontracted policemen working on Europe's behalf in catching *clandestins*. This unease ranged from political ambivalence at the top to financial resentment further down the pay scale and grew in inverse proportion to the dwindling gains in the illegality industry. When *clandestins* had been bountiful on Dakar's beaches, officers had first been able to cash in by demanding bribes or even embarking their relatives free of charge. Since 2006, this had been supplanted by Spanish largesse. The Spaniards, aware of the need to incentivize, kept some funds flowing through the E.U.-sponsored West Sahel program. But the absurdity at the heart of cooperation was hard to ignore. The Senegalese forces were now only chasing ghosts—potential clandestine migrants and smugglers who did not materialize. The basis of their business had vanished.

Instead, this business has moved elsewhere. For if Europe's border machinery has halted the migrant boats heading for the Canaries, it has not yet blocked the passage through the Sahara. Along the desert routes, African forces face a harder task than on Dakar's beaches—detecting furtive signs of an *intention* to migrate. In the process, they add a new piece to the illegal migrant under production. Already provided with a dress code, belongings, and behavior that mark him as illegal, this migrant in the border zone will be endowed with something rather more ineffable: a mind of his own.

NORTHERN SENEGAL: READING THE ILLEGAL MIND AT THE ROSSO BORDER

The road winds, potholed and dusty, towards the border. The cramped car lurches over holes gouged out of the tarmac and swerves to avoid sand pits where chunks of asphalt are missing. A Saharan haze envelops us as we drive past bone-dry outposts dotting the road to Rosso-Senegal. At times youngsters appear along the roadside to scatter sand over the potholes as we pass, hoping we will chuck them some small change. The Senegal River region's employment prospects, in a rusty bucket.

Many clandestine migrants have followed this route towards the distant Maghreb. Their long, stepwise journeys partly follow a logic different from those of the boat migrants of 2006, many of whom simply sought a quick way to Europe. These travelers have been called transit migrants, but they do not simply "transit" from A to B; instead their trips of uncertain end, often stretching over several years, trace intricate lines through the Sahel and Sahara.[5]

Among the characters on this circuit is the *aventurier*. This "adventurer," a figure first seen on air routes to Paris in the 1970s, is but the latest in a long line of fortune seekers to emerge from the febrile postcolonial cities of Francophone Africa. Like his predecessors, the adventurer embraces a life of risk taking in the face of battered regional economies and closed borders. To him, the clandestine journey is not just an escape from poverty; it is also a quest for self-realization and emancipation, however dangerous and dependent on precarious family funds. By contrast, English-speaking migrants—Liberians, Ghanaians, Nigerians—do not embark on the dangerous desert crossing as "adventurers," and neither do the women on the clandestine circuit. The latter, often simplistically treated as "trafficking victims" by European states, move ahead with the help of male companions, smugglers, or "protectors" at considerable personal cost. Yet for all their differences of trajectory, background, and vision, these travelers soon come to share in the same reality: the vortex of the borderlands and the violent reduction it performs upon them.[6]

As I dislodged myself from the *sept-place* taxi at Rosso's flyblown bus station to the calls of hustlers ("Nouakchott? Nouakchott?"), a police officer I knew from a previous visit greeted me and immediately started talking about the "new system" for clandestine migration. Moroccan truckers bringing oranges and merchandise to Dakar allow travelers to join them on the way up, for a fee. They get off before the Rosso jetty, cross the Senegal River alone, and then rejoin the trucker in Mauritania. "It's very difficult to control," the officer exclaimed, "because it's all in their head! What's their final destination? You can't stop them, you just can't know. It's just the idea," he kept repeating.

While in Dakar, police categorized travelers as licit and illicit on the basis of material and behavioral signs, in Rosso the elusive figure of the illegal migrant also acquired a peculiar mental makeup. It was the "idea in their head" that branded travelers as illegal at this border. The increasing essentialization of the illegal migrant en route was not just discursive, however; rather, illegality imposed itself upon travelers, with real effects on their mental life. As travelers were detained on the basis of their supposed intentionality, they were sucked into a circular world of trips cut short, detentions and ignominies, deportations and empty pockets. Pushed "below-board," they were entering the liminal state that anthropologist Susan Bibler Coutin has labeled "being en route": present yet absent from the jurisdictions they traverse, at turns visible and invisible to the border forces that chase them.[7]

. . .

Rosso has everything you could wish for in a border town. Turbaned Moors sit back in shacks lining its potholed lanes, half-heartedly trying to flog Mauritanian *ouguiyas* for franc CFA or euros, while their nomad compatriots take camels across the river for grazing in an ancient arrangement that is nowadays dwarfed by the postindependence border economy. This economy suffuses everything in Rosso: vendors vie for space along the road leading up to the river jetty, selling cheap electric gadgets, packets of Argentinian *gofio* flour, Spanish quicklime, and Mauritanian biscuits tasting of caked sand. And water, Mauritanian bottled water, drunk in one clean gulp to momentarily quench the thirst. Rosso is parched and hot: this is the border of the Sahara. The sun screams down through a haze of dust. Migrants stuck here complain of the heat, the dry air, the clouds of fine sand. You choke on flies and hide from the heat by drowsing on tattered mattresses and sipping a stronger green tea than that served farther south in the Sahel. Cheikh, a tall man with sugar-rotted teeth, sat on one such mattress, pouring his potent brew of *attaya* as the pot hissed on the coal stove. Known by colleagues

FIGURE 7. Views of Mauritania from the Red Cross base, Rosso-Senegal. Photo by author.

as Mr. Migration, Cheikh was in charge of the Rosso Red Cross, whose Spanish-funded mission was to provide humanitarian assistance to migrants.

Rosso has in recent years become a transit point—and dumping ground—for clandestine migrants. It is where "white" North Africa and "black" West Africa meet, and it is where Mauritanian gendarmes deport foreigners caught for supposedly trying to migrate illegally to the Canaries. As I visited on the tail end of the migration craze in 2010, Rosso was one link in the chain of subcontracted migration controls, in which local police forces and humanitarian organizations alternately detained, deported, and cared for migrants en route. As would soon be evident, however, it was a weak link, despite Europe's best efforts.

After finishing his customary third glass of tea, Cheikh took me to the Red Cross "operational base," the most visible sign of Rosso's role on the clandestine circuit. A Spanish Foreign Ministry logo branded this humble humanitarian space: a stretch of land adorned with a tent or two, with views of the border river through a frayed fence. "In 2006, we would have a hundred a day here, up to six hundred, seven hundred a week, wounded and in all kinds of states," Cheikh said. Next to us, a slight European woman squatted on the ground, smoking a hand-rolled cigarette. This was Belén, the representative of the Spanish Red Cross in Rosso. The role of the joint Spanish and Senegalese Red Cross mission was to care for exhausted deportees, who were given food and drink, a wash and a rest. Their main purpose, however, was to send migrants on to Dakar or to their Senegalese home region. Since most deportees were not Senegalese, this simply meant removing them from the border zone—often against their will. Before this removal, there was also another crucial step: escorting deportees to the police post down the main road for formalities and an occasional scolding.

The Red Cross and the border police were both subcontracted by Spain to perform different but complementary functions: treating migrants as victims in need of humanitarian assistance on the one hand, and processing them as lawbreakers on the other. This collaboration between police and aid workers did not strike Cheikh as unusual. In either case, the police had little interest in detaining or harassing deportees; in their offices, the business of the border went on in its messy, languid way, and no money was available anyhow for locking people up.

Overland travelers, Moors with weather-beaten faces, and money-changing hustlers converged around the police building down the main road. Inside, the deputy police chief, a gaunt man in his fifties, went up to a cabinet that perched precariously next to a pile of rubbish, browsed through it and found a folder labeled MIGRANTS CLANDESTINS. Data on new arrivals were collected in such folders and sent on to the border police in Dakar, he explained. That was all they could do here—"we interrogate them," he said, "but we can't detain them." He insisted that Senegal "welcomed everyone," unlike the Mauritanian security forces, with whom relations were strained. Next he handed me his CV. "You might find me some opportunities," he said in a hopeful tone.

The dearth of "opportunities"—jobs, money, promotions—again meant Spain had to provide incentives to keep their African colleagues on side. In Rosso, "Frontex" (meaning Spain) had provided a speedboat and petrol for land and river patrols, torches and night-vision binoculars, as well as the per diem payment. The task of questioning and processing deportees before the Red Cross sent them on was easy enough; the difficult task was finding any clandestine migrants *before* they entered Mauritania. All that travelers from Senegal, Mali, and the Gambia needed to cross legally was vaccination papers and a *devise,* or deposit, of fifty euros worth of Mauritanian ouguiyas. Other nationalities simply paid small bribes to the officers on the jetty in Rosso-Mauritania. "In Nouadhibou, that's where they prepare the crossing and throw away all their documents," Cheikh said. "They want to make the task harder for the police; they don't want to give away their secret. There's a serious problem of categorizing them."

This hiddenness, the "secret" in their head that both Cheikh and the border police talked about, was in Rosso becoming a key constitutive ingredient of migrant illegality. This was, after all, what the French term *clandestin* connoted, as did the Mauritanian term for illegal migrants, *siriyan,* derived from the word for secret. Making the illegal migrant speak and reveal the inner workings of his mind was hard work. Moreover, he lied; he was untrustworthy as if by nature. As a French police attaché told me: *"Le migrant, il est un grand menteur"* (the migrant is a big liar). This sentiment, echoed by other workers in the illegality industry, was not just a representation of a key imagined trait of illegal migrants, however. For travelers stuck in limbo, buffeted by Africa's subcontractors and their hopeless dreams, the blurring of truths and lies was part of their everyday experience. It was also part of their migratory toolkit, as I would discover in Rosso.

. . .

Cheikh had summoned three Liberians to talk to me in the bare Red Cross office across the road from the base. Edward was one of them, a well-dressed young man who sat waiting for me in the office's only plastic chair. "It's very difficult here with an English passport," he sighed. By this he meant documents from an Anglophone West African country. Traveling the region had never been that easy for English-speaking nationals, with especially Nigerians subjected to high "fees" at borders despite the free circulation accords covering all countries belonging to ECOWAS, the Economic Community of West African States. These free circulation provisions were still honored by Mauritania, from where Edward and his friends had just been deported, despite the country's exit from the regional body.[8] In 2010, however, Mauritania had imposed entry restrictions on nationals of all English-speaking West African countries, forcing any prospective travelers to enter by air rather than overland. Anglophone travelers, increasingly seen as illegal by definition, were targeted in crackdowns accordingly. Edward and his friends had been expelled from Rosso-Mauritania across the river, he explained, and never made it farther north. As we talked about this ordeal, his

friends arrived. He introduced Alan as his brother and Clara as a relative. Clara soon added a dissonant note to Edward's story. They were
detained and jailed in the capital Nouakchott, she said, while trying to
find work. Their purpose there was not all that clear—they alternately
said they wanted to "see Mauritania" or try to go to Europe—and their
prospects now were vaguer still. Why not take the Red Cross money
and go to Dakar, I asked? "We don't have anybody in Dakar," said Alan.
"It's hard," said Edward, "I don't know where it'd be preferable for us."
Since the Red Cross could not help them, they needed to call a relative
who could send them cash to go back home or to settle in a place farther
south. Could I give them money for a calling card?

Afterwards I met Cheikh at the base, who shook his head at the Liberians' story. They were "potential candidates" who just wanted to cross
the border again, he said, adding that I did the right thing in not giving
them money. "They say they are brothers or that she is their sister," he
said, "but no one travels with their sister in that manner." He did not
believe any aspect of their story. Neither did I know what to believe. The
Liberians were in a liminal zone where truth and falsehood had lost
their definite edges, fraying with each passing day. They acknowledged
that what they said had little value beyond the instrumental, laughing
embarrassedly as they recalled telling the local imam they were Muslim
so they could sleep for a night or two in the mosque. Everything they
did was tinged with illegitimacy and suspicion. When I returned to
Rosso a month later they had finally found a way to cross the river, one
by one, back into Mauritania.

The more clandestine migrants such as the Liberians circulated in the
system, the more money became available for the subcontractors, as
Belén hinted over dinner in a plush hotel nearby. She looked frail and
emaciated, constantly on edge, smoking cigarette after cigarette. She
had no time for the politics of the Red Cross mission or for pondering
the border patrols running in parallel to it—there were accounts to
complete, constant requests from the head office in Madrid, and the
Senegalese didn't lift a finger! Sometimes she got into a panic, she said,
and simply froze with stress. The migration project had underspent
because so few deportees had arrived lately, making for an accountancy
headache and fresh pressure from her bosses. The Spanish Red Cross,
contracted by AECID, depended on its own subcontracting to—or
"partnership" with—the Senegalese, and here there was ample scope for
improvement. Belén felt she always had to chase, prod, and remind her
local colleagues to do something, while they kept asking her for things,

"folders, papers, pens . . ." She saw them as little birds constantly opening their beaks and wanting to be fed. They were even using up the
water in the tarp-covered "bladder" in the base, which was specifically
meant for migrants! Belén shook her head, exasperated. The migrant
project would soon close for lack of arrivals and because of the end of
the funding cycle; she looked relieved that she was about to get out.

Cheikh and his volunteers saw little reason to prioritize the clandestine migrants, who might have been through a bad spell but were still
probably better off than the deprived residents of Rosso. This uneasy
interface between Western aid workers and their local counterparts is of
course far from unique, as testified by a growing body of critical studies
of international development projects.[9] In Rosso, however—as elsewhere along migrant routes—the tense interactions absurdly depended
upon the elusive presence of migrant illegality. Without it no interface
could exist, no aid would be forthcoming, and the industry would come
to an end.

In policing, by contrast, this elusiveness could help ensure a continuous cash flow, as I discovered while riding in a patrol car on a dirt road
hugging the Senegal River. Here, as in Dakar, the police were chasing
ghosts, but in conjuring a menace they would always have the ear of
European funders. "Illegal migration has become our principal task,"
said one of the four police officers as we rolled out of Rosso. None of
them wore a uniform; the only indication this was a police patrol funded
by Spain was a sticker saying POLICE taped to the car. Before, the smuggling of rice and sugar across the river was the main concern here, but
Frontex had imposed new priorities. The patrol felt strangely like a
safari, but the farther we bumped and wobbled our way into border
territory, sending up clouds of sand as we went, the more obvious it was
that there were no illegal migrants in sight. We spotted cement smugglers pushing a boat into the water, a man with a suitcase, kids playing
by the riverbed, and lone, turban wrapped figures. I snapped a picture
of the team standing in an abandoned pirogue. "Now we are illegal
migrants!" one of them quipped to laughter. The joke highlighted the
absurd impossibility of the officers' task of tracking the intentionality of
travelers along a much-traversed river and their essentialization of these
travelers as a consequence. "It's very difficult to detect the illegal
migrant," one of the officers sighed. "Just like that, he becomes a boatman, or else he appears as a simple traveler. . . . They don't exhibit their
illegality in Senegal; it's something that you can't detect." Not until
Nouadhibou, he added. At that Mauritanian "gate to Europe," police at

last apprehend the travelers as what they really are—fully formed illegal migrants, ready to board their wooden boats and brave the wild sea.

NOUADHIBOU, MAURITANIA: THE NUMBERS GAME

At the sand-swept fringes of the Mauritanian port city of Nouadhibou, some five hundred kilometers from Rosso and eight hundred kilometers from the Canary Islands, lay an abandoned school compound known as Guantanamito. Spanish soldiers had converted the compound into a holding center for boat migrants awaiting deportation in 2006, again using AECID funds. Subject to critical reports by Amnesty International and the Spanish refugee assistance organization CEAR (Comisión Española de Ayuda al Refugiado), Guantanamito housed migrants who had been either intercepted at sea and sent back to Mauritania under the readmission agreement signed with Spain or increasingly apprehended in town and accused of trying to travel clandestinely to Europe.[10]

Guantanamito, as its detractors had soon started calling it, was the product of an unusual set of circumstances. Mauritania had undergone a coup d'état in August 2005 that, while hardly the first in the country's turbulent postindependence history, triggered widespread condemnation, including from the European Union. It was a lucky coincidence that the surge in clandestine boat departures took place soon after the coup, since this forced the Europeans' hand. They now had to negotiate with Mauritania, thus recognizing the newly installed regime.[11] As clandestine boat departures grew over the winter of 2005, so did the Spanish policing presence, leading to the official launch of Frontex operations the following summer. By then, journalists were also massing in Nouadhibou, armed with cameras and notepads and an insatiable thirst for the story of a migrant exodus. Academic observers criticized the sensationalism while pointing out that Nouadhibou had for years been a magnet for *regional* labor migration. To no avail: hysteria around an African exodus was quickly worked up, and the police crackdown intensified as a result.[12]

The Spaniards kept tight-lipped about their work in Mauritania; the U.S. Embassy in Nouakchott complained that getting information on Spain's migration response was akin to "pulling teeth," according to Wikileaks cables.[13] Perhaps this was because of the legal vacuum in which migration controls took place. As critical observers such as CEAR noted, trying to migrate clandestinely to another country was not an infraction in Mauritanian law, which meant no sanction of detention or deportation could be applied to it. The deportation center's moniker "Guantanamito" was in this sense apt—as a space outside the law, though with the important caveat that migrants were kept there only temporarily (a few days in principle, often longer in practice) before being bundled into a van destined towards the Senegalese border at Rosso or the Malian one at Gogui.[14] Mauritania's government had passed a law in 2010 on migrant smuggling and was in the process of passing another on migration that would give legal gloss to the response already under way. Its eagerness to collaborate was perhaps unsurprising, given that Mauritania's new "migration strategy" was largely financed by the European Union, as were the country's recently constructed border posts, whose staff were trained by the IOM and the Guardia Civil and whose colleagues on the coast had received Spanish vessels and pay.[15]

While the Mauritanian authorities were formally in charge of Guantanamito, assistance for detainees was handled by the Mauritanian Red Crescent, with support from the Spanish Red Cross. The deportation center was the brainchild of Enrique, the Spanish policeman who had negotiated bilateral migration accords with West African states. He still took pride in his role in creating it, despite the harsh critique and calls for its closure. The center was "a green island in the middle of the desert," he insisted, "like a hotel." It was created for "humanitarian reasons" and was so well furnished that the Mauritanian gendarmes started stripping away its equipment for their own homes. By 2010, Enrique did not care to hear more about the current state of the center: rundown and derelict, it was something he'd rather forget about.

"The fiasco of Guantanamito," as one Spanish journalist put it, was complete.[16] Stripped bare of supplies by soldiers and labeled a prison by human rights advocates, the "welcoming center"—as the Mauritanian Red Crescent often referred to it—was a perfect illustration of the absurdities of the Spanish African gift economy.

It also pointed to the increasing arbitrariness of policing clandestine migration on migrants' northward journey. As the Rosso border police had said, detection was easier in Mauritania than on the border. Migrants revealed their illegality through the same signs as in Dakar when preparing for embarkation—traveling in groups and carrying small backpacks, with biscuits and euros among their belongings. But the Mauritanians threw themselves into the task of detecting "illegals" with unusual frenzy. The key characteristic of the illegality industry in Mauritania was what activists have called the numbers game (la politique du chiffre). The

Rosso police distinguished between *raflés* ("raided" foreigners) and *clandestins* deported from Mauritania. The former, they said, were simply foreign workers picked up to make up numbers, not migrants intent on migrating clandestinely to Europe. Sub-Saharan Africans were detained in Nouadhibou for wearing two pairs of jeans, this "proving" they were on their way to Europe. Once numbers of departing migrants dropped, not even this was needed as an indication of illegality: skin was enough. The Spanish Red Cross, which collected the only systematic data available on those detained, came to similar conclusions on the numbers game. Guantanamito was first a "welcoming center in citation marks," said one Spanish Red Cross officer, before being "converted into a detention center for anyone suspected of wanting to migrate."[17]

Europe's subcontracted migration controls here threatened to undermine not only Mauritania's diplomatic relations with neighboring countries but also the already fragile relations between the country's black *(haratin)* and white *(bidan)* communities by adding a tinge of illegality to the politics of skin color. The legacy of slavery, as well as the forced expulsion of black Mauritanians to Senegal following a conflict between the countries in 1999, was never far from the surface. One civil society firebrand in Dakar saw a shift between 2008 and 2010 towards the growing stigmatization of strangers, with cases of even black Mauritanians being deported to the southern borders. "Now all black people are susceptible to being [seen as] illegal migrants," she said.

. . .

Jacques was one of the migrants detained and deported in the crackdowns. Dressed in a shabby sports jacket and stained jeans, he waited for me at the Red Cross base back in Rosso. It was hard to tell his age, but I guessed he was in his late thirties. A broad, expectant grin spread across his face as we sat down on a bench next to the water bladder. He clutched a small, ragged backpack, that telltale sign of migrant illegality, in which all his belongings were gathered: a toothbrush, a grubby towel, and little else except a blanket and a soap dish given to him by the Red Cross during detention in Nouadhibou. He had only a spare shirt besides the clothes he was wearing, which under the circumstances looked relatively clean. "They stole my bag at the border between Guinea and Senegal," he said. "I arrived in Senegal with nothing but a plastic bag in my hands." Still smiling, he told me his story of growing up in Guinea; however, he said he hailed from Guadeloupe, the French overseas department in the Caribbean. He wished to enter Europe. In fact, he had a French friend who had promised to meet him in Morocco and help him sort out his papers. These he had lost somewhere en route—it was not quite clear where—and he had failed to get new ones when approaching the French Embassy in Dakar. After this far-fetched attempt at getting travel documents, he had gone north. In Nouadhibou, Jacques had paid a driver for a clandestine trip to Tetuan, an unlikely destination in northern Morocco. Like other migrants similarly fooled before him, he was instead dropped forty kilometers away and told to walk towards the West Saharan border. There, border guards promptly packed him off to Nouadhibou for a beating and a night in the cells. He refused to eat because of a "bad stomach." The next day he was sent on to Guantanamito.

Jacques smoked more and more while he ate less and less. "I was so afraid," he said. "'You have to eat!' they told me. But I said, I can't eat here, I can't eat in jail, because it smelled so badly there." Guards accompanied him when he had to go to the toilet. A "Spanish lady" from the Red Cross was there, Jacques said, but did little to help. After a few days, the Mauritanian Red Crescent came to obtain information, asking how much he had paid for his clandestine journey, if he had a relative abroad. . . . After a few days, the police sent Jacques and other deportees to Nouakchott, the capital. The policemen offered food, but Jacques recalled, "I was a bit affected by all this anxiety, I couldn't eat even a small piece of biscuit." Finally he was sent on to Rosso-Mauritania, where he again refused food. Deported across the river at night, Jacques was turned back by Senegalese border police, since he lacked a "piece of paper," he said vaguely. By the time the Mauritanians sent him across a second time, the Senegalese police had left their shift, so Jacques went ashore and headed for the Red Cross.

Jacques and many others were not registered in the Rosso police chief's dusty ledgers of illegal migrants. They were invisible. This invisibility and indeterminacy, in which authority was exercised upon the migrant body randomly, suddenly, and arbitrarily, took a big toll on the physical and mental health of deportees. Over a plate of mafe stew in the local fly-infested canteen—Jacques now ate big mouthfuls, slowly and methodically—the smile stayed on his lips. "In Senegal, there's freedom," he said. "After you pass the border towards Dakar, there's no place where they'll hassle you." But when someone dropped a plate behind him, he suddenly twitched with startled eyes. Tensions seemed to simmer underneath his taut smile and briefly burst forth in his twitchiness, queasy stomach, and cigarette cravings.

To understand Jacques's experience it is worth returning to Coutin, who sees migrants en route as experiencing an "erasure of presence" in which they undergo a "physical transformation": "When they are clandestine, migrants embody both law and illegality. Absented from the jurisdictions that prohibit their presence, migrants disappear—whether by hiding, assuming false identities, or dying. By disappearing, migrants become both other (alien) and thinglike (capable of being transported). . . . Although they 'cannot be,' migrants continue to occupy physical space. Their bodies become a sort of absent space or vacancy, surrounded by law."[18]

This vacancy was expressed in Jacques's rootlessness and wandering *(errance)*. Where would he go? Jacques had no clear answers, except for saying, "I won't go back. . . . My objective is to reach Morocco, I'll find a solution in order to continue." But this was utterly unrealistic. Jacques was down to his last savings, five hundred CFA (one dollar), "plus my cigarettes." "Once I get to Rabat, my friend can find me there," he said, before mentioning that his friend's e-mail, the only contact detail he had, was stored on his mobile phone SIM card, which he had lost. Jacques was losing everything, including his wallet on the road to Nouadhibou, where he had ended up after a police officer took pity on him and helped him into a van departing Nouakchott. Even more than with the Liberians, everything about Jacques was fleeting and unsure; everything he said blurred the lines between truth, lies, and daydreaming. That night, he would sleep as he always did, atop his spare shirt, hoping no Senegalese gendarme would wake him up. Maybe the next day a boatman could punt him across the river free of charge.

Back in Dakar two weeks later, I bumped into Jacques again; he had heeded my advice to catch the Red Cross van. In the ledgers of Caritas, the Catholic organization providing the only rudimentary assistance for migrants in the capital, he now appeared as Ibrahim, not Jacques; his age was listed as twenty-two, not verging on forty. I had tried to put in a good word for Jacques/Ibrahim, saying that he had indeed tried to migrate to Europe, which meant he was entitled to assistance. This way, I was playing the same game as everyone else in the illegality industry—invoking a traveler's intentionality as source of both suspicion and entitlement, labeling my friend an illegal migrant in the process. The last time I went looking for him, around the Laboratory for Research on Social Transformations, a university research outfit that proved a fitting place for him to seek shelter at night, he was nowhere to be found. Maybe he had gone back north for lack of options. But his aimless wandering was unlikely to lead him across the biggest hurdle awaiting West Africa's illegal travelers—the Sahara.

MALI AND THE DESERT: CROSSING AFRICA'S INTERNAL SEA

Heading north from Nouadhibou, the desert route abruptly stops. Here lies what migrants call Kandahar, a no man's land between Mauritania and Morocco-occupied Western Sahara. It is a limbo in which deportees such as Mohammadou once got stuck, ping-ponged between the border posts and forced to retreat at gunpoint. But to overland travelers, the whole desert is, in a sense, such a limbo. In crossing it, they go through their next stage in the transformation into full-fledged illegal migrants. They live off *gari,* a Nigerian staple of flour mixed with water. They learn the fleeting lingo of the border, a mix of English, French, and local words that allows them to communicate across linguistic divides. They stash what little money they have away from the sight of border guards; in Niger and northern Mali, road checkpoints have become a source of easy income for state forces targeting the presumed illegal migrant. If they are lucky enough to pass the initiation rite that crossing the desert constitutes for them, their journey—exhilarating, dreary, and deadly in equal measure—will finally have been worth it.

Before Mali's conflict in 2012, the country's vast desert borders had become the latest frontier in the drive to control migration, thanks to stiffer controls along the shores of Senegal and Mauritania. The desert was anathema to Frontex, since it was away from the external border of the European Union, so Spain had to rely on other funding instruments here. On the basis of its 2007 migration accord with Mali, Madrid had increased official development aid, funded various programs on "migration management," and (alongside the European Union) equipped seventeen border police posts.[19] The Malian border police, the gendarmerie, and the country's official migration delegations had also received Spanish-funded computers, generators, fingerprint-reading equipment, cars, and gadgets. As in Senegal and Mauritania, such personalized gifts made for good relations. The Spanish police attaché had taken the family name of one of his Malian colleagues in a sure sign of affection, and the gendarmerie colonel in charge of migration tapped his laptop contentedly, saying, "This came from Spain." But as on the beaches of Dakar, while gifts created tenuous moral bonds they also created a mechanism for articulating ever-growing demands.

"Take me to Europe!" exclaimed a Malian gendarme with a chuckle before showing me into the AC-blasted offices of his boss. The director-general of the gendarmerie had gathered his top officials on migration for my visit, and all had a word or two to say on the need for more equipment vis-à-vis the border police. "Until now, the Gendarmerie Nationale has not been equipped," said one of the colonels. "If our thirty-five [border units] are equipped, that will reinforce the control of migratory flows." Other needs came in a thick stream: they needed computers for their border offices, and solar-powered electricity, and more vehicles, and petrol for these vehicles! All this would help cut migrant crossings "upstream." Above all, they insisted on creating development projects. The chief of the border police hammered home the same point. "Europe needs to help us with projects in villages; that way people can become sedentary," he pleaded, complaining that E.U. money was only for fighting illegal migration. Then he proceeded to ask for funds on both fronts. "If you want to fight effectively against illegal migration in the north [of Mali], you have to create a system in the style of Frontex [à l'image de Frontex]," he said, invoking the Hera operations at sea. "But we too," he exclaimed, "we have an internal sea; our sea is the Sahara!" The gifts generated ever more requests, articulated through the language of the Euro-African border.

Those adrift on the "internal sea" are not just subject to the aimless errance of migrants such as Jacques. In his "auto-ethnography" of clandestine crossings, Shahram Khosravi says such crossings challenge "the sacred feature of the border rituals and symbols." To him, migrants here play the role not of initiates but of "sacrificial creatures for the border ritual." This involves their *animalization*, Khosravi and Coutin both note, evident in the terms used for clandestine migrants and their smugglers across the world: in Morocco, sheep are at the mercy of wolves; in Mexico chickens are smuggled by *polleros* (chicken farmers) or coyotes.[20]

The making of West African travelers as illegal migrants is, again, not just discursive but also played out on their bodies. Youssou, a Senegalese adventurer who had managed to cross the Sahara via Mali and Niger, recalled packing into a Land Cruiser heading north into the desert, only to be forced to abandon it to shake off the police. As the migrants marched through the desert, Tuareg bandits appeared, tipped off by the gathering's guide. "They took our money, our clothes, our bags," Youssou recalled. They tore all clothes off the migrants and made them lie naked in the sand. They ripped up soles, seams, and gris-gris in search of hidden cash. They poured out the migrants' water and scat-

FIGURE 8. Border police post, Senegal-Mali border. Photo by author.

tered their last gari. They took away four women; one never came back. As soon as the bandits left, Youssou set out again. No time to lose in the desert. He came to a waterhole, shoved a few goats aside, and drank. By then, Youssou had been reduced to a savage existence readily invoked by those who have survived. "We lived like animals" was a common remark among clandestine migrants. One survivor recalled being deported from Algeria, imprisoned with murderers, forced to drink dirty water in deportation camps, transported in cattle trucks across the desert that sent his body rocking from side to side with each bump in the road. "Am I really a goat? A cow?" he asked angrily.

As Coutin remarks, clandestine migrants are also rendered "thing-like" on the journey. Masquerading as cargo, they might manage to cross the desert. This is how Youssou finally left the Sahara behind. Smugglers told him to lie down under the tarpaulin of a truck, tucked in like merchandise in a convoy for contraband cigarettes. Arriving in this fashion in North Africa, adventurers such as Youssou have already gone through several stages in their making as illegal migrants. The clothes and accoutrements spotted on Dakar's beaches, the migrant "mind" pondered in Rosso, the racialization in Nouadhibou, and the dehumanizing experience of the desert add up to an ever more reified migrant illegality defined by the traveler's "uniform," his wildness, his deviousness, his blackness. It is to the refining of this crude illegality in North African policing that we will now turn; here, the definite touches are put to the making of illegal migrants in Europe's borderlands.

MOROCCO: THE POLITICS OF RECOGNITION

Daouda and Modou had found the shortcut. I first met them in the market town of Fnideq, on the Moroccan side of the Ceuta border, making their way between the café tables and armed with skin creams they were trying to sell. They had used the new system mentioned by the Rosso border police, going by land from Senegal to Morocco. They had not even had to resort to cargo-like transport in fruit or cigarette trucks; as Senegalese nationals they could enter Mauritania and Morocco visa-free, as long as they paid a "fee" for the stamp after crossing Kandahar into Western Sahara. They were both in their early twenties, on their first trip abroad, and lit up as soon as I greeted them in Wolof. They both seemed at ease in Morocco, learning some Arabic and moving freely from their flatshare in Tangier to Fnideq's weekly market despite their uncertain legal status as itinerant vendors.

I was surprised at this ease. Strong diplomatic bonds between Dakar and Rabat mean Senegalese benefit from preferential treatment in Morocco, but this only partly explained their relaxedness. Morocco was, as Michel Agier has noted, the first North African country in being "annexed to the security policies of European governments."[21] Seeing the country as a springboard to Europe for streams of illegal migrants from south of the Sahara, Spain and France in particular had long pushed for a strong policing response there. As relations between Rabat and Madrid thawed following the Socialist victory in Spain's 2004 elections, migration cooperation grew quickly, culminating in the tragic events of autumn 2005 outside Ceuta and Melilla. After the intense media scrutiny that followed, Rabat cleaned up its act. No more negative headlines, no wanton brutality. As a privileged partner under the European Neighbourhood Policy, Morocco was keen to be seen as trustworthy and clean. At the same time, it was increasingly becoming a *destination,* not a "transit country."[22] Besides serving as a place where sub-Saharan migrants and refugees settled owing to the "blocked" route ahead, Morocco was also attracting executives, students, and workers from fellow African states. As a result, Morocco had to walk a tightrope between clean controls, flexible entry rules, and tough crackdowns.

At the heart of this strategy was the Direction de la Migration et de la Surveillance des Frontières (DMSF), based in the town-within-a-town of cream-colored buildings and manicured lawns of the Moroccan Interior Ministry. Mehdi, the director of DMSF, navigated with expert ease between the politics of a new Moroccan era under King Mohammed VI and the mixed European calls for a businesslike discourse on migration and a simultaneous tough policing response. In a sparkling conference room, he explained how Morocco's thinking on migration had proceeded from a "global" to a "process-oriented" strategy. "We've seen an activity that is highly controlled by the mafias. We've seen lots of money involved, so it was very, very crucial to us to have a global strategy," he said in American-accented English as his aide pushed a printout with statistics on dismantled smuggling networks across the table. Morocco had first followed what Mehdi called, somewhat puzzlingly, a "multiaquarium strategy" that went beyond policing to encompass "sensitization, communication, development, security, [and] legislative and institutional reforms." Thanks to this strategy, he said, Morocco "had reached an incompressible level of ameliorations since we have narrowed by almost 90 percent the arrivals of illegal migrants to Europe." As the old strategy reached its "maturity level" in 2007, DMSF embarked on a new process-oriented approach in which "everyone will work in the same aquarium." Labeled PPP (prevention, prosecution, and protection), Morocco's latest strategy covered both the country's own clandestine migration flows—the harragas, or "burners of borders," who have crossed the Strait ever since Spain instituted visa requirements in 1991—and the sub-Saharan migrants whose journeys were to be "aborted upstream."

The key element in Mehdi's discourse was what was left unstated: coercive border policing. He talked warmly about the directorate's work with Moroccan NGOs, about "confidence building" in the monthly mixed patrols of the Guardia Civil and the Moroccan gendarmerie, and about the good relations built over several years in high-level meetings with Spain. More than money, Morocco wanted recognition and participation as an equal. I asked Mehdi about E.U. funding for the Moroccan migration response, and his reply first startled me. "What funding?" he laughed. "Well, there was a MEDA program, about €67.5 million, eh . . . I'm talking about immigration; that's a small envelope. But we are a responsible country, we are a responsible state, we are not using this card to get finance or . . . today we are combating networks that are active in this business, because first we have to assume our regional responsibility. We have to protect our nationals, OK? We cannot accept that we become a transit country for migrants or drugs or for whatever, so we have to play our role."[23]

Mehdi was of course well aware that Morocco increased its political leverage greatly with Spain and the European Union thanks to migration. It would be no surprise to him, either, that the European Union was using the migration card in its development assistance strategy, with Morocco a huge beneficiary of such aid. Morocco, it is true, has long refused to sign an agreement with the European Union on readmissions of foreigners having transited through its territory, even though a deal was progressively getting closer. Until 2012 it had also refused to accept back nonnationals under such an agreement signed with Spain in 1992, with an exception being the "massive assault" at Melilla in 2005—not to mention routine *informal* expulsions through the border fences.[24] This diplomatic reluctance has not stopped Rabat from using and even promoting its status of "transit state," however, whether in pushing for rights for its own emigrants, as a political pressure point in relation to occupied Western Sahara, or in negotiations on agricultural produce and foreign fishing rights.[25] The pressure was, of course, two-way. The E.U.-Morocco action plan, like its equivalents for other North African countries, includes clauses on "ensuring the effective management of migration flows" and readmissions, while the "mobility partnership" signed between the European Union and Morocco in 2013 has "combating illegal migration" among its objectives.[26] In the migration-related aid stream, Morocco received €654 million in funding under the European Neighbourhood and Partnership Instrument over only three years. While €40 million of this assistance was earmarked for security, the aid money was generally "clean," and so was the Moroccan strategy that Mehdi had delineated. But beyond its smooth surface lurked a rougher reality, tucked away in the backstreets and forests of northern Morocco.[27]

Starting before the Ceuta and Melilla debacle but proceeding at a quickening pace in its aftermath, irregular migration was swiftly racialized in Morocco. Blackness became, as in Mauritania a few years later, a sign of illegality. In 2003, the country's infamous law 02/03 criminalized irregular migration and introduced deportation provisions. Around that time, taxi drivers in Tangier started refusing black customers. The scruffy hostels in the city's medina closed their doors to Morocco's southern neighbors who had so far frequented them. Bona fide refugees were increasingly rounded up, bundled into police vans, and dumped in the no-man's-land of the closed Moroccan-Algerian border.

As the crackdowns intensified, sub-Saharan travelers responded by further developing their intricate means of organization and subterfuge. A constellation of safe houses sprang up across Moroccan (and other North African) cities. These ghettos, as migrants called them, were houses or flats en route, usually based on nationality or ethnicity, to which migrants gained the right of entry through adherence to house rules and usually a small sum of money.[28] Conscious of how their bodies and behavior betrayed them, migrants also developed techniques for "passing" as documented visitors rather than deportable *clandestins*. One expert on such subterfuge was Stephen, a Liberian asylum seeker in Tangier. He dressed in crisp shirts and Adidas trainers, sometimes donning what English-speaking migrants called "schoolboy glasses." As he walked through town, he pushed his weight onto the front of his feet, propelling him into a focused, fast gait. Stephen made sure to carry a bottle of mineral water in his hand, "like the tourists have." He knew who the secret policemen were: they all had the same leather jackets and sunglasses. More important, he knew that, once he spotted them, he should not turn but walk straight ahead with the air of a legitimate foreigner.[29]

Daouda and his friends did not yet have to resort to such authority-eluding performances. They laid out their skin creams on white sheets around Tangier's Casabarata market while chatting with their Moroccan colleagues. Maybe they wanted to try going to Europe, Daouda said, but seemed in no rush. He was learning the ropes of being an itinerant vendor, living abroad for the first time in a basic flatshare with fellow Senegalese and Guineans. But soon enough, his time would come to taste migrant illegality.

While in Senegal and Mauritania, the illegal migrant was recognized through his "uniform"—backpacks, double pairs of trousers—in Morocco clothes and other "props" were used to *pass* as legal rather than signaling illegality. Here blackness was enough to raise suspicion: guilty until proven innocent. With this constant threat of apprehension, the clandestine "mind" conjured at the Rosso border was also congealing into a more definite shape. In Morocco, the illegal migrant was someone who had interiorized his own illicit status and its frightening corollary, what the anthropologist Nicholas De Genova terms "deportability," or the constant threat of expulsion faced by undocumented foreigners.[30] Moroccan forces had the power to block and move migrants while sowing fears for further interceptions. Nowhere was this circle of fear and forced mobility more evident than in Oujda, on the Moroccan-Algerian border.

. . .

Oujda is a mythical and terrifying place in the adventurers' world. Some French-speaking migrants refer to deportation there as "going on pilgrimage," giving an ironic spin to the violence and despair endured by those packed off to this vortex of the border. This bustling university town is both the site of expulsion, or *reconduite à la frontière* (return to the border), as Mehdi and his forces called it, and the key overland entry point to Morocco for clandestine West African travelers. On its outskirts lies *la fac* (the faculty or "the school"), where migrants often end up after expulsion to the no-man's-land next to the closed Algerian border. Here, Western journalists and researchers have congregated in recent years in their quest for a glimpse of the illegal migrants dwelling in shacks on a field shielded by crumbling university walls. Nigerian gangs hold sway around la fac and have even taken to confiscating visitors' cameras until they pay up for the privilege of observing Oujda's migratory world. This world is rough and raw, with migrants hostage to the gangs and police, who can strike at any minute. Across the forest, deportees out of luck bide their time hiding in *tranquilos* ("peaceful" places, in adventurers' lingo). Veterans of the Moroccan migration circuits, such as Stephen, have already been deported to Oujda multiple times, some clocking more than a dozen.

As I arrived in Oujda in late summer 2010, such deportations were increasing. In recent years a drip-drip of deportations had replaced the previous mass expulsions, leading to less negative media coverage if not a sharp fall in numbers. In August that year, after a Moroccan-Spanish standoff concerning the policing of the Melilla border, the Spanish interior minister had traveled to Rabat. Deepened migration cooperation was swiftly announced, followed by a renewed crackdown on black

Africans across Morocco. And now it was the turn of Daouda, the skin-cream salesman, to experience the violence of expulsion.

Daouda had been caught up in a raid *(rafle)*, he told me when I finally got hold of him over the phone. His Moroccan entry stamp had run out in the preceding days. To renew it, he would have had to go back to his entry point at the Mauritanian border, but this was too far and expensive. After the Moroccan police stormed his flat, he and his friends were detained and "returned to the border"—only the wrong border: not the Mauritanian, but the Algerian one. "The Algerians took all the money, *tout tout tout*," is all he could tell me before hanging up. His friend Modou was out at the time of the raid but had panicked and left immediately. I caught him on a bad line in Dakhla, halfway down to the Mauritanian border, where a payment of one hundred euros would give him a *laissez-passer*. He was heading home, the adventure over.

I met Daouda a week later in Tangier, neatly dressed in what was probably loaned gear, for a meal near the port. He told me how the Moroccans had taken him to the no-man's-land outside Oujda at night and indicated the direction for heading back to Morocco. "We didn't know; we went there, but it was Algeria," he said. Next, things got worse, as for many before him. The "bandits" came:

> They were Algerian soldiers, and they stole everything, everything. They asked us, why have you entered here? They said we had to give them every-thing and if not they would kill us. They took all the money—I had seven hundred euros, my friend five hundred euros . . . They took our watches too, our mobiles, but they left the SIM card for us. They took our clothes. They left us in our underwear, and it was very cold. We walked barefoot until 8:00 A.M., through the woods. Then we got to la fac, but we didn't even sleep there. . . . It's not safe in Oujda; at any time the police may come, ask for papers, and expel us again.

Daouda and his friends finally made it to a village, where a friendly policeman paid for their bus trip to Tangier. Daouda was back, but something had changed. Unlike earlier, he was twitchy. His eyes kept darting towards the entrance of our restaurant. He talked freely but with an unusual alertness, constantly on guard. As he swallowed a piece of chicken, his eyes suddenly moved towards the entrance without his head moving at all. The effect was disturbing.

Thanks to the arbitrariness of policing, Daouda was falling into ille-gality at a dizzying rate. This dizziness was evoked by a more prosaic English term for Oujda expulsions than *going on pilgrimage*. "They [head]butt you," Stephen called it. "It's like internal bleeding," his cousin chimed in, who had just been through deportation and was now afraid of the Nigerian gangs that had helped him back to Tangier. Stephen continued: "You feel confused inside, your head spins, you start thinking, why is this happening to me? I'm getting old and am doing nothing, have no future, why?" Stephen's vocabulary and Daouda's bodily reactions both pointed to the somatization of migrants' despair at an encroaching illegality, something I had already seen with Jacques in faraway Rosso.

The mental and bodily effects of the border were deepening with each year of Moroccan collaboration in European controls. Médecins sans Frontières, which cared for the beaten, distressed, and wounded *clandestins* expelled towards Oujda until it pulled out of the country in 2013, noted how deportees' physical wounds were increasingly accompanied by grave mental health problems. Sexual violence endured by women in the no-man's-land remained horrific, bringing cases of HIV as well as depression, posttraumatic stress, and unwanted pregnancies. The children born of these encounters often faced a dark fate, in Morocco or smuggled into Europe. While access to health care had improved somewhat for sub-Saharan Africans in the country, the vicious circle could not be fixed with plasters and wound dressings. Young men had their heads and legs bandaged before staggering back into the tranquilos and forests outside Oujda and Melilla, stuck in the vortex of the border.[31]

The psychological effects of the border were affecting me, too, in a much smaller yet similarly paranoid way to the supposed *clandestins*. In Oujda I walked with fast steps around la fac, trying—like Stephen, I later realized—to perform the role of tourist or student. I saw secret police everywhere, or potential informers. I had my reasons. In Tangier I had been filmed by a suited man in a café while interviewing an activist; at another time, a Cameroonian asylum seeker was stopped, searched, and interrogated after talking to me. The border regime was producing mental and bodily effects in those it drew into its orbit, forcing the free lines of flight of the adventure into a tunnel of state-controlled movements and surveillance. This battle of attrition against supposed *clandestins* often ended—as it eventually did for Stephen—in "self-deportation," to borrow a term used by U.S. Republicans, via the IOM's euphemistically named "assisted voluntary return" program.[32]

In Morocco, the petty gift economy of Spanish-Sahelian relations had been almost wholly replaced by a politics of recognition, in which Rabat agreed to play its role as long as Spain and the European Union deepened cooperation. Here, visits by European officials, the signing of new accords, or simply the need for end-of-year statistics was enough to trigger fresh raids, detentions, and forced displacements. As in Mauritania, if not enough migrants were found who fitted the "illegal" profile, the profile could simply be expanded along racial lines without much regard for the foreigners' legal status. This meant migrants, whether on their way towards Europe or not, had to constantly recalibrate their own bodies to disprove their supposed illegality—or else attempt a crossing to Spain simply to escape harassment. In 2012, an unprecedented wave of arrests of black Africans was unleashed in Mauritania, while similar roundups picked up pace in Morocco. The clandestine migrants, like currency, had to be kept in circulation for the illegality industry to keep rolling.

CONCLUSION: ILLEGALITY PUT TO WORK

The Spanish-African border business, reaching from the aid world and security solutions of the previous chapters to the police subcontracting described in the present one, is a schoolbook example of the increasing *delegation* of migration controls. As other writers have pointed out, delegation lets states work around a central border dilemma: how to appease public fears on migration while not hurting the economy or running afoul of human rights law.[33] Moreover, the outsourced border business is cost-effective, since collaboration with especially poor West African states is cheap compared with the cost of assisting, detaining, and deporting arrivals in Spain. Yet this chapter has also illustrated a larger dilemma of delegation: as too many groups become invested in fighting illegal migration, stakes grow, conflicts arise, and perverse incentives are created.

On one level, the clandestine circuit between West Africa and Spain can crudely be seen as a simple exchange relationship, with presumed illegal migrants alternately functioning as human merchandise and cashpoint. Yet with each financial exchange, new facets have been added to the relations between African and European forces. The gift economy has created a social bond where before there was none; it has personalized Europe's border regime; and it has bound recipient and giver into a tense mutual relationship of prestations and counterprestations. Such gift relations, in turn, have also added new facets to the constitution of migrant illegality in what, following Coutin, can be seen as a process of gradual *becoming* en route. Spanish per diem payments to the Senegalese police have procured an extension of migrant illegality, moving it away from actual infractions and towards material and behavioral signs. Gifts to the Mauritanians—ranging from patrol boats and cash to political recognition—have boosted the number of detainees while adding an edge of racialization to migration controls. Development aid and diplomatic favors have compelled the Moroccans to apply well-measured force to the increasingly fearful and furtive migrant body that, stripped of its rights and resources, can then be robbed at gunpoint by emboldened criminal gangs and Algerian soldiers.

But the migrant can also, through this growing vulnerability, become a recipient of kindness from ordinary people, aid workers, and police. In this gradual, complex manner, the illegal migrant emerges not just as a discursive but above all as an embodied figure while approaching the external E.U. border: he is alternately a hounded but pitied prey and a ghostlike, prohibited presence.

None of this means that Europe has simply had its way with its southern neighbors, as the ambivalence and complaints of officers from Dakar to Rabat have shown. Nor does it mean that the traveler readily gives in to or unquestioningly appropriates the imposed category of migrant illegality. While this chapter has presented the becoming en route as linear, with illegal elements gradually added to the migrant "product," the process is more intricate than this—and so are migrant adoptions of illegality. The migrant's presence is here not simply under erasure, as Coutin suggests: by adopting the role of the adventurer, some overland travelers also forge a distinct *presence* for themselves through clandestine skills honed on the margins of the law. While some such adventurers somatize despair, others instead press ahead ever harder, taking pride in their predicament. While many travelers self-consciously start adopting the terms *illegal migrant* and *clandestin,* others do not. Yet the main point remains: Europe's streamlined strategy on irregular migration crumbles in the borderlands, where an absurd circle is created. The more gifts and favors for the outsourced African manhunt, the stronger the pressure to find fresh prey. Border controls perpetuate, thanks to their very success, the "problem" they are meant to combat. In the process they also produce a lived modality of migrant illegality, embodied in the figure of the clandestine traveler as he approaches the final hurdles on his way to Europe: the Mediterranean and Atlantic waters and the tall fences looming around the Spanish enclaves of Ceuta and Melilla. Their fraught crossings into European space—and the border spectacles unfolding there—are the subject of the next section.

PART TWO

Crossings

SCENE 2

The Capsized Correspondent

BRAVE HACK TAKES MIGRANT BOAT TO SPAIN, FAILS
TO SELL STORY

*The blue wooden boat surges forward with each swell. The prow cuts
through the heavy waves, sending up spray along the sides and rocking
the African migrants who huddle aboard in bright yellow raincoats.
Each on his own. One man is curled up in front, his head resting below
the anchor, oblivious to the waves or just plain seasick. Next to him sits
a beautiful young woman, wearing a black hat to ward off the cold: she
briefly looks towards the stern, then goes back to staring ahead over the
waves, clutching a wet tarpaulin spread across the boat. The tarp catches
the Atlantic winds and fills with fresh, salty air. No safety to be found
underneath. The only sound is the splash of the waves and the drone of
the motor, which should be comforting, a sign of civilization out on the
high seas, but all it produces is a sharp, incessant rumble, like a tired
chainsaw. It's been only twenty-four hours aboard, and a silent stupor
has already descended on the thirty-nine travelers. The skies are a com-
pact gray; the boat lurches like a drunkard across the livid sea.*

*The correspondent comes into the room and puts a plate of fruit on
the table. "I want to have your comments! Bad and good," he says as I
pop a grape into my mouth and praise his camera work. We turn up
the volume, the rumble of the motor increasing. On-screen unfolds his
oeuvre: the only successful journalistic attempt to join boat migrants
from West Africa towards the Canaries.*

133

Laurent, a French former war correspondent, had put everything at stake in his trip. He had left his base in Rabat and gone to Nouadhibou in 2007, bent on joining a migrant pirogue. Though other journalists had done the hop from Western Sahara to the eastern Canary Islands, this longer trip was something no reporter had successfully accomplished before. (One Spanish reporter's desperate call for help soon after setting off caused much laughter among border guards, who had to rescue him.) Laurent had been a sailor and knew plenty of preparations would be needed. The adventure took him two years, including two long stints in Nouadhibou, where he had to draw on the skills his experience as a war correspondent could offer. "In Nouadhibou there's nothing," he told me with a slight American drawl in his villa outside Rabat in 2010, comfortably switching among English, French, and Spanish. "There's prostitution, drugs, sand, and an incredibly rough ocean and weather conditions, very windy, and it can be very cold, and it's awesomely corrupt and beautiful at the same time." But Laurent was no poetic layabout: he was a tough-skinned hack who knew how to get a story before anyone else. Some fellow correspondents saw him as a buffoon, and he readily admitted as much. "You have to be prepared to stand on your mother's head [to get the best story]," he said, "because if you don't, someone else will. It's a cutthroat business."

In Nouadhibou the media stampede was abating when Laurent arrived for one of his stints in 2007, but he still embarked upon what he called, with a laugh, "a completely crooked strategy." He entered Mauritania with a forged journalism permit and, once installed, presented himself as an aid worker, armed with business cards for a fictive NGO. On the streets, his newly cultivated beard and Moorish turban made him blend in with the locals. In his own words, he was "incarnating different characters"—a Western reporter to security forces, an NGO paramedic to migrant acquaintances, an elderly Moor to passersby.

Laurent soon started going native. Living in a fish-smelling hovel rented from a Spaniard, his daily existence came to resemble that of the clandestine migrants he was there to report on. Smugglers took his money, and African travel companions disappeared. The venture was funded by his own savings. "Who else would pay for such a crazy thing, lasting for so long?" His wife in Rabat, six months pregnant, was angrily urging him to return home instead of risking his life on a boat. But much like his migrant contacts, Laurent saw no way of giving up. "When you're in the middle of the river you don't switch horses, because then you fall or you lose everything," he said. "I had invested so much time, energy, and money into it, it would have been a disaster if I had given up."

Laurent realized he had to try another strategy. In the Nouadhibou quagmire a new role was slowly creeping upon him: that of people smuggler. "I ended up being the organizer of the fight," he said, using his favored migrant term for the sea crossing. He took his fellow travelers, a dogged bunch of West Africans, to task, asking them what they had achieved and "what was missing, what were the fears, how much we were going to give to the customs officers, and so forth." If clandestine migration involved constant transformations, journalists such as Laurent were experts among the shape-shifters, as he himself acknowledged. His last incarnation as people smuggler highlighted how boat migration was anything but the spontaneous African "exodus" of media fame: it was rather a spectacle in which journalists, humanitarians, police, and migrants all played their converging and confusing roles.

Laurent and his passengers finally departed. They stacked petrol canisters, water supplies, a satellite phone, and two GPSs into their pirogue and set off towards the Canaries, eight hundred kilometers to the northwest. Laurent's voice-over says they are leaving "the waste land of Mauritania" for "El Dorado."

Social divisions were soon apparent onboard. Under the tarp in front huddled the "cattle," the poorer copassengers, while the stern was the "VIP area." Those skilled enough took turns at the outboard motor. Then the engine spluttered and choked. The "devils" who had sold them the petrol—corrupt Mauritanian customs officers—had mixed it with water. After the first night onboard, tensions started showing. "Every inch you abandon is taken," says Laurent's voice-over. Then disaster struck. Water seeped into the boat; the passengers were "bailing like robots." They shot a flare, to no avail. Alone on the high seas, they finally spotted a big ship heading straight towards them. Laurent turned off his camera and helped the skippers, who revved the engine back into life just in time to avoid being chewed by the approaching ship's propeller. On the third day, Laurent got hold of the Spanish emergency services over satellite phone, who obliged a Russian tanker to rescue them. As they were finally pulled aboard, Laurent again stopped filming as they ascended a flimsy ladder. The Russians were reluctant hosts: still, the Africans scattered across deck and Laurent, assigned to a cabin, sensed hope. They would be taken to Spain. A boat finally approached, without flag. Spaniards, they hoped. Then a Moroccan flag was suddenly raised. "The trap is closed," says the voice-over. "One of my guys *hides in a garbage bin." Diverted to Western Sahara, Laurent was again separated from the others, interrogated, and eventually set free. His companions were detained, deported, and forgotten. "Who cares about Africa?" the voice-over asks as the film comes to a sad, frustrating end.*

Laurent had failed. He had not reached the Canaries, and, what's more, he had let his copassengers down. Three years on, he struggled to hide his disappointment. A shorter version of his documentary had been aired on Spanish television, and his arrival had generated the expected sensation. His story had also traveled farther afield, to northern Europe and the United States. But "people were more interested [in] the odyssey, the explorer" than in the "backstory" of Africa's plight. The full version of his epic journey, meanwhile, had still to find a buyer. "Un clou chasse un autre," Laurent sighed—one nail hits another in the world of news. In 2010, editors yawned, when a few years earlier they had salivated at a juicy migrant story. "I lost so much money and reached so little, I could be bitter about it," he said. What had motivated him was not fame and money, he insisted, but the "professional challenge" of filming the journey, and something else too: to show it as a "deterrent." "I thought it was very important to say, 'Guys, don't do this.'"

Laurent's story was meant to depict a "sinking continent" and its exodus—the film's cover showed Africa as submerged under the ocean, with a migrant boat floating atop it—but instead became framed as a rescue. "When we eventually arrived in Dakhla there was a TV crew waiting for me, there was an ambulance waiting for me, there were two doctors and three colonels in uniforms," Laurent said. His image—a bedraggled, bearded Westerner staggering ashore together with the black migrants—became the story, a "propaganda tool" in his words. The capsized correspondent ended up unwittingly mirroring the fate of the clandestine migrants he had first emulated and then groomed and steered towards the Canaries: he had been incorporated into the spectacle of rescues unfolding at Europe's southernmost borders.

CHAPTER 4

The Border Spectacle

Amadou had spent many days lying in wait on the rocky slopes outside Ceuta.[1] *He was observing, his eyes scanning the fence like a camera. He would lie in hiding for two or three nights, watching the Guardia Civil officers on the other side, their routines, their comings and goings. All he had to eat were a few dry dates and a handful of sweets. In the end he learned everything. He knew they went on patrol for five minutes to one side, twenty to the other. He would have to time his attack just right.*

Breaching the fence, this multimillion-euro armor, was a finely honed skill for Amadou. As he waited, every nerve in his body had to work in concert. No stray thoughts. Full, absolute concentration. No fear. If you are afraid, the Moroccan soldiers' dogs will bark and attack. But fix your eyes sternly on the dog's eyes, and it will stay calm. Amadou had learned this the hard way, on one of his ten attempts to climb the Ceuta and Melilla fences: a fellow adventurer took fright while they hid in the bushes, and they were promptly detected, beaten, and imprisoned. Amadou learned with each attempt, each expulsion to Oujda, each endless walk back by foot to the fences. He was training himself. Sooner or later, his time would come.

For the clandestine migrants, Europe's external border is a threshold between worlds. Behind them, the violence of the borderlands they have trudged through for months or years; ahead, a space of "human rights" and the promise of freedom. As they prepare for the final crossing, in silence or in hiding, they know that success depends upon their adventurer skills, their cool-headedness, and the "grace of God." This is their chance, the one moment their long journeys have been building towards. They must not miss it.

For the border guards, Europe's external border is their workplace. Their patrol boats speed across vast stretches of sea; their sentinels look out across fences for sightings of approaching intruders. As they scan the horizon, they know success depends upon reaching out to their colleagues across the border and to aid workers, journalists, and politicians within. In these interactions, the border becomes a resource in which the avowed business is to make sure no one enters. They must not lose it.

Migrants and border workers are bound together in what has been called the border spectacle or border game. To the political scientist Peter Andreas, border policing is an audience-directed "ritualistic performance" aimed at "recrafting the image of the border," making it more solid and real. To Nicholas De Genova, building on Marxist theorist Guy Debord's notion of the "society of the spectacle," it is a show of enforcement in which migrant illegality is made spectacularly visible. Through the interplay between enforcement and an excess of discourses and images, he says, the border spectacle "yields up the thing-like fetish of migrant 'illegality' as a self-evident and *sui generis* 'fact', generated by its own supposed act of violation."[2]

The crossing offers a first glimpse for European audiences of the clandestine migrant who has until then remained hidden beyond the border. This is where illegality is transformed into something different, something bigger, what in Spanish media and politics has come to be known as the *avalancha*. The prey-like migrants of the borderlands gather here into two distinct human "avalanches"—either a huddle aboard sinking boats or a frightening horde "assaulting" the fences of Ceuta and Melilla. This chapter is about this double transformation and about the similarly two-faced spectacle within and without which it unfolds.

The transformative power of international borders is not reserved for "illegal" travelers alone. As border theorists have noted, people become part of a new system of value when they cross state boundaries. Much as sweatshop shirts become fashion items and bags of cocaine turn into gold-like dust, migrants go through what the anthropologist Michael Kearney calls "reclassification"—a pun indicating how they are both labeled anew and potentially switch social class in the crossing. While the U.S.-Mexican border is the classic site for the study of such shifts, its emerging Euro-African counterpart is perhaps the steepest value threshold in the world right now: a deep economic divide loaded with symbolic, legal, and political potency for those who cross it.[3]

This chapter will delve into these transformations and the scene on which they occur, but it does so by complementing the Marxian perspective on value underlying the perspectives just cited. Clandestine migrations—and especially the movements between West Africa and southern Europe—do not neatly map onto the economic terrain but rather follow their own tangled logics. While critical authors such as De Genova correctly identify the obscene, "off-scene" reality behind the larger border spectacle as the continued need for illegalized labor in the West, this chapter will reveal another "off-scene" within and on the margins of the spectacle itself, in the realities that fall outside its visual order.[4]

In Spain, the border spectacle is fundamentally double-edged, in accordance with the peculiar geography of its southern frontier: the dispersed border at sea versus the sharply demarcated land borders of Ceuta and Melilla. These borders, in turn, are endowed with distinct humanitarian and military logics. In enforcing this conceptual divide between land and sea, the Spanish state has since 2005 largely avoided the fate of Italy and Greece, where the "tough" and "humane" sides to the border spectacle are muddled and mixed.[5] Yet this Spanish success is far from complete. The splitting of the border spectacle into two distinct acts veils how both settings depend upon a similar militarization and mixing of agencies in the border encounter. Moreover, the spectacle cannot detach itself from what falls outside its visual order—a visceral backstage world that sometimes escapes from the wings and intrudes into the theater of operations.

This chapter, then, is a spectacle in two acts: sea and land, rescues and repulsion, huddle and horde. In the first act, it travels to the coasts of the Canary Islands and relives the 2006 spectacle unfolding there; in the second, it visits Ceuta and Melilla, whose steel fences stand as a monument to the 2005 "assault" on the enclaves, before returning to the present and the distressing new arrivals of 2012–14. The chapter is about the masks donned in these border encounters—not only by the migrants, but by border workers as well. Among these workers are the journalists, the Red Cross emergency teams, the sea rescue service Salvamento Marítimo, and not least the security force charged with securing Spain's land and sea borders: the once so fearsome Guardia Civil, whose captains and commanders stand center-stage in the spectacle of the border.

ACT 1. THE CANARY ISLANDS: GUARDIAN ANGELS OF THE HIGH SEAS

¡Oh ciudad de los gitanos!
La Guardia Civil se aleja
por un túnel de silencio
mientras las llamas te cercan.
(Ai, city of gypsies!
The Civil Guard saunters away
through a tunnel of silence
leaving you in flames.)
—Federico García Lorca, "Romance de la
Guardia Civil Española"

Heavy is the gate to Europe, and hunched under the weight of history are the gatekeepers, the Guardia Civil. Spain's military-status police force calls forth images from Spain's darkest decades: the regime of Generalísimo Franco, the attempted coup in the fledgling days of Spain's democracy, and the persecution of gypsies and the poor evoked by Lorca at the time of the Spanish Republic. But something has happened in the past two decades. The Guardia Civil has fanned out across the world, its comandantes and *coroneles* talking warmly of humanitarian missions. And clandestine migration has played no small part in the security force's revived fortunes.

There were few better representatives of this brave new era for La Benemérita (the force's nickname, the noble or "meritorious" institution) than Comandante Francisco and his maritime surveillance colleagues. Francisco had even made a video, called *The Drama of Immigration*, illustrating this transformation to his visitors.

Sitting in his Madrid office, Francisco pressed play, and familiar images flicked by on-screen to West African guitar music. Wooden boats groaning under the weight of their human cargo. Black Africans scattered across the deck of a Spanish rescue vessel. Unmarked graves dug in Mauritania. Migrants suspended atop the water surface, balancing on the submerged remnants of their boat. *Afrika-a-a-ah*, sings Senegal's Ismael Lô in a bluesy voice on the soundtrack. *Nous sommes des enfants d'Afrique*. Another packed boat in the crosshairs of a Guardia Civil camera, half the deck covered by a makeshift canopy. A patrol boat pulls up, edging closer with each swell. The migrants squeeze against the side, reach for the hands of the guardias, and are dragged aboard the patrol vessel, one by one. "The Guardia Civil has carried out a job that

FIGURE 9. An award-winning picture of a sea rescue in the Canaries. Photo courtesy of Juan Medina.

has often gone unnoticed," says Francisco as his soundtrack segues to the New Age songs of Sheila Chandra, a melancholy voice atop an Indian drone. A uniformed guardia holds a listless African woman in his arms; another officer cradles a baby; a third carries a child on his back. Bloated corpses on Spanish beaches. A man on his knees in the Canarian sands, oblivious sunbathers blurred in the background. A corpse in silver wrapping. A drenched body, stiff with rigor mortis, pulled onto an inflatable raft. *I ride the waves . . . of each deathly breath,* sings Chandra. Then, in the night waves, the eyes and heads and arms of four drowning men grasping for the hands of their saviors. "We've saved lots of lives," says Francisco, almost sounding defensive. "You have to avoid them putting themselves in danger." The final text rolls, in Spanish, French, and stuttering English: the Guardia Civil, together with its African colleagues, has since 2006 "rescued more than twenty thousand people, preventing them from putting in danger their lives embarking in small and dangerous canoes towards Europe." La Benemérita's emblem lingers afterwards: the crown of Spain, a sword, and a fasces. Comandante Francisco pressed stop.

Since the time of the boat crisis in the Canaries, a flurry of images has brought the distress of clandestine migrants to a global audience. An exhausted man on his knees in the sand, motioning for something to drink; a white girl in a bikini, her hand on the shoulder of a male migrant tightly wrapped in a Red Cross blanket; a gaudily painted cayuco packed with people as it glides into port. These pictures provide a window onto the first act in the Spanish border spectacle: humanitarianism and its Guardia Civil protagonists.

Many commentators have looked at Europe's border regime through the rather distressing lens provided by the philosopher Giorgio Agamben and his influential reading of the ancient Roman figure of *homo sacer*—the banished, "sacred" man who can be killed but not sacrificed. Like a modern-day *homo sacer*, one argument goes, the clandestine migrant is subject to a state of exception in which the sovereign power to "let die" is exercised. But as was seen in chapter 2, border controls are as much about the power to "let live," the other side of Agamben's notion of bare life—a vulnerable life that can be rescued in action, just as it can be killed by omission. And high-ranking Guardia Civil officers are consistently on-message on the importance of saving lives. They are the "guardian angels of the high seas," in the words of one former Socialist government delegate in the Canaries, whose recollection of the boat crisis was encapsulated in the picture of the drowning migrants towards the end of Francisco's video, shot by the award-winning Reuters photographer Juan Medina (figure 9). In the photo, one of the migrants was being sucked into the night-time waves "with a face of fright, his eyes almost out of their sockets, clinging onto the hands [of his savior]," the delegate recalled. "They drown, they are drowning, and you stretch out your hands to whomever you can."[6]

In Spain's sea rescues, the illegal migrant appears not as the abstract flow of risk of Frontex maps, or as the hounded prey of the borderlands, or as a naked life that can be killed but not sacrificed. On the high seas emerges, rather, a body in need, stiff with cold and fear, whose image can be captured, circulated, sold, and shown. The images, much like cognate pictures of African refugee flows depicting a "sea of humanity" without a past, fix the notion of the clandestine migrant as a helpless, nameless body, sinking into the dark waters.[7] In rescuing this drowning body a virtuous circle is born, where the tasks of patrolling, caring for, and informing on clandestine migration blur into one another.

The production, distribution, and appropriation of images—in short, the visual economy of clandestine migration—mirrors and even facilitates this mixing of roles.[8] The mixing was on display in Francisco's video and many others like it, in the rescue pictures adorning Guardia Civil corridors, and in televised snippets of sea interceptions. On the walls of the Tenerife Comandancia, it was spelled out in a framed Red Cross letter thanking the security force's maritime service (SEMAR) for its "humanitarian assistance." Through such mixing, the guardias, African forces, journalists, and Salvamento and Red Cross workers forged what sociologist Craig Calhoun calls an "emergency imaginary." This imaginary, Calhoun says, is activated when officialdom "takes hold" of events such as refugee crises in such a way that these emerge as a "counterpoint to the idea of global order."[9] This is what happened in the Canaries boat crisis of 2006, to which we will now return.

Part 1: Symbiosis

Abdou had tired of talking about his amputated feet. "I have four articles and three DVDs, and it hasn't helped me at all," the young Malian told me in a charity-run migrant shelter in Gran Canaria, where he had arrived after a brutal ordeal on the open Atlantic. "You can look me up on the Internet; it's all there. I have talked a lot, and it doesn't help me. I'm tired of all that." We looked down his legs, towards the Spanish-provided prostheses hidden under trainers, socks, and jeans that I had already seen in a TV documentary. His despair had dripped off the screen as the camera tracked his hands seeking out a picture of his mother or his eyes as he recalled the toxic mix of gasoline and saltwater that had destroyed his feet in the hull of the boat. "I spent seven months in hospital," he told me as other migrants crowded in around us. "I spent four months learning to walk. Since I came to Spain, I haven't worked a single day." A tone of despair infused Abdou's voice, just as in the documentary. I had long since stopped taking notes; we fell silent and the drizzle subsided in the gray patio.

For a few years after 2006, the tragedies of Abdou and other capsized West Africans were the most poignant example of the spectacle of clandestine migration into southern Europe. Yet the full-blown emergency they represented had been preceded by a drip-feed of no less tragic arrivals to the easterly Canary Islands. And it was there, partly outside the media spotlight, that a coherent humanitarian response to clandestine migration was initially forged in the archipelago, providing the groundwork for the symbiosis among the media, police, and aid workers that was to follow on Tenerife and Gran Canaria a few years later.

Emilio, a Red Cross worker now based in Las Palmas, was a veteran of this early era and looked back at it with something akin to nostalgia. In the late 1990s, pioneering pateras had started reaching the island of Fuerteventura, first with Sahrawis and later with sub-Saharan Africans and even Asians onboard. At night, the locals "heard the screams of people as the pateras turned over," Emilio recalled. "The next morning bodies appeared on the shore. . . . People wanted someone to do something."

In 2003 the authorities asked the Red Cross for assistance, and soon Emilio's emergency response team (Equipo de Respuesta Inmediata en Emergencias, ERIE) rushed to the beaches and ports to wrap migrants in blankets and to give them first aid, a hot drink, and a medical checkup. The rough terrains of Fuerteventura made Emilio's work even more taxing. "We had to traverse a dirt track for eight kilometers, set up motors, field hospitals, and everything else," he said. "This was something that I thought of in terms of work in the field, as in the earthquake in Haiti." As in such a natural-disaster scenario, the Red Cross had to create an emergency protocol for intervention. "The field came to us," Emilio said. But for a time, the outside world did not seem to bother.

Then Emilio had an idea: call the media. He started contacting journalists, without telling the authorities, each time a patera arrived. "No one knew what was happening there until we created a Red Cross–press symbiosis, though we kept it quiet," he recalled. "The Guardia Civil asked, 'But who the hell called the journalists?' I said, 'How would I know? Maybe they tune in on the radio.'" Emilio recognized that his efforts only paid off in part, however. It was not until large cayucos started arriving in Gran Canaria and Tenerife that a wider emergency imaginary was activated.

Emilio recalled some roughness in relations with the Guardia Civil, with overworked guardias "screaming and pushing" the migrants. He took a forgiving view, however, and insisted that the guardias "had the same heart" as Red Cross workers, with many of them traumatized by what they had seen. "The Guardia Civil assisted a lot of immigrants in their quarters, they paid for sandwiches with their own money, and their wives brought clothes for the immigrants."

On the high sea, the situation was even more delicate. Utmost coordination and professionalism was needed to intercept and save dozens of migrants, stiff with hypothermia, from a sinking wooden boat at night amid raging waves. This was the drama played out in the photos circulated by guardias, the government, and the media: the *performance*—in the sense of both spectacle and professional task—of the rescue.

As Guardia Civil launches reached a patera, frayed nerves and hot tempers initially often led to disaster. Migrants stood up in fright or expectation of a rescue, making their boat overturn. Specialized Guardia Civil divers had to throw themselves into the cold waters or search for hands to grasp, hoping to drag drowning migrants aboard. It was such a capsized boat that Juan, the Reuters photographer, had captured in the waters off the Canaries. Soon staff were trained and risks minimized, heralding a first, strange sight of Europe for boat migrants: rescue workers bedecked in full protective gear who took them onboard, isolated them as pathogens, and safely steered them to port.[10]

Before their arrival, someone always called the journalists. Contacts were close among aid workers, border guards, and select reporters, and, by 2010, the sight of arrivals had become routine on Spanish television. First, shots of a Salvamento boat gliding into port. Next, rescued migrants streaming off the deck under the watchful eye of the Guardia Civil to the snaps and flashes of photojournalists. Finally, Red Cross volunteers wrapping migrants in blankets and lining them up for a medical check followed by transport to detention. The moral narrative of a professional, streamlined labor of rescue—the reassuring end to the emergency imaginary—was repeatedly broadcast and brought to its expected denouement, just as it had been at the end of Comandante Francisco's video.

The port spectacle showed how the "symbiosis" pinpointed by Emilio concerned more than just relations between aid workers and journalists. Along with the humanitarian protocol first developed on Fuerteventura and around the Strait came an increased mixing and blurring of roles among the different agencies working on migration. A few examples of this mixing should suffice.

First, information gathering. The Red Cross conducted short interviews with recent arrivals, and Salvamento Marítimo took pictures of cayucos during rescues. Emilio and his team shared and contrasted data with the Guardia Civil—information that was then sent on to the Spanish Interior Ministry. Salvamento provided the Guardia Civil and police with their footage so that these could ascertain the "captain," for detention, as well as the possible origin of the boat. In this way, the images attained value as evidence, temporarily exiting the larger media circuit of border imagery to which the agencies all contributed.

Second, the circulation of staff, know-how, and resources. In their spare time, guardias on Fuerteventura volunteered in Red Cross emergency operations. Roles were more clear-cut on the bigger islands and

FIGURE 10. A rescue in the Strait of Gibraltar, September 2012. Photo courtesy of
Salvamento Marítimo.

along Spain's mainland coasts, but there too staff switched agencies and
roles. A former ERIE team leader on Gran Canaria was now a policeman; a long-time Red Cross worker in Tarifa became a Salvamento captain; a Red Cross spokesman became a renowned reporter on boat
migration. Equipment circulated as well. The Red Cross took over not
only old Yamaha motors from the cayucos but also Salvamento and
Guardia Civil launches in a sharing and recycling of resources that mir-
rored the circulation of border imagery. The Red Cross, Salvamento,
and sometimes the Guardia Civil also held joint exercises, contributing
to what one Salvamento chief called a "feeling *diferente*" among the
agencies working on migration.

Third, translation and interrogation. A former Red Cross volunteer
in the Canaries, Senegalese by origin, recalled rushing across the
island in 2006, often attending to one boat arrival after another in the
same night. He translated for the Red Cross, explaining, "They came to
me and spoke; they weren't reticent." He then found out where the
migrants were from or took an educated guess. Relations between
the Red Cross and police were friendly thanks to an understanding
commissioner, he said. "He gave me a job in the end. When you finish
you go straight to the police and you have work; you collect data [do

interviews], and the government pays, and they paid me *very, very* well." Here the police could tap into the goodwill generated by an African Red Cross volunteer to retrieve information from boat migrants. Similar setups facilitated the sharing of tasks across agencies in other settings too.

Fourth, migrants' perceptions of these mixed roles. It was hard to develop trust with migrants, Emilio said; in the beginning they mistook Red Cross workers for police. Around the Strait, migrants often said they had been picked up by the Red Cross, which usually turned out to mean Salvamento Marítimo or, at times, even the Guardia Civil. In Nouadhibou, Spanish Red Cross efforts to disown Guantanamito clashed with the Mauritanian Red Crescent's reference to it as "our center" or the "welcoming center." Red Cross volunteers in Rosso-Senegal said that deportees often refused to go see them, since they saw the organization as part of the coercive state apparatus they had already encountered in Nouadhibou.

Part 2: Transformation

The Red Cross brand had been identified with Spain's humanitarian regime—and had, as the Tenerife delegate insisted, received a huge boost in resources for this reason. In the Spanish migration response as a whole, the Red Cross had come to exemplify the concept of *acogida,* translated as welcoming, reception, or sheltering. The Socialist government put acogida into practice through a reception and integration fund by which NGOs gave recent boat arrivals shelter, food, and other support for a short initial period. Several civil society groups turned down participation because of the fund's short-term nature, "even though it would have sorted our accounts out quite well," as one NGO worker put it. The Spanish Red Cross embraced it, however, alongside longer-term reception, assistance in port, and humanitarian aid in Rosso, Nouadhibou, and select migrant reception and detention centers (CIEs). Its large body of volunteers, its established role as auxiliary to the state, and its institutional imperative of discretion were all factors that soon helped make the Red Cross indispensable. As its role grew, however, so did a muted criticism. Some activists and policemen dismissed the Red Cross as only "putting on plasters," while others highlighted the organization's role in legitimizing controversial policing operations. The Red Cross was aware of these dilemmas and was present in only a few CIEs for this reason. In such centers "roles can become confused," said one officer in Madrid. "To work as the auxiliary to public powers has its pros and cons."

One international Red Cross representative in West Africa was blunter. "The Red Cross has become the jailer," he said, adding that national societies worked on "projects that are not always humanitarian. . . . This is a problem within the movement." His comments illustrated an unease that was usually expressed more diplomatically by his colleagues in the International Committee of the Red Cross (ICRC), the custodian of the Geneva Conventions at the heart of the movement, about the role of national Red Cross societies in Europe's migratory operations. A different concern was voiced by North African Red Crescent societies: like good auxiliaries to the state, they—unlike their European counterparts—saw no need to prioritize foreigners on their soil.

While these clashes reflected long-standing differences between a cosmopolitan ICRC and the "patriotic" national societies, they also highlighted a larger humanitarian dilemma. A gray zone has in recent decades emerged between combatants and aid workers in war zones—as seen, for example, in the military appropriation of the Red Cross emblem in Iraq and Afghanistan. As a result humanitarianism finds itself, according to anxious voices, at a crossroads. While some trumpet a golden era brought on by the multiplication of aid into billions of dollars and of agencies into the thousands, others see humanitarianism politicized, its universalism questioned, and its workers ambushed. Humanitarianism has, critical voices allege, been transformed into a form of politics—an ethical configuration and mode of governance whose efficiency draws upon its very apolitical guise.[11]

Humanitarianism has, however, as many scholars note, *always* been political. Moreover, it has also been intimately linked to militarism ever since Henri Dunant founded the ICRC after witnessing the bloody aftermath of the battle of Solferino, in 1859.[12] The symbiosis between humanitarians and coast guards was thus not an anomaly; what was unusual was the depth of participation of wildly different agencies and the ensuing transformation of their respective roles.[13] This was evident in comments by the Tenerife delegate in 2010 when he attacked the then conservative opposition's calls for implicating the army in stopping the cayucos, before acknowledging, "It's true that the navy collaborates, but in a humanitarian sense." They were guardian angels watching out for huddled boat people, not soldiers pushing back an invasion.

Among the guardian angels, the Guardia Civil underwent the biggest transformation. In combining the ancient moral benefits of being La

Benemérita with the pictures, videos, and performances of sea rescues, the Guardia Civil, so laden with a heavy historical baggage, was reinventing itself within the framework of a state-sponsored emergency imaginary. Spain's grizzled border guards of yore had morphed into humanitarians. This was the story on display in Comandante Francisco's video, in the photos and plaques in the comandancia corridors. It was a compelling narrative that would look suspect, however, without the accompanying bright orange colors of Salvamento's rescue vessels and the Red Cross brand.

Salvamento's fortunes had also been transformed. "The Spanish sea rescue service is among the most highly valued in the world right now," said the Tenerife delegate, explaining this in reference to clandestine migration.[14] The same could not be said for the Red Cross, however, since its role at the border was constantly under threat from the "humanitarian" conflicts within the movement, criticism from without, and funding cuts from above. The organization had certainly proved helpful in branding Spain's migration operations, but as its usefulness declined it could be cast off like migrants' Red Cross–emblazoned blankets.

Not only were the agencies transformed in the border spectacle, but so were their targets, the *subsaharianos* (sub-Saharan Africans) and *magrebíes* (North Africans). The racial typology was based on the only easily observable fact from afar, workers insisted, yet these groups were also differentiated as *kinds* of migrants. The subsahariano was seen as orderly, rule-obeying, even docile; the *magrebí*, meanwhile, was a potential troublemaker. The subsahariano would sit down on the beach and wait for the rescue workers to arrive, while the Moroccans and Algerians disobeyed orders, self-harmed, and tried to run away. While workers alternately grumbled and took a forgiving view about the North Africans' behavior, black migrants were often talked about with notes of respect and awe. "Sub-Saharans are superstrong in character," said one Red Cross coordinator, impressed with their lack of agitation despite the drama at sea. "They don't cave in the way we do."

These complex frontline categorizations were brought into sharper relief by the border imagery. Whether in Guardia Civil videos, border surveillance brochures, or news reports, it was the subsaharianos, not magrebíes, who were the chief humanitarian subjects. The pictures that acquired high iconic, symbolic, and financial value in the visual economy were those of black migrants on rickety boats, hands outstretched towards their European saviors. The Red Cross blankets, clothes, and kits provided the uniform of these new boat arrivals, the guise in which migrants were seen on television screens—huddled and wrapped up, sandals or clumsy plastic shoes on their feet, all alike, perfect images of the anonymous rescued migrant.[15]

In one journalist's words, the potency of the images beamed out from the Canaries in 2006 lay in the surreal encounter of "Stone Age man" and twenty-first-century bikini-clad girl on a tourist beach. Wild-eyed with salt-streaked hair, clothes wet and in tatters, speechless on his knees in the golden sands of Tenerife, the boat migrant in these pictures briefly appeared as a primitive man rescued from the seemingly most irrational of journeys.

Part 3: The Rescue Image

The extraction of such images from the complex realities of boat migration is at the heart of the spectacle of the border. As noted in other humanitarian settings, the "emergency" needs a visual and narrative frame.[16] The images and headlines are, in a word, *agentive*, not descriptive: where the media look, money and official attention follows. It was in the largest circuit of the visual economy—where rescue pictures circulated as news commodities—that the emergency imaginary found its frame; it was also here that the gaps and cracks in this frame were most clearly beginning to emerge.

The media's power to force political action in response to emergencies is often referred to as the "CNN effect," and its existence is still widely debated. In the chaos of the Canaries in 2006, however, the process seemed inverted: politicians actively *sought* to create the emergency frame. For the Canarian and national opposition, the rescue imagery was an indictment of a floundering government; for the Socialists, it was a means to pressure the European Union into action. The journalists came to play a role in these battles, at times as hapless extras, at other times as active protagonists, alongside the other workers in the illegality industry.

The "guardian angels" and journalists did not just share in the emergency imaginary; they also mixed and depended on each other to do their jobs. Journalists embedded themselves aboard patrol boats, were called by police contacts to quays and piers, and mingled with aid workers on beaches, at times lending a helping hand. This mingling applied in particular to the journalists who tried to go beyond the "avalanche" story. The media fascination with boat migration has reached its apogee among this intrepid breed of journalists, who have, like Laurent the capsized correspondent, disguised themselves as clandestine migrants and embarked on journeys in trucks and boats, camera in hand. They have traveled to migrants' home villages with news of deaths and tracked deportees to deserts and detention centers on African soil. Members of this intrepid reporters' club seek not quick scoops but the recognition of their peers, among whom the skill in chasing a story is what counts, much like the qualities admired among the migrant adventurers.[17]

For all the reporters' efforts, the "emergency" kept framing their interventions. One award-winning British TV reporter sighed at the fact that migration sold only if it was "something about us being under siege," exasperated at editors who changed his program titles to invoke this fear. Others had their book titles tweaked, with "African" becoming "illegal" migration, or their investigative pieces on migrant abuse in the borderlands framed by scare stories on an impending invasion. Rafael, a Spanish correspondent in Morocco, took a pragmatic view after his many years of "doing migration" for a conservative daily, insisting he got the leeway he needed despite the paper's official line. Others were not so understanding. These included Juan, the Madrid-based photographer whose iconic pictures from the Canaries had featured on countless front pages, in Francisco's video, and in the Tenerife delegate's recollections.

Juan insisted he was an immigrant himself, hailing from Argentina, and like the immigrants he photographed, he also became a focus of the media's attentions. A documentary for Al Jazeera, *Photographing the Exodus,* presented Juan as someone who "has taken the plight of these desperate souls to heart," not only in "photographing their misery," but also in keeping contact with them long afterwards. On-screen, Juan and a guardia thumb his award-winning pictures from the capsized boat; next Juan travels to Mali and shows the pictures to the families of the survivors. The guardia and family members react in the same fashion: voices lowered, eyes softening. "This is utter desperation," says the brother of one of Juan's survivor friends, shaking his head. Another cries inconsolably.

Juan's work was a conscious criticism of the "speechless," one-dimensional depiction of boat migrants in the mainstream media. Yet his work also seemed to be the most striking manifestation of the role assigned to this migrant: a bare, naked, drowning life. Juan knew this. "The photographer is like a remote control," he told one conference gathering: editors could make his images appear instantly on their homepages or newscasts at the press of a button, without context and without consideration of the photographer's intentions. The most extreme example of this was perhaps the Guardia Civil's numerous "humanitarian" videos, set to soft music to differentiate them from heavily soundtracked drug interception clips. By appropriating and reframing Juan's rescue image, the Tenerife delegate and Comandante Francisco could present it as evidence of humanitarianism, not of what Juan denounced as the "cruel and macabre obstacle course" created by the government and the guardias' very efforts.[18]

Juan's feeling of being a remote control—like Abdou's tragic and tired recollections—highlighted how the rescue image was alienated from its producer and "object" alike. This alienation of course applies to any commodity, as Marx long ago noted, yet strange things happened once the rescue image was put into circulation in the visual economy of clandestine migration. Juan's image-as-commodity mingled with imagery from mainstream broadcasters, humanitarian organizations, and security forces and was appropriated by these image producers in turn. While the confident "humanitarian" framing in Guardia Civil videos indicated that the government had taken control of the story of clandestine migration since 2006, the imagery escaped any easy encapsulation. As it circulated, it took on a range of complementary and at times competing values. It served as memento for traumatized Red Cross volunteers, guardias, survivors, and their families; as iconic sign of humanitarianism in Guardia Civil corridors and brochures; as glue for a collegial experience among agencies; and as evidence in interchanges between Salvamento and police. At other times, the image took on qualities of self-perpetuation and agency, as predicted by Debord's notion of the spectacle and by the Marxian theory of the fetishism of commodities that underpins it. One Guardia Civil captain had asserted this fetishistic potency in saying that one of the most iconic Canaries photos, of "the blond girl embracing the black man . . . had a tremendous pull effect on would-be migrants in Africa." To counter this potency, Spain had in turn broadcast images of death in Africa as deterrence.

The rescue image, like a patera filling with water, struggled to contain all it was assigned to do; the visual order of the border spectacle was bursting at its limits.

Part 4: The Backroom of Migration

One hot summer afternoon I went to a Red Cross *asamblea* (local headquarters) to watch videos of rescues. "Ah, those were my times," said a Salvamento captain who had joined his Red Cross colleagues to watch the footage: guardias aboard Salvamento launches, beached pateras, corpses pulled aboard rescue boats, plastic gloves inflated as balloons for migrant children. The captain knew everyone, trading anecdotes about Guardia Civil sergeants appearing in the videos. But as we saw a guardia carrying a child on his back, he snapped. "It's not real!" he exclaimed. "That's what I don't like about all this." What, I asked? The captain mentioned examples: guardias putting their three-cornered hats on children's heads or on adult migrants to protect them from the sun. He had videos of the "backroom of migration" *(la trastienda de la migración)*, what happened after the journalists left—shoving, shouting, and violent beatings.

The border spectacle, as Juan and other journalists were well aware, revealed but a small slice of the border encounter. It left out the "backroom," or backstage world, of violence shielded from view by the state, as well as the trauma and drama at sea. In part, this chimes with Debord's prediction for the society of the spectacle—that is, replacing the real world with a narrow selection of images that "succeed in making themselves regarded as the epitome of reality."[19] The violent backroom of the border, excised from the visual realm, was instead relegated to the visceral backstage world of smells, touches, and noises. And this world both reinforced and undermined the forms of "bare" migrant life seen in the border spectacle.

Emilio, the Red Cross emergency chief, had desperately wanted the media's attention but was still not happy with the slick images churned out by the news organizations he had summoned. He took friends and family along to make them experience how different the realities of a boat arrival were from the "cold" representations on television. Waiting on the seafront to begin an intervention, he recalled, "people readied themselves, with the smell of the sea on the pier before they arrived, the sound that grew stronger because you could hear the patrol boat at a mile's distance, you knew they were arriving." Besides the noise, the adrenaline, and the whiff of the sea, the strongest memory was the smell of the patera itself. Emilio talked of the "characteristic smell of the paint of the patera impregnated in their clothes":

Many times we knew. We went somewhere, and those smells might be there, on a beach, and there's an abandoned patera there, and we arrive, smell it, and say, it smells of intervention. It was a special smell. Everything smelled the same, of people in an enclosed space; it smelled the same, something like patchouli perhaps, something characteristic, and people of black race have a characteristic smell; the interventions had their characteristic smell. It was the mix of the paint, the gasoline, and, well, the situation in which they arrived—they basically relieved themselves where they sat.

The patera smell haunted Emilio's memory and helped create a special space for interventions in his mind. It also marked out the characteristics of boat migrants as rescuable and racialized: the heady brew of saltwater, gasoline, paintwork, and strong bodily odors also recognized by Guardia Civil and Salvamento colleagues. As one guardia told a Spanish journalist, it was a "concentrated human smell" that reached them before they saw the boat: "It smells of misery."[20]

Another aspect of rescues beyond the spectacle was the migrants' gaze, their *mirada*. "They don't say anything, but [the mirada] is superexpressive. . . . It says 'help me,'" one Red Cross volunteer said. To Emilio, the mirada "told you a lot; it told you that this person has just left their whole life behind, risking many things and losing so much, for nothing."

The mirada, the smells, the noises—these impressions could not be neatly encapsulated in the border spectacle or distributed within its visual economy. In the film produced by Laurent, the capsized correspondent, the camera was off at the most dangerous and defining moments—during the night when the migrants scrambled to fix the motor as a ship approached and when they clambered up the ladder to the waiting Russian tanker. "You don't film when you're dying," he told me. However, the resulting gaps were indispensable, contributing to the aura of his video and persona.

Juan similarly recalled how he took the iconic picture of the drowning men. "I heard how the patera capsized; the memory I have is of the sound," he told his conference audience. It was utterly dark; he staggered up a ladder onto the patrol boat and snapped pictures with his flash on, without seeing anything. The most iconic picture of boat migration was, then, a glimpse of the unseen, of something beyond the journalistic and humanitarian gaze. In the Al Jazeera documentary, his guardia colleague recalled the shouts—of "resignation," not desperation—from the pitch-black water. His memory of rescues was "how they grip on to you, how tightly they grab your hands and arms." Touch, noise, smells—this was the harrowing backstage world, the very human side to the border encounter only hinted at by the humanitarian spectacle.

This darker side would, however, become central to the second act at the border. This is where the backstage world of violence had been relegated and where the spectacle once began: the tall fences around Ceuta and Melilla and the tragic mass attempts to climb over them in the autumn of 2005.

ACT 2: CEUTA AND MELILLA: KEEPERS OF THE GATE

CEUTA, JULY 2010. It was a dazzling day, the light breeze pungent with the smell of wild herbs. The patrol car had swerved through the hills, leaving zone Bravo and entering Charlie. It stopped at the highest-lying sentry box, with breathtaking views in all directions. "Take pictures!" exhorted the Guardia Civil officer in charge of Ceuta's border barrier. As I snapped away, Teniente Federico gazed across the twin fences dwarfing our car and slicing the North African hillside in two. To the left they undulated down into the valley, disappearing at the official Spanish-Moroccan border of Tarajal next to the sea. To the right, they snaked towards the fishing hamlet of Benzú, on the other side of the enclave, at a steep angle. Here, as in Melilla, thermal cameras and sound-and-motion sensors tracked movement in Moroccan territory. Guardia Civil vehicles and officers patrolled the Spanish side; through the steel mesh, it was just about possible to make out the Moroccan soldiers and auxiliary forces, known by migrants as the "Alis," ensconced in whitewashed, E.U.-funded sentry boxes. The *valla* or *perímetro fronterizo*, as the Guardia Civil interchangeably called the barrier, seemed unconquerable.

Before the humanitarian spectacle, the Euro-African border had first been a fence. Until the early 1990s only patches of tangled and weed-strewn coils of barbed wire had marked the international boundaries around Ceuta and Melilla, but as Spain joined Schengen, they now became the European Union's only terrestrial borders in Africa. With the marking of the E.U. border arrived new, Europe-bound migrants. These migrants—bedraggled, poor, black, of uncertain origin or destination—were quite unlike the Moroccan laborers, Indian merchants, and Andalusian workers who had entered the enclaves in an earlier era. As their numbers grew, so did the fences. First these were flimsy affairs, easily cut open or washed away by the rains. As more migrants arrived, the fences were slowly fortified with the help of E.U. money. Galvanized steel mesh eventually rose more than three meters above the ground, undulating across Ceuta's hills and Melilla's plains. Sensors, cameras, and bright spotlights were strung out around the perimeters. Migrants were pushed onto other routes, across the Strait and to the eastern Canaries, where Emilio and his Red Cross colleagues tended to them.

FIGURE 11. Between Ceuta's twin fences, July 2010. Photo by author.

Then came the 2005 asaltos with which this book began: hundreds of migrants "storming" towards the fences, leaving at least fourteen dead in soldiers' gunfire and many more expelled to the desert. Soon after, the barrier was strengthened yet again. The valla—triple fencing in Melilla, double in Ceuta—eventually towered six meters above the ground, enclosing the enclaves in a perfect armory. There is a before-and-after-2005 in Ceuta and Melilla, with the fence as its memento, like a vast scar etched into the hills.[21]

Walls and fences increasingly circle nervous polities, attempting to guard against the "lawlessness lapping the edges of nation-states," as the border theorist Wendy Brown puts it in her seminal study *Walled States, Waning Sovereignty.* The U.S.-Mexican border is now sealed by physical barriers and "virtual" fencing that stretch from the Pacific Ocean to the mouth of the Rio Grande. The Israeli "security barrier" undulating through Palestinian olive groves seeks to keep terrorists out, while its more recent counterpart between the Sinai and Negev Deserts targets African refugees and migrants. On the Greek-Turkish land border, a similar anti-migration fence has been erected. These fortifications are not meant to keep out the armies that have traditionally threatened the polity. Instead they target transnational threats—including, most strikingly and prominently, the clandestine migrant.[22]

To some critical border scholars, the main purpose of such barriers is broadcasting deterrence rather than guarding against the dangers lurking outside them. Brown goes further than this, seeing them as monuments of folly to the waning sovereignty of nation-states and, with a Freudian twist, as a "psychic defense against systemic failures." In unsuccessfully defending against the dangers that threaten to penetrate the nation, these barriers reinstate the sacred aspects of sovereignty in producing "an imago of the sovereign and his protective capacities." Nation-state walls, Brown concludes, are "modern-day temples housing the ghost of political sovereignty," conferring magical protection against incomprehensible powers.[23]

The awe-inducing vallas seem, at first glance, to prove Brown right: as a show for anthropologists, E.U. delegates, the media, and other select visitors they were unbeatable. Yet as at the sea border, their show was partial and incomplete. What fell outside the spectacle was in fact what rendered the vallas so effective.

Ceuta and Melilla's history in walling out unwanted outsiders goes back to the times before the vallas. As African garrison outposts and penal colonies *(presidios)* since before the Spanish colonial period in northern Morocco, the enclaves have always been sites where central state ideology clashes with the messy realities of the frontier.[24] From within Melilla's medieval city walls, the Spaniards organized raids on Rifian Berbers, who in turn raided and laid siege to the enclave. Despite these *razzias,* intense cross-frontier trade also developed between enclaves and hinterland. Since Morocco's independence, tension and trade have likewise fluctuated, with one constant: Rabat's nonrecognition of Spanish sovereignty over the enclaves. This is the context in which the vallas incongruously emerged in the past two decades as a protection against new transnational "threats": unlike the old city walls and moats, they defended not against Moroccan tribesmen or soldiers but against the sub-Saharan (and Asian) avalancha.

For migrants, politicians, and police alike, the valla was indeed a near-sacred object of the kind evoked by Brown. For migrants, it was so in the most concrete sense: like the West Bank barrier or the old Berlin Wall, it was surrounded by lethal prohibitions. "It's untouchable," said Pepe, an NGO leader in Melilla and one of the foremost enemies of the border regime. If a migrant approached it, the Moroccan soldiers would shoot; if he managed to breach it, he would be informally returned to Morocco through doors in the fences. This was so because of the immense symbolic power of the vallas to Brussels and Madrid, Pepe said: "If you cannot safeguard ten kilometers of valla [Melilla's approximate terrestrial perimeter], how will you be able to control all of the E.U.'s terrestrial borders?" There, "the only objective is that not a single one passes," he said. "The statistics have to say zero entries when they send it up high."

As a result, the vallas were the dark side of the double act at the border. Here militarization took on its violent guise, inflected by the enclaves' martial past rather than by Red Cross humanitarianism. This militarization of the border incorporated not just the Guardia Civil and Moroccan forces but also the troublesome Spanish Legion and the Regulares del Rif, an indigenous force stemming from Spain's colonial past in northern Morocco; in the 2005 crisis at the vallas, both these forces were mobilized to seal the border.

Part 1: Mimesis

MELILLA, OCTOBER 2010. "It was here that it happened." Ramón had driven his Guardia Civil car to the edge of Melilla, where the enclave's border fence suddenly forked in two and then ended abruptly at a sheer drop down to the waves and coastal road far below. This was "Ao," the final section of Melilla's fence, more commonly known as *hito* 18 (boundary post 18), in reference to the official border radius traced by cannonballs fired in 1862 from central Melilla. Ramón was standing at the spot that Spain's Socialist vice president María Teresa Fernández de la Vega had visited five years earlier, on the eve of the 2005 asaltos. She was escorted round the fence when the guardias suddenly sensed imminent danger. Migrants were waiting in the undergrowth brushing against the Moroccan side of the fence. "Because of the smell we knew that people were hiding there," said Ramón. It could be "thousands of them," they advised the vice president, who was promptly escorted off-site. After her dramatic experience at the border, the government decided to make new fencing, which would initially cost twenty million euros and would swiftly rise even higher.[25]

As border controls and discourses have become militarized in Ceuta and Melilla, so has migrant praxis in a play of reflection and mimesis ricocheting from forest hideouts on the Moroccan-Algerian border to the control rooms of Madrid and Rabat. Guardias noted how the early arrivals of the 1990s gradually lost their fear, their tactics changing along with those of border guards and the gradual growth of the fences. The migrants created intricate communities in the hills outside the enclaves, with structures of *chairmen,* or rotating leaders, for each national community, UN-styled "blue helmets" to keep the peace, and democratic structures for decision making. As Moroccan security forces stepped up harassment in 2005, the migrants' organizational prowess was diverted towards the border. Here the very materiality of the fences helped trigger the asalto masivo, since a critical mass—a horde—was now needed to climb them. "The only way to enter is on a mass scale; if not they cannot climb the fences," acknowledged one Guardia Civil comandante. The words that migrants, guardias, and journalists used for these attempts were, incidentally, the same—*attack* and *asalto.*[26]

Pierre from Cameroon was one of the organizers of the 2005 *grande attaque* from the slopes of Mount Gurugú, the mythical hill outside Melilla. It was the Spaniards who rigged the trap, he said, retelling his story in Mali's capital, Bamako, where he and many other adventurers had ended up after the ensuing ordeal. The Alis (Moroccan auxiliary forces) came to speak to their chairmen in the hills, assuring them that the next morning the coast would be clear. They should know—they were in constant contact with the guardias. Migrants started preparing. "We gave the Alis some whisky and Nigerian women," said Pierre, with no signs of remorse. It was the law of the jungle. Then they made their way downhill. First went the *cibleurs* (scouts, "targeters") who surveyed the terrain, then came the men with the ladders, then the women. They went in stages, advanced a bit at a time. When they arrived close to the fence, helicopters were circling above. Someone had betrayed them that night. Someone—they never knew who—had called the guardia chief, selling the information for passage to Spain. Then the Moroccan forces pounced. The migrants fanned out, Pierre escaping into the underbrush and onwards to the border village of Farhana. He tried to hide in a black refuse sack, but someone was already inside. It was an *ancien soldat* (old soldier), Pierre explained, the term for those who had tried to attack the valla several times without luck. He chose another refuse sack, and next day the two decided to "attack the town." The metaphor points to how far clandestine migrants have militarized the simplest daily acts, such as crossing a residential area without being detected. They made it into the forest, though their safety would not last. The Moroccans were searching the bushes and border hamlets, eventually catching Pierre in a shop. Forced expulsion awaited in one of the big buses he had seen leaving the forest in the aftermath of the attaque. Activists and journalists trailed them, trying to record their forced removal. They were told to get off in the Sahara, and two pieces of cloth were laid on the ground. "Walk between them, straight ahead," the soldiers said, "and you will get to Algeria." The sands to the sides were mined. Pierre's tragic adventure had just begun. It would continue through Western Sahara, Mauritania, Senegal, and Mali, where he was still stranded five years on.

Pierre's recollections, however partial, point to the shared militarism of the border language among security forces and migrants, as well as to their intricate social links. These were not the only groups acting in agonistic concert across the valla, however. The Red Cross attended to the wounded at the fences and in the enclaves' reception centers. In 2005, activists and aid workers such as Pepe had entered the hills of Gurugú and Ben Younech outside Melilla and Ceuta with provisions, and soon news teams arrived as well. Demand was rocketing for images and stories such as the one Pierre had told me. As the attacks reached their denouement, seemingly tipped-off journalists were already mingling among the soldiers.[27] One Spanish journalist had come to Gurugú before the grande attaque and offered to pay migrants if they would go and attack the fence so that he could film it. "He went to speak to the Cameroonians, who do anything for money," recalled one Melilla veteran in Bamako. The Cameroonian adventurers agreed, attacked, and failed, their bruising filmed by the cameraman, like tragic reality show contestants.

As controls extended away from the vallas with greater efficacy after 2005, other militarization effects also appeared on migrant circuits. Sites of departure were called striking points; migrant ghettos became known as bunkers. "The adventure—it's like going to war," said one Melilla veteran, "and we're like soldiers." Militarization also reached into the social circuits of the adventure. Nigerian smuggling rings— known as the "task force" or the Taliban, replete with fearsome "commandos"—had set up their own bunkers, including a "prison" in Rabat, where migrants were taken hostage until relatives paid up. The "mafias" that officials kept referring to were coming into existence thanks to the very controls supposed to fight them. The only routes that remained relatively free from organized smugglers, however, were precisely those where the Spanish government accused them of dumping migrants—the short sea route into the enclaves, or across the Strait over their fences. Here a crossing attempt was mainly dependent upon the traveler's own wit, strength, and cunning.

With the help of European money, the vallas, seemingly a sharp divide, had become a medium for increased cross-border cooperation. They acted as a catalyst in a militarized alignment of fence technology, Moroccan forces, guardias, journalists, and migrants. Yet, unlike at sea, this mixing and hybridization were hidden from view. Here the show was wholly the fence itself, its glistening and tall steel divide, its promise of absolute separation.

While showing it off, guardias constantly had to shield its darker workings from view by escorting the audience off the scene, much as they had done with the Spanish vice president before the 2005 "assaults." Once the audience departed, a visceral reality replaced the visual splendor of the vallas. The smell of migrants, the touch of their hands on the cool steel mesh, and the sound of their advance became incorporated into the very fabric of the fence, and so was the guardias' ambivalence in their double role as guardian angels and gatekeepers of the external border.

Part 2: Ambivalence

What one guardia called a double standard *(doble moral)* suffused the show of force at the border. He did not elaborate on what he meant, but he hardly had to. Locals still reminisced about how, during the 2005 *saltos* (jumps) preceding the final autumn attacks, black men staggered into central Melilla with gaping wounds. In Ceuta, aid workers saw migrants arrive with gashes that looked like "when you slice a chicken fillet." Rafael, the Spanish correspondent, pegged his memories of 2005 on the deadly razor wire. "Some of them were just hanging there, looking like chorizos."

Melilla's new valla was the star in the range of "advanced security solutions" offered by the Spanish company Proytecsa; it was, in the words of the Socialist vice president, not only "more efficient" but also less harmful and aggressive than the one it replaced.[28] Planned for both enclaves, the "humane" fence was eventually erected only in Melilla, leaving Ceuta with its newly fortified but still "aggressive" razor wire. Thankfully, there the border was hidden from view in hilly terrain traced by the guardias' closed perimeter road.

The "double standard" was built into the very fabric of the Melilla fence. As in Eurosur and the Spanish radar and satellite systems, technology was waved as a magic wand, promising migration controls shorn of violence and politics. The external fence was inclined outwards, making climbing it more difficult and limiting the need for razor wire, most of which had been removed in 2007 to media fanfare.[29] Those who still managed to climb the outer fence faced a moveable upper panel that, once movement was detected, descended and trapped them underneath. If the climbers made it into the middle section, they soon found themselves snared in an intricate mesh of metal cables known as the *sirga tridimensional*. The sirga tensed upon contact in order to immobilize the migrant, like an insect in a spider's web. If against all predictions the intruder got past this mesh, next was a lower middle fence; then, finally, the inner fence, again six meters tall. "It's sold as not being harmful," said Ramón about the sirga, adding defensively, "Those who would have to make sure it isn't are the politicians or the company [Proytecsa]." Sensors and cameras (104 in total) detected any movement along the fence. In the event of a bigger asalto, peppered water would be sprayed upon the attackers, accompanied by disorientating sharp flashes of light. "It has never had to be used, thank God," said Ramón.

Along sea routes, humanitarianism—on display in the rescue images—helped border guards overcome any qualms about having to play "the role of the baddie." Enrique, the Spanish policeman stationed in Africa, recalled a row with a Red Cross worker. "I asked her, who has saved more lives, you or me? You give them blankets, something to eat, and so on when they arrive in the Canary Islands, but we are out there rescuing people." The police work was "99 percent humanitarian," he said: "What I want to do is to save lives. . . . I might have been the baddie but my conscience is clear." The guardias along the fences, however, could not invoke such a humanitarian role. From the valla, no comandante-edited video collages emerged trying to put the record straight.

Attempts to gloss over the cracks between humanitarianism and violence, between the guardian angel and gatekeeper roles, took unexpected expression at times. Along the restricted road at hito 18, cut-off water bottles had been tied to the fencing. "It's something they [guardias] put there for the birds to drink," Ramón explained. The tenderness of the gesture contrasted brusquely with the three layers of fencing, the razor wire and soldier cubicles, and the grills blocking rivulets and streams flowing into the enclaves. In its privileging of wildlife over people, the gesture also recalled other attempts to humanize the walls around the West, whether in concerns over the free flow of animals across the U.S.-Mexico barrier or over the threat that Australia's refugee detention center on the remote Christmas Island poses to the welfare of migrating crabs.[30]

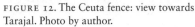

FIGURE 12. The Ceuta fence: view towards Tarajal. Photo by author.

FIGURE 13. Close-up of the Ceuta fence from the Moroccan side. Photo by author.

The cables, wires, sensors, and cameras—not to mention the birds' water bottles—did not remove violence from border controls. "They market the valla as an obstacle," said Pepe, in reference to Guardia Civil claims that the fence gave them only a few extra minutes. "But it's not an obstacle; it's a hunter's trap." Migrants had fallen onto the *sirga* and been ripped open; ambulances could not enter between the fences. Instead the new valla achieved something else. It grasped the intruder via the smallest bodily signs—footsteps, breath, odors, noises, hands on wire. Unlike at sea, these physical and visceral signs fell within, not without, the border regime. The migrant's hand was not there to grasp, but set off an alarm in the control room; his smell signaled not misery but danger. The visceral and the visual here combined in a backroom show meant only for the guardias in the Ceuta and Melilla control rooms, who saw red lights illuminated on their digital maps once a furtive bodily sign activated the valla's sensors.

The valla was sensitive to the smallest poke or caress, like a skin tingling with nerve ends. Along Ceuta's fence, a guardia watchman had opened the doors and let us into Morocco. Razor wire adorned the outer fence: coiled into concertinas of knife-sharp spikes, it staggered up for several meters. Teniente Federico pointed to the sensors snaking through the layers of steel mesh, cables, and military-grade razor wire. They set off the alarm easily, he said, so the guardias would use cameras or binoculars "to see whether it is an animal, a *negro* (black man), or a *mokhazni* (Ali)." If the thermal cameras spotted an intruder at night, the Alis would be contacted to scour the bushes with patrol dogs. Sometimes the Moroccan soldiers "pass right by without seeing them," he said. But the guardias guided the Alis with their night vision: "You have them at your feet now, you're almost stepping on them!"

The fence technology and its networked manpower—the "living system" of the valla, as Ramón called it—provided more than just the "magical" protection explored by Wendy Brown. It was effective, but only in a peculiar manner intimately related to the border spectacle. Above all, the vallas had steered the horde away from the land border, making it reappear instead as a huddle of rescuable migrants at sea. It had also reproduced the prey-like presence familiar from the borderlands in the internal workings of the vallas, where the traces left by lone migrants were easily confused with those left by gusts of wind, wild animals, or straying Moroccan soldiers. The vallas had, moreover, fomented a trickle of clandestine entries into the enclaves by sea and via the official border posts. However, images depicting such methods— heads sticking out of car seats, the migrants' bodies replacing the upholstery; barely glimpsed body parts soldered into the underbelly of trucks; migrants on Jet Skis or hydropedals in the Strait—were but part of the border workers' curiosity cabinet. The spectacle was under control.

This success came at a substantial cost. "The valla is almost a bottomless pit," Teniente Federico said in Ceuta. No matter how much money was poured in, more was always needed for the constant upkeep—bringing big profits for security companies, as well as more staff and resources for the Guardia Civil, whose primary task in the enclaves was the "sealing" *(impermeabilización)* of the border.

There were also social consequences. The low-ranking guardias charged with keeping the migrant avalanche at bay grumbled about tough working conditions and the uncertain legal status of their interventions. Besides such professional complaints, the sealing of the border has also created larger dilemmas. If the European Union has increasingly come to resemble a gated community, Ceuta and Melilla are its most concrete manifestation. As ethnographers have noted, the gating of wealthy enclaves is a contradictory enterprise: aimed at shutting dangers out, they may help foment the very fears they guard against.[31]

Among these fears was not just an impending avalanche but also grow-ing tensions with the walled-out neighbors. In Melilla, Pepe explained with some relish, the boundary markers, or hitos, were now outside the fence. Because of Moroccan protestations on entering "their" territory to construct the valla—notwithstanding the no-man's-land officially circling the enclaves—Spain had had to cede ground. This meant, Pepe said, that when a migrant ran towards the fence and started to climb it, the Alis would shoot or fight him back in what was, really, Spain.

These problems added to the Guardia Civil officers' ambivalence in showing off the vallas. While Federico had reeled off a list of official visits, he admitted he might not last long in Ceuta because of the claus-trophobia produced by this very barrier. In Melilla, Ramón remarked that some people compared the valla with the Gaza–West Bank wall. "I don't think so, there's no other way to . . ." His sentence trailed off, unfinished. Heading away from the cliffside, he talked about the Melilla of his childhood, pointing to the pristine coves across the fence. "There I used to go swimming as a child," he said. "We caught fish with our bare hands." He fell silent for a moment. "Migration has closed this city a lot; it has transformed it." Relations with Morocco had worsened because of the valla, he acknowledged, even though the fence was only meant against the subsaharianos and asiáticos. Then Ramón switched gear, with a newfound certainty. "It seems we are always on the defen-sive," he said. "But well, get rid of the fence then; let millions of people come!"

Ramón had confirmed Pepe's talk of the valla as the new "de facto border" without much elaboration as he drove along it. Up against the Melilla fence on the Moroccan side were the sentry boxes of the Alis. The Moroccans had advanced, snapping up the few meters of ceded ter-ritory. The same process was under way at the official Beni Enzar cross-ing, where the no-man's-land had been gradually occupied. A Forces Auxiliaires sign even hung on the Spanish side of the dry Río de Oro, just outside the official entrance to Spain. And this is where the next instalment in the spectacle at the vallas would play out in the summer of 2010.

Part 3: The Spectacle Hijacked

As Ramón drove along the fence, the noise grew louder and louder. Sud-denly we turned a corner and there it was, in all its glory: Barrio Chino, a zone of warehouses and hangars on the outskirts of Melilla. The whole area heaved with adrenaline-fueled waiting, walking, packing, shouting, queuing, and scuffling. Walkways undulated along the fence, and along them old women staggered towards the gates, double-bent with huge bundles on their backs and parcels roped to their bellies: coiled-up mattresses, bulks of toilet-paper rolls, packets of underwear. A young man tried to squeeze past, and a scuffle ensued; one guardia hit out with his baton indiscriminately. Further ahead, another guardia shouted at a restive congregation of men perching on top of their parcels. Once they got the go-ahead they would roll bundles of blankets or tires coiled into one another uphill, like huge dice. Ramón sighed. *"Sin novedades en el Barrio Chino"* (no news from Barrio Chino) is the best thing you can hear when returning to the comandancia.

The *porteadores* (porters), like the day laborers streaming into the enclaves, were allowed to enter without a visa in what was an exception to Schengen rules for residents of the neighboring Moroccan provinces of Nador and Tetuan. They queued from early morning at special entrances in the fences and would then be sent through walkways to the shopping hangars on the Spanish side. The ensuing pandemonium was on display not just in Melilla's Barrio Chino but in Ceuta as well. "Atypical commerce," Ramón labeled it, using an official euphemism. "If they don't do this, what would they live off?" Their illicit trade was also the lifeline of the enclaves and of bribe-extracting Moroccan officers. The value of the border trade in Ceuta alone has been estimated at €1–1.5 billion a year, or up to 70 percent of its economic activity.[32]

The arrangement by which goods moved out without Spanish controls, while Moroccan forces were meant to curb any illicit movement of people on their side, was unbalanced to say the least. The valla tipped the scales further, yet not in the negative economic sense at times asserted for other fortified borders. By channeling the border trade, the valla had boosted business in making the step in the value chain even steeper.[33] The point of tension rather concerned its effect on the workers, carriers and traders—in short, the humiliation of the valla.

The valla was a tale of two animalized flows: domesticated herds at officially sanctioned crossings, feral hordes away from them. "Look!" exclaimed an NGO worker as she drove past the fenced-in walkways in Melilla. "We are not animals!" The ignominy of being forced through such corridors "like cattle" affected Moroccan nationals rather than Spaniards, and some of the latter defended the fences as a necessary evil. The aid worker's *we*, however, referred to a cross-border identity underpinned by the enclaves' official view of themselves as havens of *con-*

vivencia (peaceful coexistence) among their Christian, Muslim, Jewish, and Hindu communities. While this view had always contrasted with a reality of discrimination, things were hardly made better by the valla. The setting was ripe for protest.

In July 2010 it came. Moroccan activists decried racist mistreatment of their countrymen at Melilla's border post of Beni Enzar and promptly launched demonstrations at the valla. Civil society organizations, which many observers suspected of being agents of the Moroccan secret police, blocked the importation of cement, bricks and fresh produce. Activists plastered posters across the border area that mocked Spanish police-women, whom they accused of insulting its citizens.[34] Spain's conservative opposition leader and premier-to-be, Mariano Rajoy, visited Melilla, journalists thronging around him and hunting angry activists at the border. Meanwhile, in an unusual move, Morocco accused the Guardia Civil of abandoning sub-Saharan migrants on a raft outside Ceuta.[35] Along with these tensions came an influx of clandestine migrants into Melilla at a rate not seen in years, prompting speculation in the Spanish Congress and media about Morocco letting them through, flung like projectiles into the enclave in their improbable, inflatable "toy" boats.

If this was so, it was hard to know exactly what the Moroccans wanted. The status of Ceuta and Melilla, as well as of Western Sahara, remained an open wound in Spanish-Moroccan relations. Added to these concerns were rumors of outstanding E.U. aid, as well as royal whims. The Moroccan king, holidaying near Melilla, had been annoyed by the military helicopters roaring past towards the Spanish-occupied islands and outcrops scattered around the northern Moroccan coast. These tiny *plazas de soberanía* (sovereign places) had, like Ceuta and Melilla, been held by Spain for hundreds of years yet had long been claimed by Rabat. To these political issues were added the smaller ones at Melilla's border, where alleged mistreatment was not the only problem. The valla imperiled the old order of small bribes and big gains, the life blood of the frontiersmen around Melilla. For the protesters, the Spanish policewomen were a convenient target in representing the Europeanization of Melilla's border; the sub-Saharan migrants, meanwhile, could serve as a weapon to enforce their aims. At the valla, uninvited actors were hijacking the border spectacle for their own purposes on behalf of a larger geopolitical order.

By late August, the Spanish interior minister had visited Rabat, and mutual "misunderstandings" had been corrected. Upon this followed the expulsions in which Daouda, the skin-cream salesman, was caught up in the previous chapter, as well as protests reverberating *within* the enclaves, as will be seen in the next.

Despite the Spanish security forces' insistence that relations with their Moroccan colleagues were excellent, they often repeated, "If migrants pass, it's because they want them to pass." Mehdi, the Moroccan director of border controls, diplomatically made clear the enclaves were pull factors *(facteurs d'appel)* for migrants. "They can put cameras, they can put whatever they want. But the truth is that it's not sufficient if you cannot stop these flows upstream. . . . Once you have them in Melilla and Ceuta, that's it; you get stuck with them, that's it."

The valla did not detract from the enclaves' attraction; instead, it raised the stakes. Like the gating around a community, it marked out Ceuta and Melilla as wealthy havens and potential sites of protest. As a spectacle in itself, it attracted not only migrants but also groups with varied grievances—including, besides the Moroccan nationalists, transnational activists protesting against the E.U. border in annual commemorations of the 2005 tragedies.

In guarding against the migrant horde, the valla had created a new set of problems. Placard wavers, marchers, and merchants could now deploy the ancient technique of the siege at the fences. This did not deter the valla, however, which simply drew more groups into its embrace. The Alis' sentry boxes snuggling up against the fences, the journalists, activists, and agitators congregating near it, the restive crowds at Barrio Chino or gathered along the border walkways all became participants in the network created by an ever-more intricate anti-migration barricade. The insatiable valla kept growing; the spectacle unfolding in its shadow was no longer under the control of its presumed directors.[36]

Part 4: Backstage Entrance

It was Amadou's final attempt at the Ceuta fence. He had guided a group of four over the mountain passes at night. By now he knew everything. The weather had to be right. It should be raining or cold, since the soldiers were then less likely to be out; windy, so that the dogs did not smell you; and foggy, to reduce the guards' visibility. They should climb one of the highest passes, where not even soldiers entered but where falling meant death. They had to be utterly silent, Amadou admonished his companions. Look, the fence! It was so close. A noise escaped one of the nervous migrants, limiting their options and forcing them to attack, even though the guardias were patrolling along the other side of the razor wire.

By now, Amadou had understood each component part, each sense, of the valla—sniffing guard dogs, the watchmen's routines, the yielding razor wire, the sensors and poles and doors, the concertina and wire mesh. He was ready to take the valla system apart, as a skilled car mechanic dismembers a vehicle.

Amadou and his companions went one by one. To cross, you needed to put on old clothes. New garments snagged on the razor wire. You must wear cotton, not nylon. You had to use gloves to push the concertina, then you put your foot on top of it, to avoid it catching your clothes. Blades might cut into your arms or legs, but you had to avoid getting caught in the stomach or crotch. On the top, the razor wire could entangle and kill you, but there was a trick for getting through. Then you needed to find a pole along the inside of the fence instead of getting nervous and jumping, breaking bones. It was a six-meter fall. Amadou slid down a pole. He looked around quickly. Where was the door? In the prison in Tetuan, the nearest Moroccan city, other adventurers had told him about the doors in the inner fence. Amadou had not been sure they existed until, on an earlier attempt, guardias had entered through a door and expelled him back to Morocco. Now he spotted such a door. The trick, he had been told, was to find a small opening in it, big enough for your head. If the head went in, the body did too. Amadou crawled through. He had heard of a dog kennel, la perrera, where migrants used to hide from the guardias. In search of the kennel, he made his way into the hills, finally into Spain. He had crossed the most difficult of borders.

CURTAIN CALL: BEYOND THE SPECTACLE

This chapter has shown the spectacle of the crossing in its double act. In the first act, it is a rescue of the huddle sinking below the diffuse sea border. In the second act—in fact the primordial border act—the crossing is a violent repelling of the horde at the sharply drawn land border. Between the acts, chairs have been shuffled. Some actors have been relegated to the wings, and others have entered for a heroic appearance. Yet the cast is nearly the same. What changes are the props, and the scenery, and the modalities of illegality that are produced in the encounter.

It is worth dwelling for a moment on the visual order of the spectacle and on what it leaves out of the realities of the crossing—the central theme of this chapter. The spectacle can be split according to the spatial dichotomy of officialdom, and so can its intended audiences. On the sea border, the spectacle is centered not only on the rescued migrant but also on the hybrid arrangements enabling his rescue: the overlap of Red Cross emblems, Guardia Civil launches, and Salvamento boats spectacularly rendering up the life-saving state at its maritime limits for a domestic and international audience. On land, both the migrant and the mixing are off-scene, save for a Red Cross cameo or two. Here, instead, the spectacle is the border itself—the fence in all its awesomeness, not the intricate social network of the valla—and its foremost audience is the European paymasters. At sea the border imagery circulates widely; on land its circuits are circumscribed and tabooed. At sea appears the rescuable huddle, on land the frightening horde.[37]

These categories are far from static and clear-cut, however. They change according to electoral cycles, media storylines, and migrant routes and in accordance with differing terrains and technologies. In Spain's crisis-hit summer of 2012, rescue imagery was briefly reduced to the simplest of messages—Red Cross volunteers wrapping migrants in blankets in an upbeat Coca Cola–sponsored advertisement, encouraging TV audiences to get the country moving.[38]

Such rescue images render up the "fetish" of migrant illegality, in De Genova's term, through two complementary transformations depending on the potency—itself fetish-like—of the image. The double act of the border spectacle here seems to create Agamben's twin figures of *homo sacer:* the vulnerable huddle and the rights-less horde, those who can be saved and those left to die. Yet Agamben cannot get us far here. As one critic has noted, "Agamben is less interested in life than in its 'bareness.'" This bareness says little about either the differentiations in migrant illegality at the border or its economic and spectacular uses explored in this chapter.[39]

The spectacle is further complicated by what remains outside the visual order—the illicit mixing, the smells and noises, and the fantasies and fears that cannot be fully captured on-screen. These backstage features highlight how the spectacle is incomplete, conflictive, and always in excess. No single story triumphs. Unwelcome actors—Moroccan nationalists, transnational activists, critical aid workers—stand ready to jump onto the stage. Journalists, the tricksters of the illegality industry, always seek new angles to expose and complicate the official story—yet always risk being framed by that same story or by a new version of it. The travelers and smugglers of the borderlands, trickster-like too, at times seek the border spotlight for a coup de théâtre, at other times a silent backstage entry, like Amadou.

Aid workers and border guards also struggle with what is left in and out of the spectacle and with their own roles in it. They recall the reek of an approaching patera, the haunting mirada, the screams and the outstretched hands of boat migrants. For the most fundamental mixing in the crossing is that which escapes both the spectacle and any bare formulations of life in its bareness: the brief encounter of the drowning or climbing or running man and the person in his path, who meet not as border guard and *ilegal*, humanitarian and huddling sub-Saharan, but as two people joined in the strangest of encounters beyond the full grasp of either.

. . .

In the summer of 2012, something disconcerting was happening at the Melilla fence. Seven years after the "massive assault," the migrants were back again. In the dead of night, Spanish media reported, up to five hundred sub-Saharan migrants approached the fence en masse, only to be "repelled" at the last minute by Moroccan gendarmes. The Spanish government delegate in the city thanked Morocco for its "magnificent collaboration" while warning that the mass entry attempts would continue. And they did: by autumn, it was clear that the horde had returned, thrusting the vallas back into the spotlight. Over the coming year, at times this horde came in the form of "kamikaze" cars packed with migrants, ramming their way through Melilla's border crossing; at other times, it appeared in ever-more spectacular entries across the fence as migrants stripped off their clothes, ran through the streets, and sought refuge in public buildings—and even an opposition politician's home— to avoid capture and expulsion back into the Alis' hands. And then, in July 2013, two migrants died in yet another mass entry attempt, one on each side of the border.[40]

The tenor of the "attacks" was easy to explain. Just as in 2005, they been preceded by months of raids and expulsions. Moroccan media had fanned a moral panic with talk of a "black peril," with some commentators even accusing sub-Saharan Africans of being mercenaries, invoking the Libya uprising and tapping into the militarized discourse of the border. As relations between Madrid and Rabat improved in 2012, repression kept increasing—as did the desperate entry attempts. The pattern from 2005 and 2010 was being repeated, culminating in the Melilla fence yet again being festooned with razor wire in late 2013.[41]

If the horde was back, so was the huddle. Yet it was no longer playing the role assigned to it in the border spectacle.

In early September 2012, an absurd sight greeted beachgoers and journalists outside the Moroccan seaside town of Al Hoceima. On the tiny, Spanish-held Isla de Tierra, within swimming distance from the Moroccan beach, eighty-one subsaharianos loitered in the sweltering sun. Clustered around the Spanish flag crowning the island, they were thrown food and drink by Spanish soldiers, snapped by photographers, and bartered by politicians, who for several days did not know what to do with them. If they were transferred elsewhere in Spain, more would come; if the government asserted that the migrants were *not* in Europe, this backed up Morocco's claim to the "occupied" territories. Rabat had already protested at a Spanish plan to post Guardia Civil officers to its plazas de soberanía for migration control. The situation was delicate.[42]

Isla de Tierra, "island of land," was an aptly named setting for a brief third act in the border spectacle. The migrants had sought out a border space combining the logics of sea and land, where the careful split of humanitarian and militarized borders no longer applied. The Spanish government denounced the "humanitarian blackmail" of the "mafias" it accused of having dumped the migrants there. Besides a hard conservative line on migration, this accusation also revealed a growing frustration at how the state's co-optation of humanitarianism, so carefully constructed under the previous Socialist government, was itself being co-opted from below in a radical new fashion.

Thanks to the Moroccan king's intervention, a solution to the standoff was finally reached. Under cover of darkness, Guardia Civil officers hauled the migrants off Isla de Tierra and into Moroccan hands, invoking the countries' bilateral readmissions agreement from 1992, which was now finally entering into force. The usual deportation route ensued, to Oujda with its waiting Spanish journalists. In the media's blurry pictures from the darkened beach, however, the violent backstage workings of the border had finally been rendered visible, if only for a brief moment.

Backstage violence was soon to become constant prime-time news. In December 2013, Madrid was again festooning the "humane" Melilla fence with razor wire, to protests from Brussels. Two months later, fifteen migrants drowned as they tried to swim around Ceuta's fence; then citizen videos emerged, showing how guardias had fired rubber bullets into the cold February waters. Unapologetic, the interior minister claimed 80,000 migrants were waiting to cross into Spain and asked for more E.U. funds to stop them. As word circulated of further reinforcements, migrants launched the largest entry attempts since 2005 in Melilla. Some of them lingered for hours atop the fences, where they chanted and waved to cameras and guardias, briefly putting off their inevitable expulsion. Straddling worlds, they—like Isla de Tierra's migrants or Ceuta's tragic swimmers—were neither huddle nor horde, stuck on the threshold of the border in its deadly double act.[43]

Another limbo awaited those who breached the frontier. For if migrants kept filling the enclaves' reception centers, creating a headache for the authorities, many of them had in the case of Ceuta in fact been *diverted* there after trying to reach the Spanish mainland across the Strait. Those so "rescued" soon found themselves incorporated into the enclaves' new role on the migratory circuit: as offshore processing centers. Fences and walls, border theorists have observed, might shut out the unwanted but can also serve to keep people in. This is what was happening in Ceuta and Melilla.[44]

The guardias manning Madrid's control room had made note of a strange border crossing in 2011. In February that year, a Malian migrant in Ceuta had tried to climb the fence, bent on reentering Morocco. The migrant, detained by the Guardia Civil, said he had spent four years in the enclave and just wanted to go home.[45] It is to this entrapment within the valla, and the unbearable tension it created, that we will now turn.

PART THREE

Confrontations

CHAPTER 5

White Mother, Black Sons

The summer of 2010 had begun hotter than usual. The easterly Levante winds enveloped Ceuta in a humid haze for days, and the Rock receded from view across the Strait of Gibraltar. All people talked about was the muggy, relentless heat. The *caballas* (mackerels), as the enclave's inhabitants are known, laid themselves out to sunbathe on the beaches facing the Mediterranean to the east or the windswept Atlantic towards the west. But up on the hill, far beyond the prime stretches of sand and the whitewashed town center with its tapas bars and churches—as far as way as possible on Ceuta's seven square miles of land—a different reality was unfolding. The eight prefabricated modules hastily erected back in 2000 to cater to a growing number of clandestine migrants kept the heat in and its residents out in daytime. And the temperature was inexorably rising.

The tragic mass "assaults" in the autumn of 2005 had not only reconfigured the policing of the fences but had also sparked a new strategy for fighting illegal migration *within* the enclaves. Instead of sending migrants on to mainland Spain and setting them free with an expulsion order, as had been the norm during the economic boom, a politics of containment was born. The idea was to "avoid making Ceuta and Melilla a trampoline towards the [Iberian] peninsula," according to one migration lawyer. "Migrants here are being used as an example so that those who wish to enter do not do so." From having been springboards, Ceuta and Melilla became, in the words of police, activists, and lawyers alike, *ratoneras* or *trampas:* traps.

Entrapment makes Ceuta a prime migration laboratory for the authorities, journalists, aid workers, and researchers who converge there. Ceuta is a key site for regulating the irregular flows of people across the southern border of Spain and thus into the European Union. The brake put on migrants' mobility here makes them readily available for police raids, as well as for researchers and reporters on the hunt for stories, humanitarians seeking needy beneficiaries, and diplomatic missions enlisted to identify their citizens for deportation.

But in laboratories, experiments can go wrong.

The summer of 2010 was to be the moment when Ceuta's clandestine migrants—almost all black Africans—invaded the city, bringing a loud protest to the heart of this European outpost. It was not to last long. But Ceuta's brief summer of discontent reveals the contradictions in the European Union's migration policies: on humanitarianism versus control, on locking people up or setting them free, on hiding or parading society's undesirables, on fear or pity towards Europe's ultimate Other. This chapter is about the protest and its backstory of containment and despair among the immobilized migrants at Europe's southern borders. It is also about the progressive racialization and infantilization of illegal immigrants and the shades of black that defined their life in the enclave.

THE CAMP

The road wound uphill, past rubbish-strewn slopes lined with flattened Landerbräu beer cans, chocolate drink bottles, fag ends, and plastic bags. A long climb ensued, heavy steps in humid African heat, before reaching the hilltop gate. Flowerbeds and eucalyptus trees lined the perimeter fence. Next to the sun-flecked entrance with its security booth, a big sign indicated who was in charge of the reception center inside: the Spanish Ministry of Labor and Immigration and the State Secretariat for Immigration and Emigration, with financial support from the European Union. Three flags fluttered atop the fencing: blue and yellow for Europe, red and yellow for Spain, black and white for Ceuta. Migrants walked up to the turnstiles, swiping cards and resting their fingers on a reader. This was their home, the home of the homeless, where clandestine migrants found themselves stranded on their long journeys towards the north.

Migrants called it the Camp. The CETI, or Centro de Estancia Temporal de Inmigrantes—temporary reception center for immigrants— was separated from the rest of Ceuta by acres of forested hills and a few miles of coastal road. Unlike in the foreigners' detention centers of the

Spanish peninsula, the CIEs, the clandestine migrants and asylum seekers who lived here could freely come and go before the gates closed at night. They slept in eight prefab modules of eight rooms each, 8 dorm beds to a room: 512 beds in all. In early summer 2010 about four hundred people were staying in the camp, many of them for two to three years or more. By the end of the season, fresh arrivals would push the number over five hundred and beyond capacity.

Almost all of the residents were black Africans who had arrived after arduous journeys by foot and truck through deserts, by dinghy and makeshift rafts, using infinite cunning and determination. These travelers had been through what the camp's director called a "Darwinian selection" along the clandestine routes stretching deep into the Sahara. Only the strongest would arrive or even survive. Many had died in the desert, found themselves stranded in Morocco's "ghettos" and "bunkers" or been deported, penniless and paperless, to the dust bowl of northern Mali. The migrants in Ceuta were thus an exclusive crowd. Having finally breached the E.U. frontier, they thought fortune was smiling at them—but Ceuta, they soon found out, would only flash a grim grin of irony. Here a new role was designated for them, a new modality of migranthood that stood in sharp contrast to both their earlier adventurer selves and their wild incarnation on the other side of the border. As prime objects of scrutiny, intervention, and pity, they would become Europe's most abject Other, fully formed "illegal immigrants."

In *Managing the Undesirables,* Michel Agier has glimpsed a "return of the camps" to the borders of Europe, as well as a worldwide "extension and greater sophistication of various forms of camps that make up a mechanism for keeping away undesirables and foreigners of all kinds— refugees, displaced, 'rejected.'" In these camps, care and control interact in intricate ways through what Agier labels humanitarian government. The CETI, run under a mixed-management system in which the authorities leave much of the care work to aid organizations (particularly the Spanish Red Cross), is a "sorting center" in Agier's terms. Here migrants are screened, recorded, and assigned identity categories in an elaborate process of "flow management." As critical migration scholars have pointed out, such sorting centers serve as "airlocks" or "speed boxes" that regulate the flux of people according to the fickle needs of the European labor market. But as a sorting center or speed box, the CETI of Ceuta had one particularity: by the summer of 2010 the flow had been reduced to near zero. Almost no one was sent on to "the peninsula," as migrants and caballas referred to mainland Spain across the Strait.[1]

In calling it "the camp," the migrants explicitly likened the CETI to the refugee camps of Africa. They had a point. Refugee camps, ethnographers have noted, are usually characterized by their remoteness, their ambiguous status as transitory spaces, and the tight control over the movement of their residents, who are all presumed to be vulnerable. The same was true of the CETI. Liisa Malkki, in *Purity and Exile,* her study of Burundians in Tanzania, observes that refugees are people out of place, an aberration in the "national order of things." Because of this "polluting" nature they are relegated to the margins, the threshold of their host society. And on this threshold, the camp resident comes to be *constituted* as a refugee, that peculiar contemporary "object of knowledge and control" in humanitarian government. The Ceuta camp, as will be seen in this chapter and the next, worked similarly upon its reluctant residents; only it was not creating the refugee role to which many travelers aspired but rather producing an even more aberrant one in the national order of things—that of the illegal immigrant.[2]

In the summer of 2010, adventurers stuck in Ceuta would challenge the logic of the camp, but in doing so they flipped the coin of their nascent migranthood, embodying and confirming fears and stereotypes of the Other lodged deep in the Western "geography of imagination."[3] In Agier's terms, they went from being tolerated and contained to being rejected and deportable. Rather than being seen as innocent victims in need of education and integration, they came to incarnate European fears of the not-so-noble savage already glimpsed on the high seas and at the enclaves' fences: wild, dangerous, and out of control. Clues to the sudden switch in their fortunes will be sought in the contradictory interplay of fear and charity, camp space and city space, in Ceuta's summer of discontent, in which journalists, police, camp workers, and migrants were all to play a part.

SPAGHETTI AND CIGARETTES

3 JULY 2010—*EL FARO DE CEUTA*—LATEST HEADLINE: "TWO IMMIGRANTS INTIMIDATE AND HURT CETI SECURITY GUARDS AFTER URUGUAY-GHANA MATCH." NEXT DAY'S FRONT PAGE: "THE RINGLEADERS OF THE DISTURBANCE IN THE CETI WANTED TO STIR UP A REVOLT, ENCOURAGING OTHER MIGRANTS."[4]

The trouble had started with a cigarette. It was the time of the 2010 World Cup, and football fever was gripping migrants and caballas alike. Big plasma screens, suspended from the ceiling of the camp's canteen, had been showing the Uruguay-Ghana game. A spat erupted between a guard and a migrant who was smoking, and a brawl ensued. That, at least, was what migrants said. Ghana lost, tempers flared, and security guards were attacked, was how the local media portrayed it. Security guards had been hurt, and prosecutors were calling for stiff sentences for the supposed instigators. Meanwhile, a dozen or so failed Congolese asylum seekers had decided to camp outside the police *jefatura* (headquarters) in town, demanding transfer to the peninsula. The protesters curled up on cardboard spread across the pavement, in front of a row of suitcases covered by more cardboard to protect against the rains. "We would rather die than go back to the CETI," said their protest signs.

Discontent was brewing, but calm had been restored back at the camp. It was set out over two levels: upstairs lay the offices, and down two flights of steps, with dazzling views across the Strait and the taunting sight of the Rock of Gibraltar, lay the living quarters and a sports pitch. The upstairs parking lot was as desolate and sun-drenched as a de Chirico painting, furnace-like, the sun pounding down through the wispy clouds onto the asphalt. Around it lay an office building labeled *control*, classrooms, a health center, showers, and the canteen with its metal wipe-down tables and plasma screens. Occasionally a migrant would saunter up to the phone booths outside the canteen, put a hard-earned euro coin into the slot, and speak for a minute to relatives at home or in a future destination, in Cameroon or Catalonia. Messages rang out on the speakers set up around the camp. *Ding-ding-dong . . . "attention s'il vous plaît"* in French or "attention please" in English, followed by a list of migrants called to the office or to a class.

Mamá, as the residents called her with a fair amount of affection, sat at her desk in a bare office inside the *control* building, a map of Africa covering the wall behind. Her kind, tired eyes scanned documents on the desk: lists of the living modules below and the residents of each module scribbled into the appropriate slots. There were reports to send off, new arrivals to tick off, *bajas* (residents who had escaped to the peninsula) to cross out. She was one of three *técnicos,* as the female workers who did the rounds of the living modules were called. They were collectively known as the *madres* by camp colleagues and migrants, but none was more motherly than Mamá. Stern, smiling, and stressed in equal measure, she navigated a steady stream of nationalities, defused rows, sorted out residents' cleaning rotas, and accommodated new arrivals.

Mamá heated her coffee in the microwave and went out to smoke a cigarette on the landing behind *control,* looking down across the fence encircling the camp, where a steep slope gave way to the road below. "So you are here to study migration?" she asked me. "They are an object worthy of study," she said of the residents. She meant this not in the sense of "guinea pigs" but because of their experiences. You could see everything here: the best, the worst. Mamá had a final puff on her cigarette, flung her small bag over her shoulder, and took me downstairs. As a camp volunteer, I would get a rare view of that hotly sought object of study for journalists, researchers, police, and NGOs alike—the recently arrived illegal immigrant.

Downstairs, Cameroonian *makossa* music streamed out of speakers resting on the windowsill of a men's dorm, young men dancing to the beat in the doorway. Mamá went up and confronted one of them. She called him Comando or Guevara. He looked the part, all rebellious cool in black beret and shades, balancing a plastic glass with one hand as he swung the other in a lethargic dance move. Here he will be called El General, echoing the journalists' epithet for him during Ceuta's impending protests.[5] "You are endangering the special curfews for the *feria*!" Mamá exclaimed. The feria, or fair, was Ceuta's party week of the year—a seven-day extravaganza of *sevillanas* dancing, *fino* swigging, and funfair rides down at the port. The director had extended the curfew for the residents; normally it was back at 11:00 P.M., doors open at 7:00 A.M. El General did not care. His voice was a drawl, his breath smelled of alcohol. "I don't want to go to Spain; I want to go to the United States," he said in French. I translated. "Go wherever you want, but in here you have to follow the rules," Mamá said, pursing her lips. A friend intervened and pleaded, "We have been here a very long time," he said, "without girls, without drinking . . . at least a little bit of music!" The party people more or less fit the profile of the average camp resident: a twenty-six-year-old man, single, sub-Saharan, asylum seeker, and a *balsero* (having arrived in Ceuta by dinghy), with a stay of over one year. In 2005, the average stay had been three months. Now it was one and a half years.[6] It was a long time and was growing longer.

Mamá sniffed their drinks and inquired sternly if they had been drinking alcohol. No, they said. Her friendly face shrank into a sour grimace. She had moved into their room, a damp eight-bed dorm with scribblings from previous residents on the bare walls: *la vie est un combat,* "Kurdistan," "Love Jesus." She confronted the circle of Cameroonians around her. They were lying! "Are you Christians?" she asked.

"Why are you doing this?" She threatened them with sanctions and went off but only after doing a few impromptu dance moves. *Ah, maman!* they exclaimed. "Tell her how much we like her," quipped El General. A confrontation had been temporarily averted.

Mamá fought such small battles every day, and, next to music, laundry was a prime casus belli. Washing hung everywhere: on the railings next to the eight living modules and above the sports pitch, along the fences encircling the camp, and draped over the wooden benches, tables, and shrubberies scattered round the central courtyard. Mamá removed every piece of washing she found, day after day. She left towels in piles, waved bras in the air, and sometimes dropped trousers onto the sports pitch to teach residents the house rules once and for all. But next day the laundry was back. Its constant reappearance hinted at protest and at the residents' wish to occupy the space of this anonymous camp, making it the most unlikely of homes. "It's for the sun," the camp's female residents pleaded, but Mamá would have none of it. In Ceuta the state ran the show: migrants were no longer adventurers dependent on their own wit and cunning. Instead they were objects of state intervention in the uneasy mix of coercion and charity seen on Mamá's daily rounds.

While applying sanctions, calling the guards, and waving clothes about were coercive sides to the madres' work, tobacco was a symbol of charity and a sign of freedom in the camp. On her tours of the living modules Mamá pulled out her silver cigarette case and roommates queued up, each waiting for his turn. "I'm not permitted to give them anything," Mamá said. "No clothes, nothing. So at least I give them cigarettes. What else can I do?" Migrants soon learned the game. *"Cigarillo por favor, no trabajo, no dinero"* (cigarette please, no work, no money), they said as Mamá meandered her way around the lower reaches of the camp. Sometimes she had to correct them, telling them that, next time, say *"mamá, un cigarillo, por favor."* The young migrant would repeat with an unsure smile and pronunciation. *"Mama cigari-lo por favor."*

Mamá finally made her way up after our round of the modules. "I'm dying for a cigarette," she said. A final cigarette was getting soft in her hand. She never had the time to smoke it.

The work of the madres was hard and often thankless. Most caballas had little interest in the migrants' plight. Unlike the Red Cross emergency teams along the coasts, aid organizations laboring both outside and inside the gates had problems attracting volunteers. One worker said she had sometimes cried at night because of the impotence of seeing police deport residents they had worked with for months or years.

Mamá and her colleagues, though, found the energy to continue. She had learned much during her six years in the camp. "I have changed as a person; I am not the way I used to be," she said. Then small things kept the mood up. In her office, she flicked through her gray steel cabinet, looking for letters from former residents. There it was. A handwritten letter from a migrant who was now in Madrid. In a sprawling hand, it thanked everyone working in the camp. Now he was writing a book about "sub-Saharan migration" and wanted replies from the camp workers on topics of interest: the idea that migrants take jobs away from Spaniards, racism, and so on. Mamá treasured this handwritten letter. It was special. There was a second letter too, written on computer, that all workers had received a copy of. It was from an Indian migrant, who thanked everyone in perfect Spanish. The camp psychologist had helped him write it, Mamá explained. She found no more letters.

. . .

The CETI, to Mamá and her colleagues, was not a camp. She saw it as an *albergue,* a hostel. Migrants were there so they did not have to sleep on the streets. Workers simply referred to them as *residentes* or *usuarios,* residents or users. New arrivals signed a paper saying they were in the CETI of their own free will because they were unable to provide for themselves. This legal mechanism meant the camp, as an open center, was not covered by the same restrictions that applied to the CIEs in mainland Spain, where migrants could be held for only sixty days. The migrants received clothes upon arrival, free meals three times a day, and a bed free of charge. Even language courses, workshops, and sports were on the menu. "They have everything here," quipped a guard. Camp workers said the residents "don't know how bad things are in the peninsula," where *la crisis* was ravaging Spain's economy and social services.

As the CETI director put it, Spain gave a much better reception, or acogida, than its neighbors Italy and Malta. And only Spain, he said, carried out humanitarian rescue in the Strait. The CETI was a manifestation of the benevolent Spanish approach to migration honed in the Socialist years—humanitarianism not crackdowns, dialogue not dictates, integration instead of rejection. The implication was, simply put, that staying in the CETI was better than going hungry on the streets of Madrid, and both were preferable to being left to Berlusconi's devices.

Many residents appreciated the effort. "They are trying," they would concede. "The camp is not the problem," said one. "The camp is taking care of us but not of all that we need." Praise was showered on the new director, a former diplomat appointed after the demotion of his unpop-ular predecessor. Residents said he was an educated man. He wanted to help them. He took pregnant women to the hospital in his own car. He addressed migrants in French as *vous* and just as politely in English. He inquired about their health, organized sports sessions and paella out-ings, allowed soft drinks into the compound, and added some spice to the bland canteen food. But to the travelers fresh off their boats, the goodwill was dwarfed by their misery. They had just made it to Europe and expected the freedom to work, travel, and send money home. None envisaged idly living off handouts for years or spending their time on sexual health courses, drawing workshops, and *clases de alfabetización* (literacy classes), as the near-compulsory Spanish lessons were often called. At the camp, said one migrant, "you sleep, you eat, maybe you go to a Spanish class, you sleep a bit again . . ." It was not enough. "We are not newborns," he said angrily. "We are men."

The camp residents were in a bind: they were not permitted to work or move on and so had no choice but to accept any handouts coming their way. They had become charitable objects in the eyes of the *caballas*, and any discontent was interpreted as ingratitude. In a clumsy stab at affection, they had become known in town as the *negritos,* a diminu-tive of *negro,* which reflected their racialization and growing infantiliza-tion. This uneasy race talk accompanied the migrants' transformation into passive welfare recipients. "We are paying big amounts of money to knock them to bits, little by little," said Paula, a nun who was among the few critics of migration policy in Ceuta. "We are teaching them to become dependent on the Spanish benefits system."

The migrants navigated this fraught terrain of pity, charity, and rejec-tion by accepting the cigarettes while complaining of the food. The food at the camp was bad, they said. The rice was hard or overcooked. The fries were stale. The fruit juice was artificial. There was no spice. Always spaghetti, spaghetti, spaghetti. The ignominy of accepting handouts was most evident in the daily ritual of lining up in the canteen, beeping the entrance card, and getting a fill of bland slop—as they saw it—while watched upon by matronly kitchen staff and baton-equipped security guards. As a result African women's makeshift food stalls, offering cheap yet tastier fare, were thriving in the hills outside the camp gates.

Food was state-sanctioned charity that, along with the bed and assis-tance offered up by the camp, was near-compulsory. Like the sacks of rice and cans of cooking oil handed out in African refugee camps, it reduced residents to passive, reluctant recipients.[7] But cigarettes were outside the state domain. Through tobacco and other little gifts, camp workers tried to personalize and counter the power relations inherent in humanitarian government. In this uphill task, family provided a useful organizing metaphor to counteract the rhetoric of camp or prison. New arrivals were told to cooperate with the camp mothers. Cigarettes changed hands daily to friendly calls of "mamá, por favor." Tensions were thus kept in check, but at a price: the camp was now reproducing the unequal power relations in an incipient infantilization.

BROKEN SLIPPERS

14 AUGUST 2010—*EL FARO* SPLASH: "UP TO 17 SUB-SAHARANS HAVE ARRIVED IN RUBBER DINGHIES IN LESS THAN 24 HOURS." INSIDE THE PAPER: BIG PICTURES OF RED CROSS WORKERS AND MIGRANTS IN CEUTA'S PORT, TOPPED BY THE TEXT "FEAR OF PRESSURE FROM MOROCCO ON MIGRATION."[8]

The long walk up the same rubbish-strewn road got hotter and more tiring as the summer wore on. Heading uphill, I often had company. There were women carrying crates of beer cans on their heads, disappearing up the forested slopes; Punjabi migrants who had been smuggled into Ceuta via the Sahara and were now hiding in the hills, fearful of deportation; and an Algerian migrant, tall and well-spoken and utterly out of place. He had been expelled from France to Algeria and was now trying to make it back to his family and home by land. Would he need to join the language classes, sports sessions, and disease prevention workshops of the camp? We walked up the hillside and discussed ways of leaving clandestinely via the port. Why did he not arrange to see the camp lawyer? I suggested. He saw no point to it. "They just want us to sign their papers so they get paid," he said. "Migrants are merchandise. . . . If they let the migrants go, unemployment would spike in Ceuta," he added. "It's big business here." He had a point. About eighty people were employed at the camp, not counting the plentiful private contractors. The high unemployment rates in both Ceuta and Melilla meant that the camps were seen as "something positive" among locals, in the words of a migrant lawyer.

A shortcut led up to the cliffs and promontories above the road. A dreadlocked Liberian showed the way, jumping up the slope with deft movements, gripping branches as he went. It took forty-three minutes to walk to the city center, he had explained on the bus, where he had paid the driver with the ten-cent coins he earned by begging and carrying shopping bags outside a supermarket. I followed him up the slope, slipping in my sandals. The path carved its way through the dry cracked mud towards a clearing. There, on plastic chairs atop a mat of leaves, rusty tins, and plastic bottles, sat three adventurers. One was eating spiced rice cooked and served up for a euro by one of the women of the camp. Others held beer cans. They all stared at the impromptu visitor. Here they were in charge. The tables were turned. It was a brief glimpse of a space more akin to the migrant ghettos or bunkers of Tangier, Rabat, and the forests outside Ceuta and Melilla than to the regulated regime of the camp. Here no one would ask mamá for a cigarillo.

During the summer new migrants arrived at the camp in a steady trickle. Whether Morocco was sending them across the border, as Spanish news reports alleged, was hard to know. Whatever the reason, tension was building at the border, and the camp was filling up. A small group of migrants had been rescued on the Strait this August afternoon and were now fresh out of the shower in their CETI-provided jogging suits. "Addadis," said the fake-brand label. One of the newcomers was Algerian, the others sub-Saharan or—as camp workers called them—*morenos* (dark-skinned). Normally applied to a sun-tanned Spaniard or a North African, the term *moreno* has started to be used across Spain to describe black Africans, especially in the context of migrant assistance. Through this term, camp workers tried to avoid the negative connotations associated with the term *negros*, or "blacks." Migrants soon caught on, and the French-speakers among them started referring to themselves as *moriños,* surely inspired—football fans as they all were—by Mourinho, the Real Madrid coach.

The morenos clutched black refuse sacks stuffed with the damp clothes from the journey. Their first steps on Spanish soil were eased by the smooth procedure for new arrivals, in which all participants played their roles in a professional relay race. First a police visit downhill, followed by entry to the camp and a shower. Then a health check. Next, registration—fingertips gently pressed down on a scanner, photo snapped. After this, a meeting with *social,* the state-employed social workers who explained the running of the camp, admonished migrants to attend Spanish classes and listen to what the *mamans* told them. Finally, out of a machine popped the green CETI entrance card, which would be the new arrivals' only form of identification in the enclave. Over the next week followed a series of meetings that residents were required to attend and tick off on slips of paper, known as the *protocolo.* This way a dossier was built up for each arrival:

step by step, the hitherto unknown migrant became categorizable and interventionable.

Unlike the segregation by nationality so common in refugee administration worldwide, in Ceuta nationalities were mixed in the dormitories to avoid creating "ghettos." Whereas the ghetto in the adventurers' world referred to safe houses based on nationality, in Spain the term came to connote a negative communalism. Mixing people of all backgrounds and breaking up close-knit groups were liberal gestures, but in their liberal individualism they also made people anonymous, substitutable. Incidentally, this was an important step in the crafting of the migrant illegality sought by journalists, researchers, and politicians in Ceuta. The camp's very spatiality, in splitting linguistic groups and assigning residents to nonnegotiable slots and bunks, did the groundwork for their reconfiguration as generic illegal immigrants.[9]

If the "no ghetto" policy rendered residents both individual and replaceable, the next step—according to the logic of a sorting center— was nevertheless to differentiate and classify. The four main migrant categories, a Red Cross worker explained, were Moroccan, Algerian, (South) Asian, and sub-Saharan. Moroccans fell outside the scope of the CETIs, thanks to their government's nonrecognition of Ceuta and Melilla and thanks to the ease of repatriation. As a result, some Moroccans claimed to be Algerian, with whom they also shared the colloquial designation *moros*. Among sub-Saharans came a further division: Anglophone versus Francophone. Another categorization followed the psychological (or intelligence) test: educated versus illiterate. Courses were organized along the intersecting vectors of colonial language and literacy levels. The typology also generated informal assessments. The *anglófonos* had been upset about the earlier camp brawl, workers said, because they were afraid of repatriation. "It's harder here for the *anglófonos* than for the *francófonos* because of the language," Mamá said. "They find Spanish difficult."

The Francophone morenos came out of *control* and took their first steps in a process that would construct them as a new type of migrant, assembled from materials that defined their existence in Ceuta: CETI card, protocolo slip, cigarettes, blankets, slippers. Mamá took toilet rolls, bedsheets, and shower cream out of a cupboard, and the migrants stuffed the items into a second black refuse sack. Then, in a small troupe, they headed downstairs, a sack flung over each shoulder.

As the troupe made its way down the steps, the camp appeared in a new light alongside the big-eyed adventurers finally entering "Europe": the unfamiliar familiarity of this tucked-away place, this strange raucous mix of African youth and music and laundry and barracks that came at us suddenly, hidden behind the somnolent parking lot and the empty canteen. The dream of a clean, modern West, evoked by the name "Hilton," which road-weary migrants had at one point given to the camp, was dissipating with each step. The migrants remained silent, fretful, and amazed, clutching their sacks. "A lot of foreigners here," observed Emmanuel, one of the youngsters from Cameroon, the home country of those in today's troupe of black African arrivals and of most of those waiting below. "It's like a boarding school." "People are nice here," was all I replied with tenuous reassurance as we made our way downstairs, into the swirl of football and ping-pong players, African women doing their laundry, and screams and banter emanating from wide-open doors.

Emmanuel and his companions peeked inside a room. It was the standard layout: three bunks, eight beds in all. Metal cupboards with locks bought by migrants in Ceuta's Chinese one-euro shops. A small table and a chair. Residents had found ingenious ways to establish privacy by tying sheets to the bunks' poles, screening the beds from view. Bits of broomsticks served as support for the top-bunk sheets. This was prohibited, Mamá said, but she let it be. Posters and cut-outs were taped to the walls—scantily dressed Western women and a random selection of news clippings. An African woman leaned in through the small window, inspecting the beds. Emmanuel's young face twitched. "Is this a room for women?" It was not, Mamá assured him; women had separate dormitories. She told a resident to remove the luggage piled on the top bunk and then inspected the foam mattress. It was dirty, but it would serve for the time being. "When will everything start here?" Emmanuel asked, still hopeful. "Now it's still like vacation." He must have seen it as the strangest sort of boarding school, where they would be waiting for the director's good word to be able to leave.

These hot days in August, it did not take long for new arrivals to figure out how things worked at the camp. Rumors spread like fire from bunk to bunk, room to room, community to community. People stayed here for three years, Emmanuel and his friends were told. It's like Guantánamo, said another. It's a prison. "Why do they keep us here?" asked some *anciens,* as French-speaking long-termers were known. There were two simple replies. *La crisis*—the economic crisis throttling Spain's economy and squeezing any need for unskilled migrant workers—was said to be the reason they could not be sent on to Seville, Madrid, or Barcelona. But many believed that something rather more sinister lay

behind their predicament. The Algerian gentleman was not alone in seeing migrants as a lucrative business. "Human trading," one migrant
called it. They "consume," thanks to us, said another. *Ils travaillent sur
nous,* said a third, echoing Mohammadou in faraway Dakar: they have
work, thanks to us.

This was the logic of the march on the city center that would soon
follow. Migrants called it a "strike," not a protest. This made sense,
since they saw themselves as *working for* the camp and the authorities,
who in turn saw themselves as working for the migrants. The strike was
to be a rare reckoning with the absurdity of the illegality industry and
its abiding assumptions about its captive human material. According to
the camp's logic, residents' undocumented status signaled a larger social,
psychological, and cultural "lack" that needed time and treatment; the
residents were their product. To the strikers, however, the camp produced nothing except illicit profits, thanks to their own unpaid labor of
doing time. These antagonists, as will be seen, were both right and
wrong: the camp and its residents *did* produce something, but not what
the workers—or the strikers—wished.

In short, the scope of misunderstanding between workers and residents was acute and became more so as tempers flared in the summer
heat and the rumor mill started processing the news from across the
border. For the time being, however, direct confrontation gave way to
petty annoyances. Slippers broke. Sheets were not washed on time.
T-shirts frayed. They had no money for calling home. The food was
bland. More slippers broke. Every day, these slippers—residents would
come and show Mamá, look, it snapped! Could I get a new pair? Mamá
sighed. "We spend a fortune on slippers here. What do they do with
them?" Often the residents would dutifully find some needle and thread,
sowing the toe-strap back on so that the slipper would last another few
weeks. The forty-three-minute walk to the center and the climb up the
forested shortcut were taking their toll. Even when going to the police
commissariat for interviews, the migrants had to walk for miles, carving
the ignominy of camp life into their footwear. But by complaining about
clothes and slippers, migrants had come to collude with the official view
of them: as needy people who lived off charity. These were the negritos
of the popular imagination: poor black people who did not have it easy,
who always asked for help. *Los pobres* (poor things), workers, caballas,
and even police would say, shaking their heads in pity.

A few days later, Emmanuel cornered Mamá on her daily round of the
modules. He had questions. Would he get some skin cream? He showed

his compulsory TB injection, looking a bit inflamed. Suddenly he looked insecure, twitchy. "How long will we stay here?" That depended, said Mamá. Did it depend on good behavior? Yes, Mamá confirmed, good behavior was important. She added that they—it was not clear who "they" were—might also look for a particular profile instead of sending away the well-behaved ones. Politics, nationality, many things played a part. Emmanuel nodded. "But one day we will leave this place?" he asked. "We will not stay here forever?" "Yes, you will leave," said Mamá, "but we don't know when." Emmanuel said he had heard of people staying here for three years. It could be one week, one month, two years, said Mamá. As we left, Emmanuel flung another question at me: "How does one do to live here?"

THE YELLOW CARD

6 AUGUST 2010—MOROCCAN FOREIGN MINISTRY'S LATEST COMMUNI-QUÉ ON THE OCCUPIED CITIES OF CEUTA AND MELILLA: "MOROCCO VIG-OROUSLY CONDEMNS THE ABANDONMENT OF EIGHT SUB-SAHARAN IMMIGRANTS BY THE SPANISH CIVIL GUARD ALONG ITS COASTLINE."[10]

Rumors stirred in the camp. Moroccan newscasts that residents watched on the canteen screens, over their mobile-Internet-connected laptops, or on television sets they had affixed to their bunk beds showed Spain abandoning black migrants in a raft outside Ceuta. The migrants had later been rescued and hospitalized and recounted their stories—true or fabricated—to Moroccan journalists. Someone had also started talking about an E.U. delegation's impending visit, and soon the camp swirled with questions. Would they come tomorrow? Would they listen to our problems? The camp was like a pressure cooker simmering with rumors and resentment.

Emmanuel's face had changed. He looked surly, bitter, standing out-side the canteen and looking out over the Strait. "Here we do nothing," he said. "We're adventurers; we're used to struggling for our survival." The camp was the opposite of the adventure, I suggested. Yes, Emmanuel said, "here it's like staying with daddy and mummy." He grimaced. "To me, the adventure is not yet over."

A few residents had gathered on the benches behind a module, next to the sports pitch and the camp's swings. El General was among them, decked out in his usual sunglasses and beret. My Algerian friend hov-ered in the background. One resident, a well-spoken Cameroonian I had previously met for discussions outside the camp gates, asked me, "If you come back after a year and I am still here, would you be happy?" Others chimed in: "It's a prison." "We are treated like savages." "It's the slave trade all over again." An older man spoke up. He was a veteran of the migrant circuit: he bared his thigh to show two big round scars from a bullet fired during the asalto in 2005. "Look above," he said, pointing towards the horse-riding center that had been constructed right above the camp and regularly sent clouds of dust down over the parking lot. "Here they keep some beasts next to others." "*Aucun blanc peut vivre ici*" (no white person can live here), they said.

Mamá had arrived, and questions and accusations flew in her direction. Why, the gathering asked, if our *tarjetas* are valid in all of Spain, can we not travel to the peninsula?

The Spanish authorities gave the *tarjetas amarillas*, the yellow cards, to asylum seekers whose applications had been accepted for processing. In earlier times, the tarjeta had been a passport to the peninsula. Then, in late 2009, the situation changed. Spain's new asylum law made it much easier to have one's application considered, and the national police promptly decided not to accept the cards as identification in port. As a consequence, the previously much-desired yellow cards came to threaten stagnation rather than promising mobility. Asylum seekers felt cheated, and newcomers were discouraged from even applying, as UNHCR would note in a critique of conditions in Ceuta more than three years later.[11]

Mamá had disappeared upstairs but came back, waving a printout with information she had found online. Ceuta and Melilla were Schengen territory, she read out to the eager and ever-growing gathering amid the swings, but they had a special disposition to carry out passport controls at the port. I translated into French. Questions were fired rapidly at her. "Why can't we leave?" Europe wanted to halt migration at its external borders, explained Mamá. So the camp was the responsibility of the European Union? asked residents, confused. No, it was Madrid's responsibility, said Mamá, "but Madrid depends on Brussels, and there they are afraid you will continue north and spread across Europe." "Why can't the Europeans speak directly to us?" asked the veteran of 2005. And why, "if the camp depends on the E.U., do we need to learn Spanish here? Why not another language?" "Anyway, why have they taken us here? We did not ask Spain to rescue us at sea!" One resident after another chimed in, in a furious, unstoppable barrage of questions.

The biggest problem in the camp, residents said again and again, was the lack of information. While this will be looked at in detail in the next chapter, suffice to say here that this predicament seems endemic to sorting centers, as Michel Agier notes. In Poland, a doctor in one such center deplored "the detainees' lack of information about their rights, and the fact that they do not understand why they are detained for so long."[12] In Ceuta, residents experienced a similar uncertainty. Everyone even seemed confused about who was in charge. Some migrants had heard in Morocco that the Portuguese ran the camp and would channel workers to Lisbon. Many knew that the European Union gave Spain money for running the camp, thanks to the flag at the gate. But who to call, who to plead to, who to criticize? No one could say. Even the camp workers seemed unsure. It was "Europe" that wanted to keep migrants here, not they or even Spain, the workers often said. Was it the Spanish government delegation in Ceuta that was in charge of assuring this, however? One worker had even insisted, erroneously, that the Interior rather than the Labour Ministry ran the camp. Confusion reigned.

El General finally spoke, and all listened to his whispery voice. He called for a big meeting at the camp, to air all concerns. The authorities shouldn't worry about money, he said. If they were permitted to leave they would go back to their homes clandestinely, with an inflatable Zodiac. Mamá nodded, then warned them their stay would be *para largo* (for long). All listened attentively for the final word on their fate. Maybe one day the politics would change and they could go, Mamá added. No one could say when. The silence broke, and her explanations were drowned in a tide of exclamations. "*Racistes!*" a young man screamed. The mood was changing. Mamá retreated, anthropologist and residents trailing her. One pointed at a little girl: "Why is she here?" "Well, her parents shouldn't have entered without papers," said Mamá. "Would you leave your son here?" they asked. "I send my son to places like this for fifteen days, but *paying*," retorted Mamá, referring to a *campamento* (holiday camp) rather than the *campo* for refugees that the residents saw themselves as inhabiting. But this was no time to debate the semantics of makeshift lodgings. "Leave!" someone screamed behind Mamá. He seemed unhinged, angry beyond measure. "We will close this place down!" Mamá went upstairs, lips pursed, fast steps. There would be no big meeting, that much was clear.

Upstairs new arrivals were waiting in the classroom building, sitting in sofas with the usual plastic sacks in front of them. Mamá opened a cupboard and handed out the kit, mechanically, in silence. Blanket, jogging suit, T-shirt, hygiene kit, slippers. On the way to the shower, an *ancien* sauntered up. "*Ici c'est Guantánamo!*" he screamed to the new arrivals. Outside the canteen, the residents had gathered, dozens of people sitting on windowsills, loitering in the doorway. It was mealtime, but they were not eating. No more spaghetti. Instead they occupied the dining tables and watched a Barça game in silence, interspersed with commercials. It was the quintessential camp protest: occupying space and refusing food, the poisoned gift that was their due. Security guards hovered in the wings.

It was the night before the migrants would erupt in strike.

A CARDBOARD REBELLION

27 AUGUST 2010—*EL PUEBLO DE CEUTA*—FRONT PAGE PICTURE: NAKED TORSOS, ANGRY MEN MARCHING. "FROM THE CETI TO THE CENTER: SUB-SAHARAN IMMIGRANTS SHOW THEIR ANGER OVER A STAY OF SEVERAL YEARS IN CEUTA." *EL FARO:* "ABOUT A HUNDRED SUB-SAHARANS, WELL COORDINATED, ORGANIZE A DEMONSTRATION ASKING FOR FREEDOM."[13]

It had started to the tune of whistles and slippers hitting the pavement as a stream of strikers came running up Ceuta's sleepy shopping street. They gathered at Plaza de los Reyes, the seat of their target: the gray bulk of a building that housed the Spanish government delegation. The square was the leafy heart of Ceuta where the children of the local elite used to play under the watchful eyes of their nannies. Now riot police formed a neat line of helmets and shields against the waves of protesters clad in their "Addadis" jogging trousers and often little else, bare-chested or stripped to their underwear, their camp T-shirts torn and twisted into turbans or scribbled upon as makeshift placards. "CETI is a prison," read one. "CETI Guantanamo Libertad," said another.

The final spark for the strike had come from the arrival, that very morning, of the much-awaited E.U. fact-finding delegation. Its intention was to question migrants on the topic of sexual violence endured en route, but as the delegates' car pulled up at the camp the strikers were already massing at the gate. The delegates took fright and sped off downhill, trailed by a horde of screaming migrants, as the camp director later explained with an ill-suppressed chuckle at the bizarre imagery. The research site must have looked ideal: a camp where migrants were gathered, immobile and ready to interview. It was not to be. "They'll never come back to Ceuta now," the director said.

The protesters had gathered round the square's central fountain, arms aloft or wrists crossed, as if shackled. *Ooh-oh Afri-cah, oh-oh-*

FIGURE 14. Strikers in front of the government delegation in Ceuta. Photo by Cristina Vergara López.

Africa, oh-oh-liberté, they sang in a melodious chorus, mixing in football chants and Shakira's *waka waka.* The whine of whistles mixed with loud claps; a beat was coaxed out of plastic water bottles transformed into makeshift drums. The caballas and tourists stopped to look and listen, snapping pictures at a safe distance. Journalists with cameras and notepads milled with the crowd, trying to pry quotes from migrants but without much luck. They had their spokesmen and leaders.

One of them, a bespectacled English-speaker, laid out the strikers' case for the benefit of the TV cameras. "After two, three months we should be liberated," he said, as in "all the other camps," meaning the closed CIEs on the peninsula. Protesters gathered into a knot around him, screaming agitatedly, one of them waving a broken slipper in front of the camera. The speaker pushed it out of sight. Here the issue was freedom, not handouts, he said. "Prison!" shouted someone next to him. "You as a journalist," the speaker finally asked, "could you live here for ten months with one set of clothes and one pair of sandals?" The life of the slippers, from camp gifts fresh out of the plastic packaging to grubby footwear that snapped apart, had become a metonym for the degradation of the strikers' hopes and their impoverished life after entering Ceuta.

El General led a chant at the fountain: *Gouverneur! Gou-ver-neur!* They wanted the Spanish government delegate, but he was away. His holidays had begun. Getting hold of someone responsible for their predicament would prove impossible. But except for the delegate, everyone was there. Representatives of most sectors in the burgeoning illegality industry had finally gathered: a mix of journalists, aid workers, police, and the odd anthropologist congregating around the disheveled migrants. On this square, the finishing touches were being put to the construction of Europe's illegal Other. An NGO worker from the camp stood by, shaking her head. "In the end, it makes me sad," she said. "What will they achieve?"

"You know they met yesterday in the hills," said a journalist with one of the local papers who stood observing the throng of protesters from behind police lines. She had a scoop from last night's forest get-together, where migrants had debated their options for action. "It's normal, they have been here for three years, nothing more than eating and sleeping, eating and sleeping." On the whole, news reports were sympathetic. The carnivalesque nature of the strike, the splashing of water, and the football chanting mitigated the discomfort of naked torsos lined up against riot police and the piles of cardboard now cluttering the neatest, nicest square of the city. But the goodwill was not to last.

PRIMETIME NATIONAL TELEVISION: MIGRANTS WITH BANNERS IN CENTRAL CEUTA. THEY FIND THEMSELVES VIRTUALLY "IMPRISONED," ACCORDING TO THE VOICE-OVER. IN *EL FARO*, ANOTHER CORD IS STRUCK: "THESE, THE PAPERLESS, WITHOUT PLACE, WITHOUT NAME OR SURNAME, EVEN WITHOUT CLOTHES, EXUDING AN AIR OF RESTLESSNESS AND UNTRUSTWORTHINESS, TO THE POINT WHERE THE PEOPLE SITTING IN THE CAFÉS GET UP AND REORGANIZE THEIR CHAIRS, SCARED, UNSURE, SURPRISED, ASHAMED."[14]

On Monday morning, Ceuta woke to the sound of pistol shots. Down the somnolent shopping street they came, a ragtag contingent of angry black men, to the loud *clack-clack-clack* of folded pieces of cardboard hitting the pavement, slapped down with force and anger. Caballas looked out of their windows; Moroccan daytrippers stopped and stared; housewives and flaneurs quickly gulped down their coffee.

The weekend had passed, and something had changed. The police chief had come out to talk to the migrants on the square but had given no ground. They would have to wait in Ceuta. Soon after, the fervor of the first days had been whipped into a frenzy. The cardboard that the protesters slept on and that had served as canvas for their scrawled messages had acquired a new function: that of a soundbox or a weapon. The protesters were militarizing, the media said, and their leader was El General. He did military salutes outside the national police jefatura, and his soldiers responded, some face-painted, most still dressed in their CETI jogging suits. "*Assis!*" a helper screamed out, and all sat down. One journalist capturing these scenes said it reminded her of images of Africa's civil wars. Rebel armies run wild. Her camera zoomed in on a red-eyed, bare-chested man, his face contorted into a grimace as he banged away on a makeshift drum.

The militarization of the protest was, of course, no accident. To the authorities and the mainstream media, it was a sign that the leaders of the strike were former guerrilla fighters or paramilitaries. What they failed to see was that the salutes and mannerisms above all pointed to the larger militarization of clandestine migration circuits discussed in the previous chapter. The strikers only had to dip into the existing imagery and paint an image of themselves that suited their objectives. In the process they fueled the latent militarized discourse in the press, which was swiftly switching from depicting migrants as victims to portraying them as a menace.[15]

The change in coverage brought new, fruitful angles for the press. Police released files showing that the "hard core" of strikers had in fact not been stuck in Ceuta for years. Their calls for transfer to a CIE and then even deportation were read as a devious tactic; they knew full well they would be released once on the mainland. News spread that they had roughed up fellow residents who did not want to participate and had threatened "camp workers," which turned out to mean the previous director. A German journalist filming the strike had also been threatened. "Destroy her camera!" they had screamed, but she kept filming. She knew some of them well, but they had changed. I knew El General and the others too, their doubts and frustrations. Now I peered from balconies and out of bars, hovered around the scene. I was not to be trusted, some of them said. "Why should we speak to you? You will leave, and you will earn money from your report. You earn money from us but you give nothing. What will you do with our story?" Of Emmanuel up at the camp, I would see little more. His sullen face would occasionally flash by before quickly disappearing out of sight, avoiding any small talk.

The German journalist's camera trailed a striker rushing towards a newspaper kiosk. He furiously hit the pavement, his cardboard fraying more with each sharp slap. "Guantánamo!" *"Liberté!"* his brothers-in-arms screamed. Another striker followed, and soon, in a circle, they were beating the ground in unison. Locals looked on in anger. *"¡Echad-los a todos!"* an old woman shouted to the camera: throw them all out.

But police stood by. The aggression was only against the asphalt, against the very soil of Ceuta. "If I knew what door to knock, I would knock it," one Cameroonian had said before the protests. There was no door to knock, no one who listened, nothing on which to vent this unbearable frustration. So they pounded this ground, as if to punish it. This is what they hated, this African soil, this fake Europe on display along the shopping street targeting Moroccan daytrippers and transiting tourists—Zara boutiques, electronics shops, Supersol supermarkets, Cortefiel clothes, outdoor *terrazas* and bars where tourists sipped cold beers. The protesters moved on down the road, their noise receding in the distance.

. . .

The politicians woke up late to the severe sense of crisis sparked by the strike. "With *cartonazos* no one is going to the peninsula," warned the government delegate, using the by now oft-heard term for cardboard on pavement.[16] The media had turned on the strikers and reserved a fair amount of vitriol for the politicians too. A veteran journalist bemoaned, "We find police who don't even know what to do: they put on their helmets, they take them off, they take up their shields, they circle the square, they come and go." Spain's migration policy was going up in smoke, ended her piece, one of many scathing assessments.[17]

Yet the wavering between laxity and repression—and the latter finally came—was not a failure: it was a *result* of a policy straining under its own contradictions. Spain's supposed soft touch—its propensity to engage in dialogue, to extol humanitarianism, to care for migrants—was paired with a rather steelier set of objectives coming from both Madrid and Brussels. Care and control both fueled and fed off each other, much as they did on the high seas and in other instances of humanitarian government—a contradiction neatly glossed by anthropologist Didier Fassin as "compassionate repression."[18] As was usually the case on the clandestine circuit, the migrants were the first to grasp these contradictions. One latecomer to the strike, banished from the camp for violence against a guard, said that migrants in Ceuta were like a sacrifice giving "a good image for Spain in all of Europe." A Cameroonian asylum seeker similarly put the finger where it hurt: "France seems nasty with migrants," he said, "but they treat them well in the end. In Spain they seem nice with migrants, but then they leave us like this!"

The mix of directives tied the hands of Ceuta's decision makers and stirred a growing frustration shared by journalists, camp workers, the public, and the migrants. What could they do? The strikers could not be imprisoned, not all of them: what would be the point, how high the cost? They could not be sent on to the peninsula, or the wrong signal would be sent out to other migrants. They could not be fined, because they were penniless. One police chief couched the dilemma in the inclusive language so characteristic of the Socialist government's migration response: "What they're doing is perfectly legal; anyone has the right to demonstrate," he had told me as strikers chanted at the plaza. "We have to tolerate it . . . [and] maintain the rule of law, the strict rule of law." The further the strike went, however, the more this façade started cracking. Migrants and authorities were stuck in the same frustrating limbo, of which the protest was simply the culmination and catharsis. But in giving an absurd riposte to absurd policies on behalf of everyone, the strikers also risked fast becoming the fall guys of Ceuta's summer of discontent.

ON VEUT LE RESPONSABLE!

"THE SUB-SAHARANS TURN DOWN THE DELEGATE, TEAR UP HIS RESOLU-
TION AND WILL PROTEST 'UNTIL DEATH.'" EL FARO, 8 SEPTEMBER 2010.
PICTURE UNDERNEATH: A BLACK HAND HOLDS UP THE YELLOW CARD TO
THE CAMERA, WITH THE INSCRIPTION "THIS DOCUMENT IS VALID ONLY IN
SPAIN" VISIBLE, THE PHRASE ASYLUM SEEKERS INVOKED FOR THEIR RIGHT
TO TRAVEL TO THE PENINSULA.[19]

The sub-Saharan crisis, as the media dubbed it, was ratcheting up the temperature across Ceuta. The Spanish government delegate had finally penned a resolution banning the protests, citing insecurity and danger for Ceuta's inhabitants. The strikers first signed it, then threw it onto the tarmac, ripped it apart, and streamed down the street to loud cheers and shouts. "Heated spirits, tribal chants and a lot of pressure" was how the media summed up the standoff. To some caballas, memories were stirred of violent conflicts between migrants and authorities before the camp existed. After all, it was a riot by African migrants in 1995 that had sparked the initial fortification of the border, and smaller protests in later years had hardened the resolve to maintain migrants on the geographical margins of the enclave. Some locals still shuddered at memories of the earlier standoff, recalling how black Africans had trailed them or their families in town. With the strike, similar sentiments were now resurfacing across the city.[20]

Up at the lofty heights of the camp, tension was everywhere, eroding workers' motivation like a toxin. They had tired under the weight of incessant demands. For those on the frontline, camp practicalities, residents' wishes and fears, and the differing objectives of the Interior and Labor Ministries had to be juggled every day. Mamá, an expert in such juggling, kept sending off her weekly reports, checking on modules, and assisting new arrivals. After many years in the camp, a protest would not shake her resolve. She greeted the strikers when passing them in town, but snapped and confronted anyone accusing workers of racism. The strike did not lead her to question the camp's mission or the needs of its beneficiaries. Rather, she split the good from the bad—the instigators from the integrated. Other workers and the authorities did likewise, in an emerging categorization that would soon have consequences for the strikers.

One of the Spanish teachers, David, called for migrants to congregate in the big hall of the camp for an announcement. About twenty of them showed up, taking their place on the school benches. On the walls hung residents' drawings from a disease prevention workshop: condom exhortations competed for space with a map plastered with AIDS ribbons. "They think all illnesses come from Africa; just look at the map," said one of the men in the benches, twisting his face into a grimace. Another promptly went up to the map and moved a few ribbons from African to European countries. Now it was more equal, they said. "They make all types of tests on us when we arrive here," they exclaimed. "AIDS, syphilis, tuberculosis . . . but when white people go to Africa, they are not even asked for vaccination papers!"

David entered and announced he would open the camp gym, one hour two times a week. He explained the rules and took questions, which came thick and fast. What did they need to bring? Their green CETI card and covered shoes, for safety. So would they get shoes, since they didn't have any? No, David said, adding, "Well, if you don't have any it's OK, just be careful." But why did the football players get shoes, not those using the gym? David could not say; he was not responsible.

People in the audience laughed, a flat bitter laugh. *"On veut le respon-sable!"* There was no one responsible, David said. He was opening the gym as a favor. For longer opening times or shoes or anything else they would need to speak to *social*. It was an interdepartmental thing; he could not do it. The meeting closed.

David lingered in the parking lot, smoking a cigarette and shaking his head. A resident came up, asking for one. "But it's bad for your health," said David. The resident insisted, got one, left. David sighed. Before it had been different: he took people to the cinema, to Ceuta's aquatic park, on excursion. He organized a book fair right next to *con-trol*! But now nothing interested them, he said. All they did was ask for things, all the time more things. Camp workers talked wistfully about how the new arrivals were somehow different from the gentler migrants of earlier times. The new ones would refuse slippers or food. Some flirted with the female staff. Others created trouble from the first day. *Ya vienen aprendidos,* said Mamá: they arrive having learned the rules of the game in Morocco, where NGOs or "mafias" or fellow travelers tell them all about Ceuta.

I left the camp in David's car, speeding past the steady streams of migrants making their way into town. David had had enough, and the protest was proving the final straw. "You know, they have always been the negritos del CETI," he said. *"Ay que pena* [what a pity] people would say"; how good they are, these poor people. "But that is when they are ensconced in the CETI. Now as they have come to town, they have become *negros,"* he said. Where would this rancor, newly stirred in Ceuta's inhabitants, lead?

. . .

In town, the strikers seemed to be losing the battle. Their cardboard and whistles had been impounded. Still, camp residents kept coming: a rumor had spread that police identity checks on strikers would lead to people being ticked off and sent to the peninsula.

Shorn of whistles and cardboard, the strikers came singing in a tightly packed group down the shopping street teeming with caballas fresh from their holidays. They stopped in front of an ice-cream parlor and faced a growing police contingent, still singing. Later one striker told me they had tried to say sorry to the caballas. This the media ignored. The female journalist of the other day had lost sympathy for the strikers. The authorities would open public order cases against them, she said. "If you had seen the state in which they left the square . . ."

Two strikers silently held a white cloth banner towards the passersby. It read, in rather good Spanish: "We are like you, we are not evil or wild animals, but a reflexive and conscious generation. We claim only our rights. We are tired of stay in prison, please government. FREEDOM— FREEDOM!!!"[21]

Three young policemen in discreet vests and fashionable hair approached the strikers, motioning to them with black-gloved hands. They carried out an identity check, calling forward a handful of protesters at a time, eyeing their camp cards, patting them down, and depositing them some thirty meters ahead. The singing had died off, and an expectant silence reigned. Onlookers were congregating—reporters, passersby, Moroccan daytrippers, policemen. All watched the same proceedings, in which the hidden phenomenon of clandestine migration was made visible. It was hard to tell who was a bystander, who a journalist, who an undercover police. Cameramen sat atop a statue and lingered on terraces above; photographers snapped pictures. Surveillance was everywhere. The strikers with the banner dutifully folded it, went up for the body search, and unfolded it again on the other side. Finally the police read out names from a list. A handful of strikers went up and were put into waiting police vans. The vehicles filled up and sped off, leaving the remaining strikers and police standing silently in front of each other for a wavering moment. Then, tentatively, the chanting picked up again in the remaining crowd—CETI *no bueno*, CETI *no bueno*. They moved forward slowly, squeezed into a tight procession behind their banner. Finally they turned the corner round the Plaza de la Constitución, waving their yellow cards in the air and leaving an indeterminate feeling of sadness and futility in their wake.

As the strikes started unwinding, Europe's "deportation machine" was revving into gear.[22] A police van took the detainees to the camp, where they sat for an hour in the heat, waiting for their belongings to be picked up from their rooms. A worker peeked inside: they looked like wild animals, she said, tucked into that small hot space, starving, thirsty . . . They pleaded for food and finally got a sandwich that they tore into like "wild dogs." Fourteen detainees were sent on to the peninsula. The reason they took these fourteen was that they did not have the asylum seeker's yellow card, which meant they could be transferred to detention in a CIE. From there, the next step was deportation.

The strike seemed to have failed, but maybe success or failure was not what mattered. It bore witness to the "climate of exceptionality" that, according to Agier, reigns in the camps and their environs. "Protest has no proper place in these sites," he says, "and itself takes exceptional and exacerbated forms, before being rapidly and violently repressed." The repression came slowly in Ceuta, however, and in the meantime the strikers had managed to craft another form of migranthood out of the meager resources at their disposal—the stuff of pitiable negritos and interventionable morenos. Their fake-brand "Addadis" clothes, a supreme sign of their neediness and anonymization, made a perfect uniform for a ragtag army. The handout T-shirts morphed into bandanas and placards. And the cardboard, the free cheap cardboard they slept on as dejected migrants out on the square, became, temporarily, a weapon against the invisible enemy of E.U. migration policy. Their street performance distinguished them from the apolitical *clandestins* spotted in other camps across Europe, who only want to travel on, invisible, imperceptible, unmolested. They were stepping into the realm of politics as subjects, not objects. The strikers were hailing the state rather than the other way round—a state that was not even their own—to see them, to detain them, to *do anything*.[23]

In their attempts at hailing the state, Ceuta's strikers followed a logic similar to that of the *sans-papiers* (undocumented migrants) on the streets of Paris or the Latinos with their million-strong marches across the United States. The migration scholar Anne McNevin, commenting on the latter, sees irregular migrants as situated at the "frontiers of the political in the context of neoliberal globalization." Their political claims, she argues, "challenge those sovereign practices through which they are constructed as apolitical and illegitimate intruders." This was true in Ceuta as well, yet the strike there took the challenge to the state one step further—or one step back. It was simply over the right to leave and even the right to be deported. While the clandestine migrants had already had to assume their own "deportability" in Morocco, here they sought to *deploy* it, calling the illegality industry's bluff in the process.[24]

The strikers' appropriation of space spoke of a similar story. By rejecting their containment on the faraway hillside and marching on the pristine city center, they challenged the spatial order by which illegal immigrants were rendered as separable, pitiable, and researchable. But in doing so, the strikers had re-created the flipside of the helpless and innocent clandestine migrant, the negrito. They had become the wild and dangerous *negro*. To quote Frantz Fanon, one "galaxy of erosive stereotypes" had been substituted for another—"the Negro's *sui generis* good nature" replaced by "Mama, see the Negro! I'm frightened!"[25]

THE CORDON

5 SEPTEMBER 2010—*EL PUEBLO*—FRONT-PAGE PICTURE OF WORKERS IN PROTECTIVE GEAR AND FACE MASKS ON THE CENTRAL SQUARE, CAPTIONED: "THE CITY CLEANS A SOURCE OF INFECTIONS GENERATED BY THE IMMIGRANTS WHO SLEEP IN THE PLAZA DE LOS REYES."[26]

The road to the camp wound uphill, past the same old rubbish-strewn slopes. I walked it as so many times before, heavy steps set in humid African heat, until reaching the hilltop gate. Two riot police vans were parked in the shade. At the turnstile stood a young security guard with muscled, tattooed arms. He was squeezing a hand exercise gadget, producing a squeaky repetitive noise.

Residents walked up to the turnstiles, swiping cards and resting their fingers on the reader. When they entered, the guard stopped squeaking, put their bags on a table inside the gates, and rummaged through them with black-gloved hands. Out through the gates came three black guys, one dressed in a beret and sunglasses. It was El General. He looked subdued. "The only thing left for us to do now is to swim," he mumbled hoarsely.

The turnstile stopped one member of the party from getting through. The guard's colleague in the booth opened the gates, and the friends headed downhill. "Fuck!" exclaimed the reception guard: that one's card was disabled. "*Curva* [curve], do you copy?" The walkie-talkie crackled. "Look," the guard told his colleagues manning the length of the fence, "El General is heading downhill with two morenos." One had a deactivated card, he said: "Send him back up." The moreno with the blocked card came dutifully clambering back up the sun-drenched hill.

After the protest, a *cordon sanitaire* had been set up around the camp, and another one was firmly in place in the city center. Ceuta's spatial order was swiftly being reestablished. Late at night uniformed police kept watch on a huddle of protesters who stood in a corner of the square, motionless. Their cardboard had been confiscated. Outside the police jefatura, a zigzag of riot fences had been put up, blocking the sleeping space of the Congolese. A police car sharked up behind them, the officer pointing at a small piece of cardboard that they dutifully deposited in the rubbish bins nearby. They slept straight on the asphalt until Ceuta's cleaning brigade descended in the early mornings in their unending task of polishing the town center. "Here the moriños are treated differently!" exclaimed one of them, dirty and agitated from lack of sleep and excess adrenaline. "But our force is here, in our heads," he said, pointing to his temples. They would not be defeated.

Next morning, the strikers were gone from the square. Space had been reclaimed for the Spanish kids, the elderly flaneurs, and the Moroccan shoppers, and the stone benches where migrants had slept had been put in nice symmetrical order again. But the whiff of illegality would linger. Two impressions stayed, however unfairly. A group of posh schoolkids had gathered in town: one of them, a teenage boy, picked up a piece of cardboard from a skip and proceeded to slap it against the pavement to the laughter of his friends, slapping and slapping until it echoed in a faint reminder of the strikers' cartonazos. An old couple was talking at one of Ceuta's frequent military parades: "Let's see if they do anything with the *negros*," said the wife. "What they should do is circle them all in the square and bang-bang-bang," replied the man.

Mamá sat in her office with a handwritten list on the table. It enumerated the strikers who had persisted despite the official resolution. "They have taken them all to the *calabozo de Tarajal*," said Mamá, the prison next to the border. They were back on the threshold of thresholds, ironically enough, the limbo of the *frontera* they had desperately tried to escape. Their bedding and clothes had to be collected downstairs, Mamá said. She got out her typed-up list of rooms, scribbling notes on it in an ever-more complicated mesh of doodles. It was in a mess, she said. The migrants who just arrived this morning after a dramatic sea rescue still had to be added.

Nine of the fourteen strikers previously taken away in vans and transferred to the peninsula—the "bad ones," as the authorities saw it—were deported back to Cameroon, thanks to an impromptu bilateral deal. The strikers who had remained in Ceuta were released and prosecuted, but the case failed in the courts. Meanwhile, a new strategy was unveiled at the camp. Migrants' good behavior was now going to be rewarded by their being sent to *centros de acogida* (reception centers) in mainland Spain. The sorting mechanism of the camp was being refined. Nationality took on a new importance, since most of the strikers had been Cameroonian. The good and bad elements were sifted. The presumed ringleaders *(cabecillas)* were sorted under "bad" and were scheduled for removal or simply left in place, more stuck than ever.

Despite this, El General managed to escape, the local papers reported during the autumn. How he had done it no one knew; maybe he had stowed away in a lorry, as had many before him. Ceuta calmed down, and the camp launched new activities for residents: more workshops, on-the-job training in the camp, sports and cultural interchanges with caballas, and even a special course at the local university. The crisis had officially been wrapped up and resolved.

Barely a month after the strike, some of the deported Cameroonians had already made it back to Ceuta. As hardened adventurers, they fast-tracked through the borderlands, despite the fences and radars and sub-contracted police blocking their path. Perhaps the returnees sought to follow El General's example, but the threat of stagnation in "Guantánamo" still made their return seem surreal, inconceivable. Like with the strike, the logic of the return has to be sought in the battle over migrants' time, the subject of the next chapter—their captive present, their past on the road, and their imagined future. There was simply no going back for the clandestine migrants of Ceuta.

. . .

The strike and its aftermath had shown that the products of Europe's illegality industry were not simply the rationally classified subjects of a sorting center; they were also redolent of fears, myths, and magic. Here it is worth returning to Malkki's observations on refugee liminality, how camps can conjure new roles out of the old. Ceuta is nothing if not a liminal space, an "out-place" in Agier's terms, artificially construed as the ultimate threshold of Europe—and the camp is a limbo within a limbo. "It is in liminality that *communitas* emerges," the anthropologist Victor Turner once said, referring to the sense of togetherness forged outside the structures, hierarchies, and normative orders of society. Turner would, perhaps, have found that Ceuta's migrants were in the liminal middle stage of a rite of passage, much like the kind Malkki describes for Burundians-turned-refugees. The "elders" of their host society kept them separate, as initiates often are: far away in their camp and on the threshold of both Ceuta and Europe, suspended in time and place until their turn came to be incorporated into or rejected by Europe's symbolic order. But the rite had broken down. Liminality had switched to stasis. And then, the strikers—as a group of initiates rebelling against the prevailing order, a "generation" in their own words—created their own rite and their own *communitas* by marching on the town center. The result was a down-grading of the migrants' status, not incorporation into Europe. The strike and its structural causes in containment, policy contradictions, media attention, and policing prerogatives had turned needy subjects into savages. It had made *negros* of the negritos and morenos. Mamá's stray children had finally abandoned the nest.[27]

It was my last visit to the camp, but it was hard to tear myself away. Migrants kept coming up to Mamá, asking the usual questions: "What about my visit to the lawyer?" "Can I get new slippers?" I finally extricated myself, said furtive good-byes. To catch the bus in time for the ferry I had to run downhill, sandals slipping, heat pounding, running away from it all, from the Trap and its miseries, from the camp and its unfinished stories, where Emmanuel and his friends remained, stranded, waiting. The bus stop was far away, but I made it, got on the bus bouncing along Ceuta's sea-hugging road, and finally ran into the port building. A female police officer flicked through my Swedish passport and flashed a smile. Isn't it the Swedes who always underscore Spain in Eurovision? *"Spain, un point,"* she said as she handed back the precious document that let me through this almost invisible barrier of luggage scans and ticket checks and friendly faces, the frontier that made strikers chant *liberté* all the way to jail. Ceuta, finally, receded in the distance.

In the Father's House

THE STORY OF A SPANISH MONK, *TIME* MAGAZINE, AND THE BLACK BABIES OF THE STRAIT

Across the Strait from Ceuta on Spain's southernmost shores, the Father waited with open arms for migrants washing up in their boats and rafts.[1] The iconic pictures of him appeared in news magazines the world over: dressed in his black habit with a white cross dangling around his neck, he stood knee-deep in the Atlantic waters holding an African baby. If the fourteen-kilometer crossing of the Strait was akin to a religious deliverance for those lucky enough to make it, here was the midwife of God fast at work: humble and caring, embodying Christian love for humanity's outcasts. TIME Magazine once named him one of its global "heroes of the year," and reporters kept doorstepping him at his offices.

The cool, dank reception of the Catholic charity to which the Father belonged was adorned with the iconic pictures of him, but the gray-haired, youthful sixty-five-year-old who received me seemed a different person altogether in his sandals, relaxed trousers, and loose shirt. He welcomed me with a pat on the shoulder and a chuckle, then showed me into the dining hall, where he served the elderly poor housed by the charity. His fame, needless to say, came not from caring for the elderly—he was the human face of clandestine migration, thanks to his work in helping rescued African women and their little children.

"Let's go back to year 2000," the Father said, retelling his story. "The security forces come with two pregnant women who just arrived. What will you do? Throw them out on the street?" The police and Guardia Civil kept bringing him migrant women and children in order to keep them apart from the men detained upon arrival. Coping with the influx was a struggle. "God is great and God helped me, but through what?" he asked, a twinkle in his eyes. "Through the news media. They came [and took] a photograph with the Father, a picture with the little children, and I always resisted but you know what I said later, look, bendito sea [it's a blessing], God had brought them to me."

With the news came money, gifts, donations. Or as the Father put it: "Faith moves mountains, and the media move hearts. . . . Each time they saw me, I got more donations." He received checks for large amounts, letters addressed to "the Father" with five euros inside, and donations of diapers and food. Local women even did crochet work for the babies.

At the height of arrivals, the Father had half a dozen reporters or more waiting on his doorstep each morning. And the journalists— whether French, Germans, or Spanish television teams—all wanted him robed, with children in his arms and preferably knee-deep in the Atlantic. "When the journalists come, I always put on the habit, always, always, always." Why? "They say it's more effective [llena más]. It shouldn't have to be necessary, but we're humans, aren't we?" He chuckled again.

The strategy paid off. "If you go to YouTube, you'll find at least five hundred [clips] of me," he said. The Father's charisma seeped out of the screen as he was filmed stacking vegetable crates, slicing garlic, serving soup, playing with the Nigerian children. He cracked his favorite words of wisdom about preferring roses with spines and the humble work of helping others, always with that childlike chuckle. He played his role of Samaritan and savior to perfection, and the more he played it, more funds came—and more migrants. "My news story was [broadcast] on a national level, so whether you like it or not the black man who's in Madrid hears that a monk receives women migrants with children, then what do they do? They call these women in Morocco."

The Father was not, in fact, a priest; he was a Franciscan monk. A Spanish journalist invented his nickname, which quickly caught on. "It's affectionate, isn't it, this Father thing?" he said. The women he received, most of them Nigerian, called him "Papá." Journalists came and filmed *his negritas, as he sometimes called them, while they bathed their babies, prayed, and praised his work. "I happy house of Father, thanks to God,"* said one woman to camera in stilted Spanish. *Papá gave them food and shelter; when they gave birth, he was there at the bedside.*

The Father's biographer, a Catholic TV presenter, described him as a *"bandit of the Strait,"* taking from the rich and giving to the poorest. For her book cover, she weighed her options: either his hand over the Bible, transmitting his idea of Christian humility, or one of him kissing a black baby on the cheek. *"This one would be polemical,"* she whispered. But the polemics were not restricted to touchy images of men of faith kissing black babies. Some in the church, she sighed, saw the Father as a *"bad example to follow."* In that case, she said, *"why not call into question Mother Teresa?"* For her, the Father represented that *"other church"*—not the stiff-collared Catholicism of the Spanish mainstream, but a more humane faith. *"His law is love."*

The Father acknowledged that many priests were unhappy about his work, *"I don't know why."* The same was true, however, among aid workers. Some saw his media stardom as grabbing attention from both migrants and the work of tending to them. Around the Strait, as elsewhere on the migratory circuit, aid organizations battled over scarce resources and beneficiaries. Here the Father had a winning card, as he himself recognized. The black fatherless babies washing up on Spain's shores were the perfect, innocent humanitarian subject, and the black-robed Papá was their fatherly savior, inserting the migrant story into a frame of Christian charity.

In this he was not alone. The Catholic organization Caritas is everywhere along migrant routes, and so are the Scalabrini Fathers and the Jesuits. If humanitarianism is suffused with *"legacies of the sacred,"* as critical scholars have recently remarked, the Father pointed to the continued prominence of openly Christian care and advocacy on behalf of the world's migrants and refugees.[2]

But in the past five years, the Father's work had dwindled. Arrivals across the Strait had receded, and the Red Cross had supplanted him in receiving *"vulnerable"* migrants. When I met him between my trips to Ceuta, Melilla, and Morocco, he sometimes looked haggard and frail. He grumbled about the protests by migrants in Ceuta and by Moroccans in Melilla, about *moros* who did not integrate and about prostitution among the Nigerian women formerly under his care. *"The migrant never tells you the truth, because he's afraid of the mafias,"* he said. This was not the voice of childlike chuckles and Christian humility on the *media record: it was more like that of an elderly Spanish man concerned about the perils of globalization.*

In the corridor, the Father stopped to look at a framed magazine clipping of himself standing knee-deep in the Strait. "The photographer must have earned good money from that," he said. "At least he should send [a copy] to me, don't you think?" Despite the Father's success in leveraging the illegality industry, he controlled neither his image nor his name. As I left he gave me a hug and a jokey slap on the head.

CHAPTER 6

Stranded in Time

Darkness falls over the shacks in Melilla. John takes another swig of his lukewarm whiskey mixed with cheap energy drink and sways to the mix of Fela Kuti and hip-hop streaming out of a speaker atop a rickety bench. "Fela was a *prophet*," he says. "He stood up for Africa." The whiskey glass circulates among his Nigerian friends in our little circle, seated on ripped-out car seats and plastic petrol cans. Around us, women stir black metal pots, dragging children along with them wherever they go. These are the *chabolas,* or shanties, as migrants call their makeshift dwellings, which they have furnished out of pallets and tarp. Like Ceuta's hillside forests, the chabolas offer a brief reprieve from the observatory of the enclave—the turnstiles and camp cards, the patrols and surveillance cameras. Reprieve, but no escape. From here, Melilla unfolds as a world of multiple fences: the fence around the migrant camp downhill, the mesh shielding the golf course next door, the high-tech valla separating the European Union from Morocco around a bend in the border road. "This place they call Europe, but I think it's Africa," says John, his hand fanning out over the dust-coated misery of the chabolas and the distant Mount Gurugú from where migrants once descended en masse towards the valla. The whiskey glass is filled and shared out again. John's friend, sporting fake Raybans and a neatly trimmed beard, raps along to the hip-hop. "We are like convicts," he sings. A captive colony: the chabola dwellers have been stuck in Melilla between one and three years, waiting for their chance to go to the Iberian Peninsula.

FIGURE 15. Protesters enact their sense of imprisonment by "shackling" one another in front of the cameras during Ceuta's "strike" of 2010. Photo by Cristina Vergara López.

Eventlessness defined migrant life in the enclaves. Ceuta's strike in the summer of 2010 was an exception—the migrants in Ceuta and Melilla were above all sucked into an endless, dreary, patient process of *waiting*. The days ground on, each like the next. The long wait endured by the "convicts" was in part a result of the economic crisis, which had cut off any Spanish—if not European—demand for Africa's wayward laborers. More important, however, the crisis had pushed the illegality industry into a phase of consolidation, in which it was developing its own discrete logics that sometimes dovetailed with and sometimes contradicted European demands for a drip-feed of undocumented labor. The enclaves' politics of containment, the reason for the strike and the subject of this chapter, was one such logic.

For the police, migrants were quite simply blocked in the enclaves in order to strangle the finances of the "mafias" who brought them there. Marcelo, the chief of the police immigration bureau in Ceuta, illustrated this by positioning himself as a hypothetical trafficker: "If I pick up *[capto]* one hundred women in Nigeria to bring them from there and put them in Madrid [for prostitution], I have an estimated cost of, I guess, €6,000 for each one" in smuggling them into Spain. The women paid €3,000 each up front and the rest once they arrived, €300,000 in total; this meant the smuggler had to invest the remaining €300,000. "If you withhold fifty of them in Ceuta and you repatriate another fifty, my business will be in ruins!" he exclaimed. "I've lost, because the poor woman who was heading there [to the peninsula] can't pay. I've lost €150,000, and you've withheld the other women here for two years, that's two years that I have immobilized capital, that's another €150,000 lost." The strategy, then, was to remove Ceuta and Melilla from the smuggling route by selectively retaining and deporting migrants. In this policing effort, the time migrants spent in the enclaves constituted *capital* withheld from the presumed smuggling rings. What Marcelo failed to mention, however, was that in 2010 most sub-Saharan migrants had arrived through their own efforts, rather than with the help of professional smugglers. For these migrants as well as for their trafficked or smuggled counterparts, retention constituted collective punishment, reducing them to indefinite confinement in ways akin to the island detention practices in Australia and elsewhere along the fringes of the West.[1]

As a result a silent battle was being waged in the enclaves over time withheld and stolen, emptied time, time bought and given, time retrieved for observation, scrutiny, and care. Yet as theorists of temporality have long noted, time cannot be separated from space: indeed, the waste of migrants' time was predicated upon their spatial immobility. Ceuta and Melilla were gaps in the migration circuit, in which a regime of inter-locking time-spaces, unevenly stretched over the enclaves' tiny territo-ries, seemed to regulate migrants as a population while disciplining them as bodies in the "biopolitical" fashion familiar from the works of philosopher Michel Foucault. Their time-space of confinement, ephem-eral yet inescapable, soon became a burden weighing heavily on their shoulders.[2]

This time-space regime did not simply confine migrants in what activists called the "sweet prison" of the enclaves.[3] Like ship castaways, they rather seemed stranded in a topsy-turvy world with its own rules and routines, a world of mimicry and make-believe. In its strangeness, this world was reminiscent not only of the refugee camp existence invoked by migrants but also of the "total institutions" of Western social states. Like the mental asylums and prisons once studied by the sociologist Erving Goffman, enclave confinement inserted the reluctant "inmates" into an institutional order with its own logics. As in prisons and asylums, these inmates went through a process of "mortification" that sought to eradicate their previous adventurer selves: they were cleansed, checked for diseases, and sparsely clothed and accommodated, their camp life documented in thickening files. And again as in these institutions, their recalcitrance was interpreted along moralistic lines suitable to the authorities' objectives. They were, as John's friend had hinted, captives in an offshore, self-contained world.[4]

The migrants were not hapless victims of this contradictory world, however, but participated in its very creation. After all, Ceuta and Mel-illa were just the most extreme example of the imposed waiting that defined the migration circuit: waiting for contacts, for money transfers, for a clandestine crossing, for papers. If the migrant strike had hinted at a new impatience among the hardened adventurers of Ceuta, there were numerous other strategies techniques of waiting—in the migratory repertoire. Some tried to render themselves invisible to avoid apprehen-sion; others sought to accumulate "good time" and be rewarded with passage to the peninsula; yet others, such as John and his chabola friends, aimed to stretch their time in the enclaves while hoping for deliverance. This multifaceted battle over time in both Ceuta and Mel-illa reached from abstract time-as-capital through the camp's day-to-day schedules all the way down to the briefest of time slots: the half-second pause in speech before migrants revealed their names and nationalities to strangers.

BUYING TIME: PAUSES, LIES, AND PARKING LOTS

A THURSDAY IN AUGUST, 1:30 P.M. *Ding-ding-ding-dong* rang the microphone of the Ceuta camp as I called out for the five latest arrivals of an increasingly busy summer. They had already showered with an antiparasite shampoo while one of the camp security guards kept watch, as was the routine, and had then been escorted to the camp clinic for a medical checkup and the TB test, indicated by inked squares on their upper arms. Eventually they came into reception and sat down, waiting for a meeting with the social workers. Four of the migrants, whose natty dreads hinted at their previous rough living in the forest of Ben Younech, outside Ceuta, had come together in an inflatable boat. The fifth had set out alone, seeking to paddle across the Strait in a tiny raft before being spotted by a commercial ship and picked up by Salvamento Marítimo. He was called Patrick, a twenty-nine-year-old Cameroonian in shorts, slippers, and a sun hat. "I don't know why they sent me here; I was trying to go to Algeciras," he said. His voice stayed calm, but he was visibly frustrated. He had good reason to be. This was his second time in Ceuta. He had first come eight years previously, in 2002. Deported back to Cameroon, he had set out again and been on the road ever since. "Now they conserve people longer here," he remarked. Before, it had been a matter of weeks, not years, before people were sent on. Patrick was unique in having tried to paddle alone across the Strait, but in two other respects he was typical of the African migrants arriving in 2010 in Ceuta and Melilla: he had spent many years on the road and had not made use of the smuggling rings mentioned by the police chief. As a bona fide adventurer, he took pride in his skills in skirting borders without assistance; he also lacked funds for expensive smuggling trips. The time he was losing in Ceuta was his own.

The microphone that had summoned Patrick was at the heart of camp life, its amplified *ding-ding-ding* and "attention please" lending an uneven daily rhythm and sense of purpose to the long, hot days of summer. Lurking in a corner of reception, it was a source of banter and ambivalence, an instrument of camp authority occasionally subverted when migrants grabbed it and called out names to everyone's laughter. Usually workers would reluctantly go up to the mike, press the red button, and call out names for workshops or meetings in basic French or English. Often no one would show up despite the repeated calls of names. "It's because they haven't memorized them yet," said Mamá with characteristic frankness. The migrants were not used to hearing the names "they had been assigned" by the smugglers. "Many times you ask for their names and there's a pause, then they look it up on their [camp] card."

Captivity yielded knowledge. The immobility of migrants in Ceuta and Melilla meant collecting data on them should be easy: names and nationalities, backgrounds and biometrics, routes and destinations. But the authorities faced a formidable adversary. The lies and pauses, the microphone and its unheeded calls, were symptoms of the war over time and knowledge that was silently waged between the Spanish state and the migrants, with the camp workers as uneasy go-betweens.

. . .

In the daytime, migrants dispersed across Ceuta and Melilla. They loitered in parking lots in the merciless sun, occasionally waving drivers into parking spaces. This work they called *tira-tira* (pulling). Besides waiting in shop doorways to beg and help customers with their bags—or, in Melilla, "doing *limpiacoches*" (washing cars) to remove the dust blowing in from Morocco—tira-tira was all they could do to make a few euros. I often sauntered up, asking innocent questions. "What is your name? Where do you come from?" There was usually a pause before the reply, a wavering, a brief silence before a West African might utter Somalia as his country or Mohamed as his name. In this pause lay the silence of their predicament, their thoughts and doubts bundled into a half second. I soon learned to stop asking about country or name and to inquire instead about the measure of all things in the enclave: "How long have you been here?"

The pause, often accompanied by a brief quiver across the lips, hinted at the fear of not being believed, of being caught lying. And many migrants lied. How could they not? The goal was the peninsula, and the end justified the means. The twisting of truth arose out of their captive predicament, but to workers and locals it became, rather, a sign of their migranthood, just as it had for the police on the hunt for illegal migrants across deserts and seas. Everyone knew that migrants invented nationalities and names. They claimed physical symptoms and diseases according to what might take them to the peninsula, camp workers said. If there are no good dentists in Ceuta, everyone suddenly had a rotten tooth.

To the migrants, Ceuta itself represented a pause, a holding of breath before their push across the final hurdle into Europe. This was so in a strictly official sense. Migrants were not permitted to join the municipal register *(padrón municipal)*, which meant the time they spent here did not easily count towards the Spanish *arraigo social* (social embeddedness), whereby irregular migrants could apply for a residence permit if they were able to prove that they had lived in the country for three years.[5] The migrants were acutely aware of this, complaining of having to start from scratch if they ever made it to the peninsula. "You have to remember that one year is a long time for them," said Luis, a ponytailed lawyer at the camp, whose office was bedecked with pictures of the West Bank wall and magazine clippings about the Senegalese "mother victims of the cayucos." "These are their best years."

The pauses were ambiguous. On the one hand, migrants aimed to reduce them. They did tira-tira for this reason—to get away from their doubts and from "only thinking," as one documentary on Ceuta's migrants put it.[6] If the pause swallowed your whole world, you would go crazy. "There are mad people up there," migrants said of the camp: listless, absent, psychotic. They had succumbed to the pause, fallen into the crack that constituted their existence. On the other hand, the invocation of Somalia or Sudan was itself a way of *extending* the larger pause of Ceuta. In this effort, migrants' make-believe nationalities interacted with the paperwork produced about them. Foremost among these documents was the yellow card that had been held aloft by Ceuta's strikers.

Asylum seekers filed their demands with the Immigration Office in the center soon after arrival. The yellow card they then received was valid in all of Spain—so it said on the card—and inserted the paperless travelers into a documented order. But since police, following Spain's new asylum law, no longer accepted the cards as documentation in port, the freedom of movement promised on the cards was phony. In this sense, the cards were what anthropologists have called "make-believe documents," or a phantasmatic form of state-produced certification. To complicate matters further, the yellow cards were a fake-upon-a-fake, based as they often were on invented nationalities. Ceuta's asylum seekers remained, in the words of the police chief Marcelo, "completely undocumented."[7]

If fake nationalities and asylum applications held little promise, they at least insured migrants against immediate deportation and kept the hope of a laissez-passer to the peninsula alive. This was the strategy of the Nigerians, whose government had a readmissions agreement with Spain. Asylum seekers from other nationalities coveted what was known as the *fuera* (out!), the Spanish word used by migrants in Ceuta to refer to the steps of their expulsion order following a refusal of asylum. After three fueras, migrants hoped for transfer to detention on the mainland, followed by deportation. Like Ceuta's strikers, they *sought* rejection of their claims and transfer to the CIEs, since they knew deportation was unlikely to be carried out for lack of readmission agreements between their countries and Spain. However, even this was denied them: in 2010 the fueras were painfully slow in coming.

John, who had a family in the chabolas, had little reason to invent a nationality. Instead he hoped for papers, an impossibility in the crisis-racked Spain of 2010. Patrick, who went by several names, sought none of the above: he neither applied for asylum nor invented a nationality. Instead he was biding his time, waiting for the possibility of a clandestine passage to Europe.

. . .

The mystery of migrants' origins, journeys, and stratagems was a source of banter and intrigue among camp workers, who used the extended pause of Ceuta to guess and classify at leisure. How could they not? This was after all their task in a sorting center, and like any professionals they wanted to understand their "users," categorize them, and assist them accordingly—here with the added challenge of the truth being hidden. Yet in their search for truth they became, for migrants, complicit in the regime that kept them stranded and deportable. Mamá's attempts to list the camp's Muslim residents for special Ramadan mealtimes were hampered by suspicion; anxious residents inquired whether new faces in the camp, such as myself, were really undercover police.

Theories and tricks for ascertaining nationalities were often aired during breakfast breaks in the coffee room. Some so-called alleged nationalities were easy to expose, said Luis. Nigerians might say they are from Sudan, then "you ask them about the capital, Darfur, and *janjaweed,* and they don't know anything." Mamá read nationalities off residents' gait and bodies—the tall, long-limbed, and lanky ones were Senegalese, the Cameroonians thick-boned and broad-faced, the Nigerians similar to the Cameroonians but louder, "very Anglophone." Almost despite myself, I too had started taking a forensic approach to nationalities. Why did that Gambian speak French, not English? Do Ivoirians have that type of tribal scar on their cheeks?

Such guesswork was constant among camp workers and involved defining not only physical but also temperamental traits. One day I entered the coffee room and there was the big, friendly head of *social* together with the former director, now relegated to an administrative role. A map of Somalia was spread across the table. "And the African stuff, have you learned it yet?" the former director asked me, meaning whether

I had started to recognize different nationalities by their traits. He gave me a crash course, contrasting the "docile" and easy-going migrants from Côte d'Ivoire, Mali, and Senegal with the Nigerians and Cameroonians, who "create more trouble" *(dan más guerra)*. The new director added a more analytical angle: the Congolese and Cameroonians were well-organized, the former outside and the latter inside the camp, while the Nigerians had lost dominance and instead engaged in shady "business."

This game of guessing and classification could, once frustration was factored in, easily take on the more sinister air of intelligence gathering. "They lie about everything," said one camp psychologist. Migrants started "playing the victim" in one-to-one sessions, he said, inventing mental and physical ailments, "but I start noticing incoherencies quickly." Stories circulated of a resident who had taken to reading the newspaper upside down and another who just stared listlessly in front of him. Eventually these migrants had been sent on to Red Cross reception centers on the mainland. "They are faking it, but you can't have people like that in the CETI," said one worker. Others were more sympathetic, even attributing migrants' madness to their captivity. "I've seen people who are OK, normal, when they enter," said one workshop leader. "Then they change completely; it's like they are a different person." Even the symptoms of the fakers could start to become real the longer their performance went on and the longer the pause of Ceuta was extended.

The guessing game clashed with camp procedures, which depended on *certainty* in pinpointing migrant identities. And such pinpointing was central to camp life; how else could entry cards be produced, forms filled in, data collected, names called out? The result was an awkward splintering between the documented existence of residents and the hidden truth about them, a game of make-believe played out both inside and outside the camp. In the tira-tira world, the Francophone migrants complained that the Somalis and Sudanese had all the best parking spots. Camp workers invoked fictitious nationalities in discussing slots for using the gym with migrants and bantered with them about the threat of deportation for Somalis. The game went beyond jokes and gym times to encompass central aspects of camp organization. The green camp cards—key in allowing for exit, entry, meals, and any interaction with the workers, who relied on cards rather than name or facial memory as means of identification—listed the "alleged nationalities" and names. In such interactions, workers and migrants soon became uneasy accomplices in the game of make-believe played out in the time-space gap of Ceuta.

The card conundrum in Ceuta exemplifies the power of documents, noted by anthropologist Mathijs Pelkmans, to forge or impose state-sanctioned identities in interaction with their holders. Also noting this disciplinary power, fellow ethnographer Tobias Kelly argues in a study of the Palestinian West Bank that documentation may serve to *increase* rather than reduce uncertainty. By opening a gap between legal and physical status, he says, documents allow for degrees of manipulation that produce fears and anxieties among their holders, who in this way come to embody the indeterminacies of their documents. In Ceuta and Melilla, documents did both produce new identities and uncertainty around these, yet with a twist. Here, the "gap" between legal and physical status was built into documented reality itself, with the connivance of the authorities. Anxiety resulted not from uncertainties in the interpretation of documents but from the *certainty* that documented reality itself was arbitrary and devoid of meaning. The documents' imposed identities were shallow, instrumental, and phony; no one would destroy them in the way Pelkmans describes passports being torn at the Georgia-Turkey border; no one would ask whether the identity given by the document was *really* in correspondence with its holder, as Israeli soldiers did at the Israel-Palestine checkpoints discussed by Kelly.[8]

One day Mamá wanted to show me a newborn baby. We went into the camp clinic and met an Anglophone West African woman in the corridor. "Congratulations!" Mamá called out and hugged her. On a hospital litter inside lay the little newborn girl. We inspected the newborn's camp card with its photo of her small, sleepy baby face. The card stated her name along those of her parents, as well as her country of origin: Somalia.

The African women were in the worst bind of all. Their bulging bellies, a common sight in the camp, attested to the fluctuations in the Spanish policy on detaining, liberating, and deporting pregnant women. When they realized pregnancy no longer guaranteed transfer to the peninsula in late 2008, the psychologist said, several of them suddenly carried out abortions. In 2010 pregnancy insured women against deportation—but by cutting short the transfer to a CIE, it could also keep them stuck in Ceuta for even longer. One male resident pointed to a pregnant woman walking past. "She's been here for three years; now she's pregnant, which means she'll be here for five years! Everyone teases her about it, but she just cries."

If migrants emerged from this make-believe world as untrustworthy figures, so did the authorities. One of the Congolese protesters, a musician and holder of a yellow card, had seen his high regard for Europe shattered during his seven months in Ceuta. "The Spaniards lie a lot," he said: the police promised them decisions and meetings, but nothing came of it. The institutional side of the camp was eyed with a similar mistrust, especially under the previous director, who some residents scolded for his alleged close links to security. And then there were the journalists, in cahoots with the state. I had bought the local rag and walked past a Ugandan friend tending to a supermarket entrance, and he shouted out, "That paper is no good, it's all lies!" He pointed at the front page, scolding the paper's journalist, who always wrote bad things. "Every Wednesday he comes, when they prepare rice, and they take photos." Nice food called for promotional shots. The seemingly arbitrary decisions that kept him stuck in Ceuta added to his anger. "We have no facts," he said. "They don't tell us the truth, because we are immigrants."

The lack of information was made worse by the camp policy of using Spanish even with the most recent arrivals. The pause when asked about names and in heeding the microphone's calls was as much about the pitfalls in easing residents into the pidgin Spanish of the camp as it was about lies and outright evasion.

One day a new resident came to reception, upset. "I've signed a piece of paper, but I don't know what it means," he told me. "It's only in Spanish." He wanted to see the social worker who made him sign it. "She explained something in French, but she doesn't speak it well, so I didn't understand." We went into the *social* office, where one worker was adamant that her colleague had translated it: "Well, I was here and I heard it! But of course I can explain it again." So she did, along these lines, and I translated: the paper said only that the migrant was at the camp voluntarily, that he would follow the camp rules, and that all he had told the workers was true. It was "nothing strange," everyone signed it as they entered, and it would not affect him in any legal way. "Okay?" The resident nodded, asked me to offer his excuses for taking up her time, and left without asking for a copy of the text he had signed.

Camp life ticked over through the circulation of make-believe documents: the signed entry forms, the yellow asylum cards that gave phony access to the whole of Spain while offering little chance of a full asylum procedure, the green camp cards with their mix of fictitious and real nationalities and names. Meanwhile the black migrants of the camp could use their generic categorization as subsaharianos in inventing nationalities and their bodies as defense when they invoked health problems or sought pregnancy. But if camp life was a game, it was one of "who blinks first." In mouthing half truths and lies, migrants risked being found out or getting stuck even longer. In pushing the make-believe further, camp workers risked the captives' wrath, as had happened in the strike.

The make-believe and arbitrariness, codified in documents, created real effects in camp relations and in the lives of migrants, as attested to by the real-fake bouts of madness, the pregnancies, the Somali parking monopolies, and the chance of being sent to the peninsula. It also impinged upon that more formal circuit of information—the regular reports sent by workers and police to the ministries in Madrid. A constant production of information, including the psychological questionnaires amassed on new arrivals, data provided to the police and *social,* and any incidents registered by the madres, accompanied the circulation of half truths within the camp itself, remaining out of reach of migrants yet helping to structure their daily rhythms in the camp.

KILLING TIME: SCHEDULES AND DOSSIERS

A TUESDAY IN AUGUST, 5:45 P.M. The smell of fried potatoes wafted out of the room next to the canteen. Inside, a group of residents stood around a table with catering hairnets on their heads, chopping tubers for a Spanish tortilla under the stern gaze of two women from the NGO Accem, a major contractor in Spain's outsourced migration assistance programs. "What's this called?" one of the workshop leaders inquired while waving the skimming ladle. She looked from face to face before homing in on an unfortunate African woman. The woman did not know. "An *espumadera,*" the leader said, admonishing her pupil. The workshop leader pointed at objects in the small makeshift kitchen, making the woman repeat vocabulary—*aceite* (oil), *patata* (potato), *sartén* (frying pan). The head of *social* had come along to watch proceedings, in a welcome relief from the tensions generated by the strikers. "They've spent three weeks here and then start screaming 'Guantánamo,'" he said, standing on the ledge behind the cooking room and observing a ping-pong game outside the residential modules below. Finally the tortilla was ready, and the head of *social* and I joined the director, camp workers, and kitchen helpers to eat the moist, golden slices.

This was the good work of the camp that had been overshadowed by the strike. Workshops, language classes, and IT sessions, psychological assistance and health checks, sports and excursions: the opportunities served up by the Spanish authorities for irregular migrants were unmatched by any other southern European country. The first task at the camp was a "recuperation of human dignity," the director had explained, followed by social integration through learning Spanish and other skills. But the picture had grown more complex the longer migrants were stuck in limbo. During the Spanish economic boom, migrants were taught how to register with local authorities and where to look for work once on the peninsula. Those who made an effort to participate in courses "were rewarded with exit to the peninsula, [but] from 2006 onwards, this was cut," said one Red Cross officer in Melilla. "The work of integration got somewhat lost." With the withdrawal of the reward of exit, the courses that took place in the camps in 2010 merely filled—or killed—the time of migrants. As one worker put it: "There's little hope for them at the moment, but we do what we can. At least the things they learn here are something they can take with them. We have to encourage them but without giving any expectations."

This logic of passing time through what Erving Goffman calls "removal activities" is familiar from other modern, total institutions. The "sense of dead and heavy-hanging time" in asylums or prisons, Goffman says, might lead to a premium being placed on voluntary, unserious pursuits among inmates: "If the ordinary activities in total institutions can be said to torture time, these activities mercifully kill it."[9]

Even allowing for this distractive function, however, the integration work of the camps remained an absurd exercise. How could anyone learn Spanish ensconced on a faraway hillside, suspended in time and fearful of deportation? How could you integrate while held captive as a collective punishment, unable to work or register with the local authorities? The enclaves, in their extreme juxtaposition of incompatible goals, simply brought to a head Spain's—and Europe's—contradictory migratory logics on integration and control, as already noted in the strike.[10] These contradictions, in turn, were unevenly played out across the enclaves' "geography of time."[11] If the time-space of control stretched from fence to port and forest to camp, camp time itself was further subdivided into fields of surveillance, integration, and indifference.

In Ceuta, the camp layout—offices upstairs, residential modules downstairs—helped create two distinct but complementary rhythms. Upstairs, old-fashioned time discipline reigned. Camp life was defined by schedules and governed by the clock, much as in a school or factory.[12] Mealtimes at 1:00 P.M. and 8:00 P.M., one hour each, with the guards congregating at the door once the canteen was about to close, to make sure it was emptied on time. Curfew at night and early morning, when everyone had to be in or else be registered on their cards as absent:

three nights of absence and the residents lost their beds, as well as *anti-güedad* (seniority) once they came back. And they always did come back: banishment meant sleeping rough in the forests with little chance of an income or even nourishment.

In this regimented time, paperwork gave the impression of progress. As migrants arrived fresh from being rescued, they were admonished to keep their documents safely. These included the "affiliation" paper, a thin slip the police gave to new arrivals listing their temporary identification number (NIP); the medical card, another flimsy piece of documentation cataloguing the compulsory medical tests and other notes from the camp clinic; a paper delineating the camp rules; and the protocolo slip with its list of compulsory meetings. A stamp marked attendance for each meeting, which were all to take place in the new residents' first week in the camp: medical screening, a psychological test, a compulsory Spanish class introduction, and a presentation on their rights to claim asylum.

If paperwork, clockwork, and compulsory meetings created a distinct upstairs temporality, time downstairs in the dorms sagged and melted like a surrealist clock. This world, visited only by the madres and the guards, was bereft of routines, if not of activity. The sleeping modules, exposed to the scorching sun and the winds and rains lashing the hillside, were alternately hot and freezing. They were also cramped and claustrophobic. In one female dorm, water had been seeping in from the next-door shower, creating a puddle under one of the beds. A baby cot stood next to the bunk. "The baby can't sleep like that!" the women complained, asking Mamá for another dorm. But the only empty module in these busy August days was closed because the ground below it had cracked and sunk, in part thanks to the construction of the horse-riding center just uphill from the camp. In other rooms, the electric sockets were coming loose, exposing live wires. Black mold stains spread across the cracks between wall and ceiling. "They shower with hot water in here in winter," Mamá offered as explanation. "I tell them that can create problems with humidity." The modules had no running hot water, so the women resorted to boiling water themselves. Eventually sockets would be fixed, floors cleaned, and rooms fumigated, but the atmosphere of neglect was evident in the futile attempts at keeping the decay of the modules at bay.

. . .

ANOTHER WEDNESDAY, 5:30 P.M. It was the hottest time of August, a couple of weeks before the Ceuta strike began, and I was loitering in the camp courtyard. An elderly Moroccan gardener hosed the trees in the yard while sipping mint tea from a plastic glass. Many of the camp's contract workers hailed from across the border, with its plentiful supply of licit and illicit labor. "This tree," the gardener said, pointing to the large poplar in front of us, "I planted it in 2002." This was the year that Patrick, the lone boatman of the Strait, had first arrived in Ceuta. As the gardener moved on, Patrick sauntered up. He had not been feeling at ease since arriving. "I feel lazy and I don't know why," he said in his usual manner, thoughtfully and slowly, as if weighing every word in his mouth. Could it be the heat? No, he said, "maybe it's the food, though sometimes the food is good. You don't know. All we can do is wait and see what they give us. All I want to do is sleep." He was starting to doubt himself. Like the other residents, he was "thinking too much," especially when stuck inside the camp, going over the lost decade of his adventure. "I keep asking myself, why me?" he said. "Trying, trying, trying to become something, but it's impossible."

The "pragmatics of time that comes with living in shelters," identified by the ethnographer Robert Desjarlais in his studies of the homeless mentally ill, was already taking its toll on Patrick, the disjointed rhythms of camp life triggering a bodily unease in him much as they led to bouts of madness among others: "The episodic quality of shelter life, where you need to live one day at a time and not get ahead of yourself and where nobody does anything, fixes time as a diffuse and sporadic order. There are eddies when the mundane occurs, and whirlpools when someone is restrained or hospitalized, but much of the day, week, and month consists of a vast ocean of routine."[13]

In this fleeting, endless present—again reminiscent of the "heavy" time encountered by Goffman in asylums—hope took on a phantasmatic quality. Much as migrants were given phony promises of upstairs time, they also harbored rosy thoughts of the future once they made it "up" (en haut) to the peninsula. These make-believe futures festered in the gap of the enclaves, in the empty time-space wedged between the rough world of the adventure and crisis-hit Spain.

As hope dwindled with each passing month, the effort to enforce upstairs time became more difficult. Instead, workers used what Goffman calls a "privilege system"—nudges, rewards, and punishments—to sort and sift good from bad migrants. The nudge was the dossier kept on each resident that might, after all, enable one's passage to the peninsula. Good behavior was not just rewarded with free cigarettes but, the madres insisted, led to a thick dossier listing a resident's attendance at the compulsory Spanish classes and protocolo meetings. Spanish course attendance was rewarded with access to the camp's computer hall and workshops, such as the cooking class with its long waiting list. The punishment, meanwhile, was the *partes* (reports) filed by social workers and madres for bad behavior. After the strike, nudges and punishments mixed in strange new ways. "Many people have been penalized," Patrick explained, "and the penalty is Spanish classes." If residents did not attend, their card could be withdrawn, and they would be stuck inside the camp. This was in keeping with the make-believe integration work of the enclaves, attesting to the absurdity of language learning among deportable migrants. Patrick, like many other adventurers, had no concentration for attending the course, which the students anyhow saw as substandard. Besides, he still had the Spanish diploma he received from the camp in 2002 in his family home in Cameroon. "What has that helped me?" he asked. Diploma or not, Patrick had still been deported.

Language, instead of aiding integration or allowing passage to the mainland, became the measure of all things in the camp. Those who dominated Spanish got to participate in upstairs time, while those who resisted or failed to learn were marooned in downstairs time. The latter group consisted, above all, of the camp's women. Sitting in their cliques around the downstairs tables, braiding hair, playing board games, or washing clothes, they were admonished by Mamá for failing to learn Spanish during their long time in Ceuta. One woman snapped back. "You've been here for seven years, and you haven't learned any English yet!" Some workers said the women *did* understand Spanish but simply pretended not to know. In either case, their refusal to participate, at least in part related to their frustration over losing the most important years of their lives, marginalized them in the camp.

Language learning also played a large role at the two other establishments for migrants in Ceuta. On the edge of town, the humanitarian association run by Ceuta's nuns provided language exchanges in addition to running workshops in making handcrafted candles, much as the camp had its cooking and Spanish classes. Another center also run by a Christian NGO, Centro San Antonio, on the slopes close to the camp, offered Internet access and Spanish courses, with class participation again the prerequisite for screen time. In these sites, a certain subject was being promoted and produced: the good, integrated immigrant, who was kept busy and connected in exchange for his linguistic efforts.

Among the "good immigrants" with reassuringly thick dossiers, the Red Cross volunteers stood out. Amadou, the adventurer who climbed the valla alone in chapter 4, was one of them. He spent his days helping the frail and elderly, his bus pass paid by the Red Cross, and even assisted relatives of Guardia Civil officers, the gatekeepers he had once eluded. "I've been in almost all the media here, on television, photos in *El Faro* and *El Pueblo*, while helping out as a volunteer," he said. Amadou's accumulation of virtue meant he was showered with attention, but his main reward as a model migrant was a busy schedule. He clocked up hours as a volunteer, attended first aid courses, and participated in Red Cross outings. For him, in contrast to Patrick and the majority of residents, time moved purposefully ahead.

The schedules and dossiers held out the promise of making time move, accumulate, produce something. This upstairs-time regime was a fragile construct, however. One camp worker, frustrated with the arbitrariness of rules and punishments, grabbed hold of a protocolo schedule, pointing at the time slots for meetings that residents had to tick off. "Look, here it says they have to go at 11:00 A.M. but it's not at 11:00 A.M. It's whenever they [the workers] feel like it! The residents go there at eleven o'clock, and no one is there, and lose confidence." The rules said residents should be expelled after three nights away, she noted, but sometimes they were expelled after only one night. The strikers, meanwhile, had not been expelled even after several nights outside. "Someone comes and asks me whether they can go out, and I can't say 'yes,' because if they throw him out afterwards, he will blame me for it. There's no coordination; everyone does what they feel like. For the residents it's very negative." The residents' protocolo slips sometimes stayed unstamped for weeks.

The camp time of rewards and punishments, schedules and dossiers, created a false sense of progress that helped disguise the fact that migrants were, to the authorities, mere numbers and their time capital withheld from the smugglers. Here the make-believe documents, as mediators between neglect and due process, played a key role in an intricate bureaucratic production of indifference as they circulated among workers, migrants, and police. Yet the paperwork also sparked strong emotional reactions, as already noted. The thick dossiers, ticked-off fueras, protocol stamps, and signed forms stirred hopes of release or, in contrast, fears of confinement or deportation. When the paperwork refused to veil the callous confinement of the enclaves—when protocol slips stayed unstamped or yellow cards failed to work their magic—it could trigger anger and rage, as a sign of the "lies" to which migrants felt themselves subjected. This is what had happened in Ceuta's strike.[14]

STRETCHING TIME: SURVEILLANCE AND ESCAPE

A WEDNESDAY IN JULY, 4:30 P.M. It was the month before the strike, and I was talking to Jean the protester in a café in central Ceuta. He had already been sleeping rough outside the police jefatura together with his fellow Congolese asylum seekers for several weeks and looked increasingly haggard. Suddenly a mustachioed Spanish man came up, flashed a badge, asked for our papers. Police control. He eyed Jean's camp card briefly, then paid my passport considerably more attention. He asked questions, took down my address, phone number, profession. A "neighbor" who had seen us talking had tipped him off, he explained. "You never know; this might be about smuggling or something illegal." After he left, Jean shook his head. "I'm not afraid of him," he said. "They always control us." He knew why the undercover policeman had checked on us: because I am white and Jean is black, his color marking him as "illegal" in the enclaves' social order.

Ceuta and Melilla, tiny militarized territories hemmed in between the vallas and the sea, were perfect spaces of surveillance. Their delicate geopolitical situation meant that undercover police and informers were everywhere, or as graffiti on a Melilla wall put it: "If snitches [chivatos] could fly, we would no longer see the sun." In Melilla in particular, police also enlisted chivatos among the migrants, who were quietly offered possibilities of a laissez-passer for gathering intelligence. As for the concerned "neighbor" informing on me and Jean, this was surely one of the many local informers eavesdropping on strangers in Ceuta's cafés.

The captive migrants, singled out by their skin, constituted readily available objects for raids, checks, and deportations. The time lag between searching for and apprehending them was minuscule. "Here they don't have to detain anyone," said the camp lawyer Luis. The police only needed to go and search for them in the camp. The camp, he clarified, "is not a detention center, but Ceuta in itself is a detention center." The port was closed, all exits were blocked. There was no escape. This is why the undercover policeman took more interest in my passport than in Jean's camp card: he knew he could find, detain, and deport Jean whenever expedient. The police, preparing "the deportation of 1, 2, or 150," simply "proceed to detain them," Marcelo explained. "You call them in, and they show up, no problem." Court summons and police notifications, written in obscure Spanish legalese, were posted on the camp notice board, next to leaflets for sevillanas dancing workshops and the like. Most residents had nothing to lose in trudging all the way down to the police offices or the courts in the hope that they would be taken to the peninsula. If they failed to show up or were to be deported en masse, the camp could be raided at any moment, a roundup yielding dozens of conationals at a time.

. . .

The camp itself was a machine of surveillance, albeit a creaking, imperfect one. A private security company—since censored by the authorities for malfeasance—kept order in the camp.[15] Some guards walked their daily rounds of the living modules with a swagger, their trousers tucked into heavy black boots and batons at the ready. Others joked and chatted with the migrants and even befriended them on Facebook. One female guard had found love with an African camp resident; a male colleague of hers had improved his English by listening to the migrants' stories "for hours at a time."

In the weeks before the strike climaxed and the policing of the camp was ratcheted up several gears, the status of the guards often seemed suspended. In daytime, they ensconced themselves in the air-conditioned cubicle at the gate or manned the reception desk when the female receptionist was off duty, cracking jokes with staff and residents; guarding the canteen entrance at night, they clapped out a flamenco rhythm with the kitchen staff while the migrants looked on bemused. But suddenly it might all change, for no apparent reason: camp cards checked, doors closed, patrolling routines reinforced. I had constant trouble being allowed past the turnstiles, even though I came several times a week; there was always someone new manning the security booth, or they wanted authorization yet again. "See, it's a prison," smiled my Algerian friend as he saw me negotiating the gate.

If the camp was a prison, it was so only in a peculiar, postmodern fashion. As punishment for any misdemeanors, individual migrants could either be shut inside or banished from the camp. Locked in or locked out, it did not matter: the divide between inside and outside was flexible, and the police could reach both those banished into the forest and those stuck inside.

In the living modules, too, the boundary between neglect and surveillance was flexible despite the official insistence on residents' privacy. The guards, police, or madres were able to enter a room at any time, peek behind the tied-up bedsheets, and ask dozing residents for their cards or for a hand in clearing a bed. Despite this "mortification," in

Goffman's sense, of having their intimate spaces invaded, some residents contented themselves with the phony privacy of the modules. Others countered their availability and deportability by stretching the time-space of surveillance as far as they could. The Algerians spent all day in port, trying to stow away on boats. Sub-Saharan migrants such as Patrick, aware of their instant availability to police, instead followed the strategy within institutions that Goffman calls "playing it cool": they tried to render themselves invisible by not participating in camp life or by participating just enough. For this reason, too, Patrick kept his involvement in the strike half-hearted. His strategy was to elbow into the Algerians' space in the port, hoping to stow away or get on the ferry with a lookalike friend's passport.

While Melilla's chabolas and Ceuta's hills provided respite and repose for the African camp residents, the open gates also allowed for temporary escape from the reach of the police. If any foreign commissions came to identify their nationals for deportation, rumors would precede their arrival. The residents could escape up the hill in time or else just stay silent, feigning ignorance. Migrants kept vigil at night, ready to jump across the fences if police vans approached. "They know everything," said the director with a note of respect.

The most radical way of stretching the time-space of surveillance was to abandon the camp and its comforts altogether. This was the path taken by Ceuta's Indian migrants. They had left the camp for fear of police raids and deportation more than two years ago and had since constructed their own community of shacks in the hills. Locals, activists, and camp workers alike urged me to go and see the *indios del monte* (Indians on the hill), among them the camp's medical assistant. "They called me the mother of the CETI," she said wistfully as she recalled being invited by them for lunch. "They put a tablecloth on the ground—it was whiter than in my home—and they used disposable plates, all so hygienic," she said. "Ask them to prepare the chickpeas and aubergines for you!"

. . .

The indios lived far uphill, past the luxurious villas of Ceuta's wealthy Indian merchants, beyond the loud barks of the *perrera* (dog kennel), and onwards into the thick underbrush. Then the first shack appeared, perched atop stilts furnished out of branches, its roof a patchwork of blankets and discarded plastic. In a clearing stood the cooking tent. Inside, five Punjabi men stooped over a big pot, slicing cauliflower, chili, and garlic that they proceeded to deep-fry for their visitors. With me was another visitor, a turbaned Sikh temporarily on shipping work in Ceuta's port. We waited for the food, seated on the forest floor; smells of spicy *sabji* wafted among the trees. "I had never thought I would meet my people living in the jungle like this!" the visiting Punjabi *sardar* laughed.

There had been seventy-two of them to begin with. The indios had come to Ceuta through prepaid smuggling packages from the Punjab at the time of Spain's migratory frenzy in 2006. They had paid more than twenty thousand euros apiece for their clandestine journeys across the Sahara, only to be dumped in Ceuta by the "mafias," who told them they had now reached Europe. Some had died on the way, in trucks crossing the desert or squeezed into Ceuta-bound dinghies. Unlike most of the sub-Saharan migrants, they had been wholly at the mercy of their smugglers. Deprived of their documents en route, they were now in hock to the Spanish authorities because of their undocumented status. "Losing your passport is like having your hands cut off," they said. While some had been taken to the peninsula and released without papers, twenty of them still remained on the hillsides.

During the long wait for any news on their fate, they had constructed a society in the hills, much as the African migrants had once done in Mount Gurugú and Ben Younech outside the enclaves. The Indians worked in teams at Ceuta's Eroski hypermarket. They bought groceries together, cooked together, lived together in shanties scattered across the forest. In the process, they had earned an enormous amount of goodwill. "The locals support us," explained Raju, a former university student and their sometime spokesman because of his Spanish skills. He and his friends were different in this respect from the subsaharianos or *negros,* who, Raju said, were especially disliked after the protest.

Their escape did not, however, put them out of reach of the police. In the enclaves, all strategies of escape were largely illusory. The sub-Saharans were marked by their physical appearance and could be apprehended at any time, as in the case of Jean. So were the indios, who the police visited regularly in the hills, exchanging pleasantries in a courteous game of make-believe freedom. Their "escape," then, was not ultimately about avoiding the time-space of surveillance. Instead it was a conscious tactic based upon yet another contradiction: the fluctuation between indifference and fascination towards the stranded migrants of Ceuta and Melilla.

TAKING TIME: LIFE IN THE OBSERVATORY

WEDNESDAY IN MID-AUGUST, 6:00 P.M. Lola, one of the three camp madres in Ceuta, was fuming. I had bumped into her outside control, where a verbal fight had erupted with a female security guard. The guard had called Lola earlier that day, saying she wanted clearance from the director before she would allow a list of female residents to leave the camp before the morning curfew, to do some sports. Lola had slammed down the phone. "You can't hang up the phone on me like that!" the guard now exclaimed, waving the list of residents. In response, Lola let out a stream of angry words and stormed into the office.

Lola's fight with security and *social* over the rights of the women to leave was nothing unusual. She seemed constantly on the warpath, her steps brisk and her temper flaring. In part, her antagonism towards the guards related to the moral division of labor in the camp.[16] In this division—again similar to those in total institutions—the social workers were aloof, the guards were alternately coercive and friendly, the director was avuncular, and the madres, nurses, and teachers were sympathetic though temperamental flak-catchers. Tensions among these groups usually took the form of occasional mutterings, but Lola wanted to show loud and clear that she was on the migrants' side, unlike the guards or social workers. "Many times my eyes fill with tears," she said. "I've been here for six years now. I've often thought I will leave it, but I can't!" Her relatives asked why she stayed, since she always kept talking and worrying about the camp. "It's just that I can't stop thinking about it," she said. "I *live* with them."

Lola was not the only one to be captivated by the captive migrants of Ceuta. Her words were echoed by Paula, the steely elderly woman in charge of the nunnery's assistance program. "We work *together* with migrants," she emphasized. This was a credo taken onboard by the young women and men with dreadlocks and African-style plaits who came and went in the nuns' cloisters, *djembe* drums in hand and bells round their bare ankles. These volunteers came to Ceuta to spend a couple of weeks in solidarity with migrants, playing beach volleyball, organizing outings, and celebrating Christmas and Easter. Then they left, taking pictures and memories, while the migrants stayed behind.

The fascination with the fate of the migrants was premised on their immobility. Their empty time in the enclaves was there for the taking. The illegal immigrants, stigmatized by their mobility, ironically stayed immobile while their visitors came and went, taking their time and stories away with them. And none did so more successfully than the journalists.

. . .

The camp was a magnet for the media. When access was granted it was a dream come true: here journalists and researchers had the possibility to come and interview illegal immigrants fresh off their rafts, almost in their natural habitat. Documentary makers, reporters, authors, research students, and fact-finding delegations all made the pilgrimage to the heights of the camp, paying their respects at the gates before being let in and put in front of their research object, the illegal immigrant. Cameramen denied access resorted to filming the camp residents through the tall perimeter fence. Journalists came every other day, said Mamá. In order to shield the privacy of residents, cameras were allowed only upstairs. There the migrants would stand and mouth their "half truths" for documentaries, newsreels, and research projects, presenting themselves as the victims the media wanted to see. Mamá said this in an affectionate way, taking the residents' part. Often they spoke too openly, she said. They should be careful. What they said might be used against them. People at home or in Spain might find out where they were, against their wishes. But after all, this was what tempted anthropologists, authors, and journalists alike to study clandestine migration—its hiddenness, its ripeness for revelation. And the camp provided just enough of a glimpse of the veiled world of today's global outcasts.

The authorities in Ceuta and Melilla were ambivalent about the media. On the one hand, journalists spread uplifting news about the nice food and good work; on the other, they loved the story of a migrant invasion. The result was yet another make-believe game—this time of media management. In the Melilla camp, where the growing number of arrivals in the summer of 2010 had led to canteen and workshop halls filling up with temporary litters, access was denied to external visitors, as usual for privacy reasons. "The ministry doesn't want to get the tents out," one camp lawyer giggled, because then the media would report on a "failure of the [government's] migration policy." And if there was one thing that could not be jeopardized, it was this: the *mediatization* of Spain's successful response to clandestine migration.

The game of make-believe was usually lost on the journalists, who faithfully regurgitated the stage-managed efforts of officials and migrants alike. Somalis appeared in videos and newspaper features, their stories of suffering taken at face value. "In Ceuta the government tries to help you," one such Somali told a journalist. "In Somalia everything's corrupt, and since there were no possibilities there [to work] I decided to leave and look for a better future."[17] One reporter in Ceuta recognized that everything that migrants said to camera might not be true, but neither were journalistic techniques of staging, for instance, their escape attempts in port. Besides this dramatic complicity, sympathy with migrants' plight and awareness of the hatred they faced from xenophobes in Europe also played a role in tempering doubts. But journalists in the mainstream media above all ignored the pauses in performance, because they usually had to slot the migrant story into either one of empathy and victimhood or rejection and menace. Doubts about nationalities and brief quivers across lips made the picture too complex, too deep and disturbing.

Along, too, came the academics. Ceuta and Melilla presented enviable research laboratories where the clandestine migrant was finally pinned down, immobilized, bored, and ready to talk in a setting that presented few difficulties, give or take some undercover police checks. Here, colonial-era academic history threatens to repeat itself. Anthropology's "savage slot"—its studying of the most absolute Other to the "civilized West"—has depended not only on spatial and temporal distance but also on the relative immobility of the object under study.[18] U.S. anthropologists had their Native American reserves; their European colleagues had colonized and corralled natives. If the clandestine migrant is the new savage at Europe's margins, he can be satisfyingly studied, observed, and written about only when immobile, when his time can be freely taken and used, much as the leading British anthropologist Alfred Radcliffe-Brown was once able to carry out his kinship studies on Aborigines, thanks to their being forcibly kept in camps on an island off the Australian coast.[19] The savage slot might no longer be the exclusive reserve of anthropology, as shown by the steady stream of political scientists, geographers, law students, and others in Ceuta and elsewhere along migrant routes. Yet regardless of the disciplinary outlook, all research efforts—not least my own—depended upon the migrants' captive condition. Such observation in captivity nevertheless held a possibility for the stranded migrants and gave a clue to why some of them had staged an escape into Ceuta's hills.

· · ·

The full glare of the spotlight of Ceuta shone upon the most reluctant of latter-day "savages," the Facebook-connected indios ensconced in their hillside shacks. The nunnery's hippies camped with them in the forest, and filmmakers and reporters made their way uphill to document their tragic journeys. The journalists behind one award-winning documentary, called *Los Ulises,* had even gone to their homes in the Punjab, filming their families and bringing news back and forth. Raju and his friends welcomed these contingents of fact seekers and sympathizers to their weekly lunches, speaking openly about their ordeals. They willingly let journalists take their time, since they had nothing to lose. Thanks to their escape up the hill, the indios had made themselves the protagonists of a transnational media spectacle with a wide, sympathetic audience of nuns and hippies, camp workers and police, journalists and academics, foreigners and locals. This spectacle suffused their time in the enclaves with the promise of something bigger, of a future deliverance.

The spicy cauliflower and puffed puri bread was finished, the plates cleared away from the forest floor. After a plastic glass of milky chai, we sat down in front of their temple, white kerchiefs covering our heads. The Sikh *gurudwara* was furnished out of branches, cardboard, pieces of fabric, and plastic sheets. Garlands and bells hung from the ceiling inside; underneath, images of one of the Sikh gurus had been placed on a small table. In front of it, one of them read from the holy Guru Granth Sahib. Occasionally he launched into chanting, and those seated next to me joined in. The sunlight shone mottled through the filigree above us. In the "jungle" of Ceuta, in front of this shrine made up of the junk of postmodernity at the fringe of Europe, a stillness descended, offering a glimpse of something beyond the Trap. We stood, clasping our hands in a *namaskar* greeting, and then holy *prasad* was served: sticky balls of godly food made of breadcrumbs, coffee, and sugar.

Ceuta's Indians were the good immigrants par excellence. This related in no small part to the prominence of the enclave's Indian merchants, for whom some of the indios del monte even worked, undocumented. However, the differing racial schemas applied to *negros,* moros, and *asiáticos* were sharpened by the last group's escape from the camp. Visiting reporters, volunteers, and researchers had filmed, danced, and slept in the hills, sharing the Indians' food, pain, and moments of worship. In Melilla, a contingent of Bangladeshis had similarly won the hearts of visitors and locals, only to be rounded up in 2010 and sent to detention centers after five years in the enclave. The outrage among *melillenses* that followed was, again, selective. The captives in the enclaves alternated between being good and bad, visible and invisible, objects of fascination and indifference. The fluctuation between invisibility and hypervisibility that other writers have identified in clandestine migration was in Ceuta and Melilla portioned out to different categories of migrants.[20] If the indios were hypervisible in their "hidden" hillside shacks, so were the dangerous *negros* in the strike. The majority of illegal immigrants, by contrast, remained invisible and neglected. Patrick was among them, as were the Nigerians in the chabolas of Melilla; even more so were the sub-Saharan women. Marooned in downstairs time, they inhabited a camp that had become both racialized and feminized through the escape of indios, Algerians, and, to some extent, the West African men who staged protests, parked cars, or tried their luck in port.

On Mamá's afternoon rounds of the dorms in August, a West African woman confronted her. "When will the E.U. delegation come?" she asked. "They couldn't enter because of your Cameroonian friends," Mamá said, referring to the confrontation at the gate that had sent the researchers speeding away downhill. "But who will listen to us then?" the woman asked. "There are many of us here who don't agree with the strike. What will happen to us?" Mamá blamed the Cameroonians, and another woman propped up on the windowsill shouted back, "Cameroonians! I'm Cameroonian! It's not about Cameroonians. It's because we have stayed here for so long, one and a half years. Is that normal?" While the women wanted to voice concerns over their captivity in Ceuta, the delegation had instead been planning to interview them about abuse suffered en route. As with refugee populations elsewhere, the visitors sought stories of the women's traumatic *pasts*, ignoring their main concern over an anxious present and indeterminate future.[21] In either case, their worries would remain unheard: the delegation had left the enclave and was not coming back.

WAITING FOR DELIVERANCE: THE TIME BEYOND

The enclaves' time-space regime stretched from the minuscule pauses in migrants' speech through the schedules, protocol slips, and microphone calls of the camp system and on to the abstract economy of time used by the police. In the complex geography of time produced by this regime, the illegal immigrants appeared as people without a past and future, stuck in an endless, anxious present. If the police stole time collectively from migrants, the emptied time slots that remained could then be filled with the rituals of the camp or dedicated to the information-gathering efforts of the authorities, researchers, and the media. These make-believe games, in turn, created their own rhythms—and their own reality. Here appeared the good and bad migrants, visible and invisible, in hock to the contradictory time-space regime and their own impossible dreams. If their immediate future had been vacated for them and their past had been temporarily disowned, the far-ahead future of deliverance became all the more real: their fate depended on the "grace of God" they constantly invoked.[22]

While the strike still raged in central Ceuta, I got on the bus heading towards the camp. At the back sat five migrants, all Anglophone sub-Saharans in camp parlance. None of them participated in the strike. I asked how they were managing, and their voices rose in raucous reply as the bus wound its way along the shore towards the camp and the border hamlet of Benzú. One of the migrants, a guy with natty dreadlocks whom I knew from my journeys on foot to the camp, stood and spoke while pacing up and down the aisle. A white plastic crucifix dangled around his neck; the topic turned to God and the Bible. "There's only one God, *un Dios, cristiano musulmán!*" he shouted with joy. Headscarfed female passengers turned their heads, bemused. "Will a savior come?" his friends wondered out loud. "How can we leave the camp?" "Ask and it shall be given," one of them intoned, "seek and you shall find!" Did Moses go from Egypt to Israel or the other way round? they asked each other. "In the Bible it says the waters parted for him," one of them shouted to cries of joy. "It could be like that for us here, the waters parting, opening a road to Europe!" Through the windows, Gibraltar Rock could just be made out in the distance.

In addition to the time of deliverance, godly time, yet another frame has to be added to time-as-capital, paused time, camp rhythms, surveillance time, and visitors' time: the electoral cycle. After the conservative Partido Popular won Spain's general elections in November 2011, it quickly removed "immigration" from the name of the Ministry of Labor in charge of the camps. In 2012, job cuts for camp workers were announced, with the camp's intricate ecology—its rhythms, its paperwork, its guessing games—hanging in the balance.

The Ceuta and Melilla camps, as workers and locals noted, nevertheless remained a necessity for the political left and right alike.[23] Yet this usefulness did not quite—or not only—stem from the Foucauldian view suggested at the beginning of this chapter, according to which they could be seen as centers of discipline preparing irregular migrants for their marginal role in the European labor market. The camps certainly disciplined their residents, but unevenly and imperfectly so—producing not just cooperative "good immigrants" and marginalized yet potentially useful workers such as Patrick, but also welfare dependents, media-savvy "hill tribes," and angry, rugged protesters. These wildly differing migrant roles were indicative of how the camps, like the migration policies underpinning their existence, were contradictory creations made on the hoof. Cheap and outsourced, they helped produce the utter indifference of officialdom towards their residents and hid the calculated use of confinement underneath a veneer of half-hearted regulations and schedules. Again, however, their ad hoc character did little to mitigate their very concrete effects. Like the total institutions they only imperfectly resembled, they helped create an arbitrary landscape of time whose spaces of punishment and privilege, visibility and invisibility, heralded an absurd disconnect in migrants' experiences, only imperfectly mediated by their invocations of God.

In this arbitrary landscape of time and the phony battle staged upon it, there were no clear "winners." The migrants—invisible and visible, good and bad, God-fearing and not—eventually made it out of there, despite their months or years lost to waiting. Amadou and the other "good immigrants" were sent on to reception centers on the mainland after the strike. The indios returned to the camp after the director had promised to help them. They were eventually sent to CIEs and set free. As their epic quest for escape ended, the audience dissipated; Raju was unhappy, finding racism stronger on the mainland than in Ceuta. In 2011, the Indians' abandoned hillside shacks were taken over by African migrants arriving in unprecedented numbers.

The Nigerians, not least the women, were in a worse position than the "good" African and Indian immigrants. In early 2011, a shack in Melilla burned down, killing three and triggering protests akin to those of Ceuta in 2010. Thankfully, my Nigerian friends were unharmed. They were still there, waiting for divine or state intervention to take them to Europe. A year later the chabolas were destroyed by the police. The authorities cited local complaints, the fire hazard, and the fact that all migrants had a bed assured for them in the camp as reasons for the long-awaited intervention.[24]

Patrick had used his invisibility to the full, sneaking onto a ferry and making it to a friend's house in Seville. "I told you I would make it," he said. As with El General and many others, the controls in port proved less stringent at times than the full surveillance the enclaves promised. Soon Patrick left Andalusia for Bilbao, the main destination for Ceuta's migrants in 2010. "You know, Seville is Andalusia; it's close to Africa," he explained. "Life is difficult there, so I decided to climb."

While Patrick climbed, I descended, heading for Bamako. My adventure in the borderlands was not yet over. The Malian capital, through which most of the migrants in Ceuta and Melilla had once traveled, has become a crucial site for the illegality industry in recent years. It is, again, a crossroads where the industry's workers clash and mingle with the deportees and stranded migrants of the clandestine circuit. In early 2011, Bamako and its Sahelian hinterland were also to become the stage for yet another confrontation in the borderlands, albeit on a larger scale: not just between captive migrants and provincial officialdom as in Ceuta, but between transnational activists and Europe's nebulous border regime as a whole.

The Jobless Job Center

THE RISE AND FALL OF THE EUROPEAN UNION'S "MIGRATION MANAGEMENT" INITIATIVE IN MALI

Far from European coasts and capitals, in one of Bamako's wealthier neighborhoods, lay one of the most trumped-up manifestations of the European Union's "global" strategy on migration: CIGEM (Centre d'Information et des Gestions des Migrations), the center for information and management of migration. Inaugurated in 2008 to much fanfare after the signing of a declaration on migration and development by ECOWAS, the European Commission, France, and Spain, CIGEM was tasked with gathering information on migration, raising awareness about the risks of irregular migration, optimizing the "human, financial, and technical capital" of expatriate Malians and—crucially, as far as the media and the public were concerned—receiving, informing, and accompanying "potential migrants and return migrants."[1] The E.U. Commissioner Louis Michel pleaded with European audiences to give this "pilot project" a chance. "Instead of demonizing the migration phenomenon, it should be supported, structured and managed optimally as a positive human element for both Africa and Europe," he said at CIGEM's inauguration.[2] The center, initially endowed with ten million euros of E.U. funds, had by 2010 developed working relations with about eighty migration-related associations, which seemed to multiply by the day now that financing was available. What it did not do was to provide jobs, despite the media's billing of it as an E.U. "job center" in Africa.[3]

I had e-mailed CIGEM, asking for an interview in November 2010, and telephoned throughout December. Now, in the run-up to Christmas, I had finally been granted a meeting with the director. The first problem was finding the center. The taxi driver asked his way around the leafy streets of Hamdallaye, far away from any poorer Bamako neighborhoods housing "potential" or "return" migrants, CIGEM's two main target groups. We finally arrived, and I entered the sparse reception. A poster on the wall said "Returning migrants. Contact CIGEM: information and advice." Few seemed to heed this call: the hall was empty except for a bored-looking receptionist. Finally the spokesman appeared, suited and curt. "The director has not arrived," he said. "You should have called beforehand." Which I had. Maybe he would appear, maybe not; I waited, flicking through leaflets on CIGEM's work on "codevelopment" and awareness raising. The director never showed up; the spokesman had disappeared. If this is how they welcome overseas visitors, how much thrift do they give to eager, impoverished job seekers? I wondered, leaving after an hour's wait in the empty reception.

While CIGEM floundered in its initial attempt to provide an avenue for legal circular migration, everyone by contrast talked about the Malian workers sent to Spain. CIGEM officers talked about them, the Spanish police attaché talked about them, the embassy and E.U. officers talked about them. It was "an example of legal as well as circular migration," enthused the Spanish embassy staff. They were referring to the contracting of twenty-nine seasonal workers for a six-month stint in the vegetable fields of the Canary Islands in 2009, with a repeat for fourteen of them the following year. But since then, none had been contracted. The job market had frozen. The Spanish government had at least "tried its best to play by the rules," said an E.U. diplomat: still, while Spain sent twenty-nine willing workers to the Canaries, Mali's emigrant population might now total more than four million, of which the vast majority remains in West Africa.[4] However, media attention for the Spanish contracts at least succeeded in pulling in around forty new visitors to CIGEM a day, hoping for interviews and jobs that never materialized.[5] CIGEM would prove similarly disappointing for me and other visiting researchers, as any attempts to talk to the wayward director failed to come to fruition.

—CIGEM bonjour?

It's 7 January, two months after my initial e-mail: for the umpteenth time I try to reach the director or his secretary.

—Appellez-vous lundi, s'il vous plaît.

Come Monday, another call. No replies all afternoon or the next day. On 12 January I reach the spokesman.

—*I'll call you back.*

He doesn't. I call the next day; finally he picks up.

—*Ah, the director just left a very big meeting with artisans and migrants, says the spokesman, who will "let him rest now."*

I start to think they are avoiding me, but then, on 14 January, the spokesman calls! I jump in a taxi and reach the same empty reception. No director shows up. No spokesman. Eventually the latter arrives. No, the director won't come this afternoon either. Maybe I can speak to a colleague? The colleague comes but has no time. "Ah, we're so tired!" Next week, maybe? Or the week after that?

I finally give up on the director and his spokesman and go to the second CIGEM reception, in which visitors are registered and interviewed. Blue-and-yellow E.U. stickers proclaiming "financée par l'Union Européenne" have been tacked onto every object in the hall: the air-conditioning, the water cooler, the computers, the TV in front of the plastic chairs lining the walls. A documentary about artisanal work, meant to convince CIGEM's visitors to stay put and find jobs in Mali, is shown in a loop—only the carpenters and bakers on-screen are all white Europeans.

The irony is lost on the chargés de mission *in the next-door office, who tell me that any images from Europe "incite" Malians to migrate. Here, they sift visitors for suitability for what little CIGEM-funded professional training is available. The visitors' details, meanwhile, allow CIGEM to build a profile on returning and "potential" migrants. Is intelligence gathering on migrants' routes and intentions perhaps CIGEM's primary purpose, as civil society critics allege?*

"It's not about tracking people [ficher les gens]," says the French adviser to the director, whom I meet upstairs after bypassing his nominal boss. He seems unsure what CIGEM is about in general, in fact. Another of its less-vaunted tasks is "assisting" Mali in legal reform, as part of E.U. attempts to tighten the country's liberal laws on migration, but this could equally be done through other channels. CIGEM is a pilot project, the adviser emphasizes: once funding ends, it will be up to Mali whether to keep it going. CIGEM's "global approach"—incorporating return,

departure, and diaspora—is its most useful legacy, he says, sounding as if trying to convince himself as much as me. Whether its role is better covered by national institutions is a matter he leaves entirely open.

CIGEM, the job center without jobs, was not even succeeding in its humble mission to send prospective trainees on to national agencies, as shown in a study by one of the intern researchers the center has hosted. All it did was to bias these agencies towards accepting candidates who said they were "potential migrants" while sensitizing visitors about the risks of irregular migration and using data on them for migrant profiles. But CIGEM was not an E.U. "watchtower," as some critics alleged: it was simply a prime site for the squandering of money in Europe's illegality industry.[6]

CHAPTER 7

Marchers without Borders

GOGUI, WESTERN MALI, JANUARY 2011. The activists come marching towards the camera, down an empty Sahelian road, holding their banner for the freedom of movement as a collective shield against the invisible enemy ahead. The enemy is Frontex, and Frontex shall fall, they chant: *"À bas, à bas, à bas le Frontex! À bas, à bas, à bas le Frontex!"* Fists are raised, calls for *solidarité* ring out, the clacks and thuds of djembe drums pierce the dull desert air. Then the activists break into chanting again, European and African voices in unison, while waving "global passports" and anti-Frontex banners: "No borders, no nation, stop deportation!" But no one hears their chants, except for the camera-wielding participants in the march, a few villagers, and a border policeman or two. The road towards the nearby Mauritanian border lies empty ahead, lined with hardy shrubs and dust-dry stretches of earth. No signs of Frontex, no deportees. What on earth are these transnational activists doing here, in a border hamlet on the potholed road between Nioro du Sahel in western Mali and Ayoun-el Atrous in Mauritania?

"The border of the European Union has arrived in Gogui," explained one of the marchers, Aboubacar, in his offices in the Malian capital. His brow frowned, his small frame tensed up, and his voice rose in indignation each time he denounced the "externalization" of policing to the European visitors frequenting the airy offices of his organization, the Association Malienne d'Expulsés (AME, the Malian association of expelled migrants). Standing at the whiteboard, he drew maps

FIGURE 16. Marchers on the border road of Gogui, Mali. Photo courtesy of Max Hirzel (maxhirzel.photoshelter.com; www.haythampictures.com).

of Mali's border areas, an X marking the spot of Nioro and arrows showing the lines of expulsion from Mauritania. Because of these expulsions, AME and its European partners had decided to make Gogui their first site of protest against Europe's border regime in the fraught roadshow that is the subject of this chapter: the Citizens' Caravan for Freedom of Movement and Equitable Development from Bamako to Dakar and the World Social Forum in February 2011. Aboubacar's AME was the key Malian partner in this ambitious collaboration, named Afrique-Europe Interact (AEI), between European activists and Malian associations around the E.U. border regime and its "war" on the irregular migrant.

Transnational activists are increasingly converging on the Euro-African border, confronting security forces and contesting state and media narratives of migration. Among these are grassroots "no-border" camps springing up across Europe, anarchist mobilizations, and direct action under the "No One Is Illegal," "Frontexplode," and "Frontexit" banners.[1] Border theorists have in recent years opened their eyes to such making and unmaking of borders by citizens, with political scientist Chris Rumford applying the term *borderwork* to ordinary people's acts of "envisioning, constructing, maintaining and erasing borders."[2] The borderwork of Aboubacar and his transnational colleagues would prove to be fraught with contradictions, however. How to enroll disparate activists, migrants, and NGOs in the common task of protesting against the border regime? And how to locate this diffuse regime, stretching as it does from the Atlantic to the Sahara, from Canaries control rooms to scattered radar systems? Here the empty Malian border road was but a foretaste of the quandaries to come en route to Dakar. In Gogui, the only visible tokens of this regime were a few signs wedged into the dry earth. One sign—STOP IRREGULAR MIGRATION, A DANGER FOR THE POP-ULATION—was adorned with the E.U. flag and the logo of Bamako's CIGEM. Another announced Gogui's defunct Red Cross mission of humanitarian assistance to deportees, modeled on that of Rosso-Senegal and financed by a Spanish regional government. Both signs were soon covered in anti-Frontex stickers and graffiti.[3] The activists would repeatedly try to locate and mark the border in this fashion in Bamako, en route through the borderlands and in their final march in Dakar against Frontex.

The activists not only searched for and conjured the European Union's borders but also enlisted the stranded adventurers of Bamako in this enterprise. The figure of the irregular migrant, obsessed over by Western states, has also become a source of inspiration for radical intel-lectuals, journalists, and activists in recent years. In their accounts and campaigns, the migrant often appears as a heroic or even revolutionary subject: a symbol of "cosmopolitan citizenship," a rebellious burner of borders, or a repository of the dream of free worldwide movement.[4] The irregular migrant and the border here become the twin rallying points for a cosmopolitan or anarchist project, linked by the latter's violence upon the former.

In the caravan, this relation among activists, borders, and migrants would be put under increasing strain. In Gogui on the Mauritanian bor-der and during the journey to Dakar, the deportees of Bamako were to become a unifier for the activists bereft of a border at which to protest. To Aboubacar and AME, they were living proof of a violent and inhu-mane border regime; to the European marchers descending on Bamako, they were its victims. As the caravan rolled towards Dakar, the deport-ees themselves increasingly participated in their own making as migrants, with quite different results from those of their repatriated brethren in the Senegalese capital. As will be seen, the caravan protests highlighted the fundamental *absence*—of location, of visibility, of responsibility—at the heart of the violent experience of clandestine migration, as well as the futile efforts to fill it among border workers, migrants, and activists alike.

To understand the dynamics among marchers, victims, and their borders, we first have to consider the migratory geography of Bamako, where the deportees found themselves stranded. Mali's capital is now the first and last safe place en route towards the desert; before the country's conflict in 2012 and 2013, it had also become an increasingly strategic point for the policing of migration in the Euro-African borderlands.

DEPORTED, GLOBALIZED, TRAFFICKED: PRODUCING MIGRANT VICTIMS

It all begins at Sogoniko *gare*. This vast, smog-filled bus station in southern Bamako, with its dozens of bus companies, hawkers, hustlers, and revving engines, is a key transport hub for West African travelers setting out on long journeys towards the north. It is also the end point for those who have already crossed the desert and failed: the *refoulés* detained in Algeria or Mauritania and dumped at the Malian border sites of Tin Zaouaten deep in the Sahara and Gogui in western Mali, respectively. An industry has grown around the stranded migrants of Sogoniko—a world of aid workers, policemen, information seekers, and activists replicating the structures already put in place in Ceuta, Melilla, Morocco, Dakar, and elsewhere on the clandestine circuit.

Sogoniko seems far away from Ceuta and Melilla, but the tragedies at the fences in 2005 lay at the heart of Bamako's strategic role in the illegality industry. Despite the Malian government's refusal to sign repatriation agreements, the country has long been a dumping ground for those caught in raids under France's increasingly strict migration regime. Such deportations, along with expulsions of Malians from Angola, had led to the creation of Aboubacar's AME in 1996. The symbolic start to the latest expansion of Mali's illegality industry, however, came with the expulsion of migrants following the attaques at the Spanish fences. Here was a global, collective victim of Europe's border regime: the deportee.

As deportees arrived at Bamako's airport or made their way back through the desert where the Moroccan soldiers had left them, one woman rose to action. This woman was Aminata Traoré, alter-globalization politician and activist extraordinaire, who in early 2006 hosted the Malian version of that year's multisited World Social Forum. On the anniversary of the tragedy, Aminata—a former Malian minister of culture and tourism—organized the first Journées Commémoratives for Ceuta and Melilla, where deportees mingled with journalists and activists flown in from Europe. She also set about mobilizing the returnees, as she was to call those forcibly deported. The result was the association Retour-Travail-Dignité (return-work-dignity), which sought to reconnect returnees with their African heritage through agriculture, handicrafts, and political action. Under her patronage, Ceuta and Melilla returnees tilled the soil together in far-flung rural areas, with some receiving Spanish development funds to do so. Though the original RTD proved short-lived, with accusations flying over who gained what, Aminata's charisma contributed to a larger ferment centered on the figure of the irregular migrant. She was now one of the figureheads of the official Bamako-Dakar caravan, despite growing tensions with the more hardline activists in AME.

In Aminata's view, the migrants made visible the malaise of Africa under neoliberalism. "When you ask those returned from Ceuta and Melilla why they left, their replies speak volumes about the real state of the continent," she said in 2008.[5] Or as a banner at Aminata's December 2010 conference on migration expressed it: THROUGH MIGRANTS, THE WHOLE OF AFRICA IS HUMILIATED. To her, they were victims of the injustices of neoliberal globalization and should be reincorporated into a proud Africa embracing its traditions.

In a similar vein, the migrants were seen as victims by the caravan activists about to descend on Bamako. Whereas Aminata focused her criticism on neoliberalism, the Europeans and AME homed in on Frontex and the border regime, whose violent workings they would seek to make visible in Gogui and en route to Dakar. The core of the activists hailed from German anti-racist and anti-deportation groups; some were neophytes, others grizzled veterans on the anti-Frontex circuit. It was a motley crowd, united in its purpose of showing solidarity with African associations and the victims of Europe's externalized borders.

The victimhood of the returnees had a global, if recent, pedigree. In *The Empire of Trauma,* the anthropologists Didier Fassin and Richard Rechtman have identified "a new configuration of victimhood" in the West. Whereas victims of war or disaster were once eyed with suspicion, they have in recent decades come to symbolize "the very embodiment of our common humanity." And this new potency of victimhood, they say, stems largely from the legitimating power of trauma. It is this trauma—the bodily, mental, or collective scar—that proves one's victim status and points a finger at the perpetrator.[6]

The clandestine migration circuit disproves what Fassin and Rechtman call the "cruel gap," borne of racial assumptions, that long left black Africa out of humanitarian trauma interventions. Indeed, migrants' victimization was, besides the activist denunciations, also the focus of aid interventions in the borderlands, with projects ranging from psychological assistance in Ceuta and the Red Cross Rosso mission to the AME's trauma counseling service. Moreover, this victimization was one key reason why journalists and academics—anthropologists not least—had taken such a keen interest in the deportees. Their suffering had bound together a diverse set of groups in a "communion of trauma" across the Euro-African border.[7]

Perhaps surprisingly, the irregular migrant was seen as a victim not only by activists, aid workers, and researchers but by Spanish police as well. "We don't consider the migrant as a criminal; therefore he is a victim of the human trafficking networks," Spain's police attaché in Bamako said. While his statement asserted the existence of criminal traffickers based on that of victims, it also allowed for a slippage between the categories of migrant and criminal, as would be evident among the stranded migrants of southern Bamako.

. . .

Not far from Sogoniko gare, up a mud lane from the Beijing IV Hotel, lay the compound of the association Aracem, a rare lifeline for migrants in the city. On the corner outside, a group of young men milled about, sharing cigarettes, mobiles, and the occasional joke. These were the refoulés sent back by Algeria through the desert. They were the quintessential victims of migration, whether for political back-to-the-soil activists such as Aminata or for freedom-of-movement voices such as Aboubacar. In the impending caravan, this was a role some of them would play to the full.

Aracem, the French acronym for the Association des Refoulés d'Afrique Centrale au Mali (association of Central African deportees in Mali), was set up by Cameroonian veterans from Ceuta and Melilla after Aminata's commemoration in 2006, though its founders had since broken with their former patron. Its task was assisting migrants at the end of a relay race conveying unwanted human cargo southwards through the Sahara. While the Moroccan security forces expelled migrants to the no-man's-land around Oujda, their Algerian colleagues in turn trucked them to the derelict desert outpost of Tin Zaouaten on the Malian-Algerian border, where they were dumped "as in a rubbish bin," in the words of one consternated Malian gendarme. There they lingered, next to the borderline and the Algerian military camp beyond it, in ramshackle ghettos run along national lines recognizable from the old encampments outside Ceuta and Melilla. Some migrants used the settlement as an abject "base camp" to head north again, cost what it may; others were simply too poor, distressed, or exhausted after their ordeals to manage. ICRC trucked a minority of such deportees to the nearest towns of Kidal and Gao. After three days in Gao's Maison des Migrants (house of migrants), funded by Caritas and a French NGO, the refoulés were sent out of the desert zone, towards Niger or Bamako. In 2010, Aracem received about 110 deportees a month in two batches. After three days at Aracem, many languished in Bamako for months or even years, waiting for money to return home or head back north. In January 2011, Aracem, together with AME, was getting ready to host and accommodate the European caravan contingent that would soon descend on Bamako.[8]

The victim role of deportees attributed by activists, NGOs, and Spanish police alike was certainly based on genuine victimization in the Algerian desert. In Aracem's patio, Alphonse from Cameroon sauntered about dressed in thick socks and plastic sandals, his foot inflamed after beatings endured in Algerian detention. "I had a good passport and a good visa," he said as we sat down to talk. "The Algerians, even if you have papers in order, they round you up." Sent back from Algiers on the well-trodden deportation route south, he was eventually dumped in Tin Zaouaten. He had seen mothers with children in detention and had, like other deportees, been forced to sign papers in Arabic before deportation. The officers refused his demands for a French translation, and "if you don't sign, you get a beating." He spent weeks in cells while the police waited to fill their "freight trucks," as Alphonse called them: "They put you inside like cattle." All he was given to eat was a piece of bread and powdered milk at noon. The police took his Algerian money and phone, leaving him with the SIM card—the same procedure reported by those expelled into the Morocco-Algeria border area, though this treatment was not common to all deportees in Bamako. "I don't have the right to have Algerian currency; the Africans come here bringing diseases; that's what they told me," he said, no trace of anger in his voice. "I don't know why they do this."

But Aracem's compound was not just for the beaten, dumped, and robbed. Here was Didier, a Cameroonian "guide" who had just come down from Morocco, promoting his smuggling services and bragging about his exploits up north. Here too was his countryman Stéphane the intellectual, with a half-finished degree and ideas of joining his sister in Canada; Pierre, the ancien caught up in the 2005 Ceuta and Melilla expulsions and since then chief of the now derelict ghetto for transiting travelers in Bamako; and Eric, a young Congolese adventurer with three years on the road, his loud, grumpy voice adding a touch of comedy to the gathering. These street corner guys were what have in recent years become known as stranded migrants—a new policy category for police, aid workers, and experts to worry about. Some were stranded because they had lost everything during deportation; others because they lacked funds to continue their journey, often after having been frisked of their money by border guards targeting *clandestins*. They all found themselves fighting for their day-to-day survival. And they all coveted one key possession: a Malian passport.

These *pièces* (documents), which enabled migrants to travel into Algeria visa-free thanks to a bilateral friendship agreement, were one of the main reasons why the deportees stayed on in Bamako. They were also a prime catalyst for the slippage between migrant-as-victim and migrant-as-criminal hinted at by the Spanish police attaché. This slippage was spelled out in big, bold letters on the façade of Mali's border police in central Bamako: "The Malian Passport Is a National Document. It Should Only Be Delivered to Nationals. Any Author or Accomplice in the Delivery of a Malian Passport to a Foreigner Will Be Severely Punished."

The passport trade was a main target for policing cooperation, with Canada and Spain helping Mali set up a national identity database to combat it. Malian officers, aware of the thriving trade and its ramifications, were keener to stress the criminal than the victimhood discourse. "We can't reject them," said the gendarme colonel in charge of irregular migration, but he went on to link the "threat" of stranded migrants to their victimhood—and the need for more resources. "We need to have a transit center in Kidal or Gao and another in Bamako; it's what we told [the Spaniards]. If not, once they arrive here they have nothing; they'll steal, rob, even kill, or they can be recruited by AQIM [Al Qaeda in the Islamic Maghreb]. It's a big problem."

The repercussions of this criminalization were felt on the Aracem street corner, where most adventurers had either paid someone for a passport or helped fix one. Cyrille, a Cameroonian veteran of the 2005 events now responsible for the welcoming of deportees, despaired at the police raids without warrant during the autumn. "They searched through everything!" he said, his soft voice momentarily rising. They threw documents on the floor, accusing Aracem of forging Malian passports. "That day, I really thought I would leave," he said, in anger over their unrecognized humanitarian work for deportees. "You know, we've even assisted Malians here."

From the Aracem street corner, Bamako looked grim, poor, and dusty. Eric and his friends complained of the fine dust and thick fumes cloaking the city, the heat and the food, the police and gendarme harassment. We looked out over the late-afternoon street as a golden haze descended over the city, as it always did at sundown. The mud road was strewn with flattened garbage colored ocher by the dust: water bottles, old flip-flops, plastic sachets. Children played at the shuttered shop fronts. Three Malian girls walked past, swinging their hips lazily. "Bamako, c'est la merde," exclaimed one of the stranded Cameroonians. The misery among the deportees was palpable as the days dragged on, much as they did for the captives of Ceuta and Melilla. But the street corner guys knew what they were in for and took pride in their survival. They were neither victims nor villains.

. . .

At the other end of Bamako in Djelibougou, AME had gathered representatives from the numerous Malian associations and NGOs that were meant to join the caravan. The European activists, who had raised money to cover the Malians' participation, were about to arrive, and seats needed to be allocated in the half dozen buses bound for Dakar.[9] Associations that had not participated in caravan preparations had suddenly showed up, and Aboubacar was busy at the whiteboard in the packed hall, whittling the number of Malian participants down to 230. Aracem voluntarily offered a cut, while newcomers clamored and pleaded to keep their allocations. Mouvement des Sans Voix, a Malian activist group, squealed when Aboubacar crossed out ten of their allotted forty places. "You're going to leave the victims behind!" As in the funding game, so in the battle for caravan seats—the more victims, the better.[10]

On the Aracem street corner, rumors were swirling about the impending caravan. "We'll have visitors tomorrow," confided Stéphane. "I think it's people from the United Nations." Another adventurer had heard the Europeans would offer work on international construction sites in Bamako. They would get something else altogether, however—a motley crowd of German radicals assigned to sleep in Aracem's compound.

WE WANT THE VICTIMS! MOBILIZING AGAINST THE BORDER

The international delegation was delayed. The "interactive space" set up by AME on a field in Djelibougou—white tarps shielding clusters of metal chairs—was empty. The Europeans had found themselves on a connecting flight in Paris with that all-too-common cargo: a migrant about to be deported. They had protested and been given the full riot police treatment and taken off the flight. Already tired and some bruised by police, dressed in caravan T-shirts with mosquito spray at the ready, they finally descended on the Djelibougou field for several days of caravan preparations. Most of the activists spoke no French and certainly no Bambara; many had never visited Africa before. One of them confided he "would never come here unless it was for the caravan": the poverty on display in the mud-cracked lanes of Djelibougou shocked him and his friends.

The caravan was but the latest and most striking example of the gradual growth of transnational activism along the Euro-African border after the Ceuta and Melilla tragedies. In November 2005, the transnational network Migreurop set up operations in Paris, eventually incorporating forty-three associations, including AME and Aracem. Migreurop's international mailing list, to which German and Malian caravaniers contributed, linked up activists, academics, and politicians who posted news on boat tragedies and Europe's externalization of borders. Activists also increasingly staged "countersummits" in opposition to E.U.-Africa summits on migration. In Rabat in 2006, a Euro-African manifesto was launched denouncing "the war that is increasingly being waged along the Mediterranean and Atlantic coastlines" and "the division of humanity between some who may freely move about the planet and some who may not."[11] More events followed during further summits as well as outside Frontex headquarters, in Oujda, and on Greek islands. Increasingly sophisticated means of protest were tried and tested: anti-racist caravans across Germany, temporary "border camps" on Europe's fringes, banners and graffiti displayed strategically around Frontex headquarters, and, in 2013, "Frontexit" street performances in which activists masqueraded as police. Such interventions were attempts to "hack the border," in the words of one German caravanier; that is, they tracked and trespassed on an increasingly fluid frontier with the aim of undermining its power. The Bamako caravan was part of this activist trajectory while seeking to broaden it beyond European space.

FIGURE 17. Anti-Frontex graffiti outside the agency's headquarters in Warsaw. Photo by author.

In this, one of its foundations was the "call of Bamako for respect and dignity for all migrants" of 2006, which decried the "murderous policies" behind the Ceuta and Melilla tragedies while urging the creation of an international migrants' rights network. By the time of the caravan, the German and Malian organizers knew each other from previous countersummits and had developed a sophisticated understanding of the need for transnational opposition to the E.U. border regime as well as of the hard work involved in consolidating disparate African and European networks. But they had perhaps not anticipated the difficulties that awaited them in Bamako.[12]

The new arrivals gathered in the shade under the canopies and took turns at the microphone to deplore the police on the flight and discuss the logistics of the caravan and the marches ahead. What about accommodation? A film projector was needed! More than beds for the night and equipment, however, they needed what scholars of activism call a "master frame" that would help them define the issues, actors, and events to mobilize around. This frame would then serve to underpin shared meanings and ideas. The activists had already started to forge such a convergence of ideas, as shown on a banner strung between two trucks next to the tents: Externalization Endangers the Freedom to Circulate in the African Space. This was the "diagnostic" dimension to the frame—spelling out the problem the caravan was addressing.[13] The prognostic element was reflected in the caravan motto, "For the freedom of movement and equitable development," which tried to suture the development-oriented goals of especially the Malian partner associations with the migration and anti-Frontex focus of the Europeans and AME. Finally there was the motivational dimension of the frame. To boost morale and mobilize activists, the Europeans had prepared a caravan song, which was sung in a jumble of voices each day of the assembly meetings:

> J'aime bien la caravane
> J'aime bien le mouvement
> J'aime bien la liberté
> J'aime bien la resistance
> Et ce que j'aime mieux
> c'est la solidarité
> Solidari-solidari-solidarité-é-é
> Solidari-solidari-solidarité-é-é
> Nous nous battons pour un monde sans frontières

> (I like the caravan
> I like the movement
> I like freedom
> I like resistance
> And what I like the most
> is solidarity
> Solidari-solidari-solidarity
> Solidari-solidari-solidarity
> We are fighting for a world without borders)

Solidarity was a powerful motif for the Europeans, who distributed their song's sparse lyrics on slips of paper to participants under the canopy. So were its accompanying terms, the somewhat uneasy bedfellows freedom and resistance. But as is often the case in emerging social movements, these motifs uneasily disguised the disparities among those they yoked together. Solidarity—"a signifier of the impossible fullness of society if ever there was one," as the philosopher Slavoj Žižek once quipped—meant supporting both African activists in their various struggles and solidarity with the deportees.[14] These aims, and the power relations each implied, overlapped awkwardly on the Djelibougou field.

"I'd like to speak to the *expulsés;* that's why we have come!" said one of the visitors during the endless canopy meetings. "When is it that we get to see them?" The AME chairman assured the visitors that "here we are all *expulsés,*" including him (though not Aboubacar). This was true, but not quite what the Germans had in mind: what they wanted were the victims of Europe's externalization policies. They wanted the street corner guys.

. . .

If the activists saw the deportees as victims of Europe's externalization policies and local police often saw them as potential criminals, these categories proved increasingly irrelevant in the gritty environs of Sogon-iko. Here was the dreariness of Aracem's street corner society but also hotels and "hustling places" frequented by sharp dressers of uncertain occupation. Mistrust marred the migrants' world, sometimes running along national lines. The Cameroonians were particularly singled out, amid talk of spectacular money-making frauds of the kind popularized by the country's notorious conmen *(feymen).* "The Cameroonians are crooks," said a Guinean friend of Eric's. Whereas he had worked in construction earning 700 CFA a day (US$1.50), the Cameroonians just sat around, asked for "loans," and created trouble.

Didier was one the adventurers whose varied roles on the migration circuit straddled the victim-villain dichotomy. He had jumped on the deportation wagon voluntarily, getting himself detained in Algeria in order to travel free of charge down through the desert. While insisting that he had lived rough for years in Morocco, he also kept up a running sales pitch to the street corner gathering on how many Cameroonians he had helped into Spain as a guide between the Algerian border and Melilla. His tall tales were not just for adventurers' ears, however: he had guided journalists through the no-man's-land between Oujda and Algeria for a fee and had received a juicy journalistic offer of filming along the desert routes from Bamako. Now he wanted to work, of all things, on preventing illegal migration, perhaps with an international NGO.

These paradoxical pursuits made sense in the surreal world of the clandestine circuit. As routes into Europe have closed up, stranded migrants have sought other means of fending for themselves *(se débrouiller).* While a few tinkered with petty fraud and many more did menial jobs, the most astute adventurers monetized their migratory project itself. Theirs was a warped, reflexive inversion of the standard aim of international migration: instead of migrating to *find* work, their migration had itself become a job. At the top of the pecking order among such "professional migrants" were the leaders of migrants' associations in Morocco. European and Moroccan NGOs active in the country—themselves at times lambasted as a "humanitarian mafia" by academics and migrants, much like their counterparts in Senegal—called upon these leaders to provide testimony *(témoignage)* in donors' conferences or else as project brokers; their countrymen approached them for advice and assorted services; journalists hungered for their stories and expertise. Some published books on their ordeal or donned titles such as "consultant on sub-Saharan migration." Didier was simply trying to tap into this market in his own small way, moving easily between Sogoniko's hotels-cum-brothels and Aracem, between Ceuta and Oujda, between journalists and smugglers. In the German caravaniers, he would soon find a new and eager audience.

ACTIVISM UNLEASHED: THE PROTESTS BEGIN

Chaos reigned in the Djelibougou field, where any European hopes for efficiency seemed to melt away with each day of meetings in the suffocating heat. Moreover, everyone had to be heard. The caravaniers had adopted the cherished "assembly format" of recent transnational activism, but assembly-based consensus democracy was proving achingly hard to practice among the disparate caravan groups.[15] The street corner guys had finally made it to the field, where they now stood studying anti-Frontex posters taped to the walls of the AME-run restaurant. "Why is everyone so nice here?" asked Eric, looking at the Europeans who kept smiling and offering him their seats. Still, he was not carried away with excitement. The caravan's citizen-journalists had filmed at Aracem, he said, but he had refused to participate unless they paid him. "After, they'll sell that and make money!" The wariness was to be expected: stories circulated about journalists and researchers visiting with hidden cameras or offering money for dangerous trips into the desert.

Under the canopy, debates had been heating up for several days. A contingent from the French sans-papiers' movement had arrived in Day-Glo vests and had mobilized the caravaniers for a protest at the French Embassy. Malians in the gathering had voiced concern about protesting without a permit, a reservation ignored by the more hardline elements in AME and in the overseas factions. The protest had ended in police beatings and bruisings. Undeterred, the activists went about organizing a precaravan demonstration targeting the E.U. Delegation in central Bamako. A flyer circulated among those attending, announcing the aim of the march: *contre l'expulsion des aventuriers et aventurières et contre les deguerpissements.* A French Bamako resident and AME collaborator saw the flyer and sighed. "Aventuriers, that means nothing!" No local would understand it, she said. Neither would they understand *deguerpissements*, which referred to the evictions campaigned against by one of the caravan organizations, the Mouvement des Sans Voix. A friend of Eric's looked at the flyer and shrugged, too, pointing at the word *aventurière*, the female form of *adventurer*, which had been inserted in accordance with the gender equality aims of the activists. "They need to take that out," he said. Such disparate concerns pointed to the failure in creating a master frame able to unite not only the factions in the activist network but a larger audience of migrants and Malians as well. The stakeholders were increasingly antagonistic, the local audience nearly nonexistent. Except for the association representatives under the canopy, the only Malians circulating among the metal chairs were a ragged bunch of local children and the occasional trinket vendor. Not surprisingly perhaps, since almost all speakers resisted using the local languages. "They should speak Bambara," said one bemused Cameroonian adventurer. "See, there are no locals here!"

These tensions did not deter Aboubacar and his fellow *militants* and *militantes.* He had failed to show up at the march on the embassy, but now he increasingly grabbed the microphone, calling for more radical action. "It's important for us to do a march here in Bamako," he said, his voice growing louder. "We're into concrete activities because we're activists!" One of the German organizers asked if the march had been announced to the authorities. "We'll pass on that question," said Aboubacar curtly. "We're not going to spend our time on authorizations." He headed off for meetings elsewhere, to coordinate with Aminata's section of the caravan as well as with another World Social Forum caravan approaching Bamako from Benin, leaving participants to voice unease at the radical turn and the growing dissent between the factions.

As tensions grew among the caravaniers, their target nonetheless acted as a unifier. For the core participants, the target was the E.U. border regime or, more specifically, Frontex. The activists, by rolling several grievances into this single "supertarget," had managed to frame Europe's whole migration management strategy—stretching from Bamako's useless CIGEM to the violent Algerian deportations—as the enemy.[16] And now the enemy had arrived at the Djelibougou field, in the form of a motorbike with a CIGEM license plate. The CIGEM spokesman skulked around the tents without having announced his presence to the caravaniers. One of the Germans spotted the motorbike and slapped an "Abolish Frontex" sticker on the license plate. "Direct action," chuckled a colleague, looking on. More radical anti-Frontex action was about to come, both at the border in Gogui and at the caravan's destination in Dakar. In the assembly, a plan was hatched for Dakar protests aimed at "the police where Frontex is based." The activists had done their homework, pinpointing Jean-Pierre's border police office. The march on Frontex, "against the death of thousands of migrants at the external borders of Europe," would be the climax of their transnational caravan to the forum.

There were smaller protests to organize before this distant goal: first Nioro and Gogui, then the E.U. Delegation in Bamako. Aboubacar rallied the caravaniers around the marches in the Mali-Mauritanian borderland, and the buses set off for the grueling journey towards Nioro. Once there, angry debates ensued about whether to continue all the way to the border. Some opposed this initial plan because of the kidnapping and terrorist threat against Europeans. When Malian police offered to accompany them, more radical elements refused "as a question of principle."[17] "There's nothing in Gogui; there's no danger in Gogui," the AME chairman assured his visitors. He was right on both counts: there was no danger for the marchers, but there was also nothing there. Camouflage-clad Malian border officers showed the marchers around what were supposedly empty huts for deportees. Activists stickered the road signs marking the E.U. border regime and sprayed anarchist symbols on a building. After all the protestations and debates, their target had proved illusory.

The logic of this march might be found in the "protest repertoires" of transnational activism. Scholars have identified three forms of activist action: the logics of damage, of numbers, and of witnessing—the first aims to destroy property, the second to achieve a critical mass of supporters, and the third to engage in direct action with high symbolic impact. A few graffitied border signs aside, the logic in Gogui was neither that of damage nor that of numbers. Afterwards, participants struggled to define the purpose of the march. Some rationalized it as a show of support to Malian authorities against the Mauritanian policing of the border, others as an attempt to listen to local concerns about poverty. But the purpose of the march had all along been to target the E.U.-Africa border invoked by Aboubacar. As such, it was a form of witnessing, but it went further in *enacting* the border for subsequent broadcast on the movement website and other visual records of the caravan. To an outside observer, however, their borderwork seemed as absurd as that of the migrant protesters of Ceuta: the anger of both was directed at an invisible enemy, which failed to appear however much it was summoned.[18]

. . .

The marchers were back in Bamako, where, on the last day of January, the Benin caravan arrived. Caravaniers new and old gathered at Maison des Jeunes, the youth cultural center in central Bamako, where speech after speech denounced Europe's border regime. Even the deportees' usual role of providing testimony was absent; looking on, one of the street corner adventurers complained about those who "speak in our name." Local associations sought to prolong their moment in the limelight, resulting in an endless talk fest that tired European and African participants alike. One of the Germans, a big mustachioed man, shouted to the camera in frustration: "Always this blah blah and no action; *das ist scheisse!*" Finally, the drums began tapping a restless beat for the march on the E.U. Delegation. The marchers snaked their way down the road, blocking traffic as they went. A French activist spray-painted the walls outside the E.U. building as people stormed towards the gates. The mustachioed German did a victory sign to the camera. But it ended there: no police violence, no further activist damage.

Back on the Aracem street corner, Eric was getting anxious about the caravan. He was on the list of participants but had now been told only those who had joined the Nioro escapade would be allowed to go. "I want to move on; I'll hang on to the back of the bus!" he exclaimed. He was growing restless in Bamako and hoped an expenses-paid trip to Dakar might propel him onwards on his adventure. Stéphane showed me a lucid analysis he had written for the forum workshops in Dakar on the fate of migrants and the inequalities of globalization. His paper denounced "internal borders" created in Africa and the contradictions arising out of the disjuncture between ECOWAS freedom of circulation accords and E.U.-imposed controls. "Our economy moves, but the people don't," he summed it up. "And the adventurers are victims of these contradictions."

It was the eve of departure. Cyrille looked out over the Aracem compound from the rooftop sleeping space. He had been assigned to stay behind in Bamako but was pondering trying to join anyhow and then get an empty seat on another freedom-of-movement caravan, from Morocco to Dakar, as it headed back up north. "I need to think of myself a little," he said. He was annoyed with the way that unequal gains of money and attention were straining relations among the Malian associations in the caravan. Political splits were widening as well. Aminata's caravan contingent, whose political objectives sat uneasily with the Gogui and E.U. Delegation marches, was now set to depart later than the buses of the more radical activists on the Djelibougou field. Despite the efforts of the Germans and AME to rally around the supertarget of Frontex, the caravan was fracturing and splintering even before leaving Bamako.

BAMAKO-DAKAR: SEARCHING FOR THE BORDER

The day of departure finally came. The Djelibougou field filled with expectant travelers, who stacked foam mattresses on top of their buses and put banners and backpacks in the cargo hold. Eric had called me before departure, desperate. He was off the caravan list. Cyrille was left behind too, but Didier and Stéphane were there with the Aracem contingent. Soon after departure, they would both try to make the most of their time with the Europeans. As the buses were boarding, delegates and unannounced travelers scrambled for seats despite the best efforts of the organizers with their official lists of participants. It was to prove a small taste of things to come in this jumbled escapade into the West African hinterland, looking for the elusive E.U.-Africa border.[19]

The buses ground their way out of Bamako slowly, caught in the usual traffic jams and the smog-packed heat of noon. I found myself squeezed into the back of the bus designated for the members of Mouvement des Sans Voix, who turned out to be anything but voiceless. A cohort of djembe drummers launched into caravan songs, and the stuffy air of the bus soon reverberated with shouts, chants, and drum beats. I had managed to get into the caravan in the role of scribe, documenting the trip for AME. Besides me and other record keepers, the caravan had welcomed a few journalists of an activist bent: an Italian reporter, two Spanish documentary makers, and the German filmmaker I had first met in Ceuta. But no big media organizations were present. Except for the Malian journalists who appeared during the initial Djelibougou days, the caravan would attract little media attention. It was instead the caravaniers' reflexive self-presentation that, as in the online shots from Gogui, gave credence to the caravan as an event. Much like the Frontex maps and control room screens it targeted, its connection to any external referent was getting increasingly tenuous.

Soon after leaving Bamako, one of the Benin buses broke down. As the caravaniers streamed out of the bus for greasy road-stop mutton and rice, Didier leapt to action. "I'm an illegal migrant," he said, presenting himself and his Moroccan adventures to other caravaniers before pitching an idea for a film on migration. The European journalists he had met in Bamako for a report on migrant routes had offered too little money, so now he was trying his luck with the activists before returning to Morocco via Dakar, he told me later. Stéphane was getting excited too, trying to make me introduce him to some German women. I interviewed him for the AME caravan record, and he launched into a political discourse: "We are about to show to the eyes of the world, to the eyes of the United Nations, to the eyes of the whole European Community, that we can change things." As we traveled on, he used any opportunity to speak up in meetings and to the Europeans, alternately presenting himself as a deportee and as an Aracem spokesman.

Lacking a clear border and a visible supertarget, the activists increasingly leaned on migrants such as Stéphane as an alternative unifier for action. The humiliated, robbed, and victimized deportee was, after all, living proof of the existence of the elusive border they sought. Clandestine migration also proved to be the glue among caravaniers. Once the drums fell silent in the MSV bus, a heated debate started raging on women's rights, with the young Europeans onboard growing increasingly frustrated with their male Malian copassengers' views. "The only thing we can agree on is migration!" one of them later said in despair.

Tensions were not limited to intellectual debates about gender equality. Increasing animosity between youth of different West African nationalities erupted once the caravan pulled up at the stadium of Kayes in westernmost Mali around midnight. Tired passengers fought and scuffled for the mattresses, then scrambled to get some food, pushing the caterers aside. Next day, in a morning meeting on the lawn, the organizers insisted that violence among the caravaniers was not acceptable. "Everyone should know that we're together!" The Germans took up the caravan song, their weak voices chanting solidari-solidari-solidarité. The huddle of activists on the lawn looked increasingly unsure, their big hopes for the caravan crumbling further with each stage of their journey.

The day that followed, with its endless talks interspersed with theater and music, failed to inject the necessary solidarité. Aboubacar's admonishing that his Malian coparticipants should stop stoking tensions with fellow West Africans fell on deaf ears. Back at the stadium, a fight suddenly broke out. A young Malian from our bus cracked a branch off a tree: people thronged, shouted, and scuffled. The No Vox bus, part of the Benin caravan, was broken. "They don't want anyone else to leave," someone explained. Now they threatened to block the route with their own bus, creating a border in our midst. Aboubacar tried to mediate, to no avail. Camera-armed caravaniers filmed the youngsters fighting in front of the parked buses. Fists and branches, Malians against Burkinabes. Most of the Germans were ensconced in their bus, suddenly reduced to the role of onlookers, like tourists happening upon a street rebellion.

"Frontex is in our heads," one of the caravaniers had quipped before the fight. "Between the idea and the reality, there's Frontex." His remark seemed to be an ironic reflection both on the failure to find a physical border at which to protest and on the tense fault lines that had appeared between caravan participants.

The No Vox passengers were finally taken aboard the remaining nine buses, which slowly snaked their way towards the Mali-Senegal border. Next beckoned Tambacounda, Senegal's easternmost city and, like Kayes, a big "sending region" for migrants.

. . .

The activists streamed out of the buses in central Tambacounda, taping anti-Frontex posters to railings and steeling themselves for another day of talks. To boost flagging spirits and launch into the action they kept talking about, the caravaniers decided to march through the city. Two Germans mounted their stilts, dressed as human fence-cutting shears and holding a banner between them calling for a world without borders. A sound system was heaved onto a donkey-pulled cart, and the marchers streamed down the main street, into Tambacounda's market, denouncing migrant expulsions over their megaphone. A few children in rags trailed behind the protesters, and market women looked on perplexed. Stéphane held the megaphone, launching into a call-and-response with gusto. "Open the borders!" he shouted, the marchers echoing his words. "No more expulsions!" A group of emaciated building workers, perhaps regional labor migrants themselves, looked at this confident, educated Cameroonian with glazed eyes. He was the migrant with the European megaphone; they, the silent, impoverished bystanders.

The Germans had taken an increasing interest in the Aracem caravaniers since the bus left Bamako. After the march, the Germans gathered in the shade, discussing the need to record the deportees' testimonies, which would later pepper the caravan documentary. There was one story that had rattled the gathering in particular. One of the Aracem deportees had told them migrants had been executed by the Spanish

Guardia Civil in the forest outside Ceuta, on the Moroccan side of the border, in 2009. He had also talked about German, French, and Moroccan police firing on migrants in the forest hideouts. The Germans were troubled by this. The German reporter and I joined their circle, voicing concerns about the plausibility of the story on the basis of our research in Ceuta. The Germans did not want to let it go, however, discussing how to verify the claim and what action they could take. One of them finally drew a conclusion. Even if the story was mixed up with rumors, he said, there could still be a kernel of truth to it, a trauma embedded in these stories, which the migrant used to make sense of it all. The gathering nodded and assented.

While this idea of the scar left by trauma rendered migrants worthy of attention, care, and assistance, for the activists in Tambacounda it was also the clearest *sign* of the existence of the border they protested against. In their view, the migrant had mixed the general tragedy of the border regime with the individual psychological shock experienced outside Ceuta in order to cope better with the latter. Then I found out that it was Didier, the professional migrant, who had told them of the killings. I kept quiet about the fact that the story had probably been fabricated to arouse the attention of the Germans. Didier surely knew that they, as activists, needed a story "designed to generate outrage and action" and that he was the man to deliver it.[20]

After another round of delays, the caravan rolled out of town for its next stop. The road to Kaolack wound westwards for hours before we pulled up late at night, exhausted. No Vox and the Bamako caravan had fallen out again, this time over sleeping spaces, and Aboubacar stood looking lost and tired among the parked buses. I saw my chance to escape the chaos of it all, saying furtive good-byes and catching the night bus to Dakar, some two hundred kilometers farther west. I arrived, dirty and bleary-eyed, just in time to attend the first global declaration on freedom of movement "by and for migrants." This was the World Charter of Migrants, finalized on the island of Gorée. Those summoned for this historic occasion included the AME leader ("as migrant, not as chairman"), but he was now marooned in Kaolack, unable to attend. They also included Pierre, Bamako's veteran ghetto chief; a clique of professional migrants who had helped organize the caravan from Rabat; free movement advocates from West Africa, the Maghreb, and Europe; and Mohammadou, my old repatriate friend, who sat silent in a corner listening to the deliberations. As the charter was joyously signed off to drumbeats and slogans, I felt a long-lost sense of relief: the journey was over, and the international civil society extravaganza of the World Social Forum was about to begin.

FINDING FRONTEX AT THE FORUM

The caravan I had abandoned in Kaolack finally rolled into Dakar. Its exhausted participants dusted themselves down, donned their stilts and banners, and joined the inaugural forum march. Central Dakar was heaving with the international NGO elite: slogans were shouted, hands shaken, banners held high, flags waved, contact books filled. Excitement was in the air, but would soon dissipate amid the orchestrated chaos that followed upon the sudden about-turn at Université Cheikh Anta Diop, the forum venue. The withdrawal of support by the university director and Senegal's government was, as noted in chapter 1, leading to chaos on campus.

In the tent village for diaspora and migration set up on the university grounds to deal with the lockout, I met Mohammadou and Omar, the repatriate association's sunglassed and smooth-talking spokesman. They were trying to organize another session on repatriation after the spectacular failure of the first one in an empty university hall, but no audience appeared. Finally Mohammadou spotted someone with a video camera and the reporters, three European university students, powered up their equipment. They asked the usual questions and got the usual answers on how the association had fought illegal migration, on the need for partners, on the false claims of the likes of Mother Mercy. Then the reporters asked Omar about his boat journey. As he launched into a tragic account of his trip to the Canaries, people started gathering around our chairs. "Were you not afraid?" asked the reporter. No, said Omar, his voice rising: "You have to throw your brother overboard . . ." The audience kept growing, almost all of them European, leaning in to hear the story. "We're doing testimonies on illegal migration," Mohammadou explained to the swelling crowd, handing out flimsy business cards and finding more chairs for the newcomers. Recording devices were thrust towards Omar as he talked of his second journey and final failure; a reporter was snapping pictures. There was a hitch, however. Rumors, unknown to Omar's eager audience, had it that he had not done the clandestine boat journey at all. Mohammadou later admitted to doubts surrounding Omar's migration story. "But he can speak if he wants to," he said with a tired smile. As in the stories of Didier and Stéphane, the narrative of the violence of the border was taking on its own life, regardless of who told it.

Clandestine migrants' traumatic stories stirred the Europeans' curiosity while the realities reflected in the Sogoniko environs and the battles of Mohammadou's association—not to mention the larger inequalities underpinning these—remained unheard and unreported.

All along, the Germans had wished to connect the story of the sea border and the repatriates with that of the deportees they had met in Bamako. As in the caravan writ large, they sought a "convergence of struggles" among migrants and in solidarity with them, and they had gone to one of Dakar's fishing neighborhoods to organize a joint cultural soirée for the purpose. Stéphane had come along to the preparatory meeting as representative for Aracem. But he was something else too. "I'm a victim of illegal migration," he said when introducing himself to the circle of local association representatives and visiting caravaniers. By now, the complex migrant victimhood he had written about in Bamako—the adventurer at the receiving end of the contradictions of globalization and migration policies—had been reduced to a convenient label for the activists' consumption.

In the Saudi-funded tent city ("Saudi Arabia, Kingdom of Humanity" read the logos, much to the activists' dismay) for all forum participants, the caravaniers were busy preparing for the Frontex march, the climax of their caravan. The offices of the Senegalese border police, pinpointed during the precaravan talks, were a good target, since they lay outside the "red zone" of central Dakar, where the authorities had prohibited protests. But no permission was forthcoming for the short march down to the Cité Police complex on the seafront either, and feeling was running high about what should be the next step. Mohammadou and his repatriate friends had been roped in as well and stood discussing plans for participation with the Germans. He asked for twenty thousand CFA to bus people from Yongor to the protest, but the caravaniers insisted participation should be voluntary. "We can get youth from Soumbedioune otherwise," said one of them, referring to the neighborhood around the corner from Cité Police. "Have you seen any [repatriates] there?" Mohammadou snapped back with newfound confidence. Suddenly, an announcement stirred the gathering: the authorities had given their go-ahead for the march.

. . .

On the morning of 10 February 2011, a knot of activists clustered outside the post office of the neighborhood Medina. Most of them were Europeans; among the few Africans present was the AME chairman.

Mohammadou had arrived alone and stood talking to a woman about the destination of the impending march. "Where are we marching?" she asked. "To the university," replied Mohammadou. "Oh, I thought it was to the French Embassy," she said. "Frontex" remained an elusive target and destination even for the marchers. As the crowd slowly grew with the sans-papiers activists and German caravaniers, so did the police presence. Officers in full riot gear descended from vans and positioned themselves around the crossing that the marchers had to pass on the short stretch of road leading to the corniche and Cité Police.

Finally, the placards started appearing—*Abolir Frontex* (abolish Frontex)—and two Germans got on their stilts, holding the usual banner. The crowd moved up the road, chanting *solidarité, solidarité*. The riot police moved ahead of them while a police van and an ambulance secured the rear. European citizen-journalists snapped pictures and filmed their slow progress. Finally, the goal of the caravan beckoned: "Frontex" and the seafront corniche.

The confrontation starts with tentative steps, in a shy dance between security forces and protesters. Police take up positions, safeguarding the front gates and perimeter wall of Cité Police. Workers gather on the balconies, looking down on the marchers. The second floor of this building houses Jean-Pierre's division; this is where Frontex has been located by the activists. The crowd starts chanting *à bas, à bas, à bas le Frontex* to the wild *tam-tam-tam* of drums. "Sit down!" someone screams into the megaphone, and the protesters start their sit-in, blocking access to the corniche. The police keep their distance, and so do I, gravitating towards the big mosque across the road. An old man in boubou and skullcap asks bemused what it is about, and the man next to him replies on my behalf, "You want a world without borders!" I feel increasingly awkward in this delicate balancing act between my police and activist contacts, but it is impossible to act the role of bystander: there are no neutral onlookers except for us and a few itinerant sunglass vendors. "They want a world without borders but they're creating a border right here!" the older man retorts with a smile, looking at the road blocked by sitting activists. Some of them have strung a banner along the perimeter wall of the Cité; then suddenly a dreadlocked German unfolds another banner on the balcony of the third floor of the DPAF building. "FRONTEXPLODE" it says, referring to the European anti-Frontex network. He had sneaked in for a relaxed chat with a high-ranking police officer, he later explained, and unfolded the banner on the way out. "It's the second floor that is Frontex really, but anyway it doesn't matter," he said, proud of his achievement.

"So you're hiding here!" Mohammadou spots me on the sidelines outside the mosque. He comes up waving an anti-Frontex poster, holding a marker pen, and flashing a smile. "Help me to write Yongor here," he says, turning the poster over on the ground. I sigh. Am I with him and the protesters, or am I not? I say I have to leave, and saunter back up the road towards the post office. On the way I meet a local man, who snaps angrily, "The forum is not for the Senegalese; it's the foreigners who come to see each other here. They come and block the road like this!" The next day, I find no news of the protest in the papers, and even the forum publications kept total silence, according to the marchers.

While this mainstream lack of interest was perhaps to be expected, the Frontex protest still brought to a head the larger conundrum already observed in Gogui, in Tambacounda, in Bamako. Europe's nebulous border regime was, as seen in chapter 2, producing a border that was no longer "at the border." It could be located only with difficulty and through painstaking research. Yet despite the activists' deft groundwork in pinpointing Frontex, the border regime remained elusive. By locating it in the DPAF offices, they pragmatically stayed out of the "red zone" of central Dakar—but it was still not clear why Frontex was faced down there, rather than at the Senegalese navy base, the Spanish Embassy, or indeed away from Dakar at the Military Palace in Las Palmas or the Guardia Civil headquarters in Madrid. The marchers' difficulty in locating the border and its regime pointed to a larger absence of responsibility for the tragedies of the borderlands. It is this absence at the heart of the violence of clandestine migration—and the absurdity it engenders among those who try to confront it—that this chapter has tried to pinpoint and to which we will now briefly turn.

PROTEST AND THE ABSENT PERPETRATOR

This account of victimhood and borderwork during the Bamako-Dakar caravan might seem overly critical, an exercise in the "misplaced cynicism" so carefully avoided by Fassin and Rechtman, which risks belittling the very real violence and victimization taking place in the borderlands. As academics and activists increasingly step on each other's toes in both their fields of travel and expertise, it might moreover seem an unfair attempt at promoting the perspective of the scribbling, sweaty anthropologist at the back of the caravan bus above those of his sloganeering fellow passengers.[21] It is important, then, to emphasize that the marchers were not simply tilting at windmills. Theirs was an audacious attempt at taking transnational activism on free movement to a new level. Given this ambition, the chaos, infighting, and outreach troubles were acutely felt by many of the participants. Evaluating the caravan for the in-house documentary, one of the Germans called it a "glass both half full and half empty." "A good many of our political plans that were a bit ambitious, such as establishing contact with the local populations and exchanging viewpoints about their and our experiences, have naturally only functioned in part," he said. Others criticized the unequal gains of Malian associations involved in the caravan and the communication problems that had marred it. What was not salient in their internal critique, however, was the deeper issue of how to mobilize protests on behalf of this particular kind of migrant at this peculiar kind of border. In taking as their rallying points the illegal migrant and the Euro-African border, the activists joined the police, the aid world, and the media in making these twin specters increasingly real. Their mobilization inadvertently confirmed the official obsession with illegality while cementing its importance in relations between European and African nations. This was the tragedy of solidarity in the borderlands: the opposition to the illegality industry could take place only on the "factory floor" of this industry itself.

The borderwork of the activists overlapped with that of the police in a play of reflexive performances upon performances. They both marked out the territory of the border—the marchers' anti-Frontex stickers, banners, and graffiti superimposed upon the anti-migration signs and property of E.U.-funded officialdom. With their placards, banners, and spray-paint cans, the marchers located and fixed the diffuse border regime in sites such as Cité Police and Gogui. Here lay the irony of their efforts: the marchers for a world without borders first had to create the walls they wanted to break down.

There is a larger point to be made about the protest as well, related to the confrontations seen in Ceuta, Melilla, and elsewhere on the clandestine circuit. The illegality industry has created new and unexpected realities in the borderlands—worlds of surreal disconnect and violent blockage that condense, in tiny enclaves and desert deportation sites, the contradictions in Europe's response to irregular migration. In these frontier zones of mixing, mimicry, and make-believe, roles shift and change, giving rise to new routes, new skills, new forms of protest. Here, astute travelers morph into smugglers or professionalize their migratory adventure; activists replicate the networks of European border police while unwittingly reproducing the borders they contest; hounded migrants don the soldierly mantle they have been handed by the authorities and the media; and each dark strategy for usurping migrants' mobility and time is confronted by new migrant countertactics.

In this world, then, arise new ways of being "illegal." This was also seen among the activists, who—much like their opponents in the illegality industry—had to conjure a certain type of migrant in their contradictory borderwork. In the caravan, the figure of the clandestine migrant underwent an inversion, from threatening villain to globalized victim. Cleansed of the dirt and dust of the border, the migrant's new victim role was, moreover, selective. As in other rallies for broad causes, the most articulate and perhaps *least* victimized by the border regime took the metaphorical and literal megaphone: strident leaders such as Aboubacar, Didier the professional migrant, and Stéphane the student rather than the limping deportee Alphonse or, of course, any impoverished *regional* migrants spotted on the sidelines. In this way, the illegal migrant was made up as a victim in a collaborative exercise between adventurers and their activist interlocutors. As Fassin and Rechtman note about survivors of disaster and war, the migrants quite logically "adopt the only persona that allows them to be heard—that of victim."[22]

As already noted, however, the perpetrator of the victimization was more difficult to identify. For the activists it was Frontex, whereas for the Spanish police it was the smugglers; for African police and migrants, it often seemed to be wild, untamed nature itself. At other times, these antagonists followed Stéphane in glossing over the question of the absent perpetrator when he said he was a "victim of illegal migration." Illegal migration itself here appeared as an increasingly reified and violent force. Absent yet present, much like the border it depended upon, it was becoming a faceless perpetrator that all actors—police, activists, migrants, aid workers, and journalists—could rally against.

. . .

The story does not end with the Frontex anti climax. Most of the caravaniers returned to Bamako, the deportees now with new journalists in tow. As I left the gathering in Dakar, Aboubacar had seemed deflated, a far cry from his strident caravan self. His firebrand performance was ending. Meanwhile, Stéphane's making up as migrant victim was becoming painfully real. A few months after the caravan, he e-mails me from Bamako. He has been deported, thrown into prison, and seen friends die in the desert. In early 2012, we get in touch again after I have seen his eloquent testimony in an e-mail sent around by a "professional migrant" on the Migreurop mailing list. He is now in northern Morocco with

Eric, waiting to cross into Ceuta. Mohammadou is still in his neighbor-hood, ever on the lookout for partners but more hopeful than before, thanks to his growing network of contacts after the World Social Forum. Cyrille finally escaped from Bamako. Rumors had it that he stole money from the street corner guys, but he told me he had to run away after being threatened by the returning Aracem caravaniers. The European activists, meanwhile, geared up for the next big protest against the bor-der regime—Boats4People, a transnational "solidarity flotilla" between Italy and Tunisia in the summer of 2012. The migration story continues, in circles of absurdity and tragedy into which the illegality industry taps at the points of its convenience.

For another actor, Mother Mercy, this industry was no longer what it once had been. Before leaving Dakar, I met her for an interview at the forum. Accompanying her was a young Belgian research student who had found out about Mother Mercy's association via a Red Cross con-tact. It had looked perfect for her research project, as it had for many others before her: "Migration, women, and development, the three issues that interest me!" Her insecure demeanor and bewildered look indicated, however, that her first impressions were already falling short of expectations.

Times were dire for her reluctant host. The Spanish money had stopped coming, and Mother Mercy had had to close her office, the sight of which had taunted Mohammadou and his friends in the years following their repatriation. "We have no more electricity, no more Internet, no more water!" she complained. "It's a real pity for our women, because we wanted to show another side of the Senegalese woman." Her main role at the forum now concerned women's rights rather than migration, and she was soon to encounter that other symbol of female empowerment, Ami-nata, on the beach of Mohammadou's neighborhood. Women from Yon-gor who had lost their sons on the sea journey, dressed in white for mourning, met with Aminata's caravaniers to light candles for their rela-tives as darkness fell over Dakar and the sea with its invisible border. At night, on the main forum stage close to the "Frontex" offices, Aminata's theater troupe acted out the journey through the desert, to the fences of Ceuta and Melilla. As the adventurers were sent back to Bamako, their elders danced, sang, and cleansed them, reincorporating them into Africa like long-lost children. *Ceuta Melilla Lampedusa Canaria* intoned a female voice, evoking those European slivers of land where the violence of the border was finally, unequivocally made real. *Ceuta Melilla Lampe-dusa Canaria.*

Conclusion

Bordering on the Absurd

They will keep coming since there exists no wall capable of
stopping people's dreams.

—text in a Guardia Civil video introducing a new migration
control center

Absurd is that which is devoid of purpose.

—Eugène Ionesco

The workings of the illegality industry, it has been repeatedly stated in
this book, are absurd. Absurdity covers a range of meanings, from the
existential to the colloquial, but what will initially concern us here is the
absurd in its guise of purposelessness pure and simple. The illegality
industry's sectors work according to their own institutional logics, and
quite rationally so. Yet taken together and assessed over a wider temporal and geographical perspective, these efforts serve little evident purpose. The illegality industry is like a sledgehammer that fails even in its
basic task of cracking a nut. Attempts to combat illegality only generate
more illegality.

Not only do clandestine migrants keep coming, as the Guardia Civil
quote above makes clear, but also their routes and methods take increasingly surreal forms. To briefly recapitulate, it was thanks to increasing
police harassment and the fortification of Ceuta and Melilla that the
small, harmless groups of sub-Saharan migrants in Morocco in the early
2000s morphed into a seemingly frightening horde. Further crackdowns
proved the catalyst for the opening of a route to the Canaries, and suddenly packed wooden pirogues appeared among European holidaymak-
ers. The closure of the Atlantic route piled pressure on Greece and then

Italy, whose neighbor Libya had perfected the political art of using clandestine migrants as a bargaining chip. The blanket control of the Mediterranean also strengthened smuggling networks and gave rise to ever stranger, and more dangerous, entry methods. The illegality industry and its contradictions—on humanitarianism and violence, visibility and hiddenness, outreach and closure—has molded its raw material of illegality into ever more distressing forms.

Yet on the frontline and in European capitals, it is business as usual. Illegality is now hardwired into institutional arrangements, from Red Cross rescue operations to Frontex risk analysis networks. It materializes in detention centers, hi-tech fences, and coastal radar stations. It is paraded in broadcasts, broadsheets, and border-guard videos. It is counted, calculated, and stacked up in ledgers by Frontex and European and African interior ministries. As the stakes grow higher, illegality is reified and refined. It also becomes ever more absurd, in the various meanings of the term: ridiculous, incongruous, senseless, and futile. Like Sisyphus in Greek mythology, the illegality industry rolls its boulder up a hill every day only for it to roll back down again.[1]

This conclusion might seem counterintuitive in the extreme. After all, this book has followed migrants' own analysis in focusing on what the illegality industry *does* achieve and on who benefits from these achievements. In fields such as development aid, sea surveillance, and humanitarianism, illegality is not just produced; it is also productive. As a "problem" to be solved, it sparks new security "solutions," NGO projects, professional networks, activist campaigns, and journalistic and academic engagements that might otherwise remain unfunded and ignored.

As has been seen from Dakar to Warsaw, each of the industry's sectors works according to its own discrete logics. In the world of sensitization, "codevelopment," and migration management, the very hiddenness of clandestine migration provides the foil for a public-private partnership in which actors large and small stand to gain power, clout, and money. In the defense industry's laboratories, the development of subsidized surveillance products is a virtually risk-free enterprise that, as with SIVE or Eurosur, creates lock-in effects for its state customers. For European police, the retention or deportation of migrant bodies constitutes a supreme form of deterrence. In border guarding, migration controls give old-fashioned outfits such as the Guardia Civil a new lease of life while spurring a relentless depoliticization of the border. And for politicians, this depoliticization is precisely the point: by handing more money to the wizards of the new frontier, a great magic trick can be performed whereby "vulnerable" borders suddenly appear secure.

While a full account of how this multifaceted industry has come to pass is beyond the scope of this book, a few notes should be made on its recent growth. Border guards have repurposed themselves since the end of the Cold War, finding new threats and problems to justify their work in today's "borderless" Europe. In the migration-development nexus of "sending countries," once-lofty international aid programs are similarly being repurposed as "strategies aimed at containing the world's 'surplus' population," as other writers have noted. Security companies and nonprofit organizations, in turn, have benefited from the outsourcing of state functions, winning contracts for anything from running detention centers and building radars to assisting "vulnerable" migrants. And the costs for such contracts can increasingly be borne by the European Union, since governments' border anxieties dovetail with a European project itself anxious to be seen as a safe container shielding the Union's common "space of freedom, security, and justice." From this perspective, Europe's illegality industry is simply one "regionalized" political response to the insecurities and possibilities generated by a patchily "globalized" world economy.[2]

The business of bordering Europe is thus a political project that might be more rational—and cynical—than this book has seemed to suggest. Three political gains from it will be flagged here, among others arising in the course of this book.

First, "race" has been deployed to maximum effect at the border. In his study of Spanish migration policy, Lorenzo Gabrielli has convincingly argued that Spain and the European Union, by focusing on the small flows of clandestine migrants from south of the Sahara, have engaged in a spectacular show of force that hides, by sleight of hand, a continuing influx of workers and tourists from economically more important regions. Sub-Saharan Africa here appears not even in its commonly invoked guise of reserve labor pool but as a frontier zone for a projection of fears and visions that serve the electoral interests of European powers. The "collateral damage" of these short-term political goals is all too evident: the increasing deaths, counted and uncounted, occurring in the new buffer zones of the Sahara, the Mediterranean, and the Atlantic.[3]

Second, the illegality industry keeps the problem of "illegal migration" productively at a distance: out of sight, out of mind. In this regard, Spain's diplomatic drive in Africa has been extraordinarily effective in blocking, hiding, and rerouting migratory "flows"—and at a relatively cheap price to boot. The "hidden" world of clandestine migration can nevertheless be transformed into a spectacle when needed, as Italy's Silvio Berlusconi did in announcing a national "emergency" during the 2011 North African uprising, triggered by his government's retention of boat migrants on Lampedusa in front of angry locals and the world's cameras. This is the creative push-pull that makes the media a supreme accomplice in the illegality industry: without the cameras, there would simply be no emergency.

Third, the creation of a subcontracting chain makes accountability impossible while enabling extensive feedback between seemingly self-contained sectors. Frontex can blame member states for human rights violations in joint operations; the Spaniards can shrug at reports of violence committed by their Moroccan colleagues or blame defense companies for lethal fence technology; the Moroccans can point a finger at Algerian soldiers, smugglers, or European push-backs; meanwhile, aid workers and security companies can argue that they simply provide specific services or products without responsibility for how these will be used. Most important, European politicians absolve themselves of blame for the tragedies and mistakes in migration controls. As in the use of mercenaries in war or the outsourcing of the welfare state, arm's-length delegation brings political leverage—at a price.[4]

These rationales help explain the growth of the illegality industry, whose price tag remains utterly out of proportion to its target. Sisyphus rolls his boulder up the hill again and again, but this is precisely the point: the illegality industry keeps the defense industry and security forces funded, the NGOs busy, and the media occupied with an external "threat," all the while providing new synergies and collaborations.

Yet this conclusion would lend too much power to the industry and its political paymasters, as well as assuming far too much unity of purpose.[5] As has been seen in this book, no one is in full control at the borders. Instead, the border business has created new frontier economies that blur the lines between the licit and the illicit, the rational and the surreal. The growing stakes in illegal migration mean that all the industry's sectors—border guards and defense contractors, aid workers and the media—have an interest in inflating the phenomenon, yet their ways of doing so clash and create new conflicts. Migrants similarly both subvert and reinforce the industry's schemes, whether as nationless subsaharianos or wild strikers, hidden *clandestins* or rescuable "boat people." These interactions perpetuate the contradictory subject position of the "illegal migrant" in his various guises, poised at the fault lines of a tense new terrain of power.[6] The circularity at play can be summarized thus: illegal migration, once formulated as a *problem* of "illegality," will keep coming back to haunt the frontiers of Europe. It will do so through the distressing presence of migrant bodies, whether packed into Melilla's kamikaze cars, paddling inner-tube boats, or stripped to their underwear at the border fence. The industry, in a sense, demands it.

The notion of "externalities" may help to bridge the industry's steely logics and its unnerving or absurd outcomes. For the fight against illegal migration does not just come with a steep price tag, bringing virtually frictionless gains for the defense sector; it also creates what can be conceptualized as *negative externalities,* in the sense familiar from environmental economics. The plans for the industry might have been costed and evaluated, but their insidious social, political, and human effects are rarely taken into consideration. As has been seen in this book, these "side effects" constantly threaten to overrun the workings of the industry. This, in turn, leads to more complex expressions of absurdity than mere lack of purpose.

. . .

One of the principal externalities was seen in the borderlands in chapter 3. When clandestine West African migration is framed as a risk and the "junk" risk is heaped onto North African partners, unforeseen tensions are stoked. This has often been starkly spelled out by the Moroccan authorities, who insist that they pay a high price for cooperating in controls. The externalities of externalization—worsening relations with fellow African states, social malaise caused by migrant destitution and blockage, a dented image of Morocco abroad—are adding up. As the tensions build, European border guards again face the "threat" they thought they had pushed beyond the border or into the algorithms of their surveillance machinery. For the migrants, needless to say, these externalities are even more acute.

For the aid sector, the negative externality might similarly be one of credibility. The lack of accountability and transparency among NGOs, as well as their dependence on funders' priorities, has been noted across contemporary Africa and beyond. These features of the global NGO expansion, however, are thrown into particularly stark relief by the fight against illegal migration, in which nonprofits and international organizations such as the Red Cross and the IOM function as a buffer between

the steely core of the border regime and its human interfaces. The ran-
corous funding battles, replicated from Senegal to Morocco and even
Spain, show a tawdry scramble for funds disbursed according to warped
short-term priorities. In these battles, local resentment builds over the
inequitable distribution of provisions, as exemplified by the repatriates'
struggles in chapter 1 and the Rosso quandaries in chapter 3.

In these two forms of subcontracting—policing and aid—migration
is turning into a privileged language for exchanges between the West
and its Others. Migrants become tokens of communication in a claims-
making process through which a small, containable "problem" is hugely
inflated, as was absurdly illustrated by Libya's Gaddafi, who in 2010
asked for five billion euros a year to "stop illegal migration" in order to
prevent Europe "turning black." A similar circularity besets attempts to
contest the industry, as was seen among the protesters of the borderlands—or, for that matter, in this book. In delving into the workings of
the illegality industry, the book risks reinforcing precisely what it sets
out to criticize: the fetish of the border, the racialized migrant, and the
emergency framing joining the two.

Those labeled "illegal migrants" are increasingly participating in
these games themselves, using their imposed status to receive recognition. Their participation highlights yet another externality for European
powers—that of perception. The migrants encountered throughout this
book, like many of their compatriots back home, exhibit a growing
disillusion with the European dream that once motivated their adventures. This disillusion is paired with a searing criticism of the illegality
industry itself—whether by repatriates in Dakar, deportees in Bamako,
or strikers in Ceuta—which migrants see as illicitly profiteering from
their misfortune. In their protests and grievances, such illegal migrants
are neither the seekers of European favors or rights amply studied by
migration scholars, nor invisible and apolitical *clandestins*. Here
appears, rather, what political scientist Andreas Kalyvas calls the "rebellious immigrant," an unexpected and bitter fruit of the illegality industry's labors.[7]

The emerging clandestine lingo reflects the radical twist to migrants'
perceptions. As seen in chapter 4, this lingo increasingly mimics the
larger industry under whose shadow the illegality industry labors, the
"war on terror." Terms such as *Guantánamo, Taliban,* and *bunker* highlight how migrants increasingly ironize their subject position as that of
the most-wanted Other of the contemporary West: the terrorist. This
new border vocabulary confirms yet subtly undermines Europe's inva-

sion myth; more important, however, it frames Europe as a wretched empire victimizing African travelers through military means. As anger and disillusionment spread through migrants' social networks and even filter into the illegality industry itself, fragments of a shared narrative of the Euro-African borderlands emerge. The end result is not pretty: Europe here emerges as a dark, cynical force finally robbed of its once so shiny allure.

. . .

To explore the world of migration controls along Spain's coasts is to travel through a landscape of ruins, structures set up only a few years ago that are already falling into disuse, thanks to the changed migratory landscape. In the Canaries, the CIEs stand empty, their detainees long departed. In Tarifa, on the Strait, the debris washed up by waves of arrivals has made Red Cross workers ponder creating a museum to clandestine migration, with artifacts displayed as in an ethnological exhibit: inflatable boats, inner tubes used as life vests, a migrant paddle sculpted out of a single piece of wood. But the Red Cross offices are themselves museum-like; made for migrant rescues, they stand empty, unused.

Even when the illegality industry succeeds, in its repressive guise, in rerouting migrants, the remnants it leaves behind hint at the futility of its efforts. These efforts are, by necessity, always in excess and never quite suited to their target. Steel fences, detention centers, and rescue facilities remain among the few tools available for politicians to signal decisiveness in the "fight" against fluid, fickle migrant routes.

The illegality industry's efforts are in excess in a more human sense as well. I began this book by tentatively suggesting that the illegality industry acts reductively: travelers with diverse origins, stories, aims, and legal statuses are gradually reshaped to fit the generic mold of migrant illegality. Yet this imposition of a one-dimensional illegality is not the whole story. As the chapters have shown, the illegality industry's workers constantly dress up the "naked" notion of illegality. In part, they do so to target and tailor their interventions—after all, everyone cannot be asked for papers, detained, deported, rescued, observed, cared for, filmed, or written about. But such instrumental aims combine with deeper motives. The illegality industry needs something to fundamentally motivate and justify its workers' efforts, which many of them openly recognize as futile. In the borderlands, backpacks and black skin hint at a dangerous, hidden illegality that calls for prompt detection. In Ceuta, lack of documents implies an essential condition of vulnerability

that justifies "treatment." In policing and aid work, the secrets and traumas in migrants' heads motivate interrogation or therapy. These excess
attributions, as a supplement, come to the aid of something that had
increasingly seemed so natural, so commonsense, so black-and-white—
migrant illegality.[8]

From the material perspective of this book, this "will to meaning" is
simply another factor fed back into the illegality industry's hybrid functioning.[9] The excess attributions materialize in the iconography of Frontex operations, in the technology of the Melilla fence, in rescue imagery,
and in the make-believe paperwork of Ceuta. Here absurdity is more
than just purposelessness: it becomes an incongruous, even grotesque
split between reality and representation, set in a feedback loop that generates ever stranger *real* results.

One of these results concerns the lived experience of migrants, who
have to endure the contradictory attributions with which their illegality
is crafted. The "illegal migrant," especially when black and male, is both
a pitiable object of rescue and a massing threat at the borders. He is
defined by the stigma and promise of mobility yet regularly rendered
immobile; he is a threatening, cunning invader but also an innocent,
ignorant victim; skin and clothing make him visible, but he is still
endowed with an authority-eluding invisibility. Out of these contradictions emerges an elusive essence of migrant illegality, produced by the
mere absence of documents in order. This "illegal immigrant," as the
preceding chapters show and as other ethnographies have similarly
pointed out, is, however, an impossible presence. Living through this
impossibility, migrants at times come to experience the absurdity of
their predicament in its existential sense of radical unmooring—or, in
the words of Albert Camus, of "irredeemable exile."[10]

Incongruousness is also on display at the border. This book has
asserted that clandestine migration is a spectacle and a staging, and as
such it might give a brief glimpse of truths otherwise left hidden about
the workings of the contemporary world. Seen through such a lens,
the strange show—discussed in chapter 4—of migrants congregating
round a Spanish banner on Isla de Tierra in 2012 seems, like the spectacles on Tenerife's beaches in 2006 and atop Melilla's fence in 2014,
to fulfill the task once envisioned for the midcentury theater of the
absurd. As Martin Esslin once put it, discussing the seemingly senseless
works of Ionesco and Beckett: "The means by which the dramatists of
the Absurd express their critique—largely instinctive and unintended—
of our disintegrating society are based on suddenly confronting their

audiences with a grotesquely heightened and distorted picture of a world that has gone mad."[11]

Perhaps it is here that the illegality industry finally finds its wretched purpose.

. . .

The illegality industry is in a constant state of disequilibrium. In 2012, Mali underwent a coup and saw its vast desert north claimed by separatists, sparking a refugee crisis that soon set alarm bells ringing in Madrid and Warsaw, while the violent aftermath to the "Arab spring" saw mass displacements farther north. In Senegal and Spain, new governments promised a different political era and different priorities on migration—as seen in the large cut in development aid for sub-Saharan Africa announced by the Spanish conservatives, as well as in battles with Brussels over their ever-tougher measures at the borders. Morocco, for its part, had by 2014 launched an unprecedented regularization and suspended its Oujda deportations, even as crackdowns continued.[12] The illegality industry grinds on, despite these changes, yet its configuration is amenable to change at a moment's notice.

One catalyst for change is economics. As the eurozone crisis deepened, southern European countries were again being seen as nations of emigrants, not immigrants. Angola offered to help Portugal in mitigating the crisis, and Portuguese workers streamed into the former colony. Job-seeking Spaniards traveled not just to northern Europe but also to new destinations such as Morocco and Brazil, with the latter enforcing tougher border controls in a tit-for-tat between governments that eventually forced Madrid to ease checks on Brazilians entering Spain. "One day Europeans will come to Africa to look for work," an adventurer in Tangier angrily predicted in 2010. That day has come rather sooner than he perhaps expected.

Perhaps one day, the inhabitants of what was once the rich world will look back at the early twenty-first century and wonder why so much time, energy, and money was spent on controlling the movements of so few. Perhaps then, decision makers will realize the folly of controlling human movement at any cost, of labeling certain travelers illegal, and of parading these "illegals" in elections, broadcasts, surveillance rooms, NGO pamphlets, and books such as the present one. But for that to happen, the illegality industry first needs to be dismantled and the product on which it works seen for what it is: nothing more, and nothing less, than people on the move.

Appendix

A Note on Method

The study of the illegality industry involves methodological considerations that will be briefly considered in this appendix. To put the central dilemma simply: How can a complex system stretching from Sahelian border posts to European control rooms be researched without its being clearly and fully present in any of these places? And how can anthropology—a discipline that has traditionally privileged long-term immersion in "local" worlds—adapt its fieldwork methods to the study of such systems?

Aware of the challenge of studying processes associated with "globalization," anthropologists have come to embrace multisited research. In migration studies in particular, researchers have for many years heeded George Marcus's call to "follow the people," especially along the U.S.-Mexican border—a call I also heeded in my initial research plan of accompanying migrants on their journeys.[1] Such multisited studies have transcended the ethnographic focus on a "local community," yet problems remain, as otherwise sympathetic anthropologists have noted. What Nina Glick Schiller and Andreas Wimmer term "methodological nationalism"—ignorance or naturalization of the nation-state and the territorial limitation of objects of study—is subtly reproduced in the community focus of many multisited studies. Added to this is the ethical problem identified by Raelene Wilding: while the anthropologist flits between locales, her informants remain anchored to specific places and identities. Ghassan Hage, writing about transnational Lebanese migrants, adds further concerns. To him, multisited fieldwork implies futile (and exhausting) attempts at studying the relation between each instance of a transnational "community" and its corresponding "site." In sum, multisited ethnography still seems tied to community and locality even in its promise of abandoning them. Or, as Ulf Hannerz notes, the anthropological ideal of immersion and "being there" lives on in the multisited world of "being there . . . and there . . . and there!" We could ask, along with Bruno Latour: "Is anthropology forever condemned to be reduced to territories, unable to follow networks?"[2]

As multisited research is being critically reassessed, some anthropologists have returned to the single field site, now reframed as an "arbitrary location" giving a view onto larger complexities or as a "node" in the world system. Another solution has been to reconfigure anthropology's relationship to locality altogether. This is the approach pursued by Gregory Feldman, who in *The Migration Apparatus* argues for a "nonlocal ethnography" that goes beyond the traditional anthropological privileging of "evidence obtained through direct sensory contact." In this, he draws upon the earlier efforts of Xiang Biao, whose study of mobile Indian IT workers made a strong case for a focus on intangible social processes. While it gains ethnographic reach, however, such nonlocal ethnography loses some of the "thick description" so cherished by anthropologists—something Xiang himself acknowledges in highlighting the lack of a "flavor of the research sites and a sense of 'being there'" in his excellent monograph. The anthropologist, instead of being there or being there-and-there, is suddenly appearing everywhere yet nowhere.[3]

There is, I believe, another option: what I would like to call the "extended field site" in a nod to the extended case method of the "Manchester school" of social anthropology. Exemplified by Max Gluckman's classic text *The Bridge,* this approach brought groups that previously had been considered as separate—tribesmen and colonizers—into an analytical conversation that reached well beyond the confines of the geographically bounded villages that it was anthropology's lot to study. My extended field site approach takes this focus on agonistic social interfaces and repeats it across diverse locales. Instead of multiplying sites or sidestepping localities, this rather involves a transversal relation to locales in which "the field" is not conceptualized within narrow geographical boundaries. In sum, I treat my dispersed research settings as a single site. The extended field site, as "one site, many locales," allows for the tracking, tracing, and mapping of the *system* of the transnational illegality industry and the modalities of migranthood it produces.[4]

This approach also draws upon forms of "interface analysis" in development studies, which have allowed researchers to bring funders, aid workers, brokers, and beneficiaries into one analytical frame. In reaching across the social interfaces created along the Euro-African border, the aim has, however, not been to flatten the account of the illegality industry or to essentialize and compartmentalize distinct subject positions, as interface analysis is sometimes alleged to do. The purpose has rather been to explore how each interface uneasily and imperfectly superimposes a new suprageographical function on towns, roads, and enclaves in the borderlands and to inquire into the production of new subject positions *through* the encounter.[5]

An "extended field site" approach provides a very different, yet complementary, vantage point on Europe's border controls from that explored by political scientists or indeed by Feldman's nonlocal ethnography. Feldman distinguishes between "tangible" but merely "symptomatic" features of the "migration apparatus" on the one hand and less tangible but generative "rationales" on the other. As seen in this book, however, Europe's evolving border regime is not just based on "intangible" processes but is also constituted through social, communicative, and financial networks reaching from distant border posts to policy makers' offices while depending on the physicality of deserts and sea borders, the geography of offshore enclaves and isles, and precarious supplies of infrastructure and manpower. Following the questioning of the policy-practice nexus emerging from recent anthropologies of development, I argue that the materialities, geographies, and social configurations "on the ground" are not simply temporary manifestations of a predefined system but rather function as key constitutive arenas. By moving away from the nebulous world of the policy apparatus and focusing on the interfaces where the border machinery rubs against specific places, people, and structures—what Anna Tsing terms "friction"— we can hopefully produce an ethnographic account that spans the overarching logics of Europe's response to clandestine migration and those crucial "grains of dust that jam the machinery."[6]

Actor-network theory provides a useful theoretical scaffold for doing just that, thanks to its focus on interactions among materialities, machines, and people. In short, this "theory" (or, rather, toolbox) approaches human and nonhuman groups as "actants" that, in the process of overcoming resistances among them, generate apparently solid systems through what Bruno Latour labels the work of purification and translation.[7] This analytical scaffold, while invisible in the chapters, has allowed for shifting the focus away from the two poles of migration studies—the (political science) perspective that privileges policy and the (ethnographic) insistence on a grounded "migrants' perspective"—towards the material, virtual, and social interfaces of the illegality industry.[8] From this vantage point, the fences, patrol boats, radars, TV cameras, and rescue equipment can be seen as "actants" in a network or "collective" made up of human and nonhuman links. The "illegal immigrants" here function as key connectors or "tokens" in the illegality industry; their circulation is the language and currency of the network.

However, it is important not to lose sight of the complicity of those subject to such circulation and categorization, as the philosopher Ian Hacking would insist. This is why, despite this being an ethnography of an industry, the migrants have been given a prominent place in the chapters, as actors and coanalysts of the system in which they find themselves stranded.

My methodological approach also draws upon journalism. As Liisa Malkki has noted, anthropology has mainly been concerned with durable, culturally transmitted experiences to the detriment of the transitory, dramatic events commonly treated by journalists. Clandestine migration is defined by such events, created and mythologized by the media in collusion with politicians, police, humanitarians, smugglers, and migrants. While this media-fueled "spectacle" has been thoroughly interrogated in this book, I do follow Malkki in using the investigative end of the journalistic spectrum to rethink the benefits of fieldwork on dramatic and staged events. As an anthropologist, I enter an overcrowded research arena where fieldwork is no longer what it "used to be" as I follow in the footsteps of journalists, academic pioneers, NGO workers, government fact finders, and policemen. In this crowded field, the investigative, intrepid reporters stand out. As noted in chapter 4, some of these have followed migrants on their clandestine journeys, often at great personal risk; others have investigated boat tragedies through long-term engagement with migrants and officials. These immersive, investigative approaches resemble and sometimes surpass what anthropologists can achieve, and a critical engagement with such efforts has therefore been a key part of my approach—whether in seeking out dramatic events, "following the money," or applying journalistic persistence to building a heavy contacts book.[9]

In a broader sense, too, my intention has been to work in as interdisciplinary a manner as the border professionals themselves, finding inspiration in their mobility and methods. Such eclecticism is a necessity in researching the secretive world of clandestine migration and in negotiating access with antagonistic and difficult-to-reach groups such as migrants and police. My extended field site approach has, for instance, allowed me to offset access limitations and potential conflicts of interest in one place with renewed access, thanks to "snowball sampling," in another.

Most important, perhaps, treating my research area as an extended field site has made me a colleague and "accomplice" of sorts for migrants, reporters, police, and aid workers. This is a treacherous yet thrilling place to be for anthropologists who, trickster-like, specialize in moving with ease between the "natives' point of view" and their own. Yet the anthropologist, as I hope the chapters show, is already "native" to the industry he writes about. He, like the workers and migrants he encounters, moves through Europe's emerging borderland and helps create it as he moves; his personal and professional networks, like theirs, reach from Mali to Madrid and beyond. As he trades anecdotes with migrants or workers about distant contacts, dreary border posts, or grueling overland trips, a shared understanding starts emerging of the Euro-African border, of the industry itself, and of the clandestine journey.

There is some comfort to be had in this shared understanding. On one level, rather than being an example of a dark and cynical industry pulling us into its field of influence, it is simply part of that age-old fellowship among people on the road. For, as many adventurers told me, "until you travel, you live with your eyes closed." The purpose of the adventure, and of anthropology, is to open them.

Notes

INTRODUCTION

1. This officially acknowledged death tally does not include those who later perished in the desert. An investigation into the deaths has repeatedly been called for without luck (Migreurop 2006).

2. See www.guardian.co.uk/world/2012/mar/28/left-to-die-migrants-boat-inquiry. On the 2013 tragedy outside Lampedusa—widely reported in the media—see www.theguardian.com/commentisfree/2013/oct/04/lampedusa-boat-sinking-no-accident-eu-migrants.

3. The term *illegal immigrant* is highly problematic, as this book will make clear. See the section "Tales of Hunger" in this introductory chapter, as well as note 36 below, for a discussion of its qualified usage in this book.

4. The figure given here is from the blog Fortress Europe: see http://fortresseurope.blogspot.co.uk. Since this figure is based on incidents reported by the media, it is very likely to be an underestimate. For similar findings on *documented* deaths attributable to European border controls, see www.unitedagainstracism.org/pdfs/listofdeaths.pdf.

5. *Illegality* used as shorthand for the term *illegal migration* has its problems, not least the fact that any criminal activities may be subsumed under it. However, I have opted for the term *illegality industry,* since it does not contribute to reifying "illegal migration" even more (see also note 36). It also helps avoid any confusion with earlier scholarly usages of the term *migration industry,* which has largely referred to the facilitation of movement (see Gammeltoft-Hansen and Sørensen 2013 for a more inclusive usage, however). Finally, it captures the emphasis on the *illegal* qualifier of *migration* in policing—as border workers would insist, it is "illegality," not the migrants themselves, that they target.

6. For a sweeping study of such illicit movements of goods across the contemporary world, see Carolyn Nordstrom's (2007) ethnography in this series.

7. Harvey (1989) defines globalization as "time-space compression"; see Bauman 1997 for an influential take on the difference between the two types of mobility discussed here, which he glosses as those of the "tourist" and the "vagabond."

8. *Jungle* is the term for the migrant encampments outside Calais, in France, next to the English Channel.

9. I will use the term *clandestine migration,* common in the French- and Spanish-speaking environs of this book, for two reasons. First, it is a relatively neutral term in English (the French noun *clandestin,* by contrast, carries the negative connotations of *illegal immigrant* and will be translated as such). Second, it points to the embodied experience of traveling through the borderlands, instead of being just a negative legal inscription. While on the road, the clandestine migrant frequently hides from police, evades border checks, and disguises himself through recourse to false documentation, ad hoc dress codes, and furtive behavior. For these reasons—its relative neutrality and its embodied connotations—I will use the term *clandestine migration* as analytical shorthand to refer to migration via land and sea towards (though not yet fully inside) European space. See also note 36 on *illegal migration.*

10. One Frontex (2011:32) report has pointedly compared detected boat arrivals with the number of unauthorized overstayers of Swedish student visas, which at 12,000 in 2010 were "roughly comparable to the 14,258 detections of illegal sea border-crossing" in that year. The latter figure increased sharply to 71,171 in 2011 (Frontex 2012:14) but still remains small in comparison with overall immigration into E.U. states, which Eurostat puts at about three million a year (with third-country residents making up just over half of this in 2009). See http://epp.eurostat.ec.europa.eu/statistics_explained/index.php/Migration_and_migrant_population_statistics. See de Haas 2007 on Europe's "myth of invasion" and Kraler and Reichel 2011 on clandestine migration statistics. Reher et al. (2008:63) give the census figure.

11. See the 22 April 2013 press release by the Spanish Instituto Nacional de Estadística: www.ine.es/prensa/np776.pdf.

12. On British and Swedish crackdowns on irregular migration, see www.theguardian.com/uk-news/2013/aug/03/illegal-immigration-issue-unacceptable-walthamstow and www.thelocal.se/46350/20130222; see Amnesty International 2011 on racial profiling in Spain. On detention, see the Global Detention Project: www.globaldetentionproject.org.

13. This situation took an interesting turn in the U.S. presidential election of 2012, when the Republicans were widely seen as having lost the Latino vote because of their draconian proposals on irregular migration.

14. Readers wishing to explore these wider perspectives could start by looking at Cohen 1987; Portes 1978; and Castles and Miller 2003.

15. The case of the "war on terror" has been discussed by Klein (2008). On border or frontier regimes, see especially Anderson 2000.

16. See Malkki 1995 on the feminized image of the refugee and Comaroff 2007 on the abject view of Africa.

17. See Andreas 2000 on the term *border game,* as well as chapter 4.

18. Alonso Meneses cited in Gabrielli 2011:397.

19. Bouvier 2007.

20. Gatti 2007:130.

21. Andersson 2005:30.

22. De Genova 2002; Agier 2011:68.

23. As Cornelius and Tsuda (2004:43) say, "Market forces and demography—not government interventions—will be the most powerful determinants of international migration dynamics in the twenty-first century." See also the blog of Oxford's Hein de Haas: http://heindehaas.blogspot.co.uk/2012/03/migration-its-economy-stupid.html. The economic case should not be pushed too far in the case of the clandestine migrations of this book, however: see chapter 4.

24. Harding 2012; see also Carr 2012.

25. Female irregular migrants and unaccompanied minors are usually treated as special "vulnerable" cases in Spain. The problem of access has also contributed to the lack of female migrants in the book; see chapter 6 for brief discussions of female versus male migrations. All men are of course not equally visible to the industry either. While those who do seek the industry's attentions will play an important part in this book, chapters 3 and 6 in particular also explore the experiences of those who remain marginal to those attentions.

26. See Gammeltoft-Hansen and Sørensen 2013 on the "migration industry" and Rodier's (2012) *Xénophobie Business*.

27. For recent studies of Spanish migration policy, see Serón et al. 2011; and Gabrielli 2011.

28. The differences between Feldman's (2012) approach and mine, as well as their complementary findings, are discussed in the appendix.

29. See http://ec.europa.eu/dgs/home-affairs/financing/fundings/migration-asylum-borders/index_en.htm. The €4 billion figure includes €1.8 billion specifically for the external frontier. Home Affairs funding as a whole will see a planned 40 percent increase to €10.9 billion in the next period—a large portion of which will again be set aside for migration, now through two separate funds. For Spanish figures, see www.salvamentomaritimo.es/sm/conocenos/plan-nacional-de-salvamento/ on sea rescues (which also include nonmigrant rescues) and MIR 2011. On development aid funding in migration controls, see chapters 1–3.

30. In 2013, the International Organization for Migration (IOM) said it had "observed a direct link between tighter border controls and increases in people smuggling, which is now a US$5-billion dollar a year business" (see www.iom.int/cms/en/sites/iom/home/news-and-views/press-briefing-notes/pbn-2013/pbn-listing/its-time-to-take-action-and-save.html). Estimates of the value of this "business" are, however, extremely hard to verify. The United Nations Office on Drugs and Crime (UNODC), on its part, has given an estimate of $6.75 billion a year for two of the world's principal irregular routes, from South to North America and from Africa to Europe (see web page and 2010 report, www.unodc.org/toc/en/crimes/migrant-smuggling.html); Gammeltoft-Hansen and Sørensen (2013) give an older, E.U.-specific figure of €4 billion.

31. Until January 2014, Airbus Group was known as EADS: see www.airbus-group.com.

32. The implicit framework here is actor-network theory (Latour 1993), discussed in the appendix. Aware of the disparate nature of the sectors included under the "industry" label, however, I will use *border regime* when talking specifically about the sectors involved in border controls.

33. Sampson 2010:271.

34. Hacking 1986 and 1999:10, 31. See also his later writings on "making up people" in *London Review of Books*, 17 August 2006: www.lrb.co.uk/v28/n16/ian-hacking/making-up-people.

35. Desjarlais, cited in Willen 2007b:12.

36. The criminalization of migration is well under way in countries such as the United States, Italy, Morocco, and Algeria, making the label increasingly "correct" in these jurisdictions. Elsewhere, the ethical and analytical problems with the term mean that analysts, activists, and even border guards often talk of irregular, unauthorized, or undocumented migration. The latter groups' usage highlights how these terms, as De Genova (2002) has pointed out, suffer from a similar state-centrism. For our purposes, too, they lose the useful connotations and implications of *illegal migration*. Sarah Willen (2007b) gives a robust defense of the ethnographic use of *illegality* because of "the cross-contextual applicability of the term, its substantial material consequences, and its impact on migrants' own experiences of everyday life." This is a line I will follow, while interspersing *illegal* with *clandestine* (see note 9 above).

37. Nevins 2002.

38. This book will talk about "West" Africa, since the focus is on clandestine routes through Senegal and Mali; however, it is important to keep in mind the strong presence of "Central" African migrants on these routes, including those from the Democratic Republic of the Congo and Cameroon (with the latter country often seen as poised between West and Central Africa).

39. See Gaibazzi 2010 on the Gambia, Jónsson 2008 on the Soninké, and Gardner 1995:95 on the postcolonial glorification of the West.

40. See Hann 2013 for more on the male breadwinner role in urban Senegal.

41. Lucht 2012:xii.

42. Calavita (2005) shows how "third-world" immigrants' legal Otherness in both Italy and Spain makes their integration—an official goal—all but impossible. Compare chapter 6.

43. See Cornelius 2004 on Spain's switch from labor exporter to importer; see Ferrer Gallardo 2008:136 on the coincidence of the 1991 events.

44. On the Spanish migration picture since the 1980s, see Cornelius 2004. For the interior minister's intervention, see http://tinyurl.com/9cwlh73.

45. Malmström made this comment after news that the Associated Press had dropped its usage of the term *illegal immigrant*.

46. This is known as the "migration hump" (Martin and Taylor 1996).

47. On the Italy route, see, e.g., Pastore et al. 2006.

48. Torpey 2000; see Cooper 2005:239 on the failure of full colonial dominance.

49. In the coming chapters, I will use the term *migrant* rather than *immigrant* when the traveler in question has not entered European space.

SCENE I

1. Quote from Kalyvas 2012. Migreurop's 473 figure (http://tinyurl.com /pljajr3) includes some non-E.U. countries.

2. Earlier, the limit to detention in CIEs was forty-five days. Worth noting is that other E.U. countries have much longer limits, with the E.U. Directive controversially setting the absolute maximum at eighteen months.

3. The CIEs have been heavily criticized by NGOs such as the Comisión Española de Ayuda al Refugiado and Amnesty International while also being censored in reports by, for example, the Spanish ombudsman and the European parliament; see González et al. 2013 for a full discussion and references. For the growing anti-CIE campaigns in Spain, see http://ciesno.wordpress.com and http://15jdiacontraloscie.wordpress.com.

CHAPTER I

1. Other scholars have written about Mother Mercy's association and its media impact, but I am leaving out these specific academic references to safeguard anonymity; her moniker has been modified for the same reason.

2. I will use *repatriation* rather than the legally speaking more correct *deportation* or *removal* here, following former migrants' usage and the generic term *(repatriación)* applied to their return *(devolución)* under Spain's Aliens Law.

3. See MIR 2011 for data on arrivals.

4. Passenger figure from airport website, www.aena-aeropuertos.es.

5. The argument that the announcement of Frontex patrols increased arrivals is hard to prove but was made at the time by the Canarian regional government. This would follow a pattern, seen in Ceuta and Melilla the previous year, of migratory flows accompanying or anticipating reinforcements. See *El Día*, front page, 1 August 2006.

6. No exact figures on deaths and disappearances exist. Mohammadou estimated fifteen hundred youth had died (Yongor's total population is around forty thousand), though official estimates are lower.

7. The *modou-modou* image of success is not clear-cut, however, as testified by their often barely half-built houses: see Buggenhagen 2001:376.

8. See Gabrielli 2011 on this "discovery," as well as http://seekdevelopment. org/seek_donor_profile_spain_feb_2012.pdf.

9. See De Genova and Peutz 2010, who coined the term deportation regime; Anderson et al. 2013; and individual studies such as those of Coutin (2007); Fekete (2005); and Willen (2007a, 2007b).

10. See Serón et al. 2011 as well as Gabrielli 2011, the latter of whom discusses how Spanish externalization measures became a model for other E.U. member states. Arrival figures from MIR 2011.

11. See http://canariasinsurgente.typepad.com/almacen/2007/06/informe_ del_mpa.html. The REVA funds have been discussed by Rivero Rodríguez and Martínez Bermejo (2008).

12. See Pian 2010 for more on the visa debacle.

13. On the contracts, see http://elpais.com/diario/2008/02/13/andalucia /1202858534_850215.html.

14. For the global figure, see Gammeltoft-Hansen and Nyberg Sørensen 2013:3. On the E.U. contribution given in 2007, see Hallaire 2007:87.

15. See Rossi 2006 on *sensibilisation* in other settings.

16. The right to leave one's country is enshrined in the Universal Declaration of Human Rights.

17. A 2010 agreement, preceded by a 2006 accord hampered by rights concerns, allowed Spain to start repatriating minors (Spanish ambassador, personal communication; Serón et al. 2011:75).

18. See Melly 2011 on these runaway tales among would-be migrants in 2006.

19. On the fishing crisis, see Nyamnjoh 2010.

20. On a parallel case among Ghanaian fishermen-turned-migrants, see Lucht 2012.

21. The largest CFA franc denomination is ten thousand, so what Mohammadou had in mind here was the total value of the bills.

22. On such top-down co-optation in other settings, see Gardner and Lewis 1996:126.

23. These studies are, respectively, Habitáfrica, "África cuenta: Reflexiones sobre la cooperación española con África" (online at http://archivos.habitafrica.org/pdf/AFRICACUENTA_BAJA.pdf); and Serón et al. 2011:71. The 2006–8 Africa Plan was followed by a 2009–12 plan, available at www.ccoo.es/comunes/recursos/1/doc18019_Africa_Plan_2009–2012.pdf.

24. On codevelopment, see Audran 2008.

25. The term is Bending and Rosendo's (2006). My discussion in the following paragraphs is inspired by Lewis and Mosse's (2006) "bottom-up" approach to studying development projects.

26. See Blundo and Olivier de Sardan 2001 on "everyday corruption" in Senegal and elsewhere.

27. See Gabrielli 2011.

28. Mosse 2004; Ferguson's (1990) *The Anti-Politics Machine,* a major source of inspiration for this chapter, discusses such "side effects" in development projects elsewhere.

29. Quote from Portes 1978:469; see De Genova 2002:421 on the same trend in the 2000s.

30. Prominent studies—all highly worthwhile reads—include Brachet 2009, Bredeloup and Pliez 2005, and Collyer 2007 on regional and historical patterns; Carling 2007a and 2007b on humanitarianism and fatalities; and Escoffier 2006 and Pian 2009 on strategies and networks en route. As for policy-relevant research, it is worth noting that migration was already framed as a "problem" in search of a solution in colonial times. As Gardner and Osella (2004:xi) note, migration studies as a whole are still affected by a "northern bias" that privileges international over internal migration and Western "destination" settings over so-called sending regions. The recent fascination with the clandestine migrant is but a poignant example of this larger pattern.

31. See, e.g., Nyamnjoh 2010:21.

32. Melly 2011; see also Hernández Carretero 2008 for a concise analysis of risk taking in boat migration.

33. On the World Social Forum, see www.forumsocialmundial.org.br.

34. Quote from Slavenka Drakulic, writing in the *Guardian*, 17 February 2012: www.guardian.co.uk/commentisfree/2012/feb/17 /bosnia-in-the-land-of-blood-and-honey. See Das 1995 for a powerful ethnographic study of violence.

35. Such co-optation from below is discussed in Mosse 2004:239.

36. See Hacking 1986; and introduction.

37. De Genova and Peutz 2010:8; in their volume, see also Cornelisse on the "territorial solution."

38. Melly 2011:363.

39. In this sense, the boat migrants' journeys were an exercise in mutual "interpellation," to borrow a term from the philosopher Louis Althusser (1971). While Althusser uses it to refer to the "hailing" of subjects by the state, here the process was two-way. See chapter 5 for similar dynamics elsewhere on the clandestine circuit.

CHAPTER 2

Portions of this chapter originally appeared in *Anthropology Today* 28(6) (Andersson 2012). Significant additions include the chapter introduction and parts of the conclusion, the section "Hardwiring the African Frontier," the italicized vignettes, and extra explanatory material on securitization.

1. The critical literature on Europe's borders is vast. See Parker, Vaughan-Williams, et al. (2009: 586) on the "seismic changes in the nature and location of the border"; Andreas and Biersteker 2003 on "rebordering"; Guild 2008 and Balibar 1998 on the proliferation of controls; Braudel 1975 on the Mediterranean; and Walters 2006a on the border as firewall and limes (Walters 2004).

2. This exercise of seeing the border from "above" and "below" is inspired by Anzaldúa (1999).

3. Beck's early conception of risk has been widely criticized by anthropologists for being too universalistic and ignorant of power (see, e.g., the edited volume by Caplan [2000]). By contrast, see Beck 2009 for the more complex perspective on "staging" discussed here.

4. An existing Spanish-Mauritanian readmissions agreement, first signed in 2003, was reactivated in 2006 along with a patrolling deal. Other agreements from 2006 and 2007 include a Spanish-Senegalese memorandum of understanding in August 2006 on cooperation in the fight against illegal migration; a Spanish-Malian framework cooperation agreement in 2007; and a July 2007 migration accord between Spain and Mauritania, formalizing cooperation already under way.

5. Frontex 2010:37. Besides Hera and Indalo, a third Frontex operation, Minerva, has targeted southern ports.

6. Quotes from Arteaga 2007:6.

7. The military's Noble Centinela operation ended in 2010.

8. Bigo 2001. See Andreas and Price 2001:31 on the militarization of policing and "domestication of soldiering," as well as on the shift from war fighting to crime fighting in the U.S. context.

9. See Tondini 2010:26.

10. Under international law, national sovereignty extends for twelve nautical miles from the coasts; next follow a "contiguous zone" of limited sovereignty for another twelve miles, the "exclusive economic zone" of up to two hundred miles, and, finally, mare liberum.

11. The agreements, which have not been made public, differ from country to country. Senegal allows non-Spanish Frontex boats and planes to patrol in the exclusive economic zone; Mauritania allows only the Guardia Civil to patrol and only in the contiguous zone (Guardia Civil, personal communication).

12. See Gammeltoft-Hansen and Aalberts 2010:17 on the amended rescue regimes, and HRW 2012 on the death count and "distress at sea."

13. Guardia Civil, personal communication with officers in Algeciras (2013); Ceuta (2010); and Madrid (2010).

14. See Walters 2011, who uses the term *uneasy alliance,* on Lampedusa's Praesidium Project; Guild 2008 on the "migration of sovereignty"; and Arteaga 2007:6 for the security argument cited here.

15. Quotes from Feldman 2012:95.

16. The budget has stabilized since 2010, excluding a peak to cover the 2011 boat arrivals from North Africa. However, other projects such as Eurosur are continuing apace, with separate funding. See figures in Frontex 2010:10 and its amended 2013 budget: http://frontex.europa.eu/assets/About_Frontex /Governance_documents/Budget/Budget_2013.pdf.

17. These comments resonate with the controversy surrounding Frontex operations at the Greek-Turkish border. See HRW 2011.

18. Hernández i Sagrera 2008:4.

19. On thought-work, see Heyman 1995.

20. See http://w2eu.net/frontex/frontex-in-the-mediterranean/.

21. See, e.g., Frontex 2009a:16–17, 20; and Frontex 2009b.

22. A secure system, ICONet, is used for sharing such sensitive information. Frontex also trains non-E.U. states on risk analysis, for example, through the Africa Frontex Intelligence Community. As Julien Jeandesboz (2011:8) notes, risk management techniques in policing preceded the establishment of Frontex.

23. During the full period of the 2011 JO Indalo (May–December), 12,274 kilograms of hashish was seized. See official press release at www.lamoncloa. gob.es/IDIOMAS/9/Gobierno/News/2011/27122011_OperationIndalo.htm.

24. This definition is part of the updated common integrated risk analysis model (CIRAM) used by Frontex analysts (Frontex 2012:9).

25. The original "Copenhagen School" formulation of securitization as a speech act (Buzan 1991) is complemented by Bigo's (2001) focus, followed here, on securitization through *practice*. See Léonard 2011 on Frontex and securitization, as well as Gabrielli 2011 and Huysmans 2000 on longer-term securitization in the European Union. Some scholars have contrasted the logic of risk with that of securitization, arguing that the latter is not necessarily dominant in European migration policy; however, the most recent Frontex definition of risk shows how "risk" and "threat" discourses are becoming intricately entangled.

26. A facilitator is anyone who has "intentionally assisted third-country nationals in the illegal entry to, or exit from, the territory across external borders" (definition provided by Frontex via e-mail).

27. Frontex risk analyses talk of "risk countries" in contexts in which such countries are likely to refer to senders of refugees. See, e.g., Frontex 2011:50.

28. See Gledhill 2008 and Martin 2004 for explorations of the twin notions of securitization similar to the one proposed here.

29. On financial securitization and its effects, see Tett 2009.

30. In its revised 2011 mandate, Frontex was given powers to colead joint operations and the right to purchase or lease its own equipment. However, its deputy director indicated in an interview that co-ownership of assets was the likeliest option because of budget constraints.

31. See MIR 2011. Aeneas, which ran from 2004 to 2006, was superseded by a "thematic program" on migration and asylum for the 2007–13 period.

32. MIR 2011.

33. The ICC is located in Madrid when both Indalo and Hera are active, otherwise in Las Palmas.

34. Kristof cited in Donnan and Wilson 1999:48.

35. See Walters 2004:682; and Beck 2009:188.

36. Spanish border workers nowadays use the term *patera* as shorthand for any migrant vessel. "Zodiac," a brand name for an inflatable boat, is sometimes also used by migrants to refer to fiberglass vessels. See glossary.

37. See Frontex (2010:62) on RAU as the "brains" of the agency. See the Guardia Civil's SIVE book (2008:109) on the funding rationales underpinning the switch from drugs to migration control. On Indra's exploits, see www.indracompany.com/en/sectores/seguridad-y-defensa/proyectos /sive-romania's-black-sea-border.

38. This is similarly the case with Eurosur, as Jeandesboz (2011:6) notes. SIVE screens covering the Strait do indicate "borderlines" in the form of edges delimiting the Autopista del Estrecho, the passage designated for commercial vessels.

39. Guardia Civil 2008:93.

40. See www.laverdad.es/alicante/v/20110211/provincia/augc-denuncia-falta-per sonal-20110211.html.

41. See Bigo 2005 on the technological fix across Europe. The Guardia Civil and the Moroccan gendarmerie exchange liaison officers, hold two annual high-level meetings, and carry out monthly joint patrols on the basis of a bilateral agreement.

42. See www.gmes-gmosaic.eu/node/112.

43. Quote from the commentator Arteaga 2007:5–6. See Frontex 2010:55 for a list of border control initiatives.

44. On these lobbying activities and export arrangements, see Lemberg-Pedersen 2013. See also http://ec.europa.eu/enterprise/policies/security/.

45. See Talos project: www.piap.pl/en/Scientific-activities/International-Research-Project/Projects-completed/TALOS (video available at www.youtube .com/watch?v=jpxZ24Daxlk).

46. The earliest sketches for a system akin to Eurosur were drafted by the Centre for Information, Discussion and Exchange on the Crossing of Frontiers and Immigration (CIREFI), created in the 1990s by the Council of the European Union, and took SIVE as inspiration. On CIREFI, see http://europa.eu /legislation_summaries/other/l33100_en.htm. For more on SIVE as inspiration for Eurosur, see Guardia Civil 2008:133.

47. The new system, called the Joint Operations Reporting Application, or JORA, runs in parallel to the Eurosur interface.

48. This quote highlights several discursive elements in the border regime: the conceptualization of people on the move as a source of risk, the scramble to monitor their movements, and the rendering of a desperate humanitarian situation as a so-called push.

49. Hayes and Vermeulen 2012. A more recent official figure, covering a shorter time span and thus including less expenditure, is €244 million for 2014–20. See http://europa.eu/rapid/press-release_MEMO-13-578_en.htm.

50. The Guardia Civil also uses Eurosur for sharing drug-related information, showing how national priorities can benefit from E.U.-funded systems targeting migration. The aim of saving lives was inserted into the Eurosur mandate only after the issue was raised by E.U. politicians. Future usage of Eurosur is envisaged for other fields, as part of a common information-sharing environment (CISE) for the European Union's maritime domain.

51. Until the revisions of its mandate, Frontex was unable to process personal data and is not allowed to send data to "third countries" (non-E.U. member states).

52. The "Seahorse Mediterranean" system is also being planned, on the basis of Spain's Atlantic system.

53. The politics involved in information sharing was illustrated by Spain's refusal to sign off on Eurosur in the autumn of 2013. While this did not stop Eurosur becoming operational—as Madrid knew—the no vote was a symbolic protest against U.K. participation in information sharing, following bilateral tensions over Gibraltar earlier in the year. See http://politica.elpais.com/politica/2013/11/04/actualidad/1383585272_066452.html.

54. Vaughan-Williams 2008:77.

55. Beck 2009:14.

CHAPTER 3

Portions of this chapter originally appeared in *Anthropological Quarterly* 87(1) (Andersson 2014).

1. Spanish ambassador (personal communication). For the state secretary's quote, see www.abc.es/agencias/noticia.asp?noticia=1012233.

2. Agier 2011:50. For the ethnographic studies inspiring this chapter, see Coutin 2005; Lucht 2012; Willen 2007a, 2007b; and Khosravi 2007, 2010.

3. The strategy later changed to one in which migrants were seen as victims of smugglers, bringing the Senegalese approach into line with Spanish priorities.

4. See Cooper's (2005) argument on the simultaneous incorporation and differentiation of the colonized Other in French West Africa, and Parry 1986:454 on anthropological theories of gift exchange.

5. See Collyer 2007 and Düvell 2006 for a critique of the "transit migration" concept, widely used and promoted by especially the IOM.

6. See Bredeloup 2008 for the biography of the aventurier given here.

7. See Coutin 2005, who uses the terms *above-board* and *below-board* in talking about the relation between the licit and the illicit in Central American migrations.

8. See Serón et al. 2011:51 on Mauritania's reciprocal entry agreements with ECOWAS countries.

9. See in particular Long's (2001) pioneering work on the application of social interface analysis to development projects.

10. See Amnesty 2008 and CEAR 2008 as well as Migreurop/La Cimade 2010:18 on reasons for detaining migrants in Nouadhibou.

11. Spain was also aided in negotiations by the weak position of Mauritania's postcoup government.

12. For a poignant critique of the "exodus" narrative, see Choplin and Lombard 2007.

13. See http://dazzlepod.com/cable/09NOUAKCHOTT379/.

14. With the migrant handovers money changed hands from Mauritanians to Malian officers, according to Migreurop/La Cimade (2010:32), though the exact arrangements are unclear.

15. For more on E.U./Spanish involvement, see Serón et al. 2011:51–60.

16. See http://elpais.com/diario/2008/07/10/espana/1215640817_850215.html.

17. On the numbers game, see Migreurop/La Cimade 2010. See Amnesty 2008 on the use of clothing as evidence of illegality and Cruz Roja Española's report (undated) for data on Nouadhibou detainees.

18. Coutin 2005:196, 198–99.

19. See Serón et al. 2011:74–75 for details on this cooperation. France has also been involved in funding the Malian border police: see Trauner and Deimel 2013:24.

20. Khosravi 2007:322, 324; Coutin 2005. See Driessen 1998 on Morocco and Kearney 1998 on the U.S.-Mexican border.

21. Agier 2011:31.

22. On the "transit country" misnomer, see Cherti and Grant 2013.

23. MEDA is a financial assistance program for the European Union's southern neighbors: http://europa.eu/legislation_summaries/external_relations/relations_with _third_countries/mediterranean_partner_countries/r15006_en.htm.

24. See chapter 4 and http://politica.elpais.com/politica/2012/09/03 /actualidad/1346702660_647547.html.

25. On Morocco's usage of "transit" migration, see Gabrielli 2011 and Natter 2013; the latter author also points to the *domestic* political logics behind the (at least partly self-imposed) framing of Morocco as a "transit state," as well as the regional political gains it has involved for Rabat.

26. See http://ec.europa.eu/world/enp/pdf/action_plans/morocco_enp_ap_final_ en.pdf and http://ec.europa.eu/dgs/home-affairs/what-is-new/news/news /2013/docs/20130607_declaration_conjointe-maroc_eu_version_3_6_13_en.pdf.

27. Figures from EMHRN 2010:61. Aid figures also include €390 million under a 2003 Spain-Morocco agreement (see www.foreignaffairs.com /articles/67566/behzad-yaghmaian/out-of-africa).

28. Valuable studies of life in and around such ghettos include Laacher 2007 and Pian 2009.

29. In Bauman's (1997) terms, he tried to enact the role of the "tourist," not the unwanted "vagabond."

30. De Genova 2002.

31. See report by MSF (2013).

32. On "self-deportation" in the United States, see www.washingtonpost.com /opinions/the-self-deportation-fantasy/2012/01/25/gIQAmDbWYQ_story.html. For a coruscating critique of the IOM's returns programs, see Hein de Haas: http:// heindehaas.blogspot.co.uk/2012/10/ioms-dubious-mission-in-morocco.html.

33. Lahav and Guiraudon 2000:5.

CHAPTER 4

1. This story is based on one of the interviews undertaken during fieldwork in 2010 with migrants in Ceuta.

2. See De Genova 2012:492; Debord 2004; and Andreas 2000.

3. See Heyman 2004:324 on border crossing points as sites where value "steps up or down" in the world system; Donnan and Wilson 1999 on value switches at the border; and Kearney (cited in Donnan and Wilson 1999:107) on "reclassification."

4. Mexican irregular migrations to the United States do follow economic trends more clearly than their European counterparts, which depend upon the rather different dynamics created by a maritime border. This is especially so in the West African case, which is bound up in the competing logics of the illegality industry, family demands, refugee considerations, and the individual quest for emancipation as this book shows.

5. These dynamics have been pinpointed by Cuttitta (2011) in the Italian case.

6. Agamben 1998. See Albahari 2006 for one interesting—and distressing— exploration of the practice of "letting die" on open seas.

7. See Malkki 1996:377 on the depiction of refugees as a "sea of humanity."

8. Like Poole (1997:8), I use the term *visual economy* to highlight the transnational social relations and channels of communication implicated in a particular organization of the visual field.

9. Calhoun 2008:85.

10. Workplace health regulations also included special insurance covering tropical illnesses for Salvamento staff and separate ventilation for rescued migrants on large Guardia Civil patrol boats.

11. See Ticktin 2006:33 on humanitarianism-as-politics. Forsythe (2009:74) discusses the tensions in the Red Cross movement. See also Pandolfi 2010:227 on the appropriation of humanitarian symbols and Barnett and Weiss 2008:3 for the contemporary humanitarian dilemma.

12. The larger debates on the politicization of humanitarianism will not be discussed here: see Weizman 2011 for one recent intervention.

13. Fassin's (2007:155) writings on the "militaro-humanitarian moment" are pertinent here; see also Walters 2011.

14. See funding figures in the book introduction.

15. Besides the examples in Comandante Francisco's video and others like it, another poignant example of the absolute predominance of sub-Saharan migrants in rescue pictures is the Guardia Civil's *SIVE* book (2008).

16. See Robinson 2000.

17. Much of this in-depth journalistic material is not available in English. Spanish books include Naranjo 2006 and 2009; Pardellas 2004; and Fibla García-Sala and Castellano Flores 2008. See Gatti 2007, Kenyon 2009, and Del Grande 2007 on the Libya-to-Italy route.

18. See Malkki 1996 on "speechlessness" in refugee depictions. Juan's conference appearance was at Encuentro de Fotoperiodismo de Gijón, 2010 (website now defunct). For the Al Jazeera documentary, see www.aljazeera.com /programmes/witness/2007/04/2008525194208 52346.html.

19. Debord 2004:17.

20. Aldalur 2010:164.

21. See Ferrer Gallardo 2008 on this backstory of the current fences.

22. Quote from Brown 2010:83; see Andreas 2003 on the shift towards targeting transnational threats.

23. See Andreas and Snyder 2000 on the broadcasting of deterrence; quotes from Brown 2010:131, 133.

24. See Driessen 1992, on "frontier praxis" in Melille.

25. Monetary figure from Ferrer Gallardo 2008:143, who also discusses the expansion of militarized discourses on migration in the next paragraph.

26. The mimesis theme here is inspired by Taussig (1993); see Laacher 2007 on the community structures in the hills.

27. Migreurop 2006:31.

28. Citations from old Proytecsa website: compare www.proytecsa.net /en/.

29. See www.publico.es/espana/17862/retiradas-todas-las-cuchillas-de-la-val la-fronteriza-de-melilla. The sharp razor wire was in fact added to the fence after the 2005 asaltos, showing the continuity between the Socialist and later conservative strategy despite official appearances.

30. See www.wilderness.org.au/campaigns/marine-coastal/detain_ci.

31. The guardias, in expelling migrants, admitted to treating the territory around the fences as virtually "Moroccan": see http://politica.elpais.com /politica/2013/09/21/actualidad/1379786530_154160.html. In 2014, the interior Minister similarly asserted that migrants had not "entered" Spain until making it past the guards. See Low's (2003) findings on gated communities, as well as van Houtum and Pijpers 2007 on Europe as such a gated community.

32. Figure from Ferrer Gallardo 2008:138.

33. See Heyman 2004 and chapter introduction on the steps in the value chain at the border.

34. See http://www.lexpress.fr/actualites/2/tensions-entre-le-maroc-et-l-es pagne-accusee-de-racisme_911851.html.

35. See www.jeuneafrique.com/Article/DEPAFP20100806T175949Z/.

36. See Low 2003:131 on how gating marks enclaves as wealthy, and Brown 2010:120 on the technique of the siege.

37. Phrased in Latour's (1993) terms, at sea the "work of translation" and its hybrid creations are put on display, on land the "work of purification," and the two are kept apart through another purification separating sea and land borders.

38. See www.youtube.com/watch?v=FTHn8X895cI.

39. Quote from Lemke 2005:8; De Genova 2012.

40. For the initial 2012 event relayed here, see www.elfarodigital.es/melilla /sucesos/101560-marruecos-repele-un-nuevo-asalto-masivo-de-inmigrantes-a-la-valla-fronteriza.html. On further entries in 2012–14, see the running coverage of *El País:* http://elpais.com/tag/melilla/a/.

41. See MSF 2013 on expulsions and their relation to better bilateral relations. The headline "Le péril noir" covered the *Maroc Hebdo* front page in November 2012.

42. See http://politica.elpais.com/politica/2012/09/03/actualidad/1346679500_929352.html.

43. On the new Melilla razor wire, see http://politica.elpais.com/politica /2013/10/31/actualidad/1383248597_158835.html. On the Ceuta tragedy, see http://euobserver.com/justice/123681.

44. See Pelkmans 2012 on this enclosing function in the case of the old Iron Curtain.

45. See www.elmundo.es/elmundo/2011/02/04/espana/1296817060.html.

CHAPTER 5

1. Agier (2011:3–4 and 47) uses the term *humanitarian government* in a somewhat different sense from Fassin (2007 and 2012: see also notes to chapter 4). See Rodier and Blanchard 2003 on "airlocks"; and Tsianos et al. 2009 on "speedboxes."

2. Malkki 1995; see also Turner 2010.

3. This term is Trouillot's (2003).

4. See http://elfarodigital.es/ceuta/sucesos/12134-dos-inmigrantes-acorralan-y-lesionan-a-vigilantes-del-ceti-tras-el-uruguay-ghana.html for article from 3 July 2010 and *El Faro* front page from 4 July 2010.

5. Journalists said *el general* was the term by which the other strikers addressed him but showed delight in using this military terminology themselves.

6. Figures provided by the CETI director.

7. See Turner 2010 on the negative effect of handouts on refugees.

8. *El Faro,* 14 August 2010.

9. See Malkki 1995 on the administration of refugees.

10. See www.aufaitmaroc.com/actualites/maroc/2010/8/6/le-maroc-con damne-vigoureusement-labandon-par-la-garde-civile-espagnole-de-huit-sub sahariens-au-large-de-ses-cotes.

11. See www.elconfidencial.com/ultima-hora-en-vivo/2013/06/acnur-decen as-inmigrantes-ceuta-niegan-acogerse-20130613-160432.html.

12. Agier 2011:49.

13. *El Pueblo* and *El Faro* front pages, 27 August 2010.

14. See www.elfarodigital.es/blogs/jorge-lopez/17535-entre-pitos-y-flautas. html.

15. The Consell de l'Audiovisual de Catalunya, in an exhaustive study of the media treatment of the 2005 tragedies (CAC 2006), detects an oscillation between depictions of migrants as helpless victims and as dangerous aggressors.

16. José Fernández Chacón cited in *El Faro*, 2 September 2010. See www .elfarodigital.es/ceuta/politica/18035-fernandez-chacon-a-los-inmigrantes-a-cartonazos-nadie-se-va-a-la-peninsula.html.

17. See www.elfarodigital.es/blogs/carmen-echarri/18553-con-la-resoluci on-en-la-mano.html.

18. Fassin (2005:362), writing about the old Sangatte camp outside Calais. Compare Agier 2011:144.

19. *El Faro* front page, 8 September 2010.

20. See Ferrer Gallardo 2011:30 on the 1995 events.

21. The original read: "Somos como vosotros, no somos malvados ni animales salvajes, pero una generación reflejado y consciente. Reclamamos solamente nuestros derechos. Estamos cansado de quedar en carcel, por favor el gobierno. LIBERTAD—LIBERTAD!!!"

22. Fekete 2005; see also De Genova and Peutz 2010.

23. Quote from Agier 2011:52; see Papadopoulos 2011 on the invisibility sought by clandestine migrants. The hailing of the state by Ceuta's strikers has some similarities to that of Dakar's repatriates. On a theoretical level, it also recalls Judith Butler's corrective to Althusser's (1971) theory of interpellation. To Butler (1995:24), the subject is not only hailed by the state but is in "passionate pursuit of the reprimanding recognition by the state" in a process that she terms "subjectivation."

24. See McNevin 2007 on the U.S. marches. See De Genova 2002; and chapter 3 herein on "deportability."

25. Fanon 1967:112, 129.

26. *El Pueblo* front page, 5 September 2010.

27. See Turner 1974:97–100; Malkki 1995; and Agier 2011.

SCENE 3

1. The Father's nickname has been changed.

2. The quote is from Bornstein and Redfield 2010:17; see also Bornstein's chapter on the "value of the orphan" in the same volume.

CHAPTER 6

1. See Mountz 2011 on such detention practices elsewhere.

2. See, e.g., Foucault 2008. For the time-space theorization informing this chapter, see Munn 1992; and Thrift and May 2001.

3. This was the term used by Ceuta's nuns.

4. Goffman 1961.

5. In 2011, the new conservative government swiftly moved to curtail this right. See http://politica.elpais.com/politica/2011/11/24/actualidad/1322125831 _984714.html.

304 | Notes to Pages 218–239

6. *Only Thinking,* by Gabriel Merrún: available at www.socialsciences .manchester.ac.uk/disciplines/socialanthropology/visualanthropology/archive /mafilms/2009/.

7. See Navaro-Yashin 2007 on make-believe documents. While Navaro-Yashin's case from northern Cyprus concerns documents not recognized beyond the (unrecognized) state producing them, in Ceuta the failure of recognition has occurred between two authorities within the same state.

8. See Pelkmans 2013; and Kelly 2006.

9. Goffman 1961:67.

10. Calavita (2005) has argued that the mismatch between the temporary legal status of immigrants in Italy and Spain on the one hand and the government emphasis on "integration" on the other stems in part from the legal inscription of these immigrants as cheap labor. What this chapter shows, however, is how these economic and legal logics have to be seen in relation to logics developed within the illegality industry itself—in this case, the use of migrants' time as withheld capital.

11. The term is from Glennie and Thrift 1996:280.

12. The classic study of "time-discipline" in such settings is Thompson 1967, an inspiration for this section. Worth noting is that the Melilla camp, unlike Ceuta's, was not divided into upstairs and downstairs spaces.

13. Desjarlais 1994:895.

14. On emotions and make-believe documents, see Navaro-Yashin 2007; on the bureaucratic production of indifference, see Herzfeld 1992.

15. See www.elfarodigital.es/ceuta/economia/16148-el-misterio-de-econo mia-y-hacienda-prohibe-la-contratacion-de-serramar.html.

16. The term *moral division of labor* is from Hughes 1958; also cited in Goffman 1961:107.

17. This example is but one among many in Spanish and international media.

18. Johannes Fabian (1983) uses the term *denial of coevalness* in his influential analysis of the temporal distancing involved in ethnographic representations of research subjects.

19. See Trouillot 2003 on the "savage slot," and Silverstein 2005 and Andersson 2010 on migrants as new "savages" in anthropology and related disciplines. The Radcliffe-Brown example is from Lindqvist 2008.

20. See Coutin 2005 on invisibility and hypervisibility.

21. For a discussion of this focus on past traumas in the official construction of refugeeness, see Mann 2010:235–42.

22. See Guyer 2007 for an influential anthropological argument on the "evacuation" of the near future occurring in contemporary societies. Among Ceuta's migrants, unlike in Guyer's American examples, this evacuation seemed to be a conscious effect of encampment.

23. See, for example, a diatribe by the camp doctor at www.elpueblodeceuta .es/201201/20120115/201201158203.htm.

24. See www.europapress.es/ceuta-y-melilla/noticia-desalojan-melilla-campamento-medio-centenar-chabolas-inmigrantes-levantado-hace-ocho-anos-20120529161926.html.

SCENE 4

1. See the CIGEM homepage, "Objectif et missions": www.cigem.org.

2. European Commission press release: www.carim.org/public/polsoctexts /PS3MAL001_EN.pdf.

3. CIGEM received funding from the 9th and 10th European Development Funds, with the scheduled total reaching eighteen million euros. For more detail on CIGEM and Malian migration policy as a whole, see Trauner and Deimel 2013.

4. The figure is an estimate for the year 2000 based on migratory patterns in preceding years; no exact data on emigrated Malians exist. See Sally E. Findley, "Mali: Seeking opportunity abroad," at www.migrationinformation.org /Profiles/display.cfm?ID=247.

5. Funakawa 2009:40.

6. The intern study is by Funakawa (2009).

CHAPTER 7

1. See http://noborders.org.uk and www.noborder.org on "no border"; www5.kmii-koeln.de/?language=en on No One Is Illegal; and http:// frontexplode.eu/ on Frontexplode. See www.frontexit.org/en/ for the more recent (and mainstream) Frontexit campaign.

2. Rumford 2008:2.

3. I stayed in Bamako during the Gogui march; this section is based on recollections of participants and audiovisual material. See www .afrique-europe-interact.net/index.php?article_id=384&clang=1.

4. The aim here is not to simplify the sophisticated arguments put forward for the subversive potential of irregularity, however. See Papadopoulos et al. 2008 and Kalyvas 2010 and 2012, the latter of whom uses the term *cosmopolitan citizenship*, for intriguing explorations of this theme.

5. See www.oecd.org/dataoecd/5/63/41682765.pdf.

6. Fassin and Rechtman 2009:23.

7. Quotes from Fassin and Rechtman 2009:183, 18. Joel Robbins's (2013) discussion of anthropology's recent focus on the "suffering subject" is highly relevant here; as seen in chapter 6, however, the discipline's previous research object of choice—the "savage"—still lingers in other modalities of illegality.

8. On Tin Zaouatene (Tinzawatene), see in particular Lecadet 2013.

9. The caravan was funded by individual fund-raising efforts and support from charitable foundations and NGOs (AEI 2011:119).

10. MSV focuses on evictions, and so its "victims" were not necessarily migrants.

11. See http://no-racism.net/article/2814/.

12. Walters (2006b) sees the trespassing and "hacking" of the border in, for example, border camps as a creative response to the fluidity of power. The challenge that he poses for such protests—that is, "how to fashion a form of action that protests and even disrupts the machinery of the border, while avoiding a position that fetishizes the power of borders" (Walters 2006b:35)—is highly pertinent to this chapter. On the Frontexit action, see http://vimeo.

com/62428750. For the history of AEI, see www.afrique-europe-interact.net
/index.php?article_id=38&clang=1.

13. On the frame analysis drawn upon here, see della Porta 2006:67; and
Snow and Benford 1998.

14. Žižek 1999:178; see James 2007:29 on a similar dilemma in contemporary South Africa.

15. See della Porta 2006 on the assembly format; her study informs this
chapter as a whole.

16. This was an example of what the political scientist Sidney Tarrow calls
"frame condensation" (cited in della Porta 2006:70)

17. Information from the recollection of participants, along with video and
textual material, including the MSV caravan report: www
.mouvementdessansvoix.org/IMG/pdf/Rapport_sur_la_participation_du_
MSV_au_FSM_de_Dakar.pdf.

18. See della Porta 2006:238 on the logics of protest.

19. "E.U.-Africa" is used here in keeping with the AME's differentiation
between the E.U. and European borders; the rest of this book uses the broader
"Euro-African" to highlight the border's dispersal.

20. See Fassin and Rechtman 2009 on the "scar" of trauma; quote from
Merry 2005:241.

21. On activist-academic overlaps, see Merry 2005.

22. Fassin and Rechtman 2009:279. See James 2007 on a similar selective-
ness in asserting victimhood in South Africa.

CONCLUSION

The text of the first opening epigraph, from the middle of a video section on
migrant rescues, is a shortened version of the more poignant phrasing of Rosa
Montero in El País: "They will keep coming and keep dying, since history has
shown that there exists no wall capable of containing people's dreams." See
http://elpais.com/diario/2006/06/18/eps/1150612022_850215.html.

The second opening epigraph is Ionesco cited in Martin Esslin's *The Theatre of
the Absurd* (1972:23).

1. See Luper-Foy 1992:97 on the various meanings of the term *absurd;* and
Camus 1942 on the Sisyphus myth.

2. Quote on "'surplus' population" taken from Walters 2012:74, who in turn
cites the work of Duffield (2007).

3. See Gabrielli 2011:341.

4. The point about accountability has been made by critics of Frontex operations, including by contributors to Gammeltoft-Hansen and Nyberg Sørensen
2013.

5. The latter argument—concerning the state's lack of internal unity on migration—has been made forcefully by Nevins (2002:168) in the case of U.S. controls.

6. Bayart's (2007) writings on the production of "global subjects" under
conditions of globalization have inspired these lines; however, his rather grand
assertions about these subjects need to be considered in light of the obsession
with illegality discussed throughout this book.

7. See Kalyvas 2010.

8. The use of *supplement* here is akin to that of Derrida (1976).

9. The term *will to meaning* is from Robbins 2006:213.

10. Camus 1942:18; see Coutin 2005, Ngai 2004, and Lucht 2012 on how irregular migrants come to experience such an "impossible" subjecthood.

11. Esslin 1972:400.

12. Morocco's new migration politics, launched in September 2013, did not put an end to the violence and raids, as NGOs such as Caritas and HRW noted. Instead of being expelled towards Oujda, migrants were sent to Morocco's big cities, displacing the humanitarian crisis to major urban centers. Regularization, meanwhile, held little promise for most clandestine sub-Saharan migrants. On the 2013–14 situation, see, e.g., http://elpais.com/m/politica/2014/04/01/actualidad /1396373829_144060.html and www.hrw.org/news/2014/02/10/morocco-abuse -sub-saharan-migrants.

APPENDIX

1. Marcus 1995; for U.S.-Mexico studies, see especially Alvarez 1995.

2. Glick Schiller and Wimmer 2003:598; quote from Latour 1993:116; see also Wilding 2007; Hage 2005; and Hannerz 2003.

3. Feldman 2012:184; quote from Xiang 2007:117.

4. This approach thus follows attempts to move away from anthropology's "spatialization of difference" in "bounded fields" towards a methodological focus on "shifting locations," without approaching this as a multisited proliferation of field spaces or a nonlocal ethnography (Gupta and Ferguson 1997; on the extended case method, see van Velsen 1967 and Gluckman 2002). By talking of an "extended" field site, however, I also wish to acknowledge the continuity with earlier anthropological research. Anthropology has of course always been much more than "single-sited," as testified by Malinowski's classic explorations of the Kula ring or the early Torres Straits expedition. Indeed, the discipline has throughout its history sought to connect scales and places, as Hage (2005) among others acknowledges in his call for a neo-Kulan ethnography.

5. On interface analysis, see Long 2001 and Rossi 2006 for the critique; see Ortner 2010 for another take on "interface ethnography."

6. Feldman 2012; Tsing 2005; quote from Agier 2011:7. On the policy-practice perspective followed here, see Mosse 2004:13.

7. See Latour 1993.

8. Actor-network theory also allows us to move beyond two of the scientific tendencies Latour (1993) warns against: "Sociologization," or studying people among themselves, and "discursivization," or the analytical privileging of language and signification.

9. Malkki 1997; and Faubion and Marcus 2009. For journalistic work, see note 17 to chapter 4.

Selected Glossary

ACOGIDA Welcoming or reception; used to refer to migrant assistance in Spain.

ALIS Nickname for the Moroccan auxiliary forces, active at the fences of Ceuta and Melilla.

ANGLÓFONOS Term used in Spanish migration assistance for English-speaking sub-Saharan migrants.

ARRAIGO "Embeddedness," used in assessing whether an irregular migrant may qualify for a Spanish residence permit through work or residence.

ASALTO Term used by the Spanish media for a mass migrant attempt to climb the fences of Ceuta and Melilla.

ATTAQUE Term among *aventuriers* for an attempt to climb the enclaves' fences.

AVENTURIER "Adventurer," term of self-designation used by some Francophone sub-Saharan Africans on clandestine journeys towards North Africa and Europe.

BUNKER Alternative term for a migrant ghetto, or safe house, in the Maghreb.

CABALLAS Nickname for residents of Ceuta (literally, "mackerels").

CAYUCO Spanish term for the large wooden fishing boats used in clandestine migration from West Africa towards the Canary Islands.

CHABOLAS "Shanties," used to refer to ramshackle dwellings constructed by migrants in Melilla.

CHAIRMAN Term among French-speaking adventurers for leaders of ghettos or nation-based groupings en route.

CLANDESTIN French for "illegal (im)migrant."

COMANDANCIA Guardia Civil provincial headquarters.

CODEVELOPMENT An approach to development assistance that involves seeing migrants as a factor in developing their home countries.

CONVOYEUR Migrant smuggler, from the French for "courier."

COXEUR Migrant hustler or smuggler.

FACILITATOR Term used by Frontex for any migrant smuggler.

FRANC CFA The name of two African currencies: the West African and Central African CFA, which are both set at a fixed exchange rate to the euro and are guaranteed by the French treasury. The former, of concern to this book, is shared by countries belonging to the West African Economic and Monetary Union.

FRANCÓFONOS Term used in Spanish migration assistance for French-speaking sub-Saharan migrants.

GAAL GI Wolof word for wooden fishing boat; compare *cayuco* and *pirogue*.

GHETTO A safe house or flat for West African migrants in the Maghreb, usually based on nationality or ethnicity.

GLOBAL APPROACH An E.U. approach that involves a three-pronged strategy of fighting illegal migration in collaboration with "sending countries"; fomenting development in these countries; and promoting legal migration.

GRIS-GRIS Religious amulets or charms used in countries such as Mali and Senegal (known as *tere* in Wolof).

GUIDE Term for migrants who facilitate clandestine crossings for other migrants, often in return for a relatively small sum of money.

HARRAGA Moroccan term for the country's own clandestine migrants, from the root *to burn* in reference to the "burning" of borders and papers.

INTERNO Roughly *intern* or *detainee* in Spanish.

JEFATURA Spanish police headquarters.

LAISSEZ-PASSER A pass of safe conduct.

MAGHREB Northwest Africa (Morocco, Algeria, and Tunisia).

MAGREBÍ Person hailing from the Maghreb. Used in Spanish aid operations in contrast with *subsahariano*.

MARABOUT Muslim religious leader or teacher (*serigne* in Wolof).

MBËKË MI Wolof term for the clandestine boat journey, literally, "hitting one's head."

MODOU-MODOU Term used for migrants in Senegal, usually connoting a rags-to-riches journey from relative poverty to success in Europe.

MORENO "Dark-skinned" in Spanish; increasingly applied to black Africans, especially in migrant assistance contexts.

NEGRO "Black" or "black person/man" in Spanish.

NON-REFOULEMENT In international law, the principle of not returning refugees to countries where their lives or freedoms could be at risk.

PASSEUR "Smuggler" in French.

PATERA Literally referring to the small wooden fishing boat used by Moroccans crossing to Spain in the 1990s, *patera* has become the generic term for "migrant boat" used by all agencies working on migration.

PIROGUE French term for *cayuco* or *gaal gi*.

RAFLE A raid on migrant dwellings.

SANS-PAPIERS French for "undocumented migrant." Increasingly used by activists and migrants themselves in the vindication of rights.

SUBSAHARIANO "Sub-Saharan person" in Spanish. Used in aid operations and the media, often in contrast with *magrebí* and without the assumed negative connotations of *negro*.

TOY Term used by Spanish coast guards in referring to small inflatable boats used by migrants around the Strait of Gibraltar.

TRANQUILO Makeshift shelter used by *aventuriers* in Morocco (from the Spanish word for peaceful).

VALLA Spanish term for fence, barrier, or barricade. Used by the media, locals, and border guards in referring to the perimeter fences around Ceuta and Melilla.

ZODIAC The brand name of a small, fast inflatable boat used in crossing the Strait of Gibraltar in recent years, though the term is sometimes used by migrants in referring to semirigid vessels as well.

Bibliography

AEI (Afrique-Europe-Interact). 2011. *Mouvements autour des frontières/Grenz-bewegungen.* AEI report, November.

Agamben, Giorgio. 1998. *Homo sacer: Sovereign power and bare life.* Stanford, CA: Stanford University Press.

Agier, Michel. 2011. *Managing the undesirables: Refugee camps and humanitarian government.* Cambridge: Polity.

Albahari, Maurizio. 2006. "Death and the modern state: Making borders and sovereignty at the southern edges of Europe." CCIS Working Paper 137, University of California, San Diego, May.

Aldalur, Martín. 2010. *Clandestinos: ¿Qué hay detrás de la inmigración ilegal?* Barcelona: Ediciones B.

Althusser, Louis. 1971. "Ideology and ideological state apparatuses (notes towards an investigation)." In *Lenin and philosophy and other essays,* edited by L. Althusser. London: Monthly Review Press.

Alvarez, Robert R. 1995. "The Mexican-US border: The making of an anthropology of borderlands." *Annual Review of Anthropology* 24:447–70.

Amnesty International. 2008. *Mauritania report: Arrests and collective expulsions of migrants denied entry into Europe.* Amnesty International report, July.

——. 2011. *Stop racism, not people: Racial profiling and immigration control in Spain.* Amnesty International report, December.

Anderson, Bridget, Matthew J. Gibney, and Emanuela Paoletti, eds. 2013. *The social, political and historical contours of deportation.* New York: Springer.

Anderson, Malcolm. 2000. "The transformation of border controls: A European precedent?" In *The wall around the West: State borders and immigration controls in North America and Europe,* edited by P. Andreas and T. Snyder. Lanham, MD: Rowman & Littlefield.

Andersson, Ruben. 2005. "The new frontiers of America." *Race and Class* 46(3):28–38.

———. 2010. "Wild man at Europe's gates: The crafting of clandestines in Spain's *cayuco* crisis." *Etnofoor* 22(2):31–49.

———. 2012. "A game of risk: Boat migration and the business of bordering Europe." *Anthropology Today* 28(6):7–11.

———. 2014. "Hunter and prey: Patrolling clandestine migration in the Euro-African borderlands." *Anthropological Quarterly* 87(1):119–48.

Andreas, Peter. 2000. *Border games: Policing the US-Mexico divide.* Ithaca, NY: Cornell University Press.

———. 2003. "Redrawing the line: Borders and security in the twenty-first century." *International Security* 28(2):78–111.

Andreas, Peter, and Thomas J. Biersteker. 2003. *The rebordering of North America: Integration and exclusion in a new security context.* New York: Routledge.

Andreas, Peter, and Richard Price. 2001. "From war fighting to crime fighting: Transforming the American national security state." *International Studies Review* 3(3):31–52.

Andreas, Peter, and Timothy Snyder, eds. 2000. *The wall around the West: State borders and immigration controls in North America and Europe.* Lanham, MD: Rowman & Littlefield.

Anzaldúa, Gloria. 1999. *Borderlands = La frontera.* San Francisco: Aunt Lute Books.

Arteaga, Félix. 2007. *Las operaciones de última generación: El Centro de Coordinación Regional de Canarias.* ARI Report 54, Real Instituto Elcano, May.

Audran, Jérome. 2008. "Gestion des flux migratoires: Reflexions sur la politique française de codéveloppement." *Annuaire Suisse de Politique de Développement* 27(2):1–12.

Balibar, Étienne. 1998. "The borders of Europe." In *Cosmopolitics: Thinking and feeling beyond the nation,* edited by P. Cheah and B. Robbins. Minneapolis: University of Minnesota Press.

Barnett, Michael N., and Thomas George Weiss. 2008. *Humanitarianism in question: Politics, power, ethics.* Ithaca, NY: Cornell University Press.

Bauman, Zygmunt. 1997. "Tourists and vagabonds: The heroes and victims of postmodernity." In *Postmodernity and its discontents,* edited by Z. Bauman. Cambridge: Polity Press.

Bayart, Jean-François. 2007. *Global subjects: A political critique of globalization.* Cambridge, MA: Polity.

Beck, Ulrich. 2009. *World at risk.* Cambridge: Polity.

Bending, Tim, and Sergio Rosendo. 2006. "Rethinking the mechanics of the 'anti-politics machine.'" In *Development brokers and translators: The ethnography of aid and agencies,* edited by D. Lewis and D. Mosse. Bloomfield, CT: Kumarian Press.

Bigo, Didier. 2001. "Migration and security." In *Controlling a new migration world,* edited by V. Guiraudon and C. Joppke. London: Routledge.

———. 2005. "Frontier controls in the European Union: Who is in control?" In *Controlling frontiers: Free movement into and within Europe,* edited by D. Bigo and E. Guild. Aldershot, UK: Ashgate.

Blundo, Giorgio, and Jean-Pierre Olivier de Sardan. 2001. "La corruption quotidienne en Afrique de l'Ouest." *Politique africaine* 83:8–37.

Bornstein, Erica, and Peter Redfield, eds. 2010. *Forces of compassion: Humanitarianism between ethics and politics.* Santa Fe, NM: School for Advanced Research Press.

Bouvier, Nicolas. 2007. *The way of the world.* London: Eland.

Brachet, Julien. 2009. *Migrations transsahariennes: Vers un désert cosmopolite et morcelé (Niger).* Paris: Croquant.

Braudel, Fernand. 1975. *The Mediterranean and the Mediterranean world in the age of Philip II.* London: Fontana.

Bredeloup, Sylvie. 2008. "L'aventurier, une figure de la migration africaine." *Cahiers Internationaux de Sociologie* 135:281–306.

Bredeloup, Sylvie, and Olivier Pliez. 2005. "Migrations entre les deux rives du Sahara." *Autrepart* 36:3–20.

Brown, Wendy. 2010. *Walled states, waning sovereignty.* New York: Zone Books.

Buggenhagen, Beth Anne. 2001. "Prophets and profits: Gendered and generational visions of wealth and value in Senegalese Murid households." *Journal of Religion in Africa* 31(4):373–401.

Butler, Judith. 1995. "Conscience doth makes subjects of us all." *Yale French Studies* 88:6–26.

Buzan, Barry. 1991. *People, states and fear: An agenda for international security studies in the post-Cold War era.* Boulder, CO: L. Rienner.

CAC (Consell de l'Audiovisual de Catalunya). 2006. "Televisión e inmigración: La televisión y la construcción de una imagen pública de la inmigración." *Quaderns del CAC* 23–24.

Calavita, Kitty. 2005. *Immigrants at the margins: Law, race, and exclusion in southern Europe.* Cambridge: Cambridge University Press.

Calhoun, Craig. 2008. "The imperative to reduce suffering: Charity, progress, and emergencies in the field of humanitarian action." In *Humanitarianism in question: Politics, power, ethics,* edited by M.N. Barnett and T.G. Weiss. Ithaca, NY: Cornell University Press.

Camus, Albert. 1942. *Le mythe du Sisyphe.* Paris: Gallimard.

Candea, Matei. 2007. "Arbitrary locations: In defence of the bounded field-site." *Journal of the Royal Anthropological Institute* 13(1):167–84.

Caplan, Patricia. 2000. Introduction. In *Risk revisited,* edited by P. Caplan. Sterling, VA: Pluto Press.

Carling, Jørgen. 2007a. "Migration control and migrant fatalities at the Spanish-African borders." *International Migration Review* 41(2):316–43.

———. 2007b. "Unauthorized migration from Africa to Spain." *International Migration* 45(4):3–37.

Carr, Matthew. 2012. *Fortress Europe: Dispatches from a gated continent.* New York: New Press.

Carrera, Sergio. 2007. *The EU border management strategy: FRONTEX and the challenges of irregular immigration in the Canary Islands.* CEPS Working Document 261, Centre for European Policy Studies.

Castles, Stephen, and Mark J. Miller. 2003. *The age of migration.* New York: Guilford Press.

CEAR (Comisión Española de Ayuda al Refugiado). 2008. *Informe de evaluación del Centro de Detención de Inmigrantes en Nouadibou, Mauritania.* CEAR report, December.

Cherti, Myriam, and Peter Grant. 2013. *The myth of transit: Sub-Saharan migration in Morocco.* Institute for Public Policy Research report, June.

Choplin, Armelle, and Jérôme Lombard. 2007. "Destination Nouadhibou pour les migrants africains." *Revue Mappemonde* 88(4). Available online at http://mappemonde.mgm.fr/num16/lieux/lieux07401.html.

Cohen, Robin. 1987. *The new helots: Migrants in the international division of labour.* Aldershot, UK: Gower.

Collyer, Michael. 2007. "In-between places: Trans-Saharan transit migrants in Morocco and the fragmented journey to Europe." *Antipode* 39(4): 668–90.

Comaroff, Jean. 2007. "Beyond bare life: AIDS, (bio)politics and the neoliberal order." *Public Culture* 19(1):197–219.

Cooper, Frederick. 2002. *Africa since 1940: The past of the present.* Cambridge: Cambridge University Press.

——. 2005. *Colonialism in question: Theory, knowledge, history.* Berkeley: University of California Press.

Cornelius, Wayne A. 2004. "Spain: The uneasy transition from labor exporter to labor importer." In *Controlling immigration: A global perspective,* edited by W.A. Cornelius et al. Stanford, CA: Stanford University Press.

Cornelius, Wayne A., and Takeyuki Tsuda. 2004. "Controlling immigration: The limits of government intervention." In *Controlling immigration: A global perspective,* edited by W.A. Cornelius et al. Stanford, CA: Stanford University Press.

Coutin, Susan Bibler. 2005. "Being en route." *American Anthropologist* 107(2):195–206.

——. 2007. *Nations of emigrants: Shifting boundaries of citizenship in El Salvador and the United States.* Ithaca, NY: Cornell University Press.

Cruz Roja Española. Undated. *Migraciones africanas hacia Europa: Estudio cuantitativo y comparativo, años 2006–2008. Centro no. 6 de Nouadibou, Mauritania.* Spanish Red Cross report.

Cuttitta, Paolo. 2011. "Borderizing the island: Setting and narratives of the Lampedusa border play." Paper given at ABORNE workshop Fences, Networks, People: Exploring the EU/Africa Borderland, University of Pavia, Italy, December.

Das, Veena. 1995. *Critical events: An anthropological perspective on contemporary India.* Delhi; New York: Oxford University Press.

Debord, Guy. 2004. *The society of the spectacle.* London: Rebel Press.

De Genova, Nicholas. 2002. "Migrant illegality and deportability in everyday life." *Annual Review of Anthropology* 31:419–47.

——. 2012. "Border, scene and obscene." In *A companion to border studies,* edited by H. Donnan and T.M. Wilson. Oxford: Blackwell Wiley.

De Genova, Nicholas, and Nathalie Mae Peutz, eds. 2010. *The deportation regime: Sovereignty, space, and the freedom of movement.* Durham, NC: Duke University Press.

de Haas, Hein. 2007. *The myth of invasion: Irregular migration from West Africa to the Maghreb and the European Union.* IMI research report, University of Oxford, October.

Del Grande, Gabriele. 2007. *Mamadou va a morire: La strage dei clandestini nel Mediterraneo.* Rome: Infinito.

della Porta, Donatella. 2006. *Globalization from below: Transnational activists and protest networks.* Minneapolis: University of Minnesota Press.

Derrida, Jacques. 1976. *Of grammatology.* Baltimore: Johns Hopkins University Press.

Desjarlais, Robert. 1994. "Struggling along: The possibilities for experience among the homeless mentally ill." *American Anthropologist* 96(4):886–901.

Donnan, Hastings, and Thomas M. Wilson. 1999. *Borders: Frontiers of identity, nation and state.* Oxford: Berg.

Driessen, Henk. 1992. *On the Spanish-Moroccan frontier: A study in ritual, power and ethnicity.* Oxford: Berg.

———. 1998. "The 'new immigration' and the transformation of the European-African frontier." In *Border identities: Nation and state at international frontiers,* edited by T. Wilson and H. Donnan. Cambridge: Cambridge University Press.

Duffield, Mark R. 2007. *Development, security and unending war: Governing the world of peoples.* Cambridge: Polity.

Düvell, Franck. 2006. "Crossing the fringes of Europe: Transit migration in the EU's neighbourhood." COMPAS Working Paper 33, University of Oxford.

———. 2008. "Clandestine migration in Europe." *Social Science Information* 47(4):479–97.

EMHRN (Euro-Mediterranean Human Rights Network). 2010. *Study on migration and asylum in Maghreb countries: Inadequate legal and administrative frameworks cannot guarantee the protection of migrants, refugees and asylum seekers.* EMHRN report, July. Available online at www.refworld.org/pdfid/515018942.pdf.

Escoffier, Claire. 2006. "Communautés d'itinérance et savoir-circuler des trans-migrant-e-s au Maghreb." PhD dissertation, Université Toulouse II.

Esslin, Martin. 1972. *The theatre of the absurd.* Harmondsworth, UK: Penguin.

Fabian, Johannes. 1983. *Time and the other: How anthropology makes its object.* New York: Columbia University Press.

Fanon, Frantz. 1967. *Black skin, white masks.* New York: Grove Press.

Fassin, Didier. 2005. "Compassion and repression: The moral economy of immigration policies in France." *Cultural Anthropology* 20(3):362–87.

———. 2007. "Humanitarianism: A nongovernmental government." In *Nongovernmental politics,* edited by M. Feher, 149–60. New York: Zone Books.

Fassin, Didier, and Richard Rechtman. 2009. *The empire of trauma: An inquiry into the condition of victimhood.* Princeton, NJ: Princeton University Press.

Faubion, James D., and George E. Marcus, eds. 2009. *Fieldwork is not what it used to be: Learning anthropology's method in a time of transition.* Ithaca, NY: Cornell University Press.

Fekete, Liz. 2005. "The deportation machine: Europe, asylum and human rights." *Race and Class* 47(1):64–91.

Feldman, Gregory. 2012. *The migration apparatus: Security, labor, and policy-making in the European Union*. Stanford, CA: Stanford University Press.

Ferguson, James. 1990. *The anti-politics machine: "Development," depoliticization, and bureaucratic power in Lesotho*. Cambridge: Cambridge University Press.

Ferrer Gallardo, Xavier. 2008. "Acrobacias fronterizas en Ceuta y Melilla: Explorando la gestión de los perímetros terrestres de la Unión Europea en el continente africano." *Documents d'Anàlisi Geogràfica* 51:129–49.

———. 2011. "Territorial (dis)continuity dynamics between Ceuta And Morocco: Conflictual fortification vis-à-vis co-operative interaction at the EU border in Africa." *Tijdschrift voor Economische en sociale Geografie* 102(1):24–38.

Fibla García-Sala, Carla, and Nicolás Castellano Flores. 2008. *Mi nombre es nadie: El viaje más antiguo del mundo*. Barcelona: Icaria.

Forsythe, David P. 2009. "Contemporary humanitarianism: The global and the local." In *Humanitarianism and suffering: The mobilization of empathy*, edited by R. Wilson and R.D. Brown. Cambridge: Cambridge University Press.

Foucault, Michel. 2008. *The birth of biopolitics: Lectures at the Collège de France, 1978–79*. Basingstoke, UK: Palgrave Macmillan.

Frontex. 2009a. *General report 2009*. Frontex, Warsaw.

———. 2009b. *Programme of work 2009*. Frontex, Warsaw.

———. 2010. *Beyond the frontiers: Frontex: The first five years*. Frontex, Warsaw.

———. 2011. *Annual risk analysis 2011*. Frontex, Warsaw.

———. 2012. *Annual risk analysis 2012*. Frontex, Warsaw.

Funakawa, Natsuko. 2009. "Le CIGEM—Centre d'Information et de Gestion des Migrations (Mali): Sa place face aux défis des politiques migratoires." Master's thesis, Laboratoire Migrinter, Université de Poitiers.

Gabrielli, Lorenzo. 2011. "La construction de la politique d'immigration espagnole: Ambiguïtés et ambivalences à travers le cas des migrations ouest-africaines." PhD dissertation, Université de Bordeaux.

Gaibazzi, Paolo. 2010. "Migration, Soninke young men and the dynamics of staying behind." PhD dissertation, University of Milano-Bicocca.

Gammeltoft-Hansen, Thomas, and Tanja E. Aalberts. 2010. "Sovereignty at sea: The law and politics of saving lives in the Mare Liberum." DIIS Working Paper 18, University of Copenhagen.

Gammeltoft-Hansen, Thomas, and Ninna Nyberg Sørensen, eds. 2013. *The migration industry and the commercialization of international migration*. Abingdon, UK: Routledge.

Gardner, Katy. 1995. *Global migrants, local lives: Migration and transformation in rural Bangladesh*. Oxford: Oxford University Press.

Gardner, Katy, and David J. Lewis. 1996. *Anthropology, development and the post-modern challenge*. London: Pluto Press.

Gardner, Katy, and Filippo Osella, eds. 2004. *Migration, modernity and social transformation in South Asia*. New Delhi: Sage.

Gatti, Fabrizio. 2007. *Bilal: Il mio viaggio da infiltrato nel mercato dei nuovi schiavi*. Milan: Rizzoli.

Gledhill, John. 2008. "Anthropology in the age of securitization." Joel S. Kahn lecture at La Trobe University, Melbourne, December.

Glennie, Paul, and Nigel J. Thrift. 1996. "Reworking E.P. Thompson's 'Time, work-discipline and industrial capitalism.'" *Time and Society* 5(3): 275–99.

Glick Schiller, Nina, and Andreas Wimmer. 2003. "Methodological nationalism, the social sciences and the study of migration." *International Migration Review* 37(3):576–610.

Gluckman, Max. 2002. "'The bridge': Analysis of a social situation in Zululand." In *The Anthropology of politics: A reader in ethnography, theory and critique*, edited by J. Vincent. Malden, MA: Blackwell.

Goffman, Erving. 1961. *Asylums: Essays on the social situation of mental patients and other inmates.* Harmondsworth, UK: Penguin Books.

González, Tania, Sandra Gil Araujo, and Virginia Montañés Sánchez. 2013. "Política migratoria y derechos humanos en el Mediterráneo español: El impacto del control migratorio en los tránsitos de la migración africana hacia Europa." *Revista de Derecho Migratorio y Extranjería* 33:245–67.

Guardia Civil. 2008. *SIVE: Cinco años vigilando la frontera.* Madrid: Guardia Civil.

Guild, Elspeth. 2008. Sovereignty on the move: The changing landscape of territory, people and governance in the EU. London Migration Research Group seminar at London School of Economics, 4 November.

Gupta, Akhil, and James Ferguson. 1997. "Discipline and practice: 'The field' as site, method and location in anthropology." In *Anthropological locations: Boundaries and grounds of a field science*, edited by A. Gupta and J. Ferguson. Berkeley: University of California Press.

Guyer, Jane I. 2007. "Prophecy and the near future: Thoughts on macroeconomic, evangelical, and punctuated time." *American Ethnologist* 34(3): 409–21.

Hacking, Ian. 1986. "Making up people." In *Reconstructing individualism: Autonomy, individuality and the self in Western thought*, edited by T.C. Heller et al. Stanford: Stanford University Press.

———. 1999. *The social construction of what?* Cambridge, MA: Harvard University Press.

Hage, Ghassan. 2005. "A not so multi-sited ethnography of a not so imagined community." *Anthropological Theory* 5(4):463–75.

Hallaire, Juliette. 2007. "L'émigration irregulière vers l'Union Européenne au départ des cotes sénégalaises." Master's thesis, Université de Paris Sorbonne (Paris IV).

Hann, Agnes. 2013. "An ethnographic study of family, livelihoods and women's everyday lives in Dakar, Senegal." PhD thesis, London School of Economics and Political Science.

Hannerz, Ulf. 2003. "Being there . . . and there . . . and there! Reflections on multi-sited ethnography." *Ethnography* 4(2):201–16.

Harding, Jeremy. 2012. *Border vigils.* London: Verso.

Harvey, David. 1989. *The condition of postmodernity: An enquiry into the origins of cultural change.* Oxford: Blackwell.

Hayes, Ben, and Mathias Vermeulen. 2012. *Borderline: EU border surveillance initiatives.* Heinrich Böll Foundation report, June. Available online at http://il.boell.org/downloads/Borderline.pdf.

Hernández Carretero, María. 2008. "Risk-taking in unauthorised migration." Master's thesis, University of Tromsø.

Hernández i Sagrera, Raúl. 2008. "Frontex: ¿Proyección a nivel europeo de la visión de España sobre el control de fronteras?" In *España en Europa 2004–2008,* edited by E. Barbé. Bellaterra (Barcelona): Institut Universitari d'Estudis Europeus.

Herzfeld, Michael. 1992. *The social production of indifference: Exploring the symbolic roots of Western bureaucracy.* New York: Berg.

Heyman, Josiah. 1995. "Putting power in the anthropology of bureaucracy: The Immigration and Naturalization Service at the Mexico-United States border." *Current Anthropology* 36(2):261–87.

———. 2004. "Ports of entry as nodes in the world system." *Identities: Global Studies in Culture and Power* 11:303–27.

HRW (Human Rights Watch). 2011. *The EU's dirty hands: Frontex involvement in ill-treatment of migrant detainees in Greece.* HRW report, September. Available online at www.hrw.org/sites/default/files/reports/greece0911webv-cover_0.pdf.

———. 2012. "Hidden emergency: Migrant deaths in the Mediterranean." HRW report, August. Available online at www.hrw.org/node/109445.

Hughes, E.C. 1958. *Men and their work.* Toronto: Collier-Macmillan.

Huysmans, Jef. 2000. "The European Union and the securitization of migration." *Journal of Common Market Studies* 38(5):751–77.

James, Deborah. 2007. *Gaining ground: "Rights" and "property" in South African land reform.* Abingdon, UK: Routledge-Cavendish.

Jeandesboz, Julien. 2011. "Beyond the Tartar steppe: EUROSUR and the ethics of European border control practices." In *Europe under threat? Security, migration and integration,* edited by J.P. Burgess and S. Gutwirth. Brussels: VUB Press.

Jónsson, Gunvor. 2008. "Migration aspirations and immobility in a Malian Soninké village." IMI Working Paper 10, University of Oxford.

Kalyvas, Andreas. 2010. "An anomaly? Some reflections on the Greek December 2008." *Constellations* 17(2):351–65.

———. 2012. "The stateless citizen." Paper given at London School of Economics and Political Science, November.

Kearney, Michael. 1998. "Transnationalism in California and Mexico at the end of empire." In *Border identities: Nation and state at international frontiers,* edited by T. Wilson and H. Donnan. Cambridge: Cambridge University Press.

Kelly, Tobias. 2006. "Documented lives: Fear and the uncertainties of law during the second Palestinian intifada." *Journal of the Royal Anthropological Institute* 12:89–107.

Kenyon, Paul. 2009. *I am Justice: A journey out of Africa.* London: Preface Publishing.

Khosravi, Shahram. 2007. "The 'illegal' traveller: An auto-ethnography of borders." *Social Anthropology* 15(3):321–34.

———. 2010. "*Illegal" traveller: An auto-ethnography of borders.* Basingstoke, UK: Palgrave Macmillan.

Klein, Naomi. 2008. *The shock doctrine: The rise of disaster capitalism.* London: Penguin.

Kraler, Albert, and David Reichel. 2011. "Measuring irregular migration and population flows—what available data can tell." *International Migration* 49(5):97–128.

Laacher, Smaïn. 2007. *Le peuple des clandestins: Essai.* Paris: Calmann-Lévy.

Lahav, Gallya, and Virginie Guiraudon. 2000. "Comparative perspectives on border control: Away from the border and outside the state." In *The wall around the West: State borders and immigration controls in North America and Europe,* edited by P. Andreas and T. Snyder. Lanham, MD: Rowman & Littlefield.

Latour, Bruno. 1993. *We have never been modern.* Hemel Hempstead, UK: Harvester Wheatsheaf.

Lecadet, Clara. 2013. "From migrant destitution to self-organization into transitory national communities: The revival of citizenship in post-deportation experience in Mali." In *The social, political and historical contours of deportation,* edited by B. Anderson, M.J. Gibney, and E. Paoletti. New York: Springer.

Lemberg-Pedersen, Martin. 2013. "Private security companies and the European borderscapes." In *The migration industry and the commercialization of international migration,* edited by T. Gammeltoft-Hansen and N. Nyberg Sørensen. Abingdon, UK: Routledge.

Lemke, Thomas. 2005. "A zone of indistinction—a critique of Giorgio Agamben's concept of biopolitics." *Critical Social Studies* 7(1):3–13.

Léonard, Sarah. 2011. "Frontex and the securitization of migrants through practices." Migration working group seminar at the European University Institute, Florence, February.

Lewis, David, and David Mosse, eds. 2006. *Development brokers and translators: The ethnography of aid and agencies.* Bloomfield, CT: Kumarian Press.

Lindqvist, Sven. 2008. *Terra Nullius: A journey through No One's Land.* New York: New Press.

Long, Norman. 2001. *Development sociology: Actor perspectives.* London: Routledge.

Low, Setha M. 2003. *Behind the gates: Life, security, and the pursuit of happiness in fortress America.* New York: Routledge.

Lucht, Hans. 2012. *Darkness before daybreak: African migrants living on the margins in southern Italy today.* Berkeley: University of California Press.

Luper-Foy, Steven. 1992. "The absurdity of life." *Philosophy and Phenomenological Research* 52(1):85–101.

Malkki, Liisa H. 1995. *Purity and exile: Violence, memory and national cosmology among Hutu refugees in Tanzania.* Chicago: Chicago University Press.

———. 1996. "Speechless emissaries: Refugees, humanitarianism, and dehistoricization." *Cultural Anthropology* 11(3):377–404.

———. 1997. "News and culture: Transitory phenomena and the fieldwork tradition." In *Anthropological Locations: Boundaries and grounds of a field science*, edited by A. Gupta and J. Ferguson. Berkeley: University of California Press.

Mann, Gillian Robertson. 2010. "Being, becoming and unbecoming a refugee: The lives of Congolese children in Dar es Salaam." PhD thesis, London School of Economics and Political Science.

Marcus, George E. 1995. "Ethnography in/of the world system." *Annual Review of Anthropology* 24:95–117.

———. 1997. "The uses of complicity in the changing mise-en-scène of anthropological fieldwork." *Representations* 59:85–108.

Martin, Philip L., and Edward J. Taylor. 1996. "The anatomy of a migration hump." In *Development strategy, employment, and migration: Insights from models*, edited by E. J. Taylor. Paris: OECD, Development Centre.

Martin, Randy. 2004. "America as risk/securitizing the other." *Interventions* 6(3):351–61.

McNevin, Anne. 2007. "Irregular migrants, neoliberal geographies and spatial frontiers of 'the political.'" *Review of International Studies* 33(4): 655–74.

Melly, Caroline M. 2011. "Titanic tales of missing men: Reconfigurations of national identity and gendered presence in Dakar, Senegal." *American Ethnologist* 38(2):361–76.

Merry, Sally Engle. 2005. "Anthropology and activism: Researching human rights across porous boundaries." *Political and Legal Anthropology Review* 28(2):240–57.

Migreurop. 2006. "Guerre aux migrants: Le livre noir de Ceuta et Melilla." Migreurop report, June. Available online at www.meltingpot.org/IMG/pdf/livrenoir-ceuta.pdf.

Migreurop/La Cimade. 2010. "Prisonniers du désert: Enquête sur la situation des migrants à la frontière Mali-Mauritanie." Collective report by migrants' rights associations, December. Available online at www.lacimade.org/publications/47.

MIR (Ministerio del Interior). 2011. "Balance de la lucha contra la inmigración ilegal 2010." Spanish Interior Ministry press release, 18 January.

———. 2013. "Balance de la lucha contra la inmigración irregular 2012." Spanish Interior Ministry press release, 24 January.

Mosse, David. 2004. *Cultivating development: An ethnography of aid policy and practice*. London: Pluto Press.

Mountz, Alison. 2011. "The enforcement archipelago: Detention, haunting, and asylum on islands." *Political Geography* 30:118–28.

MSF (Médecins sans Frontières). 2013. *Violencia, vulnerabilidad y migración: Atrapados a las puertas de Europa: Un informe sobre los migrantes subsaharianos en situación irregular en Marruecos*. MSF report, March. Available online at www.msf.es/newsletter/docs/InformeMarruecos2013_CAST.pdf.

Munn, Nancy D. 1992. "The cultural anthropology of time: A critical essay." *Annual Review of Anthropology* 21:93–123.

Naranjo Noble, José. 2006. *Cayucos*. Barcelona: Editorial Debate.

———. 2009. *Los invisibles de Kolda: Historias olvidadas de la inmigración clandestina*. Barcelona: Ediciones Península.

Natter, Katharina. 2013. "The formation of Morocco's policy towards irregular migration (2000–2007): Political rationale and policy processes." *International Migration* DOI: 10.1111/imig.12114.

Navaro-Yashin, Yael. 2007. "Make-believe papers, legal forms and the counterfeit." *Anthropological Theory* 7(1):79–98.

Nevins, Joseph. 2002. *Operation Gatekeeper: The rise of the "illegal alien" and the making of the U.S.-Mexico boundary.* London: Routledge.

Ngai, Mae M. 2004. *Impossible subjects: Illegal aliens and the making of modern America.* Princeton, NJ: Princeton University Press.

Nordstrom, Carolyn. 2007. *Global outlaws: Crime, money, and power in the contemporary world.* Berkeley: University of California Press.

Nyamnjoh, Henrietta Mambo. 2010. *We get nothing from fishing: Fishing for boat opportunities amongst Senegalese fisher migrants.* Leiden: Langaa & African Studies Centre.

Ortner, Sherry B. 2010. "Access: Reflections on studying up in Hollywood." *Ethnography* 11(2):211–33.

Pandolfi, Mariella. 2010. "Humanitarianism and its discontents." In *Forces of compassion: Humanitarianism between ethics and politics,* edited by E. Bornstein and P. Redfield. Santa Fe, NM: School for Advanced Research Press.

Papadopoulos, Dimitris. 2011. "The autonomy of migration: Making the mobile commons." Paper given at SOAS Department of Development Studies joint seminar series, London, February.

Papadopoulos, Dimitris, Niamh Stephenson, and Vassilis Tsianos. 2008. *Escape routes: Control and subversion in the twenty-first century.* London: Pluto Press.

Pardellas, Juan Manuel. 2004. *Héroes de ébano.* Santa Cruz de Tenerife: Ediciones Idea.

Parker, Noel, Nick Vaughan-Williams, et al. 2009. "Lines in the sand? Towards an agenda for critical border studies." *Geopolitics* 14(3):582–87.

Parry, Jonathan. 1986. "The gift, the Indian gift and the 'Indian gift.'" *Man* 21(3):453–73.

Pastore, Ferruccio, Paola Monzini, and Giuseppe Sciortino. 2006. "Schengen's soft underbelly? Irregular migration and human smuggling across land and sea borders to Italy." *International Migration* 44(4):95–119.

Pelkmans, Mathijs. 2012. "Chaos and order along the (former) Iron Curtain." In *A Companion to Border Studies,* edited by H. Donnan and T.M. Wilson. Oxford: Blackwell Wiley.

———. 2013. "Powerful documents: Passports, passages, and dilemmas of identification on the Georgian-Turkish border." In *Border encounters: Asymmetry and proximity at Europe's frontiers,* edited by J.L. Bacas and W. Kavanagh. Oxford: Berghahn Books.

Pian, Anaïk. 2009. *Aux nouvelles frontières de l'Europe: L'aventure incertaine des Sénégalais au Maroc.* Paris: La Dispute.

———. 2010. "The discursive framework for development: From discourses and concrete political actions to the range of actions by deportee associations." IMI Working Paper 25, University of Oxford.

Poole, Deborah. 1997. *Vision, race, and modernity: A visual economy of the Andean image world.* Princeton, NJ: Princeton University Press.

Portes, Alejandro. 1978. "Toward a structural analysis of illegal (undocumented) immigration." *International Migration Review* 12(4):469–84.

Reher, David-Sven, et al. 2008. "Informe Encuesta Nacional de Inmigrantes (ENI—2007)." Spanish Labor Ministry report, April.

Rivero Rodríguez, Juan, and Eva Martínez Bermejo. 2008. "Migraciones y cooperación: El Plan REVA y la ayuda española." Research report by Grupo de Estudios Africanos de la Universidad Autónoma de Madrid, August.

Robbins, Joel. 2006. "Afterword: On limits, ruptures, meaning, and meaninglessness." In *The limits of meaning: Case studies in the anthropology of Christianity,* edited by M. Engelke and M. Tomlinson. New York: Berghahn Books.

———. 2013. "Beyond the suffering subject: Toward an anthropology of the good." *Journal of the Royal Anthropological Institute,* n.s. (19):447–62.

Robinson, Piers. 2000. "The policy-media interaction model: Measuring media power during humanitarian crisis." *Journal of Peace Research* 37(5):613–33.

Rodier, Claire. 2012. *Xénophobie business.* Paris: La Découverte.

Rodier, Claire, and Emmanuel Blanchard. 2003. "Des camps pour étrangers." *Plein Droit* 58. Available online at www.gisti.org/doc/plein-droit/58/index.html.

Rossi, Benedetta. 2006. "Aid policies and recipient strategies in Niger: Why donors and recipients should not be compartmentalized into separate 'worlds of knowledge.'" In *Development brokers and translators: The ethnography of aid and agencies,* edited by D. Lewis and D. Mosse. Bloomfield, CT: Kumarian Press.

Rumford, Chris. 2008. "Introduction: Citizens and borderwork in Europe." *Space and Polity* 12(1):1–12.

Sampson, Steven. 2010. "The anti-corruption industry: From movement to institution." *Global Crime* 11(2):261–78.

Serón, Gema, et al. 2011. *Coherencias de políticas españolas hacia África: Migraciones.* Report by Grupo de Estudios Africanos de la Universidad Autónoma de Madrid, November. Available online at www.uam.es/otros/gea/Documentos%20adjuntos/INFORME_MIGRACIONES_FULL_OK.pdf.

Silverstein, Paul A. 2005. "Immigrant racialization and the new savage slot: Race, migration, and immigration in the new Europe." *Annual Review of Anthropology* 34:363–84.

Snow, David A., and Robert D. Benford. 1998. "Ideology, frame resonance, and participant mobilization." *International Social Movement Research* 1:197–217.

Steinbeck, John. 1993. *The grapes of wrath.* London: Everyman's Library.

Taussig, Michael T. 1993. *Mimesis and alterity: A particular history of the senses.* New York: Routledge.

Tett, Gillian. 2009. *Fool's gold: How unrestrained greed corrupted a dream, shattered global markets and unleashed a catastrophe.* London: Little, Brown.

Thompson, E.P. 1967. "Time, work-discipline, and industrial capitalism." *Past and Present* 38:56–97.

Thrift, Nigel J., and Jon May. 2001. *TimeSpace: Geographies of temporality*. New York: Routledge.

Ticktin, Miriam. 2006. "Where ethics and politics meet: The violence of humanitarianism in France." *American Ethnologist* 33(1):33–49.

Tondini, Matteo. 2010. "Fishers of men? The interception of migrants in the Mediterranean Sea and their forced return to Libya." INEX Paper, October.

Torpey, John C. 2000. *The invention of the passport: Surveillance, citizenship, and the state*. Cambridge: Cambridge University Press.

Trauner, Florian, and Stephanie Deimel. 2013. "The impact of EU migration policies on African countries: The case of Mali." *International Migration* 51(4):20–32.

Trouillot, Michel-Rolph. 2003. "Anthropology and the savage slot: The poetics and politics of otherness." In *Global transformations: Anthropology and the modern world*. New York: Palgrave MacMillan.

Tsianos, Vassilis, Sabine Hess, and Serhat Karakayali. 2009. "Transnational migration theory and method of an ethnographic analysis of border regimes." Sussex Centre for Migration Research Working Paper 55, University of Sussex.

Tsing, Anna Lowenhaupt. 2005. *Friction: An ethnography of global connection*. Princeton, NJ: Princeton University Press.

Turner, Simon. 2010. *Politics of innocence: Hutu identity, conflict, and camp life*. New York: Berghahn Books.

Turner, Victor. 1974. "Passages, margins, and poverty: Religious symbols of communitas." In *Dramas, fields, and metaphors: Symbolic action in human society*, edited by V. Turner. Ithaca, NY: Cornell University Press.

Urry, John. 2007. *Mobilities*. Cambridge: Polity.

van Houtum, Henk, and Roos Pijpers. 2007. "The European Union as a gated community: The two-faced border and immigration regime of the EU." *Antipode* 39(2):291–309.

van Velsen, Jaap. 1967. "The extended-case method and situational analysis." In *Craft of social anthropology*, edited by A. L. Epstein. London: Tavistock Publications.

Vaughan-Williams, Nick. 2008. "Borderwork beyond inside/outside? Frontex, the citizen-detective and the war on terror." *Space and Polity* 12(1):63–79.

Walters, William. 2004. "The frontiers of the European Union: A geostrategic perspective." *Geopolitics* 9(3):674–98.

———. 2006a. "Border/Control." *European Journal of Social Theory* 9(2): 187–203.

———. 2006b. "No borders: Games with(out) frontiers." *Social Justice* 33(1):21–39.

———. 2011. "Foucault and frontiers: Notes on the birth of the humanitarian border." In *Governmentality: Current issues and future challenges*, edited by U. Bröckling, S. Krasmann, and T. Lemke. New York: Routledge.

———. 2012. *Governmentality: Critical encounters*. Abingdon, UK: Routledge.

Weizman, Eyal. 2011. *The least of all possible evils: Humanitarian violence from Arendt to Gaza*. London: Verso.

Wilding, Raelene. 2007. "Transnational ethnographies and anthropological imaginings of migrancy." *Journal of Ethnic and Migration Studies* 33(2):331–48.

Willen, Sarah. 2007a. "Exploring 'illegal' and 'irregular' migrants' lived experiences of law and state power." *International Migration* 45(3):2–7.

———. 2007b. "Toward a critical phenomenology of 'illegality': State power, criminalization, and abjectivity among undocumented migrant workers in Tel Aviv, Israel." *International Migration* 45(2):8–38.

Wolcott, Harry F. 2005. *The art of fieldwork*. Walnut Creek, CA: Altamira Press.

Xiang, Biao. 2007. *Global "body shopping": An Indian labor system in the information technology industry*. Princeton, NJ: Princeton University Press.

Žižek, Slavoj. 1999. *The ticklish subject: The absent centre of political ontology*. London: Verso.

Index